Wakefield Press

Sweet Boy Dear Wife

Heather Rossiter is a scientist, writer and traveller who lives in Sydney. She is the author of *Lady Spy, Gentleman Explorer: The life of Herbert Dyce Murphy* and *Mawson's Forgotten Men: The 1911–1913 diary of Charles Turnbull Harrisson*, while her articles, book reviews and travel pieces have appeared in Australian and overseas newspapers and magazines.

Besides studying Eastern and Oriental Art in Oxford and Islamic monuments at UCLA, Heather Rossiter has travelled extensively in North Africa, the Middle East and Central Asia. In 2001 at Susa, Iran, she was captivated by Jane Dieulafoy's story.

Heather Rossiter's beautifully constructed and evocative work will at last introduce to a much wider audience Jane Dieulafoy's singular tenacity, endurance and character, as well as her remarkable Middle Eastern travels and descriptions of a now-vanished era in the history of Iran.

Dr John Tidmarsh, Sydney University

SWEET BOY DEAR WIFE

Jane Dieulafoy in Persia 1881–1886

Heather Rossiter

Wakefield Press

Wakefield Press
16 Rose Street
Mile End
South Australia 5031
www.wakefieldpress.com.au

First published 2015

Edited by Penelope Curtin
Cover designed by Liz Nicholson, designBITE
Text designed and typeset by Clinton Ellicott, Wakefield Press

National Library of Australia Cataloguing-in-Publication entry

Creator: Rossiter, Heather, author.
Title: Sweet boy dear wife: Jane Dieulafoy in Persia 1881–1886 /
                Heather Rossiter.
ISBN: 978 1 74305 378 2 (paperback).
Notes: Includes bibliographical references and index.
Subjects: Dieulafoy, Jane, 1851–1916.
                Women archaeologists – Middle East – Biography.
                Women authors, French – Biography
                Iranologists – Biography.
                Ceramics – Iran – History.
                Iran – Description and travel.
                Iran – Social conditions – 19th century.
                Iran – Social life and customs – 19th century.
Dewey Number: 955.0090909

**Government
of South Australia**

Arts SA

CORIOLE

McLAREN VALE

Australian Government

Australia Council
for the Arts

Publication of this book was assisted by
the Commonwealth Government through the
Australia Council, its arts funding and advisory body.

For Charlotte and John

Contents

Persia: Chronology   viii
Characters in order of appearance   x
Glossary   xii
Map showing the Dieulafoys' travels in Persia and Iraq   xiii
Foreword, John Tidmarsh   xiv

Prologue   1
Chapter 1   A daring destination   4
Chapter 2   To a land without roads   13
Chapter 3   A golden dragon caught in a net of stars   29
Chapter 4   Saving Marcel   38
Chapter 5   The Golistan two hours before sunset   50
Chapter 6   On business for the shah's son   69
Chapter 7   Isfahan, rose flower of paradise   81
Chapter 8   Caravan to Pasargadae   111
Chapter 9   The Achaemenids   128
Chapter 10   Shiraz, city of wine, of roses and of poets   149
Chapter 11   South to the Sasanids   165
Chapter 12   Smuggled into Babylonia, Iraq   182
Chapter 13   With the Shi'a to the Holy Places   200
Chapter 14   The deadly price of Susa   209
Chapter 15   Return to Susa: The cast assembles   236
Chapter 16   First season: The Lion Frieze   250
Chapter 17   Second season: The Frieze of the Archers   277
Afterword   305

Notes   308
Selected bibliography   316
Acknowledgements   319
List of illustrations   321
Index   325

Persia: Chronology

Pre-Islamic period

Pre-550 BC **Elamites:** An early indigenous people who lived on the Iranian plateau and the Mesopotamian plain. Warred with Babylon, Assyria, Sumer.

550–330 BC **Achaemenids:** Persians of Aryan descent who defeated, then integrated the Medes and many other states to create a huge empire. Monumental architecture: at <u>Pasargadae</u> built by Cyrus; at <u>Susa</u> built by Darius; and at <u>Persepolis</u> initiated by Darius. Tombs at <u>Naqsh-i Rustam</u>. After centuries of warfare with the Greeks, Susa was pillaged and Persepolis destroyed by Alexander the Great in 331 BC.

312–238 BC **Seleucids:** Macedonian (Greek) dynasty who took power in the eastern part of the former Achaemenid Empire after Alexander's death. Their capital was Seleucia on the Tigris.

238 BC–224 AD **Parthians:** Central Asian Aryans who dominated from Armenia to the Persian Gulf.

222–636 AD **Sasanids:** dynasty founded by Ardashir (Artaxerxes), who claimed descent from the Achaemenid kings and built <u>Firuzabad</u>. European culture and architecture are deeply indebted to this dynasty. Warfare between Sasanids and Romans devastated large areas of Mesopotamia. Capital at <u>Ctesiphon</u> on the Tigris was destroyed by the Arabs in 636.

Islamic period

637–1220 AD **Arab rule:** First under the Rightly Guided Caliphs, the first three of whom are regarded by Shi'as as usurpers of Ali's rightful place. A Umayyad dynasty then ruled from Damascus, until superseded by the Abbasids who built a new capital at <u>Baghdad</u>. Though the Abbasids retained religious primacy as Caliphs until 1220, from 1038 they were powerless in affairs of state.

1038–1220 AD **Seljuks:** Turcs from Central Asia whose hegemony extended across Syria, Lebanon, Turkey and Iran. Under the Seljuks Persian culture, particularly literature and architecture, revived and flourished. Seljuk architecture survives in their capital <u>Isfahan</u> (part of a jume mosque), at regional capital <u>Rayy</u> (Gombad i-Tughril, part of immamzaddé Shah Abdul Azim), at <u>Narchevan</u> (Momine-Khatun mausoleum), and at <u>Qazvin</u>

(mosque sanctuary and dome). From 1096 the Crusaders assimilated Persian architecture and decorative arts, which manifested in Europe as Gothic. The Assassins, an internal Ishmaili sect, contributed to the destruction of the Seljuk dynasty.

1220–1380 AD   Mongol domination: Persia, devastated under Genghis Khan, was rebuilt by the Ilkhanid dynasty from 1256. After converting to Islam, the Ilkhanids presided over a renaissance of Persian architecture, literature, scholarship and painting. Earthquakes and war have destroyed all Ilkhanid monuments at their capital Tabriz except the Arg. At Soltaniyeh the tomb of Uljaitu and at Varamin a jume mosque remain.

1380–1502 AD   Timurid hegemony: Central Asian ruler Timur (Tamerlane) incorporated Iran into his Turco-Mongolian state. Persian artists and writers were celebrated, Persian architects and artisans created enduring monuments in the Timurid capital, Samarkand, and at Bukhara. In Tabriz the Blue mosque was built and Shiraz flourished, its painters and Sufi poets cultivated and admired. A Shirazi architect designed the Taj Mahal.

1502–1722 AD   Safavids: Turco-Persians from Azerbaijan who made Shi'a Islam the state religion. Under Shah Abbas the borders of modern Persia were defined and Isfahan was created. Major construction of dams, caravanserais, bridges, mosques and madrasas. Decorative arts flourished. Persia opened to the Western world.

1722–47 AD   Afghani invasion: Isfahan and Shiraz devastated by Afghani warlords. Their last occupying leader, the Persianised and cruel Nadir Shah, who invaded India, was murdered by fanatics.

1747–96 AD   Zands: Indigenous Iranians from the Zagros Mountains who rebuilt Shiraz.

1796–1924 AD   Qajar dynasty: Founded by Turcoman eunuch, Aga Mohammad, who made Tehran his capital. Shah Nasr-al-Din ruled 1848–96. His sons included the crown prince Muzaffar-al-Din, Zil-es-Sultan and Naib-es-Sultaneh.

1881–82 Jane and Marcel Dieulafoy travelled throughout Persia, from the northwest to the south and into Iraq, visiting all the major cities, investigating and recording ancient Persian monuments.

1884–86 Jane and Marcel Dieulafoy excavated the ancient Achaemenid capital of Susa in two winter digs.

Cities underlined were visited by the Dieulafoys

Characters in order of appearance

Louis de Ronchaud, general secretary at the Ministry of Fine Arts, later director of Le Louvre

President Carnot, President of the Third French Republic, 1887–94

Viollet-le-Duc, influential architect engaged in restoration of Gothic monuments

Nasr-al-Din, Shah of Persia, 1848–96

Ferhad Mirza, the shah's uncle, governor of the Persian province of Azerbaijan from 1881, formerly governor of Shiraz

Muzaffar-al-Din Mirza, 28-year-old crown prince

Naib-es-Sultaneh, the shah's third son, Governor of Tehran, Commander-in-Chief and Minister of War.

Edward G. Browne, English traveller in Persia, 1887–88

Dr Tholozan, shah's French physician

Isabella Bird, famous independent traveller, best-selling author, travelled through Persia 1890

Hasan-e Fasa'i', Shirazi noble, author and Qajar chronicler

hadji **mirza Hosein Khan**, grand vizier, 1871–73

General Kouly Khan, town governor of Saveh

mirza Taqi Khan, grand vizier, 1848–52

Père Pascal, head of the Catholic community in New Julfa

General mirza Taqi Khan, Zil-es-Sultan's doctor and personal assistant

Zil-es-Sultan, eldest living son of Shah Nasr-al-Din, governor of Isfahan, Fars and all Persia's southern provinces

Kodja Youssouff, Père Pascal's New Julfa parishioner, Armenian, Isfahani merchant

Youssouff *khanum*, Kodja Youssouff's wife

hadji **Houssein**, Muslim Isfahani merchant

Houssein *khanum*, aka Ziba *khanum*, hadji Houssein's wife

Arabat, Armenian servant who accompanied the Dieulafoys from Isfahan to Bushire

George N. Curzon, English traveller in Persia, 1889–90, later Viceroy of India

Husein Kuli Khan, leader (Ilkani) of the Bakhtiari Lur tribesmen, killed 1882

Henry Rawlinson, British officer employed by the shah, later British political agent in Turkish Arabia based at Baghdad, famous decipherer of Old Persian cuneiform writing

Dr Olding, English member of the British telegraph staff in Shiraz

Sahib Divan, deputy governor of Shiraz, great grandson of the trusted vizier, *hadji* Ibrahim Khan, who betrayed the Zands

William Kennet Loftus, in 1852 identified the Susa mound as the Achaemenid city, Shushan

Mizal Khan, residing at Fallahiyah, governor of Mohammerah, Sheikh of the Muhaisen Ka'b Arabs

Torkhan *khanum*, widow of the lately deceased sheikh, head of Mizal Khan's *anderun* in 1882

Dominici, Captain of the *Mosul* which carried the Dieulafoys from Basra to Baghdad

M. Péretié, French Consul in Baghdad

Jesus, member of Amarah's Christian community

Beni La'am, marsh Arab tribesmen, notorious horse stealers and caravan plunderers

Kerim Khan, chieftain of a Bakhtiari Lur tribe

Mohammad, Kerim Khan's son

Bibi Dordoun, pregnant wife of Dizful's deputy governor

mirza Akbar Ali, town governor of Ahwaz on the Karun River

Golag *khanum*, another widow of the old sheikh, head of Mizal Khan's Fallahiyah *anderun* in 1884

M. Babin, engineer, excavator at Susa, 1884–86

M. Houssay, science graduate of l'Ecole Normale, excavator at Susa, 1884–86

Dr Ross, British Resident at Bushire

Sheikh Mohammad Taher, senior cleric at Dizful

hadji **sayyid Hussein**, Khuzestan's senior cleric

mirza Abdoul-Rahim, Mozaffer el-Molk's spy at Susa

Mozaffer el-Molk, governor of Khuzestan

Sheikh Ali, chieftain of an Arab Beni La'am tribe

Papi Khan, member of Kerim Khan's Bakhtiari tribe

Ousta Hassan, Dizfuli master mason

Ali Khan, chieftain of the powerful Segvend Arabs

M'sban, head of all the many Beni La'am tribes

Attar, tcharvadar bachy of the Dieulafoy caravan to the Tigris in early 1885 and from the Tigris in late 1885

Menchet, chief of a Beni La'am band, subject to M'sban

Jean-Marie, navy carpenter seconded to the second excavation mission, 1885–86

Fellahyé, Menchet's son imposed as guide to the returning mission in late 1885

Sayyid Ali, a mad muleteer who in 1886 transported material to the Ab-i-Diz, tributary of the Karun River

mirza Taguy, an offsider of the hateful mirza Abdoul-Rahim

Glossary

anderun = harem
bellum = small native boat
Hakim = governor, respected citizen
hadji = honorary title awarded after visiting Mecca
imam = cleric (no capital)
Imam = one of the twelve caliphs recognised by the Shi'a (capital)
khanum = wife/ Mrs/ Mme
mehala = larger native boat
prefix mirza = secretary (no capital)
Mirza suffix = Prince (capital)
sayyid = descendant of the prophet
talar = open formal reception area
tcharvadar bachy = chief muleteer

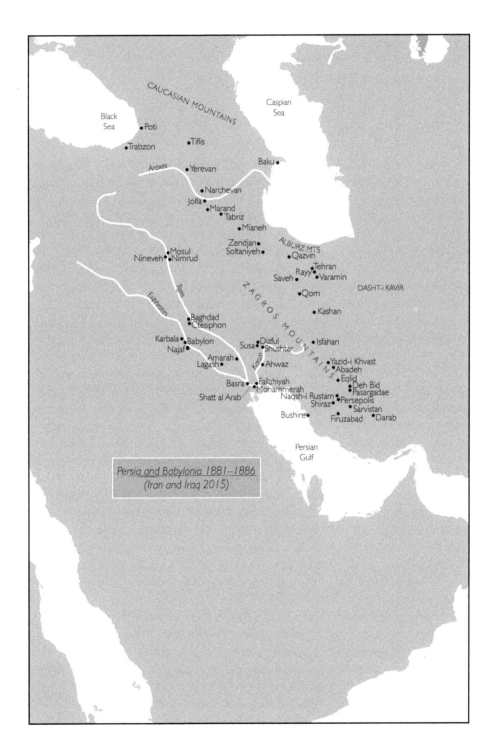

Black
Sea

CAUCASIAN MOUNTAINS

Caspian
Sea

• Poti

• Tiflis

• Trabzon

Baku •

Araxes

• Yerevan

• Narchevan

Jolfa •

• Marand

• Tabriz

• Mianeh

Zendjan •

ALBURZ MTS

Soltaniyeh •

• Qazvin

Mosul

Tehran •

Nineveh • Nimrud

Rayy •

Saveh •

• Varamin

DASHT-i KAVIR

• Qom

Tigris

Z A G R O S

• Kashan

Euphrates

M O U N T A I N S

• Baghdad

• Ctesiphon

Karbala •

• Babylon

Susa

• Dizful

• Isfahan

Najaf •

• Shushtar

Amarah •

Karun

Yazid-i Khvast

Lagash •

• Ahwaz

• Abadeh

Basra •

• Fallahiyah

• Eqlid

• Deh Bid

• Mohammerah

Naqsh-i Rustam

• Pasargadae

Shatt al Arab

Shiraz •

• Persepolis

Bushire •

• Sarvistan

Firuzabad

• Darab

Persian
Gulf

Persia and Babylonia 1881–1886
(Iran and Iraq 2015)

xiii

Foreword

The vast mound of Susa (actually four more or less separate hills) in Khuzestan, south-west Iran, remains one of the most renowned sites in Iran today and, indeed, in the ancient world. Although many of its ruins, covering an area of more than 100 hectares and representing at least 5,000 years of settlement, have been investigated by travellers, explorers and, over the past 200 years, archaeologists, the great majority of its remains are still to be uncovered.

Susa lured Marcel and Jane Dieulafoy to commence excavations there in 1885 and to return in 1886, initiating a French archaeological involvement with Susa which lasted almost unbroken until the Islamic revolution.

Initially the Dieulafoys, Marcel an engineer-turned-archaeologist and the intellectually restless Jane, had been drawn to Persia in search of Sasanian and Seljuk remains and to investigate their relationship to the origins of European Gothic architecture. Gradually, however, their attention turned more and more to Susa, culminating in two seasons of excavations. Both seasons were undertaken under particularly trying conditions with the hazards of malaria and other infections, extremes of temperature, and the difficulties of dealing with corrupt, untrustworthy, and frequently hostile government officials and tribal leaders made even worse by Jane's gender – even if she did habitually keep her hair short and wear men's trousers ('they were comfortable, practical and they kept her safe') – and their non-Muslim 'infidel' beliefs. Despite these hardships and while, inevitably for this period, many of their archaeological methods were crude and lacking in technique, the Dieulafoys along with their almost 300 workmen managed to recover (and ship to France successfully – no mean feat!) some of the finest examples of Achaemenid art and artefacts in the possession of the Louvre, objects which still form the core of that museum's Susa collection. Thus the walls of its Iranian galleries, two of which are named after Jane, boast glazed brick friezes of archers and lions, while in the centre of one gallery sits an Achaemenid column surmounted by its double-headed bull capital retrieved from the Apadana of Darius.

Heather Rossiter's major source for this book was Jane's diary and photographic plates. They record the triumphs and hardships of the Susa excavations, supplementing admirably the more archaeological approach of Marcel's *L'Acropole de Suse*, and give a vivid account of the couple's Persian travels, in particular their journey in 1881–82 from north-west Iran southwards to the Persian Gulf, then to Baghdad and, finally, to Susa. From this comes a rich and unique picture of life in late nineteenth century Iran during the reign of the Qajar ruler Nasr al-Din Shah. Accounts of decrepit villages impoverished by rapacious governors, raiding tribes and devastating endemic malaria, of the country's '*kanat*s, caravanserais, roads and bridges falling into ruin, while the shah and his sons built opulent palaces', of the formidable infant mortality (two out of every three children did not survive), and of the complete desolation and neglect of such formerly glorious cities as Shiraz and Isfahan indicate how far Persia had declined after the demise of the Safavids in the early eighteenth century.

Happily, these depressing pictures are more than balanced by many wonderful vignettes which include travelling through the wild and often spectacular Persian countryside in some of the great caravans which criss-crossed Persia before the age of the automobile, encounters with the vast Bakhtiari and Kashquai nomadic tribes (whose power was later to be severely curtailed by Reza Shah Pahlavi), her dealings with Persian men of all ranks and status – including the Shah himself – and, especially, with Persian women from tribes, villages and the *anderun* (harem). Fluent in Farsi and extremely sympathetic to their status, which was usually little more than that of a chattel, Jane was able to form firm, if ephemeral, bonds with many of the women.

Many of the monuments – both pre-Islamic and Islamic – which she and Marcel visited, such as the great Achaemenid burial ground of Naqsh-i Rustam (along with its Sasanian rock reliefs), the Achaemenid palaces of Pasargadae and Persepolis (at Persepolis Marcel filled a 200-page notebook with notes and drawings and Jane took dozens of photographs), the Sasanian palaces at Firuzabad, the Jameh Mosque of Qazvin, the Blue Mosque at Tabriz (its stunning mosaic tile work now well restored), and the architectural marvel which is the Mausoleum of Uljaitu at Soltaniyeh, are still able to be visited and admired today. Others, like the Sasanian palace at Surmaq whose mudbrick walls were being mined by village farmers for fertiliser when the Dieulafoys passed through, have now, lamentably, been totally degraded or vanished altogether.

Although Jane's copious notes recording her travels through Persia and southern Iraq and the couple's excavations at Susa have been published in French, her exploits have been largely, and unjustly, neglected in the English literature. Fortunately, Heather Rossiter's beautifully constructed and evocative work will at last introduce to a much wider audience Jane's singular tenacity, endurance and character, as well as her remarkable Middle Eastern travels and descriptions of a now-vanished era in the history of Iran.

John Tidmarsh
University of Sydney

Prologue

The Louvre Museum, Paris, 20 October 1886

Jane Dieulafoy stood self-contained and poised as the President of the French Republic pinned the cross of the Chevalier de la Légion d'honneur to her jacket.

'Outrageous,' a woman whispered as applause filled the gallery.

'Scandalous,' whispered another.

It was not Jane's receiving the honour that upset them, but her dress, or, rather, her suit – Jane had given up wearing dresses. Her perfectly tailored plain trouser suit was in stark contrast to the waisted, frilled and trimmed dresses, trains sweeping the floor, worn by the other women. As much as Pierre-Auguste Renoir loved to paint them, and they were high fashion, they were not for Jane. While fighting alongside her husband Marcel in the Franco–Prussian War, riding for fourteen months along Persia's dusty tracks and, later, excavating the secrets of Susa, she had grown accustomed to trousers. As she had explained to the Shah of Persia in the rose-scented garden of the Golistan palace in Tehran, they were comfortable, practical and they kept her safe.

The astonished shah had looked at the petite figure and exclaimed, 'What! That sweet boy is a woman?'

'Indeed, your Majesty,' Colonel Dieulafoy replied proudly, 'she is Madame Dieulafoy, my dear wife.'[1]

Thirty-five-years old and still recovering from a near-fatal miscarriage suffered in a lonely desert, Jane seemed a sparkling boyish figure in the galleries named to honour Marcel and Jane Dieulafoy. Her suit's dark cloth emphasised her fair complexion, the pearl-grey silk collar of her white shirt echoed the gleam in her intensely blue eyes. Though her features were too sharp for conventional prettiness, her vivacity and fine colouring gave her a subtle beauty.

Marcel Dieulafoy lost his air of haughty detachment and allowed his pleasure to show. Louvre director Louis de Ronchaud beamed like a proud parent, which, in a professional way, he was. Behind Jane a pride of lions strutted the wall, to her left a guard of archers paraded on fine brick panels and rearing high above her were paired bull heads atop a fluted column. Glass display cases, packed full with alabaster vases, ancient seals and antique jewellery, reflected her image.

These treasures from Susa in southern Persia, now called Iran, made an impressive addition to the Louvre's archaeological collection. They opened a new window into the achievements of the ancient Near East and the contribution of its vanished cities to Western civilisation. The enamelled brick *Frieze of the Lions* and the *Frieze of the Archers* were quite unlike anything in other developing Near Eastern antiquities collections. Berlin, London and Istanbul had only colourless stone reliefs. The Dieulafoy ceramics had sparkled in the sunshine when they lined Susa's palace courtyards millennia before; now they glittered in the Louvre's vast gallery. The clarity and delicacy of their colours, the expressive rage of the lions – no tame cats these, lips drawn back to reveal lethal incisors, muscles taut to leap off the wall – and the poise of the stylised archers, their spear butts resting on the forward foot, made this collection unique.

And it was Jane who had found the bricks and painstakingly with a small trowel had dug out their shattered fragments and in the Louvre basement meticulously recreated their design. She and Marcel had spent two difficult seasons in southern Iran excavating Susa in 1884–86. Despite dangers and deception, illness and starvation, the Dieulafoys had persevered, sharing the excitement of retrieving the old Achaemenid city from the earth and the satisfaction of safely expatriating a share of its treasures. But the enamelled brick friezes, they were essentially Jane's achievement.

In 1881–82 Jane had ridden 6000 kilometres through Persia. Always at hand was the little notebook in which she recorded not only Persia's strange beauty and its ancient monuments, but most particularly details of Persian daily life. Of necessity she mingled with people of high and low degree. Their story became part of her story, an exotic background against which she moved. Her warmth and charisma gave her access to worlds closed to her more austere husband. Her easy manner overcame administrative restrictions and reassured hesitant members of minority groups. Her humour resolved many difficult situations.

Lowly Persians, nomads, tribal chiefs, princes and functionaries fill her pages, but particularly resonant are the women, both vital tribal women and the pathetic creatures locked in the *anderun*s (harems). Jane, an early feminist nourished in the intellectual heart of the Third Republic, believed passionately that women should be free to live dignified independent lives, and their subjugation in Persia saddened her. She saw and regretted their treatment and deplored their lack of education, yet spoke to them always without condescension. 'No, the British Shah, Queen Victoria, is very powerful, but she does not have a beard and there is only one husband in her *anderun*,'[2] she explained patiently, suppressing her amusement.

Her cumbrous photographic equipment, too, was always with her. Produced using the newly developed dry-plate technique, her photographs were a revelation to Europeans who had no chance of seeing enigmatic Persia or of meeting its inhabitants. Her camera captured the mullahs' turbans, mosque interiors, the shah's nieces and the crumbling history and scenic glory of Persia.

Published in the Paris journal, *le Tour du monde*, her written dispatches and her photographs made her reputation. Her work at Susa earned her the Légion d'honneur.

The inauguration of the Dieulafoy Galleries at the Musée du Louvre and the award of France's highest honour marked Jane's day of triumph. If she chose to appear on this public occasion in an outfit that would become her hallmark, she was making no fashion statement. Rather, her trouser suit was a public declaration of how she wished to be perceived; it was a claim to equality. She never again wore a dress.

Sweet boy and dear wife – Jane was both, but she was her own person, a woman of great courage, intelligence and determination.

Chapter 1
A daring destination

Nothing was less likely for a girl born on 29 June 1851 in the French provincial city of Toulouse than that she would go to Persia; yet the first decades of Jane Magre's life seem almost designed to equip her with the skills and attitudes to survive such a chance.

The wealthy Magre family lived in a grand townhouse on the best street of Toulouse, but spent the summers and celebrated Christmas in their medieval château de Terride near Castelsarrasin. Widowed while Jane was still a baby, Estelle-Monique-Marcelle Magre ran her establishments with gentle efficiency. She was a shrewd woman who recognised early that her youngest daughter was different from her sisters. Suspecting that high intelligence explained Jane's precocious behaviour, even naughtiness, Mme Magre sent her, aged eleven, to be educated by the Sisters at the exclusive Convent of the Assumption in Auteuil, a fashionable Paris suburb. In effect exiled there, Jane applied the characteristics that would ensure her survival in Persia and make her name in the Paris salons: curiosity, courage, grit and enterprise. She learned ancient and modern languages, the history of the Persian Wars – although from a Greek perspective – and read the classic literature. When 'The Orient', then the rage in Parisian artistic and literary salons, penetrated the thick convent walls, Jane discovered Delacroix, Fromentin and Maxime du Camp and through them she was infected with ʾe oriental virus. In her art class, instead of delicate pastel drawings of the ʾt Paris bonnets, Arabs swathed in burnous and turbaned in colourful ʾloped across her paper.

Magre returned to Toulouse at eighteen desperate for something ʾer inquisitive mind. She considered the prospect of marriage. ʾtual sustenance would married life in a provincial town provide? Twice-weekly municipal concerts, afternoons studying fashion, the parochial social round that she despised – the future seemed bleak.

It is not surprising that when she met Marcel Dieulafoy she fell madly in love. Also from a comfortable Toulouse background, he had recently returned from Algeria. Jane's imagination gilded him with the glamour of the Orient and garnished him with her passion for the East. It was romantic love, a dangerous love, but she was too young and inexperienced to know there was any other kind.

In the French colonies of North Africa, Marcel had worked as an engineer of bridges and railways. Escaping the ordered European enclave in the evenings, he wandered into the scented chaos of the Kasbah and discovered another world. Confronted by early Muslim buildings, his habitual European condescension withered and he decided to explore the origins of this astonishing Islamic architecture. For four years he sweated over the iron roads by day and studied in the evening, dreaming every night of travelling to the Near East.

When he returned to France and met Jane he realised immediately she was the perfect companion. He confided his dreams born in the old Algerian towns.

Jane saw Marcel as intellectually and physically adventurous, someone who would confront life bravely and have the fortitude to take from it what he wanted, not someone who would settle for the mundane or accept what was imposed on him. She knew what she wanted from life and she believed intuitively that he wanted the same – a full life shared with a brave companion. Above all, she wanted an intellectual equal. With Marcel, she thought, she would never have to hide her intelligence or pretend to accept the conventional. She would be able to use her talents, develop her mind, and achieve what she knew she was capable of – something unique, though she did not yet know what that might be. Marcel offered an intellectual life she could share and a dream they could pursue together.

Three months after their marriage in May 1870, the Dieulafoys woke to find their beloved France invaded by the Prussians. Although excused from military service, Marcel could not remain an onlooker as French armies were humiliated and Paris besieged. When the emperor abdicated and fled and the Third French Republic was declared, Marcel enlisted as a captain in the army of the Loire. Jane would not let him go, not alone – if he risked his life, she would risk hers. She must be with him, by his side. Refused enlistment as a soldier, Jane donned the grey blouse and trousers of a *franc-tireur*, volunteer, cut off her blonde curls and pulled on the military hat, fastened spurs over her boots and picked up her riding whip. Marcel looked at her with pride and admiration. His dear wife made a sweet boy, a pretty boy whose flashing blue eyes charmed everyone. He insisted she sit for her portrait.

That neglected portrait still hangs in the house bequeathed by the Dieulafoys to the French Red Cross. She is young and confident. Her blue eyes laugh out of the torn canvas.

But as the autumn of 1870 proceeded and people began to die from starvation in blockaded Paris, Jane laughed less often. During the terrible winter when the army camped in snow and frost and undertook forced marches, she was at Marcel's side. With him she galloped to save a troop cut off by the Prussians, together they undertook a secret mission to the north and they stood side by side as the battalion was presented to General Barrail. The commandant recounted Jane's courage and coolness in moments of danger, but it was the whispered 'her uncle is Vice-President of the Admiralty Board', that earned her a deep bow. Marcel was decorated.

When Paris fell at the end of January 1871, Jane and Marcel returned to their Toulouse apartment. Slowly her health recovered from the deprivation and misery of that winter. On 29 June 1871 she turned twenty. She could now add 'experienced roughrider and crack shot' to her qualifications for Persia.

The freedom of the grey trousers, the standard issue of a volunteer, affected Jane deeply. She realised how women's cumbersome clothing restricted their lives. Later she would rebel and make trousers her signature dress, but in Toulouse during the 1870s she could not adopt them. Even with her status as war heroine, she would have shocked the conservative *haute bourgeoisie* of the southern town. Besides, in France it was an offence for women to wear men's dress.

War brought change for Marcel also. While Algeria had been mostly a battle with sand, Toulouse had few challenges for a capable engineer. On discharge, Marcel gave up trains and accepted responsibility for Toulouse's civic and historic monuments. For a few years he and Jane fuelled their oriental passion by visits to Morocco, Egypt and southern Spain to explore Islamic art and architecture, but they dreamed of the East. Determined to realise the dream, Jane began adding the Persian language, Farsi, to her accomplishments.

In 1874 Marcel met the influential architect, Viollet-le-Duc, who was restoring Notre Dame and other derelict Gothic structures vandal-ised during the French Revolution and neglected since. Viollet-le-Duc encouraged Marcel to study architecture and archaeology as twin disciplines. When Marcel suggested a link between the Gothic architecture that appeared suddenly in Europe in the early twelfth century and the ancient Persian dynasty, the Sasanids[1], who for centuries had ruled the Near East, Viollet-le-Duc shrugged and said, 'Go and see for yourself.'

A casual remark, but fuel for a fire already burning. In the 1870s few Europeans had visited Persia and its ancient structures were barely known, apart from Persepolis and Isfahan. Although the Frenchmen, Flandin and Coste, artist and architect, respectively, had in 1851 published *Voyage en Perse*, an illustrated account of their Persian travels, the detail in their lithographs did not satisfy Marcel and Viollet-le-Duc. Looking at the plates of the Sasanid site at Firuzabad, for example, they asked, 'How is it constructed? What are the dimensions?' The pictures gave no answer.

While Marcel struggled with that problem, Jane studied the travel literature, sparse and mainly in English, and the ancient sources, mostly Greek. By early 1880 the Dieulafoys had made their decision. They would go to Persia, however difficult that might be.

Jane's friends in Toulouse were appalled. They warned against it, describing the hazards of travel in Eastern countries. They called Jane 'an original', which was 'a grave accusation in the provinces'. Better, they told her, to stay home 'and hang perfumed sachets in the wardrobe, spread powder against silver fish, and inventory your preserves and saucepans.'[2] Domestic matters held little charm for Jane and she laughingly dismissed their misgivings.

Marcel took temporary leave and the Dieulafoys moved into the Paris apartment of Marcel's mother. Always practical, Jane began a three-month first-aid course centred on tropical diseases, studied Persian history and Farsi grammar at the School of Oriental Languages, and took a course in photography to learn the newly developed gelatin dry glass plate technique. In any trip to Persia, she would not go as baggage. By equipping herself she was staking out her areas of responsibility.

As he looked for financial support, Marcel refined his objectives to set before the authorities. He wanted evidence to support his theories concerning Gothic architecture, he said. Since 1868 Europeans had begun, reluctantly, to admit that its inspiration came from the East, brought back in the minds and the artefacts pilfered by the Crusaders, who for two hundred years, from 1096, had swept eastwards in successive bands to recover Jerusalem and the Holy Lands from the Muslims. Although ultimately the Crusades were a territorial failure, in lands dominated by Persia's

Seljuk dynasty the returning Crusaders had seen a rich and sophisticated culture. Coming from the regressive poverty of the European Dark Ages, envy filled their hearts when they were confronted by the dazzling beauty of cities like Damascus and their gorgeous treasures, as at Antioch. They discovered Seljuk military architecture, built their castles and fortresses in Seljuk style and took the plans home with them. Back in the squalor of their home cities with new ideas and skills and looted mechanical devices, they used their captured artisans and engineers to transform their built world. Within sixty years Europe had completely discarded the limiting round arch of the Romanesque and had adopted the pointed arch of the East, enabling elaborate stone vaulted roofs to rise above high thin walls. The great Gothic cathedrals of Medieval Europe grew from a seed planted east of the Mediterranean.

Marcel was an intelligent man with the engineer's concern for foundations. For him an unanswered question remained – where were the roots of that inspiring Seljuk architecture? After a decade of study he suspected the truth lay with the Sasanids, the Persian dynasty defeated by the Arabs when they swept into Persia aflame with the teachings of Mohommad in 637 AD. 'With the speed and violence of a desert whirlwind',[3] the Arabs shattered Sasanid political power and smashed their ancient religion, yet, like the Crusaders later, they were conquered by aesthetics. Was European architecture a grandchild of the forced marriage of Sasanid with Islam, speculated Marcel.

Accordingly, the stated purpose of Marcel's journey to Iran was to identify and record Persian monuments and ancient Iranian architecture. His wife and colleague, Jane, would be an integral part of the endeavour, maintaining a photographic record and keeping the daily log, he explained. Ironically, although her part sounded secondary, the expedition's primary success came from Jane's diary which, illustrated with her perceptive images of the Persian people and photos of the monuments, was published in installments in 1883–84 in the Paris journal, *le Tour du monde*. It made Jane's literary reputation and profoundly affected Marcel's professional life.

Hachette, the premier publishing house of the time, issued the collected articles in 1887 in a volume entitled *La Perse: La Chaldee et la Susiane*. An invaluable source for this biography, it is also most highly valued in Iran today. Her camera had captured many things now lost and her pictures not only hang on the wall of restaurants and hotels but have become the official Iranian record. In his foreword to the 1989 Tehran facsimile edition of *La Perse: La Chaldee et la Susiane*, publisher Abbas Sahab acknowledges that her illustrations 'are particularly interesting and bear witness to the monuments that disappeared towards the end of the Qadjar [sic] reign, and her finesse, precision and artistic mastery make this an exceptional work. The historical and social remarks of Mme Dieulafoy are generally of value, so much so that her book becomes a part of the archives of the Qadjar epoch.'

Jane was not considering posterity in Paris in 1880; she was busy selecting equipment and occupied with the apparent trivia of dress. Although it was the great age of frocks, there would be none in her luggage. While no one in Paris knew much about Persia, the few Frenchmen who had been there all reported that women were only ever seen swathed in shapeless black, scurrying to the markets or dashing from one house to another. Even when the call to prayer sounded from the minaret, they were seldom seen entering a mosque and certainly they were never seen drinking tea in the bazaar where the men gathered. What the women wore in their houses was unknown to the travellers. Only when Jane returned to Paris with her photographs would the French see Ziba *khanum's*[4] short gathered skirt hanging from generous hips and Ziba's breasts peeking through transparent black lace above a bare rounded stomach. Commonplace today, perhaps; hugely titillating then.

If short, slight, blue-eyed Jane were to stride safely through the Persian streets, it would not do to show her blonde curls or let a fashionable frock reveal her slim figure. European fashion in the 1880s decreed a dress that enclosed the body from neck to knee as tightly as possible. Large steps were considered ungraceful; women's knees were actually tied together to make them impossible. Below the knee the skirt flared into a shallow train – not desirable on the unpaved streets of Persian towns where sanitation was medieval.

But hygiene and convenience were not what persuaded Jane into trousers. In Persia foreign men were treated with great suspicion; a foreign woman walking openly about the Persian streets would be at risk of her life. It would be safer, Jane concluded, to be a boy.

Persia, an unusual and daring destination in the late nineteenth century, was difficult to reach. Jane and Marcel sought advice. There were two routes, they were told. They could cut down from the Mediterranean through the Suez Canal, opened twenty-two years earlier, and emerge from the Red Sea into the Gulf of Aden, and from there the pirate-infested waters along the Yemeni and Omani coasts of the Arabian Peninsula would take them

Persian woman's street dress, 1880s

Ziba Khanum

straight to the Persian Gulf. But the longer route via Karachi with a back-track up to the Persian Gulf was safer. After forty days at sea they would reach Bushire in southern Persia. There, their friends warned them, they would 'fall into the hands of savages outside the authority of the shah who would cut them into little pieces.'[5]

In Mme Dieulafoy's comfortable Paris home they considered that route and rejected it without suspecting how familiar it would become. Instead, they chose a northern access through the Black Sea and the Caucasus, from where they could skirt the foot of Mount Ararat and drop down into Tehran. Here, too, their friends warned, they would be cut into little pieces. 'The Russo–Turkish War has ended but it has settled nothing. The Kurds are raiding from the mountains, burning and murdering in the villages where you will stay, flaying and killing on the roads you will travel. The unhappy Kurds,' they said, 'are pitiless.'[6]

Marcel applied for extended leave. As Jane explained in the Introduction to *La Perse: La Chaldée et la Susiane*, 'Marcel had great difficulty getting leave . . . and could not obtain any financial assistance, only a beautiful white sheet of paper on which a calligrapher of the third order recommends him to the good offices of our diplomats in the Orient and requests the representatives of the Ministry of Foreign Affairs to facilitate his mission, that being as interesting as it was unfunded.' Marcel 'had made a good impression on M. de Ronchaud, [then] general secretary at the Ministry of Fine Arts. Thanks to his intervention the official who was blocking Marcel's request was demoted and we found ourselves free as air with a year of liberty ahead of us.'[7]

Marcel may have told the shah later, 'I am sent on a mission by the government to study the ruined monuments of Kosrow, Darius and Shapur,'[8] but it was not true. Mere travellers, the Dieulafoys had no powerful connections. To set off without official backing to a place barely known to Europeans, where they would run the gauntlet of a society notorious for its antipathy to foreigners, was almost courting danger. And there would be no comfort along the way: the country was so undeveloped that 'travel is a portion of hell fire', as the Arab proverb asserts. Their financial resources, despite their upper middle-class families, were not unlimited and nor were Jane's physical reserves. In reality a frail person, her spirit was always greater than her bodily strength. Yet Marcel's confidence in her resilience must have been substantial. Obsessed though he was by the Sasanians, he deeply loved that 'sweet boy, his dear wife', and would not intentionally have exposed her to hazards beyond her capacity. Unfortunately, the hazards were greater than he knew.

Chapter 2
To a land without roads

In February 1881 Jane and Marcel Dieulafoy left Marseilles in a ship bound for Constantinople (today's Istanbul) by way of the Piraeus, port for Athens. Although Marseilles, bathed by the Mediterranean, may have been marginally warmer than land-locked Paris in the middle of winter, at sea in the *Ava* the cold was extreme. Grey clouds hid the morning sun and the decks were freezing. The passengers gathered in the unlit saloon, their teeth chattering as they took their places for luncheon in an unheated dining room. When they complained, the enraged captain threatened to turn on the punkah fans. And, he added, 'they had best be in bed by 8 o'clock because all lights would then be extinguished.'[1] Aghast, the travellers gossiped with the crew and soon discovered what was filling the hold and all the spare cabins. The ship was stuffed with gunpowder, ammunition and arms, destined for the Macedonians in northern Greece struggling to throw off the Turkish yoke.

The Macedonians had appealed to the Europeans. The *Ava*'s cargo was a present from the French government. 'This was surprising,' wrote Jane ironically. 'In Parliament, the minister had sworn they would never send arms to Greece; in that conflict France maintained strict neutrality. With that declaration of principles, the *Ava* moored for two days at Piraeus to unload the cargo.'[2]

Taking advantage of this delay, Jane and Marcel took the train to Athens and climbed the path to the Acropolis. For a romantic who had dreamed of being carried up in a litter, or at least riding up on horseback, it was a pedestrian way to arrive at the classical monuments, but more distressing to Jane was their terrible state of ruin and neglect.

From September 1687, when Venetian mortar had blown up the Turkish powder magazine in the Parthenon, the site had been littered with fallen columns, smashed metopes and pieces of pediment too large for the local inhabitants to pilfer. When Lord Elgin arrived on the hilltop more than a hundred years after the explosion, he found Turkish houses filling the spaces between the shattered temples and the pasha's[3] ladies ensconced in the Erechtheum. Like Jane almost a hundred years later, Elgin was distressed. Some record must be made, he thought, before everything is lost.

His initial plan to have drawings and casts made of the marbles was foiled. When the Turkish pasha objected to the erection of scaffolding because infidel workers would be able to see into his harem there could be no casts, and the draughtsmen's efforts were made impossible by 'mercenary and insolent guards'. Lord Elgin rose to the challenge and shipped the marbles to Britain.

In 1830 the pasha evacuated his harem only days before the newly independent southern Greeks tore down the minaret from the corner of the Parthenon and removed the mosque from its heart. When Jane stood among the fallen columns, a further fifty years of neglect and decay had affected this once-magnificent site, and it would be another fifty before re-erection of the columns and repair of the buildings would begin. Cement reinforced with steel rods is a not inconsiderable part of the Parthenon seen today.

Surveying the chaos on the Acropolis in early 1881, Jane was a confident, even an opinionated woman, well informed about the heroic past. Since the purpose of their journey was to identify and record ancient Persian monuments, the irony of the Parthenon being their first testament to Persian history was not lost on her. Jane was well aware of the long-standing enmity between Persia and Greece.

Aeons before the Romans intervened, well before a Roman emperor founded Constantinople, ancient Greeks and Persians confronted one another on a frontier that moved back and forth through Macedonia and Anatolia (modern Turkey) and through the Aegean islands. At the beginning of the fifth century BC the Greek homeland itself became the frontier. The Persians rapidly overran the northern Greek states, but were repulsed at Marathon in 490 BC. In thanksgiving the Athenians began building a great temple on the Athens Acropolis. It was still unfinished in 480 BC when King Xerxes led the Persians back to Athens and razed it. Its replacement, Pericles's temple to Athena Parthenos, was begun only after a peace treaty was agreed.

When Jane inspected this later temple, the broken and desolate Parthenon, her thoughts flew to Susa, the city where Greeks and Persians had sat down in 478 BC to seal an accord to end that war, and where 150 years later Alexander the Great had taken Greek revenge. Although she hoped to visit the ancient site, she had no premonition of how deeply Susa would resonate in her own story.

She kicked the stones and cursed Xerxes, at the same time cursing Lord Elgin for carrying off the marbles in the name of preservation. Ironically, a similar justification would see Jane removing from Susa Persian treasures which today are the pride of the Louvre. Perhaps they were both right.[4]

Without its cargo of arms, the *Ava* danced up through the Aegean on the tops of the waves. At the entry to the Dardanelles, Jane gazed south towards a hillock where in 1873 Schliemann had found the site of ancient Troy. Like all Europe, she was entranced by 'Priam's treasure': silver vases, gold cups, earrings and jewelled headdresses unearthed among broken jars and rotted furniture, but she could not know that within five years she also would be a famous excavator.

Constantinople took her by surprise. She had, she said, 'never realised its splendours of art and nature or the magnificence of the city.' Paeans to the 'little caiques flying like golden arrows on the tranquil waters,' descriptions of 'houses painted red, yellow and blue . . . on snow-dusted slopes' and of bridges of boats thrown across the Golden Horn, accounts of the 'lively population swarming amid the disorder usual in seaports', quickly filled her notebook. Fifteen days 'were not enough to see all the Byzantine monuments and the modern Turkish edifices, to aid the sultan's prayers in the mosques . . . to twirl with the dervishes, to run through bazaars and caravanserais despite the snow and slush, to taste kebabs roasting in the open air, nor to taste the cheese pastries unequalled anywhere, to wash oneself at the seraglio, and to learn from the Persian merchants in the bazaar that the quickest and safest route into Persia is still that through Tiflis.'[5]

Almost with regret Jane and Marcel forsook the Turks they had cursed in Greece and unexpectedly come to like in Constantinople and took passage across the Black Sea for Poti, en route for Tiflis, Georgia, their ultimate destination, Persia.

The cable was brief: Take the woman, kill her.

Jane Dieulafoy shrank back against the smoke stack of the Russian steamship. Marcel put his arm around her. Down below in his many-oared boat rocking on the waves, stood the governor of Trabzon angrily waving a thin yellow paper. The setting sun glinted on his jewelled sword hilt. His slave crew rested on their oars, waiting. Looking down from the bridge high above, the ship's captain seemed undecided. The waters of the Black Sea were a clear blue.

Suddenly, violently, the ship's saloon door slammed open. A young man broke from it and ran along the deck, heading desperately towards the bridge. The governor shouted, his boat leapt on the bright blue water, the muscles of his crew flashed bronze in the evening light. Jane glimpsed a smaller figure parcelled in black running on the far side of the young man. Running. Running. The governor whipped out his pistol. From the stern of his boat two guards levelled rifles at the bridge.

'Put down your arms at once,' said the captain in a voice of iron that rang across the water almost to the Pontic Alps. 'How dare you threaten me.'

The monstrous insult of his ship being menaced had decided him. Without looking at the couple lying at his feet begging his protection, the captain ordered, 'Bring up the anchor.'

Out on the deep Black Sea waters, Jane Dieulafoy said to the captain, 'My God, the naughty sparrows! What a risk they took. What would have happened to them?'

'"Take the woman, kill her," were the pasha's instructions,' the captain replied, shrugging. 'She'd have been tied in a sack and thrown in the sea. I often meet the pasha in the Istanbul bazaar. He'd have no pity for someone who escaped his harem.'

Watching the night take away the Alps that Xenophon had crossed, Jane shivered for the girl and her Armenian lover. 'Poor little thing,' she whispered.

Jane's account of the incident[6] indicates how shocked and affected she was. Harems and the women locked away in them were part of the orientalist fantasy, the reality grimly different, this encounter priming her for later Persian experiences. She recognised, too, that both she and the girl were hiding their female bodies, the girl swathed in voluminous black and she dressed as a boy.

Jane Dieulafoy wore her trousers with panache. She had designed a very practical outfit for this journey. Her white cotton shirt was held at the neck by a light silk cravat. Over it she wore a straight-cut woollen coat buttoned only to the waist so that when she sat astride a horse, as she knew she must through the whole length of Persia and possibly into Iraq, the wide skirt panels could separate and cover the tops of her legs. She would need the warmth on her thighs, at least until the summer came. She had thought carefully about the trousers; they had to be loose enough to be comfortable in the saddle, while the cuff must be wide enough to let her unfasten her high lace-up boots. Over her ensemble she wore a thick great-coat, and yet she shivered in the ice-laden March winds sweeping across from central Asia.

The early morning light revealed small villages and steep green slopes at the eastern end of the Black Sea. In Poti the French Vice-Consul waited on the wharf. The poor miserable little town, battered in the recent Russo–Turkish War, was an important outlet for Caucasian wines and fruit, tea and hides. The customs agents understood agricultural products, but Jane's baggage baffled them. In which tax category were the leather chests filled with gelatin bromide-coated glass plates, her photographer's tripods and her cameras? And were the glass demijohns, full of chemicals and packed in boxes of straw, classed as liquor? Then there were the weapons – revolvers, rifles and ammunition. Surely they were contraband? Adroitly resolving the dilemma with a little baksheesh, the consul quickly swept them towards Marcel's theodolite, surveyor's chain and instruments and had them loaded onto the train leaving for Tiflis, the city that is today's Tbilisi, capital of the Republic of Georgia.

Tiflis lay at the heart of the Caucasus, the narrow east–west land bridge between the Black and Caspian seas, the north–south highway between Europe and Asia. For millennia invaders from the steppes of Central Asia had fought their way along its rich valleys and through its high mountain passes, Mongols and Avars, Alans and Scythians, Timurids and Cimmerians barrelling through, intent on ravishing the rich Persian uplands and the sweeping farmlands of Anatolia. At the time of Jane's journey the Russians were pressing in from the north, snatching at Caucasian territories then held by the huge Ottoman Turk Empire based at Constantinople, and threatening to overrun northern Persia. While the frontline between the three battling armies thrashed north and south, swayed east and west, the native inhabitants: Azerbaijanis, Kurds, Georgians, Chechens, Armenians, tried desperately to defend their culture, their livelihood, language and religions against the ambitions of the more powerful states. The treaty that had ended the Russo–Turkish War, the most recent outburst of Russian aggression, was an unsatisfactory affair that incensed many peoples, not only the Kurds whose lands had been assigned to Persia.

As the train rocked through sublime Georgian scenery, Marcel was filled with admiration for the engineers who had flung the railway like pages from a textbook across the Caucasian Mountains. The train sped ahead on a railbed incised into steep mountain flanks hung with emerald-green and towards sheer rockfaces before disappearing into the black of a tunnel opening. When it emerged into the dazzling Georgian sunlight, it was usually to traverse a viaduct crossing a dark ravine. The railway climbed to the top of the watershed that separates the Black Sea drainage from the Caspian, then eased down through tortuous gorges, passing at the sidings 'long lines of tank-cars [crawling] by like an army of gigantic armour-plated caterpillars'[7] carrying what made the Russians so anxious to annex the territory, oil from Baku.

In the amazingly beautiful and dramatic Georgian landscape, mountains hang down from white clouds. From their slopes water cascades into fertile valleys where the climate is sub-tropical, yet Jane's diary is filled with descriptions of miserable villages deserted and broken by war, herds of swine their only living creatures. She wondered where the people had gone.

Suddenly, she glimpsed a posse of horsemen poised watchful on a mountain flank. With a wild cry they galloped down the slope, bridles flashing with metal inlay, saddlecloths streaked with colour. Wheeling their horses, they cantered alongside the train. Jane glimpsed white teeth gleaming in tanned faces, daggers at the belt, swords waved in the air, muskets slung across shoulders, bandoliers filled with ammunition. She felt for her revolver, but the shouting Georgians had come for admiration, not booty.

'The Georgians are all princes, but poor princes,'[8] a Greek merchant told her sadly. Though Georgia had been Christian since early in the fourth century, its tiny constituent principalities had fought each other more frequently than they had repelled non-Christian invaders. Now only the church had any wealth and that, in the form of jewel-encrusted, gold-sheathed icons, was well hidden.

Tiflis hung off the side of a mountain, with the oldest part of the town sitting on the banks of a wild river. Racing along a rocky bed, the turbulent water turned the millwheels and sometimes, swollen with melt, threatened the hovels where the poorest people lived and the bazaars where they traded. Further up the mountain stood the palace of the governor, Russian Grand Duke Constantine, and many churches lined well-made streets. The once-gracious city, still scarred from its 1795 sack by the Persians, seemed to Jane's eyes nothing more than an impoverished provincial Russian town.

Anxious to begin research on the monuments, the Dieulafoys called on the French Consul and immediately began to arrange transport into Persia, but as they walked about the Georgian city they found another reason for a quick departure.

Despite a reputation for charm and courtly manners, their fearlessness and utter lawlessness made the Georgians difficult to govern. Proud of their ancient literature and refined language, they despised their coarse Russian masters. The Dieulafoys were struck by the *hauteur* of the bearded figures they passed in the street. Hatted with Persian lamb, booted to the knee, wasp-waisted in their belted tight-fitting frock coats, they were hung about with damascened small arms. The Georgian women, never having been veiled or enclosed, walked with the pride of queens – resentful queens. Like the men affronted by the Russian occupation, they seethed with bitterness and hatred. Jane sensed incipient rebellion. Adding to the incendiary atmosphere were clusters of angry Greek Christian refugees, further casualties of the Russo–Turkish War who had fled the Pontus when the Muslim Turks reoccupied it. Too many people, too few resources and too much religion, an eternal equation to disaster then as now, predicated an eruption.

Touched by Georgia's misery, yet fearful that other people's politics might prevent her from getting into Persia, Jane hurried along. A poster for a concert that evening by Tchaikovsky surprised her, but before night had fallen a dispatch arrived announcing the assassination of Russian Tsar Alexander. Twenty years to the day since he had freed the serfs, someone had thrown a bomb. 'In the cafes officers, functionaries . . . discuss nothing else . . . [though] the people go about their affairs indifferent,'[9] Jane recorded. Tiflis closed its town gates and suddenly all foreigners were suspect. Yesterday's warm regard became today's suspicion. To the Tiflis police almost 3000 kilometres from St Petersburg, yesterday's arrivals could be assassins, or at least conspirators. Taken in for questioning, Colonel Dieulafoy assumed his most imperious manner, stood tall and straight as though again on a battlefield, presented their passports, waved his letter from the Ministry of Foreign Affairs, and called for the French Consul. Despite such a display of dignity they were detained for eight hours, then forbidden to leave town. How could they? The town was closed, the gates shut.

Word that the Tsar's assassin had been captured and the anarchist leader Sophia Perovskaya arrested did not reach Tiflis until the funeral ceremonies were over. The city gates were opened.

A hired berliner, not a large carriage despite needing a team of six to draw it, wheeled round from the stables. While their baggage was being lashed to the rear platform provided for standing footmen, Jane waited in the warm sunshine. She was a very handsome boy, chic but not conspicuous in her trousers and redingote, a plain silk cravat matching the grey of her helmet, a rifle over her shoulder and a riding whip in her hand. The blonde curls were tucked out of sight. At Marcel's signal she walked towards the carriage, her stride confident and easy. Unencumbered by the knee-tie so happily left with the frocks in Paris, there was an echo of the military in the bearing of her short, slight body.

The postilions lashed the horses and the berliner rocked away. As the coach travelled south through vineyards stretched along the valleys, where spring sunshine was already coaxing tiny lime-green leaves from gnarled stems, Marcel and Jane were confident of reaching the Persian frontier in four days. Happy to leave Tiflis behind, they shrugged away regret that recent heavy snowfalls had closed the side road to Mount Ararat. 'It wasn't the mountain that lured us from France,' said Jane. The passage of armies had damaged the highway, the berliner was badly sprung, and Marcel, a tall angular man with a big head, felt increasingly cramped. It is only four days to the border, he comforted himself.

Ten days later they reached Yerevan in Armenia – and the border was as far away again. Despite the imperial pass bought in Tiflis entitling them to a change of horses at the staging posts, there had been long delays waiting for fresh animals. Accommodation at the posthouses was primitive. Ice covered the mountain passes. When a snowstorm blinded horses and coachman, the berliner careered into a ditch. 'I'm thrown left and right, then I find myself on top of my husband in a capsized vehicle.' They spent a night in a primitive village where they became infested with fleas. By the sixth day their supplies had gone and there was nothing to buy along the way.

They arrived in Yerevan starving. When their carriage rolled into the posthouse courtyard a dirty little boy with bright, intelligent eyes dashed forward, snatched their baggage and carried it into a bare miserable room. Recognising their urgent need for food, the child led them to the bazaar. From that night's diary entry drip the succulent juices of eastern cooking: 'a booth . . . On the bench is a large basin full of mutton meat cut small; a brazier with glowing embers is set alongside, ready to receive the skewer. How could we resist the temptation? We pass behind the chef who invites us to sit on a wooden bench, and we help him to make the kebab. The cook seizes a handful of meat and pushes the pieces onto a metal spike, then he takes a handful of water and drips it slowly on the meat: at one moment I think I see the artist using his tongue to fix a rebellious morsel, but I don't go deeply into a question so lacking in interest. In any case, that culinary manoeuvre doesn't do any harm to the perfection of the kebabs that are ready in a few minutes, wrapped in a small piece of bread. We devour them greedily, and, that accomplished, we are strong enough to take a look at the town.'[10]

The town's history could be read in the streets where 'the flat Russian cap and the cylindrical Persian lambskin hat are equally mixed, mosques outnumber the single church, the atmosphere is almost Persian,' and the common speech a Turkic dialect.

Still hungry after days without food, they dined again three hours later at the inn and again Jane describes her meal – a salad of fermented cabbage mixed with mutton pieces and yoghurt, rice sprinkled with dried raisins in the Persian style, sugared pig's trotters served in a dish of stewed prunes. With 'well-made wine of a golden colour', she toasted Noah, locally credited with planting the first vines at the foot of Mount Ararat.

At daybreak the Dieulafoys climbed to the top of the citadel for a clear view of the mountain where the ark supposedly grounded after the Biblical flood. At the end of a green valley and flanked by lesser mountains 'Ararat rises majestically, forever snow-crested. The summit, formed by two peaks of unequal size separated by a col, dominates the skyline.'[11]

Well fed and having slept comfortably, they were able to face the berliner and were away early. Spring had filled the fields with flowers and the rivers with floodwater – and soon they were being pulled out of a bog by a bullock team. At the next posthouse, while watching twelve horses mounted by six postilions being harnessed to the berliner, Jane asked in surprise, 'Why so many?'

'You will see,' was the coachman's cryptic response.

Ahead was a swollen river. Gathering speed and rocking from side to side, the carriage bounded over gravel and stones. The postilions dug in their spurs and beat with their whips, the coachman swore furiously and the berliner launched into the white foam. Marcel and Jane were thrown about; water flooded into the coach and soaked the cushions; soon they were climbing the bank on the far side. At the next posthouse the Dieulafoys were thankful to find a fire, for, said Jane, 'a bath in the river in the month of March is completely devoid of charm.'[12] Before leaving Persia, Jane would look back on these first few weeks in the north as the easy part of her journey.

At Narchevan they found what they had come so far to see – ancient Iranian architecture, a relic of a layered past – and Jane at last was able to use what she had spent so many hours struggling to master – Farsi, the Persian language. She wondered if the verbs acquired in France would desert her and her accent be too appalling when put to the test. Accosted at the doorway of the Narchevan inn by a breathless man dressed in Russian uniform, 'Why,' she asked, 'are you wearing the uniform of your conquerors?'

A torrent of words fell on her, most of which she understood. 'My father and my grandfather were governors of this town. When the Russians took my patrimony they made me guardian of the monuments,' he replied bitterly, and whisked the Dieulafoys off to tour his charges. Towering above low, flat-roofed, unpainted houses the Mu'mina Khatum mausoleum was in a sad state of repair. Standing twenty-one metres high, the twelfth-century Seljuk tomb had a recessed panel on each of its eight faces, and each was uniquely patterned with turquoise-blue enamelled bricks inserted into a background of soft-red unglazed bricks. 'The marriage of turquoise blue enamel and the rose tint of bricks is of exquisite delicacy', Marcel later wrote.[13] On all vertical surfaces unglazed bricks projecting from the plane formed intricate laced designs, their shadows accentuating the textural effect. Walking around the towering monument, Jane glanced up and saw beneath a cornice of muqarnas (carved stucco work) an inscription band that read: 'Everything passes. May this remain.'

Nearby, twin minarets guarded a decorative portal, a majestic entrance to a pile of rubble that had once been a mosque. While Marcel measured and recorded, Jane's camera captured its lost dignity.

The guardian led them out beyond the city walls to another ancient tomb tower, its tented stone roof crowned with a stork's nest, which Jane photographed. After accepting an invitation for tea at his house, she realised that city pride and traditional hospitality were not the guardian's only motives – he offered to sell them the second tower. Seated on carpets patterned in Caucasian angularity, Jane graciously declined. Confident now in her Farsi, she told him it would not be wise so early in their journey to encumber themselves with baggage so huge and immovable. Besides, thought Marcel, beautiful though it is, it is not Sasanid.

When the Dieulafoys, travelling down from Georgia, arrived at the Araxes River they had reached the end of the road. Across the river lay Persia, and Persia had no roads. Whatever the deficiencies of the berliner, it could go no further. At Jolfa, on the far bank, Jane's epic horseback ride began.

The Aba, the Persian customs collector, was asleep. Irritated by his curt message saying he would see them later, Jane looked around impatiently, saw a telegraph station and recognised it as a link in the line connecting

England with its most precious possession, India. Having crossed Europe and part of Russia, at Jolfa the line began its march to the Persian Gulf, where it became a submarine cable linking the Indian continent. If this is the English line, there must be an English telegraph officer, Jane reasoned.

The Aba's nap was their good fortune. The telegraphist gave them advice on hiring horses and engaging servants and tips on travelling safely. Above all, he said, 'don't pay your servants anything en route – if you do you'll be abandoned before you reach Tabriz.'[14] He also changed their Russian money into Persian kran. When the Aba finally appeared with his entourage, he put his hand on his heart and offered his services. Jane bowed, put her hand on her heart and asked if he had slept well. Taken aback, the Aba unctuously repeated his offer, but was disappointed. His nap had cost him the large commission he exacted from merchants and the 'cut' he excised from money exchanges. So Jane met, and in this instance bested, the first of the Persian functionaries who would cause her to rail time and again against a system that more than encouraged, but enforced official corruption.

On 7 April 1881 the Dieulafoys set off on horseback at the head of their caravan. Behind them came a string of mules, swaying under baggage lashed with goatskin thongs to pack saddles, and urged on by muleteers commanded by a caravan leader, the tcharvadar bachy. Perched lightly among the bundles were two boys, postilions responsible for returning the riding horses to Jolfa when they were replaced at the next staging post. A cook and a servant, encapsulated in Lord Curzon's unforgettable description as 'a kind of tattered butler', to take care of their bedding and personal needs, made up the train.

These were the basic constituents of any caravan, the only transport for baggage-encumbered travellers throughout the whole of Persia, where appalling roads made wheeled traffic impossible. Only one short stretch from Qazvin to Tehran had been cleared of bushes and stones; although it was not metalled or levelled and it intersected many irrigation ditches, it would take a carriage. Before too many weeks passed, Jane would be speeding along it in a desperate attempt to save Marcel's life. All other roads were little more than well-trodden routes, rarely a single track, usually just many small paths plaited together. No attempt was made to improve the surface, except sometimes removal of the largest boulders. The edges were not defined, there were no side ditches for drainage and bridges were rare, the rivers usually crossed by a stony ford.

On similar roads caravans had brought the rich goods of the East along the Silk Route into Europe; they had carried Marco Polo to China, and would carry the Dieulafoys over 5829 kilometres on this journey through Persia and Iraq, and probably as many again before they left Persia forever in 1886.

Later in their journey the Dieulafoys often travelled as part of a larger caravan; however, on this first day of Persian travel Jane was disconcerted when another group wanted to join their small one. With her keen eye and quick mind, she also learnt from it.

Leaving Jolfa, the Dieulafoys turned their backs to the Azerbaijan Mountains lying to the north and east, 5000 metres high, an indeterminate violet shadow, except for a startling white jagged crust defining the horizon. The route followed the twisting western bank of a river that cut across a plain until two mountain wings came down and closed in on either side, leaving only room enough for the river rushing downwards and the narrow track picking its way upwards towards a pass. Suddenly the sound of galloping horses came from behind. What to do? To gallop off and leave their baggage would be disastrous; they would have to turn and make a stand.

The tcharvadar bachy called to the caravan to close up. Jane and Marcel whipped off the thongs lashing their rifles across the saddle bows and drew their revolvers. Around the bend below, six well-mounted horsemen appeared. Keeping their arms levelled, the Dieulafoys waited for the Persians to come abreast. With both hands clearly on the reins, a sign of peace, they assured the Dieulafoys their only wish was company on the road. When the caravan moved off again the Persian troupe brought up the rear, but Jane's and Marcel's rifles remained loaded and the revolvers stayed tucked in their belts.

Beyond the pass the road ran down through low hills until it reached a wide river valley defined by high angular mountains to the west and sleeping-lion shapes on the east. The Dieulafoys were in that confusion of peaks and high plateaus where three major mountain systems collide. Here the Alburz Mountains, sweeping in an arc around the southern edge of the Caspian Sea, meet ranges pushing down from the Caucasian north, while the Zagros Ranges, lurching up from the Persian Gulf, strike them both with tectonic force.

The route crept through fertile valleys lying between the mountains, passing from one to the next over snow-filled passes. Ruined villages hid in the foothills, their unpainted mudbrick not inconspicuous enough to deceive the raiding, murdering Kurds. Broken walls disclosed clusters of introverted houses, each centred on a courtyard with only a single barred door and no windows to offer a view of a hostile world. In the surrounding farmlands watered by melt-filled streams, freezing winds swept the fields where starving, gaunt figures toiled to replace crops destroyed by the plundering Kurds.

Bitterly cold in the valleys, it was worse in the passes. Yet a touch of green was beginning to sneak up the winter-stricken gullies, wildflowers flashed among the rocks and along the roadside, and the generous vistas echoed the poets who had hymned this country. After the claustrophobic berliner, Jane was delighted to be on horseback amid such scenery. Birds called from the crags and loitered in the sky, inviting them to linger, but Jane and Marcel rode warily, checking ahead, watching the tail of the caravan.

After eight hours in the saddle they came to a caravanserai. It stood on the edge of a plain surrounded on one side by duck-egg green mountains, rose pink on the other backed by distant snow-capped peaks. From the distance they could see the caravanserai's dilapidated portico rearing up above thick square-set mudbrick walls, their corners marked by circular inward-sloping bastions. Night had fallen before they reached the high wooden door, whose leaves, banded and studded with metal, were folded back into a vaulted vestibule. While Marcel and the tcharvadar bachy negotiated with the guardian, Jane looked into the courtyard. Muleteers were lifting loads from their pack animals onto a raised central platform, horses were being watered at a well towards the back and sheep were being pushed through doorways into the corner bastions. The smell of animal manure was overpowering.

Around all four sides ran an arcade of dirt-floored lodges. Doorless, each opened directly into the courtyard through a high arch. The Dieulafoys' baggage was heaved into one of these, the muleteers being expected to sleep on the earth beside it. Jane and Marcel would occupy the room above the vestibule reserved for foreigners and dignitaries.

Caravanserai design was standard throughout the east. Although sometimes octagonal or, rarely, circular, a caravanserai was basically a spacious unpaved courtyard surrounded by lodges, enclosed by four stout walls pierced by a single entrance. Between the back of the lodges and the earth wall ran a chamber resembling a wide canal, the stables, which were entered through openings in the corner bastions. The bastions also contained the latrines. The caravanserai fee included straw and water for the animals. Although the guardian sometimes had wood and yoghurt for sale, the travellers' supplies were their own responsibility.

Caravanserais were Persia's only inns. They were strung out like beads along the route, one stage – that is, one day's travel – apart, usually within a town, though often outside it. Whatever their variety over the next year, Jane would experience it.

Eavesdropping the Persians' conversation while the baggage was being unloaded, Jane heard them congratulate themselves on travelling under the protection of foreigners – robbers rarely attack their caravans, they said, because they know they're well armed and won't submit without a fight. Jane was delighted. She laughed aloud at the thought 'that someone as small as I, and a woman, could frighten off the Kurds and the wild nomads.'[15]

Her laughter quickly stopped when the cook and the butler came to complain about the cooking equipment. Jane had kept the kitchen to a minimum, but 'these are not enough, little master, each dish must be served on a separate plate'. Promised a shopping spree in Tabriz, the sulky cook kindled a fire in the courtyard and began preparing dinner. The Persians' cook unbuckled a small saddlebag made from carpet and out came many plates and all the necessary utensils: saucepans, frying pan, samovar. He unbuckled another and there in small separate packs were the bread, the rice, meat, vegetables, sugar, tea. Jane foresaw a great deal of rearrangement before her saddlebags went back onto the mules in the morning.

The Persians' bedding was even more unsettling. A travelling rug was Jane's mattress, her rolled-up clothes her pillow, and a fur rug her only cover. Out of the corner of her eye she watched the Persians unbuckle a carpet and leather saddle roll, straighten a cotton-covered felt inside it, fold one end over to make a pillow, unroll a feather quilt and lie down on the earth. Jane's Tabriz shopping list lengthened.

In this poor village the caravanserai was very humble, its best room windowless and damp. With mountain air whistling through an ill-fitting door held shut by a piece of string, Jane and Marcel were too cold to sleep. They crept down the steep stair. The great door was bolted and barred. The guardian snored on the raised square platform in the centre of the courtyard. Inside a deserted lodge the Dieulafoy baggage lay unguarded, the muleteers having chosen the warmth of the stable. Creeping back to the upper room they gathered their bedding, then laid it out in the empty lodge. And so passed Jane's first night asleep on bare Persian earth.

'Ya Allah,' called the tcharvadar bachy and Jane was happy to rise from the hard ground, bones aching from the pre-dawn cold. While the muleteers faced Mecca to make their morning prayer she prepared for another long day in the saddle. It had been several months since she had last been astride a horse and the decrepit Persian horses were far different from the elegant animals she rode in the Bois de Boulogne. Her muscles were stiff from yesterday's ride, the inside of her thighs chafed, but saddle proud or not she must go on.

At best a loaded mule can travel about forty kilometres a day. Even on the flat, its pace is slow and in the worst passes the mule often needs an encouraging shove from behind. Jane was sometimes impatient as the mules lumbered along, but she was bound to them of necessity. How else could she transport all they needed for a year's stay in Persia? The bundles and sacks balanced either side of the pack mules held cooking utensils, food and bedding, spare ammunition, Jane's photographic equipment and chemicals, which formed the greater part of their baggage, reference books and journals and a complete medical kit, well stocked with chlorodyne and quinine, as well as a spare saddle and their clothes. The latter, although confined to the absolute minimum, had to protect them in all weathers, extreme cold and desert heat, rain and snow, while not forgetting something appropriate to uphold the dignity of France in official audiences.

Their daytime needs – binoculars, weapons, ammunition and maps – were stowed within easy reach in various pockets and packs on themselves or their saddles. Their money was a huge worry. In the saddle bags on their horses by day and under their heads while they slept at night, it was never left unguarded. Persia had no banks and no paper money. The gold toman worth ten kran was rejected by villagers, who feared counterfeit, so in large heavy one- and two-kran pieces the Dieulafoys carried enough for expenses as far as Tehran – only a few hundred kran certainly, but bulky and cumbersome.

The caravan reached Marand in two days. Looking for fresh supplies in the well-stocked bazaar, Jane ran across her muleteers who saw the 'young master' as the weak link in Dieulafoy authority. 'Advance us two toman, little sir, so we can buy a sheep and some rice,' they begged. 'We have nothing to eat and Tabriz is yet two days.'

'What have you done with the rations money we gave you in Jolfa?'

'Were we to leave our women and children to starve?'

Touched by the image, made more real by the poverty of the people shuffling through the bazaar, Jane ignored the English telegraphist's warning. 'Let them have it, Marcel,' she pleaded.

In the morning the muleteers were hung-over and sour, slow to harness and load the mules. Suddenly throwing the baggage to the ground, they swarmed around Marcel and demanded to be paid off. 'Give us our money,' they shouted.

'Not a kran until we reach Tabriz. That's the agreement.'

The men pressed closer. The flash of a knife. A dagger raised. Marcel feeling for his revolver. A muleteer grabbing his arm. Jane on the edge of the melee drawing her revolver and levelling it at the tcharvadar bachy, saying, 'If he strikes, I will shoot you dead.'

The tcharvadar stared. Her eyes were blue-cold and unblinking. He dropped his gaze, spoke angrily, and the muleteers picked up the rolls and bundles from the ground and went on with the loading.[16]

Would she have shot the tcharvadar bachy? Certainly. She and Marcel were one. She would defend him to the death. Would her aim have missed? Certainly not. The Franco–Prussian War had made her a crack shot.

Though she had upheld the foreigners' reputed resolve, it was a shaken Jane who set off again down the long slow road.

Chapter 3
A golden dragon caught in a net of stars

In Tabriz the Dieulafoys had their first meeting with the dysfunctional Qajar family who at that time ruled Persia. Handsome, intelligent, great sportsmen, infinitely avaricious, the Qajars were extremely virile. There was an oversupply of princes of the blood. Fath Ali Shah, great grandfather of the incumbent shah, had contributed fifty-three surviving sons (the forty-six daughters who outlived him were not worth a mention). Nasr-al-Din, shah since 1848, had already fathered more than forty children, among them five surviving boys, and in 1891 at the age of sixty he would contribute his ninth strong son. It was not a bad record for a dynasty begun only eighty-six years earlier by an enormously fat eunuch.

When the French Consul took Marcel off for his official audience with Prince Ferhad, the shah's uncle recently appointed governor of the Persian province of Azerbaijan, Jane stayed behind in their small suite at the consulate. In Azerbaijan's capital, Tabriz, a city dominated by fanatical clerics, it would have been unwise for the 'little master' to appear publicly as Madame Dieulafoy. Even after later meeting the shah in Tehran and being given quasi-official recognition, in private audience with governors and local authority figures it was still dangerous to acknowledge her gender.

She was quite happy that morning to linger in a European bed. With sheets! After weeks on the road, where it had been impossible to undress, to sleep in a nightgown was sybaritic luxury, but she was curious enough to interrogate Marcel on his return.

The governorship of Azerbaijan province, whose capital Tabriz was the second largest city in Persia, was usually reserved for the heir to the throne. Nasr-al-Din himself, described by a traveller as a shy twelve-year-old boy sitting wistfully under a window,[1] had once been governor. The most recent incumbent, twenty-eight-year-old crown prince Muzaffar-al-Din Mirza, had fallen prey to the mullahs, Islamic clerics. They complained to the shah that he wore European clothes, which can be interpreted as he tried to introduce Western learning. His tutor, a scholar who had studied in France and whose lessons included European subjects as well as Koranic studies, was executed, while the prince was recalled to house arrest in Tehran. His uncle, Ferhad Mirza, hung about with a brutal record as successful governor of Shiraz, took up the challenge. The mullahs had triumphed. No, Tabriz was not a place for Jane to 'come out'.

The consul and Marcel, 'too important to go on foot', Jane wrote wryly, had ridden off preceded by an armed military escort and surrounded by baton-wielding servants to clear a path. The reception room, the *talar*, was crowded. Ancient tradition made it a public place open to the citizens to which they could bring complaints, if they dared, where malefactors were judged and punished, the bastinado administered and where, since old prince Ferhad arrived, many ears, fingers, hands and several noses had fallen to the floor. Already the roads are safer and there are fewer burglaries in the bazaar, proclaimed the mullahs, nodding their huge turbans. When this prince entered the city, it was a bad day, they said, for robbers and those who do not heed the words of Mohommad.

The *hakim*[2] was courteous, offered them sweet cakes, coffee, tea and a drag on the *kalian*, the eastern pipe. As Marcel departed, the leftovers along with the hubble-bubbles were being enjoyed by the crowd who had listened attentively during the audience. Hearing Marcel's account of his meeting with the prince, Jane realised the gracious manners of the ordinary Persian and their elegant forms of address came from these opportunities to see and hear the highest members of their society. She was suddenly ashamed that the coarse tongue she and Marcel spoke owed more to the muleteers than to the Persian poets. She at once looked for a tutor.

Returning late one afternoon Jane found the French consulate in feverish activity, servants shining silver, guards beating rugs. A message had come from the governor that he would call, an unprecedented honour.

From a balcony early the next morning she watched the approach of a majestic, haughty figure. His garments were bright red, flashing metal decorated his horse's trappings, his sword was borne before him on a cushion, a military escort followed behind. A thin-faced, brown-skinned figure then appeared, much less impressive, although sitting a magnificent Turcoman horse. This was the governor, whose executioner always preceded him. Jane raced down to the reception room, took her place as 'the little master', and watched Marcel receive the governor's official permit which would allow the Dieulafoys to enter religious sites otherwise closed to foreigners.

Although she visited among the consular corps, Jane's real pleasure was exploring Tabriz and observing the local people. Their 'scowling faces and furtive grey eyes', made Tabrizis unpopular among the Persians, who derogated them with the rhyme,

'From a Tabrizi thou wilt see nought but rascality,
Even this is best, that thou should not a Tabrizi see.'[3]

Yet several Persian dynasties had made the city their capital and it remained Persia's commercial capital. Earthquakes had destroyed many of its monuments, but what survived Jane was determined to see. She had not come to Persia to drink tea with Europeans.

Slipping along earth-floored alleys in the bazaar, avoiding pannier-widened donkeys and laden carts pulled by bent old men, she found the lane where Tabrizis shopped for crockery, then to an alley filled with carpet and leather bedrolls where she remedied the shortcomings of their sleeping gear. A camel train swayed past on its way to unload in the day caravanserai, where there were storerooms for locking up goods, the camels looking with disdain at the small foreigner. Jane flicked their dust from her trousers with her riding whip, stared with desire at two turquoise-glazed bowls, and lingered in a square near the bazaar's heart. Her fingers stroked the pile on carpets woven by nomads; her eye was caught by heelless yellow shoes with long, turned-up pointed toes spilling from a dim recess. Before the bazaar closed at sunset, among Jane's purchases were a hammer and tacks and a few lengths of cotton material to hang across the window (when there was one) and over the usually ill-fitting door of the rooms in the crowded caravanserais along the route.

Escaping the Christian quarter early one morning the Dieulafoys proceeded towards the huge crumbling Arg, the citadel. Riding down from Jolfa, they had seen it from the steppe long before they reached the city – a great amorphous shape brooding in the distance. Suddenly the cloud had lifted and the westering sun broke through. Massive high walls flanking a central bastion had stood silhouetted against the glittering snow on distant Mount Sahand. As they came closer, sparkling blue domes and tall minarets surrounding the Arg became clearly visible. Saddle-proud and exhausted, chilled to the bone by five days of wind-driven snow, Jane had seen the city as a refuge.

That was not how the Mongols saw it, streaming down in the early thirteenth century. Plunder, women and power was what it meant to them. Under Ghenghis Khan the Mongols destroyed everything: cities, libraries, mosques. They razed entire towns, murdering all the inhabitants. With blind destructiveness they wrecked the irrigation systems and laid waste the farmland. Persia was almost obliterated. For generations the depopulated and ruined countryside resembled the world of the damned, where weeping desperate figures scratched at bare earth; in the cities existence was purgatory.

But in the end, Persia won. Conquerors, even when they lose power, never go home: they always leave their genes behind. At first the Mongols had sent treasure and slaves back to central Asia, then thought better of it, deciding to stay and build. By the end of the thirteenth century Persia had diluted, tamed and almost civilised her conquerors. The Mongols, who had raped the world from China across the Russian steppe, through Persia and Mesopotamia, and almost to the Mediterranean, became patrons of the arts. Persian culture reappeared, changed and revitalised. The old Persian crafts were put to work again, but the new buildings had to be bigger, taller, more solid, more elaborate than the old. People who had arrived as tent dwellers demanded splendour and magnificence from their architects.

During the Mongol hegemony Tabriz was the capital of the Ilkhanids, the 'subordinate Khans', so called to distinguish them from the Great Khans ruling in China as the Yuan dynasty. Under the Ilkhanids, Tabriz became a glorious university city full of madrasas[4], libraries, caravanserais and gardens. None remains. Of the many mosques, only one survives and that only partially: the Arg. On a colossal scale, built of sun-dried brick, the mosque's high vault crashed to the earth within decades, earthquakes toppled the slender paired minarets, and the great doors of polished alabaster were carried off as plunder. The beautiful faience tiles that covered the walls and a wide tiled band of Koranic inscription in gold and white letters against a floral background that bound the structure – they also had gone. As they fell, the pieces were pilfered for domestic decoration and so endured as evidence of the mosque's past magnificence.

A thick piece of wall and a corner tower were all that was left for Jane to inspect. After admiring its patterned brickwork, she climbed to the battlements, added later to transform the broken mosque into a citadel, an arg. Another steep stair took her onto the roof of the munitions storehouse.

The view was magnificent. The high plains of Azerbaijan province, pastureland that had once nourished the famed horses of the Medes, rolled away north and south. To the mounted Mongols coming out of central Asia it must have seemed like the garden of heaven, paradise. To Jane, seeing it in its green spring magnificence, it was a revelation of space and landscape on a scale unknown in Europe and a way of life apparently little changed since biblical times. Flocks, shepherded by men in long robes and almost naked boys, grazed their way slowly across the flanks of the hills. A stampede of horses wheeled off over a ridge. Strung out in long lines were the slowly moving caravans. In the far distance, east and west, ranges of snow-topped mountains, and in the town below, at their feet, the houses.

The suburbs were decorated with blossom: almond, apricot, cherry. Their pink and white beauty hid the litter in the courtyard that centred each house and shaded the low flat roof of the dried brick structure. Each house was a world enclosed by its wall, each family patriarchal, each woman the wife of a man with several other wives, each child born with a one in five chance of becoming an adult.

Passing feet raised little clouds of dust along narrow lanes between the closely crowded houses. Scattered among them, caravanserais and bazaars were marked out by lines of bubble domes, the mosques by blue-tiled domes, except for the Blue Mosque, which was distinguished by its fallen domes and the makeshift hovels filling its great internal space. The now powerful Shi'a Muslims had no interest in repairing an earthquake-devastated Sunni mosque.

Visiting the Blue Mosque later, Jane was intrigued by the tilework. A thick cable moulding faced with intense turquoise-blue tiles spiralled around the portal arch above the broken door. Inside, still clinging to the walls, were bright, elaborately patterned panels. Artisans had cut shapes from coloured tiles and assembled the jigsaw-like pieces into intricate designs. Gold arabesques danced around white flowers, pale-blue leaves glittered against a dark-blue background. The little pieces were set not quite flush, their slightly different angles sending the light sparkling and flashing, a technique that turned otherwise uninteresting flat or rounded surfaces into something almost alive.

Returning through the bazaar the Dieulafoys found the shops putting up their shutters. The long alleys were deserted, the beggars earlier clustered near the entrance had disappeared. The grand mujtahid, they were told, will soon present his beautiful soul to God. He will instantly be in paradise. Marcel had met the mujtahid, a senior cleric, at the governor's *talar*. His ascetic appearance and serene face had so impressed Marcel that he asked,

'Would his reverence allow a photograph?' The mujtahid had demurred, not for religious reasons, he said, only because of his age. Perhaps he knew he was dying. Ah, a second thought. 'With my vicars by my side you may make my image.'⁵

A servant carrying a bundled tripod and a leather case of glass plates had followed the Dieulafoys into the mosque. Jane carried her wooden camera and lenses wrapped in black cloths in a leather valise, Marcel only his riding crop. The mujtahid, dressed in a robe of fine white wool, his white beard curling onto his chest and his head wound round with the dark-blue silk that signifies descent from the prophet, seemed a fragile spiritual figure, his eyes looking beyond the dusty courtyard into another world. Quickly Jane unbound the tripod, turned the screws that held its platform steady and carefully set up her camera. Shaking out one of the black cloths, she flung it over the apparatus and disappeared beneath it. The servant had already undone the fastenings of the leather case. Jane pulled it into her tent, withdrew a glass plate, its surface coated with silver bromide suspended in gelatin, and dropped it into position behind the lens.

The mujtahid had called up a huddle of turbaned men and now stood in their midst. Jane uncovered the lens and began to focus. She called a muffled, 'Hold very still'. Marcel repeated the demand, embroidered with a few courteous Persian phrases. A click and the shutter opened. Jane counted the seconds, slowly, slowly, minutes, praying no one would move while her infidel's eye gathered the essence of the holy man. The shutter clicked shut.

Still beneath her shroud, Jane unfurled a second black cloth, removed the glass plate from the camera, wrapped it, and replaced it in the leather case. She flung back her own cover and stepped forward to thank the mujtahid, being careful to stay in character as the 'little master'.

The gelatin 'dry' plate, still a relatively new formula, was more sensitive, needed less exposure time than the old 'wet' plates, but still had to be developed, although not immediately like a 'wet' plate. That night Jane went up onto the roof of the consulate and in a dark corner dropped the plate into a bath of developer. After a time she removed it, washed it carefully in a water bath, then let it lie for twenty minutes in a dish of hardening fixer. Using this careful procedure, in the following months and years, Jane captured Persia and the Persians.

The mujtahid's insistence on company, said Jane, saved our lives. If he had been photographed alone, the ignorant fanatical population would have blamed his death on the foreigners' sorcery.

Mujtahid, Tabriz

As burial within two hours of death was a necessary custom in a country of searing summers and no refrigeration, people soon began lining up to follow the bier. Jane rashly pushed forward hoping to see the parade. She had yet to experience the rage of a fervent Muslim crowd and she had forgotten she was an infidel. The guide was appalled. And afraid. She would put them all in danger. 'Come away, come away,' he begged.

From the flat roof of his cousin's house she watched laughing children somersaulting along a dusty lane, expressing the joy of the Muslim crowd who saw death as release from hardship and entry into paradise. Then four men appeared, rapidly bearing the corpse toward the cemetery. A raggle-taggle crowd hurried along behind, the rear taken up by veiled ululating women. As the mujtahid was Tabriz's most senior cleric and highly venerated, Jane was surprised there were no officials, no uniforms, no representatives of the governor, only the ordinary people and the mullahs in the crowd. She began to sense the tension between religion and government, separate entities locked in a struggle for civil power and state wealth. She glimpsed the gulf that separated the justly revered mujtahids from the venal, ignorant and fanatical lesser clerics, the mullahs.

Tabriz went into mourning. The mujtahid's death closed the bakeries, the butcheries and the saddleries, making it impossible for caravans to depart the city. The Dieulafoys, who had planned to leave next day, were grounded.

Leaving their muleteers praying in the mosque, Jane and Marcel rode out through blossoming orchards to the place where Ghazan Khan at the beginning of the fourteenth century had created a remarkable suburb, raising his mausoleum at the centre of a complex of mosques, madrasas and hammams[6]. Western travellers reported a hospital, a library, an academy, an observatory and gardens that encircled administration buildings and summer palaces. The mausoleum itself was a dazzling domed twelve-sided tomb tower, banded by inscription friezes and faced with faience tiles arranged in geometric designs. Time, earthquake and invaders had done to all of these buildings what Ghazan Khan's grandfathers had done to Persia, obliterated them.

A peasant searching the rubble for usable bricks brought Jane a glazed eight-pointed tile. Wiping away the dirt of centuries Jane saw a perfect example of Ilkhanid artistry. The Mongols had introduced new techniques, Chinese clouds and Asian motifs into Persian fine arts. On a cobalt-blue baked tile an artisan had painted a writhing dragon into his design, then flecked gold dust onto its scales, before putting the tile on a rack to be refired. When it emerged from the kiln a golden dragon was caught in a net of stars and arabesques. Jane stared at the dragon and saw the durability of a tile. The brick buildings had crumbled to dust, yet the tile survived. The knowledge of medicine, mathematics and astronomy that had filled this city had been forgotten, but the dragon still writhed, the stars still gleamed on the tile.

The turquoise-blue bricks of Narchevan had charmed her, the tile mosaics in the Blue Mosque intrigued her, but this tile set her on the path to the Légion d'honneur. She did not then recognise the moment; only in retrospect did she realise that this was when her search for the enamelled brick *Frieze of the Archers* began.

In the once-elegant Paris salon where Jane's portrait hangs, a glass-fronted case contains several tiles of this period. Could one of these be the tile that in an instant transformed her from being a colleague in Marcel's enterprise into an independent and passionate collector?

But, said Marcel, gathering up the reins, there are no Sasanids here.

And then the rain began. They galloped back to Tabriz through a deluge.

Chapter 4
Saving Marcel

On 11 May 1881 Jane woke in Qazvin, 643 kilometres southeast of Tabriz, 140 kilometres short of Tehran and a long, long way from provincial Toulouse, where she and Marcel had married exactly eleven years before. The government resthouse for foreign dignitaries coming into Persia via the Caspian Sea was a palace compared with the places in which she had slept in the previous twenty days. Her head had lain in caravanserais, village houses and once a telegraph station.

East of Tabriz, the increasingly ferocious forays of the angry Kurds had made the roads too unsafe for small lone caravans, so the Dieulafoys had joined a large pilgrim caravan travelling via Tehran to the holy city of Mashhad. The tcharvadar bachy was an astute Azerbaijani who had been to Mecca and earned the title *hadji*, but was surprisingly tolerant of foreigners. Jane turned to him for information on everything from monuments to local gossip and after she treated his minor medical problem he became their protector. It was he who shamed the Soltaniyeh mob by escorting the Dieulafoys back into the Ilkhanid tomb of Uljaitu for a second visit the day after they had been assaulted and thrown out and pelted with stones by the village children.

Confident that the governor's letter would safeguard them, the foreigners had ridden on ahead of the caravan, but in Soltaniyeh the permit proved useless. Catching up with them next day, the tcharvadar turned in fury on the villagers, but his well-meant gesture was unnecessary. With all the assurance and assumed superiority of the European dealing with Easterners, Marcel had already cowed them, terrifying them with a threat to bring in the platoon of soldiers he had met on the road. The Qajar army, seldom paid, lived rapaciously off the country. The villagers knew they would have to garrison and victual the troops. In Marcel's words the headman heard empty storehouses and winter starvation.

And so the Dieulafoys had returned to the great mausoleum standing lonely on the plain, Marcel to measure the vault, larger than anything in France, comparable with London's St Paul's and Hagia Sophia in Constantinople. The Ilkhanids, who built it, knew nothing of either, but had chosen monumentality to refute their reputation as vandals. Jane explored an interior faced with exquisite glazed tilework, banded by inscriptions in unmatched calligraphy. The cream glaze, a contrite villager whispered, was mixed in gazelle's milk.

The Dieulafoys' insistence on examining an Islamic monument might be seen as culturally insensitive, yet perhaps it made the insular villagers realise that their dedicated sanctuary, the place where they bowed before Allah, had another valuable dimension – as historical testament to their ancestors' achievements. Ground down as they were by the oppressive Qajar administration, it may have given them some pride, even opened their minds a little. Certainly when the Englishman Browne visited Soltaniyeh in 1887 he found 'the European traveller meets with none of the difficulties which usually form an insuperable obstacle to visiting similar [tombs]', and, his guide boasted, 'some time ago a European engineer had spent a whole week making plans and drawings.'[1]

If *hadji* accepted them, the spiritual leader of the pilgrim caravan certainly did not. The imam swayed along, perched on an enormous pile of carpets and quilts, his head surmounted by a blue turban, his mule caparisoned in blue cloth extending from head to heels. 'Is the mule also a descendant of the prophet?' Jane asked impiously. Whenever the foreigners approached, the imam turned his head away to avoid acknowledging them. It was as well he never discovered that the 'little master' was a woman.

Followed by their baggage loaded on 150 beasts of burden, the noisy trail of mullahs, pilgrims and servants lumbered slowly along to tempi ringing out from bells hung about the animals. Fervent teenagers making their first pilgrimage clowned about on stacks of baggage loaded on tired donkeys. The rich rode fine Turcoman horses and smoked their *kalians* as they travelled. Poorer men went on foot or lay half asleep on the necks of broken-down asses, their women unidentifiable dark shapes among the bundles on the backs of the pack animals. The wives of the rich were hidden in paired, cloth-curtained, wooden panniers balanced either side of a mule. Curled up inside the baskets beneath a mountain of quilts, the women passed the whole stage, occasionally thirteen hours, seldom less than seven. Never allowed to dismount and never seen, they were heard only as a piteous cry ringing out when their animal stumbled. Feeding their unweaned babies and surrounded by children too young to ride, they were jealously guarded, no one apart from the husband and women servants allowed near them.

One pilgrim, an Aga who often rode alongside the imam, had brought his entire *anderun* of eight. The Aga's favourite and her child swayed along in panniers attached to a horse, the less-loved in paired baskets hung off mules. With the party was a cheerful young servant, Ali. Shaven head covered by a black lambskin-lined bonnet, belted jacket showing off a slim figure, he kept the beasts moving along, soothed crying children on his shoulder and ran errands for the wives. Surprised by the boy's intimacy with women who were supposedly unapproachable, Jane reined in and waited until her own servants, following in the train with the pack mules, came abreast. 'She's a Kurd who's shaved off her hair, she's dressed like a man so she can go about unveiled,'[2] they told her.

Without admitting her own gender Jane soon won the confidence of the young woman. Full of stories about her mistresses and scurrilous tales of her master, she betrayed the wickedest secret only when outraged by the Aga slapping her unjustly.

The path followed a winding river through a narrow valley guarded by weird geologic formations, whose crests reared like roosters' combs against the sky. Crossing a reed-filled marsh, the path became a greasy track. The Aga's mount slipped and lurched into the imam's. Piled quilts and baggage swayed about, saucepans and samovars clashed, and down into the swamp with a great splash went the imam, the Aga and their dignity. The boys tried not to laugh, the muleteers, coarser fellows, whooped with delight. Ali clapped her hand across her mouth but a single burst escaped, ringing out as she hurried to help her master. That devout pilgrim slapped her across the face so hard it was heard all along the file. The girl fell back to Jane for consolation, tears on her cheeks, revenge in her eyes.

'The Aga,' she said, 'will be punished. His wives will cuckold him again with the students in the madrasa.'[3]

Married young, the Aga had no success in fathering children. Despite great efforts and new wives, he remained childless. Praying devoutly for a son, he embarked on a pilgrimage to Mashhad, where he spent his days imploring Allah at the tomb of Imam Reza and debating doctrine with the senior clerics in the madrasa. While their tutors were taken up with the Aga, the students found other occupations. Soon the husband was overjoyed to learn his piety had not been wasted: his favourite was pregnant. When the other seven women announced they too were expecting he was ecstatic. 'Mashallah, mashallah, praise to Allah,' he cried, packed up and returned home. Delighted with these children, he was disappointed that their number remained eight. He is returning, said Ali, to Mashhad to beg Allah's bounteous mercy again. The women, she added, are very happy to be going on another pilgrimage.

With the beasts hung about with bells and the pilgrims with cooking equipment, the caravan clanged and tinkled along the busy route. Returning pilgrims replete with holiness hastened past. Strings of camels, each with 'an indescribable dignity . . . who seems to eye one scornfully with half-turned head as he passes majestically,'[4] padded by in the dawn laden with goods for the Tabriz bazaar. Mounted horsemen overtook the pilgrims, and troops bound for the Kurdish insurrection pushed them roughly off the path. On the flat stony plains near Zendjan the sun burned down and water ran short; on other days a bitter wind swept down from the Alburz Mountains. The nights were always cold. They crossed the great plains of Mianeh and Soltaniyeh, where the Mongols had pastured their horses, and before them the Medes, and where the Qajar shahs now raised their silk-hung tents during the hunting expeditions which they loved.

The dilapidation of Azerbaijan was left behind as the villages became less subject to depredation. Although still only a high blank wall enclosing a few rooms opening to a central courtyard, the houses were dressed with fresh mud-and-straw plaster and their doorways ornamented with stucco. Birds flashed their bright feathers in the walled orchards, where fruit trees were bursting into bloom. In the surrounding fields, irrigated from the mountains, spring crops were being planted. Bullocks pulled a wooden ploughshare through the soil while boys perched on the bovine backs directed them left and right with pebbles from their pockets. Behind them, a man dropped grain into the opened furrow.

When the caravan took a day's rest at Mianeh, a town notorious for a virulent infection, Jane and Marcel rode off to a castle, allegedly Sasanid, which much later became the lair of the dreaded Assassins. In the late nineteenth century it still had a fearful reputation. 'Our rifles,' Jane wrote, 'resting on the saddle bow, are charged with bullets, and two pairs of revolvers are tucked into our belts. I hope this artillery will frighten any robber foolish enough to covet *hadji's* horses.'[5]

Climbed to the ruined castle on top of Kaflan-kou, they were rewarded by a spectacular view across the plain. Luminous pearl-grey mountains painted with mauve shadows and beyond them snow-capped steel-grey peaks made a palette as subtle as the feathers of a grey dove. At a flooded river Jane lingered to set up her camera and photograph a twelfth-century bridge, and stayed too long to reach Mianeh before nightfall. Seeking shelter in a village, Jane and Marcel were offered a henhouse. 'We had to choose between that lodging and the inn of the stars; the icy cold after the sun goes down did not allow us to hesitate.'[6]

In every village and town Marcel, remote and formal, filled his notebook with measurements, plans and architectural drawings, while the 'little master' talked to the people. The inherent threat of a foreigner evaporated before Jane's fluent Farsi, easy charm, and her small size. Her journal filled with details of their lives and dress and her lens with their faces when they would permit. She photographed villagers and mosques, the present and relics of the past.

At Zendjan members of the Babi[7] sect asked her to make their portraits. Less then forty years before, a young *hadji*, descendant of the prophet, had called for reform of the clergy and their venal practices. He wanted to give women equal rights with men, ban polygamy and throw off the veils. He called himself the Bab, the Gate, but his many adherents were brutalised by mullahs and Qajars, massacred in thousands at Zendjan and tortured terribly in Tehran.

Despite the terror, the sect persisted. Walking with the posthouse warden through leafy tunnels where spring blossom brushed her head, Jane praised his orchard as 'a terrestrial paradise without the apple'. Succumbing to her charm, the warden confessed he was a Babi and invited 'His Excellency' home to tea. Nothing pleased Jane more than an invitation to get inside the walls and see domestic life.

The warden's sole wife abandoned her cooking to welcome the foreigner graciously. The unveiled Babi woman was confident and at ease as she sat on a fine Kurdish carpet drinking tea with a 'boy'. Her daughter continued with the pilau. Kohl ringed her dark eyes, two bunches of hair swept her forehead and a burst of carnelian threaded with amber encircled her neck. A flash of bare midriff showed as she bent to the fire. Before the light faded Jane photographed her: a light piece of red wool is flung loosely over her head, a loose cotton jacket with attached patterned sleeves hangs open over a rose silk chemise, a gathered cashmere skirt falls from her hips; white socks and leather slippers complete the ensemble.

Babi girl, Zendjan

Approaching Qazvin they were deluded by a desert mirage; when it vanished they saw walled pistachio orchards and vineyards surrounding a large city. Qazvin's streets were crowded with arriving and departing caravans, for here the trade route coming up from the Caspian over the steep wall of the Alburz Mountains intersected the east–west routes. Merchants eager to make deals flooded from the bazaar. Elegant heavily armed horsemen carelessly wheeled their superb Turcoman horses among the crowds. The pride of the shah's army and famed for their courage, the Qazvini soldiers dressed proudly in the uniform their ancestors had worn when they joined Turks and Kurds to expel Afghani invaders in 1723.

Originally built by the Sasanids, Qazvin had been destroyed numerous times since, often by earthquake, once by the Mongols. Marcel knew the Sasanid fire temple underneath the mosque's Seljuk sanctuary would be inaccessible, but surely he would be allowed to see the sanctuary's dome. 'I must see it,' he muttered, hurrying to an audience with the governor of Qazvin province. 'And the tiles,' reminded Jane. The governor, one of the shah's many brothers, received them in a graceful garden pavilion, seating them on chairs borrowed from the guesthouse. He was sympathetic, but refused them permission to enter the mosque.

Deep disappointment filled the Dieulafoys on their wedding anniversary. Eleven years before, Jane's dream had been of the East. The dream had come true. She was in the East, but she wanted more. 'The governor didn't give you permission?' teased the guesthouse warden. 'He's too cowardly to confront the mullahs. But if you follow me, I'll show you that a humble shah's domestic can sometimes be more adroit and obliging than governors and officials.'[8]

Between the morning and the midday prayer, while the mullahs gossiped in the madrasa and the merchants were busy in the bazaar, the caretaker slipped them into the mosque. No one was there to be affronted except some beggars, who were left speechless. They strode through the central court and into the sanctuary. As Marcel measured the vault, Jane inspected the tiled friezes that banded the upper walls. A double inscription of Koranic verse written in kufic lettering and nakshi script, the white ceramic letters raised above a blue ground of vines and tendrils are, 'for sheer loveliness perhaps not equalled in Islam,' claims the great authority, Arthur Upham Pope.[9] Perhaps the beauty and delicacy of the inscription reveal the true meaning of the sacred words when read by a devout Muslim.

Unfortunately, few of the townspeople could read, not even Farsi, and the inscriptions are in Arabic. Until the Pahlavis came to power in the early twentieth century Persian girls were never taught anything, left alone to transmit their ignorance and superstition to their children, while the boys' education was usually limited to the Farsi alphabet, basic arithmetic and recital of the Koran. When Jane visited few could read the great Persian poets, though many could quote them extensively. Those who could read and write effectively inserted *mirza*, clerk, before their name. (Princes had the suffix Mirza after theirs.) Most mullahs had reached this level. Promising pupils then entered the madrasas, the well-endowed lodges lining the inside of mosque courtyards. Here they learned Arabic and memorised the Koran, but studying only textual commentaries, shari'a law and revered Islamic documents no horizons were opened, while dogmatism and intolerance were inculcated. More talented students moved on to larger religious centres and made pilgrimages, but still learned nothing of the world beyond their small part of it. Such profound ignorance made them despise foreigners and led them to dismiss cultures different from their own. They disdained infidels like the Dieulafoys and treated them with contempt. Exceptional scholars, mujtahids, authorities on Islamic law were revered by the people for their sanctity and spiritual knowledge and seen as their last resort against the injustice of the Qajar regime. Sadly, the advanced science and medicine that had bloomed in Islamic countries at the time of the European Dark Ages was no longer taught. That knowledge, taken by Persian intellectuals and philosophers to the margins of the Islamic world, had entered medieval Europe, where it restored the lost Greek learning, but it was now entirely lost to the Persians.

When the sun indicated it was almost time for the midday prayer, the despised foreigners, the Dieulafoys, discreetly withdrew from the Qazvin mosque and hurried off to the bazaar. Jane had to restock their kitchen. On the following day, Friday, the Islamic holy day, the bazaar would be closed and the caravan granted another rest day, but on Saturday at one in the morning when *hadji* called, 'Yah Allah, Yah Ali,' all must be packed ready to begin the last six stages to Tehran.

Walking through the lanes next day Jane heard a rhythmic clapping of flesh on flesh coming from the jume (Friday) mosque. Usually, after Friday's midday prayer the senior cleric chided people who neglected their prayers, gave political advice, and sometimes whipped them into a frenzy of hatred. But not in Qazvin on that Friday in Moharram, the Month of Mourning.

Instead, the despairing faithful were beating their bare chests and shoulders in remembrance of the deaths of the deeply revered Shi'a figures, Ali and his son Hussein. To Jane it was a frightening, primitive beat. She hurried on.

Later that afternoon, in an open space at the end of a narrow lane she saw a huddle of people in the usual nondescript blacks and browns. Colourfully dressed figures flitted across her view. Down the lane came the sound of weeping. Edging slowly closer, moving from one shadowy doorway to the next, she realised the weepers were watching a religious play. Women sobbed, tears rolled down the men's faces, little children caught up in their parents' grief wailed loudly. This too, she realised, was in recognition of the long ago deaths of Ali and Hussein.

So absorbed was the audience that no one noticed her, or Marcel shadowing her. At the end of the lane the foreigners stopped and stood very still. They could see figures robed in green, the colour of Islam, lining a pathway down which other actors came and went. Hovering at one side was a figure all in white except for a black veil, which Jane guessed signified invisibility. The drama became more passionate, cymbals and pipes drowned the sound of weeping. A splendid figure stalked in. Dressed in red with two towering white feathers caught in a scarlet headdress, he raised his sword and struck out. A less arrogant figure in blue robe, head swathed in white, defended himself with a black shield. It glittered with gold Koranic lettering, but was no match for the sword and the man fell into the dust. Cymbals clashed and a bolt of red silk unfurled like a spurt of blood across the earth. The Shi'a audience went wild with grief and rage. Old men began mumbling the Shi'a curse, 'Oh God, curse Omar: then Abu Bekr and Omar: then Othman and Omar: then Omar: then Omar.'

The vigour and intensity of the drama had roused the audience to an emotional pitch. Jane sensed danger. She and the tall thin man beside her turned and walked steadily away. This was not the place or time for infidels. It was Ashura, the day during Moharram when Hussein's martyrdom is commemorated by all Shi'a, supporters of Ali.

Jane was learning caution.

Moved by the drama, although only half understanding it, Jane and Marcel later discussed it. They knew it represented the essence of what divided Shi'a from Sunni Islam – the exclusion from the caliphate first of Ali, Mohammad's son-in-law, then Ali's two sons by Fatima, Mohammad's daughter. Instead, outsiders Abu Bakr, next Omar, and then Othman were chosen caliph (successor). The final scene represented the battlefield at Karbala in 680, where

Ali's second son Hussein had led a doomed challenge to the Umayyad, Yazid, who then became the sixth caliph. The figures in green were Yazid's encircling army, the striking red figure was Yazid who kills Hussein, the gentler, more righteous man in blue. The supposedly invisible Ali, assassinated while praying outside the Kufa mosque in 661, watches his son's death, accepting its inevitability. Inshallah. It is the will of Allah.

'Where was Hasan?' Jane asked. She had not recognised the elder of Ali's sons in any of the actors.

'Cut from the drama, most likely,' replied Marcel. 'He was despised for being involved in a failed challenge after Othman's murder in 656.' She didn't need to ask why Omar was being so roundly cursed. She knew all Persians have a particular hatred of the man who was caliph when the Arab armies overran Persia.

After the death of the prophet Mohommad in 632 AD, the succession was disputed. Although many supported Ali, cousin and son-in-law of Mohommad, as legitimate head of the community, Mohommad's associates, first Abu Bakr, next Omar and then Othman, were proclaimed caliph (successor). Passed over again after Othman's murder in 656, Ali collected his forces on the upper Euphrates River and opened battle at Siffin. Exhausted by fighting, both sides agreed on arbitration. This was Ali's great mistake. His supporters deserted him, unwilling, they said, to accept compromise and submit the Will of God to human judgement. In 661 Ali was assassinated while praying outside the Kufa mosque.

Agitation in support of Ali's sons revived after the fifth caliph died in 680. He had named his son Yazid as his successor, but the Umayyads' excesses and the dynastic implication made that family unacceptable to many. 'Only the virtuous should rule and if he go astray, obedience should be withdrawn from him,' the disaffected pronounced, quoting a precept of Persia's old Zoroastrian faith. In the short term this principle led to a revolt by Ali's party; in the long term, although Jane was not aware of the tenet, it was undermining the Qajar regime while she was in Persia, and in the longer term it breeds the unrest that festers in Iran today.

Opposition to the Umayyads focused on Ali's sons, grandsons of the prophet through their mother Fatima. Rigid supporters of the house of Ali rejected Hasan, the eldest, who had acquiesced at Siffin, so it was Ali's second son Hussein who led a doomed challenge to Yazid onto the battlefield at Karbala. The Umayyad became sixth caliph. It is Hussein's martyrdom which the Shi'a, supporters of Ali, commemorate on Ashura day.

When the stoical Marcel complained that evening of headache and stomach trouble Jane knew it was serious. During the night his temperature surged and, while trying to dress after *hadji* made his call for departure, he fainted. He was clearly unfit for horseback travel. Except for a basic travel kit, all Jane's medicines were in the baggage train, and where was that? Beyond the city, sent on ahead.

No, said *hadji*, I will not wait while it is sent for, the pilgrims are ready to depart, we must leave at daybreak.

Is there a foreign doctor in the town?

Only the Muslim doctor.

Can he help?

He will prescribe tincture-al-Koran – sacred verse inscribed on the inside of a cup, dissolved in water and drunk slowly.

The caravan departed without the Dieulafoys. As Marcel's condition worsened, Jane knew she must find a European doctor. She could not let Marcel die in this foreign country, she must get him to Tehran at once. But how? Resourcefulness and determination were Jane's attributes. It also helped that she was now absolutely fluent in Farsi and could curse like a muleteer.

They left at three the following morning in a four-wheeled vehicle reserved for the use of ministers. Rain had turned the shah's special road into a quagmire. Five kilometres out of town they became bogged. The coachman descended and took the horses' heads while Jane sat on the box and thrashed them, but it did no good. Marcel lay delirious on the coach floor. Jane waited, raging, until daybreak, when some peasants hauled them out with bullocks. 'The shah's road is like this all the way to Tehran,' they shrugged.

She struggled from posthouse to posthouse, taking whatever horses were available, not delaying at the change a moment longer than necessary. The horses were better on this vaunted route than on any other, but even so the wretched, abused things hadn't the strength to gallop any distance. The morning passed with Marcel almost unconscious. He deteriorated in the afternoon and delirium returned. Jane bathed his forehead and cleaned him as the coach rocked along, and cursed the shah's cook responsible for making the appalling road. Marcel was now critically ill. By late afternoon Jane could see Mount Damavand. At its foot lay Tehran, inside the walls were European doctors. She must get Marcel into Tehran without delay. His life could still be saved. It must be saved. She would not contemplate any other possibility. Hurry, she called to the coachman, whip the horses, whip them.

At the last stage the post-master refused them a change of horses. Night will fall before you can reach Tehran, he said. Jane would not have it. It was only twenty kilometres to the city gates, and because a Qajar palace lay nearby the road was better maintained. Besides, she knew she was vulnerable here with Marcel unconscious, their money a temptation to the venal and only herself to defend their lives. The 'little master' became very forceful, insisted, the post-master succumbed and they galloped off once more into the rain.

At ten at night they crossed the ditch outside the walls and entered the city, fortunate that the gate was still open. The dark streets were deserted. The post-boy hired as navigator, a country lad, had lied. He had never been to Tehran. Soon they were lost in a maze of dead-end alleys. Marcel lay limp and unconscious, his forehead burned her hand. Where was the foreign quarter? Not in the pitch-black covered bazaar where they found themselves. A light showed under a door. Stop, she cried, and sprang from the carriage and beat on the wood. The soldiers were startled at having their teacups rattled by a desperate boy, so pitiful and small. One of them volunteered to show the way, but when they came to Artillery Square where four arches led into the four great streets of the city he was stumped. He abandoned them.

They were so close to the help Marcel needed, but which door concealed the doctor who could save his life? Not the first she tried in the sleeping streets, only a tea merchant closing his shop. Jane implored, beseeched him, bought him. He led them into the northern quarter and stopped in front of a teahouse. Here is the French hotel, he said, they will send for Doctor Tholozan.

Chapter 5
The Golistan two hours before sunset

In the shadow of the Alburz Mountains and dominated by Mt Damavand, Tehran stood in a hollow in the plain surrounded by stark desert. Chosen as his capital by the first Qajar ruler for geopolitic reasons, meaning it was close enough for a strategic retreat into the Turcoman homeland should the Persians rise against him, Tehran was a relatively new city. In a northern suburb, inside the sick room where Marcel fought for his life Jane was anchored by his bed. While the Sisters of St Vincent de Paul and the French Doctor Tholozan came and went, and two anxious weeks passed, Jane was oblivious to everything except his struggle. When Marcel began to recover Jane realised she desperately needed exercise and fresh air, but it was dangerous to go out alone. Instead she slipped along beside the Sisters when they visited patients too ill to come to the clinic. She found Tehran's new avenues lined by high blank walls. Behind them lay embassies, palaces and the houses of upper-class Persians. Sometimes a figure slipped through a door in the wall or a gate swung open to let a horse and carriage pass, allowing her a tantalising glimpse of gardens, small lakes, fruit trees and flat-roofed dwellings, but Jane could not enter. One afternoon when boys ran out from the only modern secular school in Persia, the Dar al-Funun, she caught sight of a secluded garden but here too she was excluded. She longed to see more.

A city of secrets, Tehran hid intrigue and power struggles behind its impenetrable walls. Private travellers without significant contacts, the Dieulafoys were denied access to Tehran's multifaceted life, in contrast to some travellers who came after them, perhaps inspired by Jane's account of Persia. Jane never saw the domestic interiors, described later by the more fortunate Isabella Bird as 'beautiful and appropriate to the climate and mode of living . . . and the same suitability and good taste run down through the trading classes till one reaches the mud hovel . . . of the workman and peasant.'[1] Jane was never invited inside. Nor was Marcel, when he recovered, invited to dinner parties, unlike the Englishman Browne, a Persian scholar who came in 1887. In Cambridge Browne had taught the sons of rich and influential Persian families. In Tehran he was a guest in one of the houses that Jane only glimpsed, where he was tutored by an eminent Persian philosopher in the refinements of Persian literature and the subtleties of Sufi mysticism. He was welcomed into the social life of upper-class Tehran and attended parties, where the guests, all men of course, sat on ancient carpets and lolled against cushions while dancing boys entertained them. Music filled the rooms and wine flowed freely. Browne thought Tehran a cultured, liberal city with a vivid intellectual life. He praised the literary and conversational brilliance of contemporary Persians, whose 'wealth of metaphor . . . flow of language and . . . sweetness of utterance'[2] he found beguiling, clearly not the same language Jane was hearing as she sat by Marcel's sickbed or paced the streets with the nuns.

Nor did the Dieulafoys have the backing of a powerful embassy, as did best-selling author Isabella Bird. A guest at the British legation in 1890, Isabella met the shah's ministers and was introduced to the grand vizier (first minister) who told her, 'I hope if you write you will write kindly, and not crush the aspirations of my struggling country as some have done.'[3] She dined with British officers employed by the shah to train and often command the Persian regiments, where she overheard talk of intrigues and political manoeuvring never revealed to Jane.

Although they were warmly welcomed at the French legation, the Dieulafoys were not official guests. Besides, the French legation was not in particular favour at the Persian court, being compromised by Dr Tholozan's ambiguous position. After many years as the shah's trusted physician, Tholozan was encouraged by the French embassy to meddle in politics. From 1876 to 1878 he lobbied for France to be granted exclusive navigation rights on the great southern river, the Karun (where early in 1882 shipping problems were to bring Jane to the edge of life), and for development rights to irrigation, dams, mines and what lay beneath the sand in the surrounding territory – petroleum.

Dr Tholozan's machinations were his downfall. Seething with resentment at his influence with the shah, the Islamic court physicians conspired with members of the royal family and the clergy – and the women of the *anderun* – to successfully undermine the scheme. With the failure of the

French aspirations, Tholozan was banished, and once more the shah found himself in the hands of doctors who bled boy babies on day three of their little lives in order to rid them of the mother's impure blood. Once again they opened the shah's veins with ruthless frequency. Not until the King of Kings fainted in his bath did the terrified Islamic physicians send urgently for the foreign doctor. Tholozan was restored to royal employment, though not to royal confidence.

Despite her isolation, Jane soon became aware of the political pressures surrounding the shah as the 'Great Game' played out in Tehran. The Russian Bear, pressing in from the north and always hungry for more territory, threatened barbaric rape. On the other side were the French and the British, with whom the shah, amorous and cool in turn, flirted. The French offered only commercial marriage, but the British were spoilers, determined to block Russia whatever the cost. 'What would happen to India, our crown jewel, old boy, if the Bear swallowed Persia?' the British legation asked. And answered themselves, 'They'd block our overland access and be into Delhi by the back door. Can't let that happen.'

The sophisticated Persians understood the complex struggle and mostly backed the British. 'Why do you like the English?' Isabella Bird asked the Khan of Rustam-i while treating his son for an infection.

'Because they are brave and like fighting . . . and because they conquer all nations and do them good after they have conquered them . . . They give one law for rich and poor, and they make just laws about land, and their governors take the taxes and no more, and if a man gets money he can keep it . . . Why don't the English come and take this country? If you don't, the Russians will, and we would rather have the English.'[4]

The Khan's reasons for inviting the English reflected Persia's domestic problems, as Jane quickly learned. More than unjust laws, or lack of law, the real issue for Persians was tax. Leaving Marcel sitting in an invalid's chair in the garden, Jane set off for the grand bazaar, discovering on the way that not all Tehran was as salubrious as the northern suburb where the elite partied. Searching the bazaar's lanes for delicacies to tempt Marcel's appetite, Jane was surprised by the quantity of cheap foreign goods that 'show . . . the extent and rapidity with which Europe is ruining the artistic taste of Asia.'[5] Bubbling with intrigue, full of spies both domestic and foreign, the souks were another world denied to Jane. But she could eavesdrop – to the merchants she was nothing more than a well-armed foreign boy surrounded by servants; as she turned over silks and fingered pomegranates they continued their conversation. Despite her exclusion from the networks that controlled

Persia, in the bazaar the people's bitterness towards Persia's corrupt bureaucracy became very apparent to Jane.

Each *No Ruz* (New Year) all offices of the Qajar administration came up for review. Whichever applicant offered the shah the most generous 'gift' was appointed. If someone else's 'gift' outbid his, an existing office holder was replaced, regardless of his merit. To recoup his outlay, the successful bureaucrat appointed his staff according to the same principle. Even down to the peasant cooperative the same iniquitous procedure prevailed. It took great courage to criticise the system, only someone confident of his power would attempt it. One who dared was *hadji* mirza Hosein Khan, appointed grand vizier in the Muslim year 1288, November 1871 in the Western calendar.

Since the Qajar dynasty filled its palaces with jewels rather than archives, the grand vizier's protest against venality survives only in the records of his contemporary, the Shirazi noble Hasan-e Fasa'i', descendant of the prophet Mohommed through Ali and his wife Fatima. The grand vizier dared to write:

> The existence of the state is bound to the prosperity of the country and the tranquility of its inhabitants. The decline of prosperity and tranquility is caused by greed and avidity. Those who are kindly disposed to the welfare of the state must eradicate ... these two illnesses ... It is an age-old custom ... to call the illness of avidity 'revenues' which they collect ... by three different means: The first ... is bribery: they pay a sum of money to an official and receive something in return ... The second is *peshkash*: the governorship of a district is conferred upon a deceitful man, and one closes one's eyes to his oppression and tyranny. The third is presents: timid people out of fear of the officials send the governor the first-born of cattle, well-tasting dishes, or horse outfits as tribute. Further, the leopard-like Persians ... if they are nursing a hatred ... accuse the unfortunate man falsely of treachery and bring him [down].
>
> The Shah has become sensitive to these widespread illnesses. When he conferred upon me the high office of grand vizier, he ... ordered me to eradicate [them]. Inshallah! one can say that ... bribery and gifts have disappeared at the royal court ... However ... the governors, proud of their relationship to the royal family ... consider themselves exempt from punishment ...
>
> 'Kingship is barren'; accordingly this [Shah] has no connection with children, relations, servants and friends; the trained army and the reliable

subjects are his children . . . The Shah has [taken] . . . a solemn vow that he will destroy . . . any governor who oppresses his subjects by increasing the taxes . . . and any officer . . . who dares to shorten the rations and pay of a single soldier.[6]

Provincial governors, bitterly resenting interdiction of their 'presents', and the shah's mother, distraught that 'gifts' no longer penetrated the walls of the *anderun*, connived to bring down vizier Hosein Khan. In 1873 he was appointed governor of Gilan, a perpetually wet mosquito-ridden province on the edge of the Caspian Sea. It was not for nothing that an angry Persian would curse his enemy, 'May he be bitten by a Kashani scorpion, or, better, made governor of Gilan.'[7] Hosein Khan's passing was soon announced; his death was still being debated in the Tehran bazaar in 1881. Only a few argued it was caused by fever, most whispered that a 'cup of Qajar coffee' was involved. Either way, the remorseless shah had murdered a second vizier.

Curious as Jane was about Persian cities and their history, empathising with the people and their problems, she was not enchanted by Tehran. For Marcel, there was nothing in this new town, no Sasanids or Seljuks, the dynasties that had brought him on the long journey. The Dieulafoys had only one objective in Tehran. For that they had to meet the shah.

Marcel was barely recovered when the Shah of Shahs, Asylum of the Universe, commanded them to an audience 'two hours before sunset'. With her clothes cleaned and pressed, her boots shining like mirrors, and her helmet pushed down on her hair, Jane felt naked. How could she step out without a rifle over her shoulder, a pair of revolvers in her belt and, most reassuringly, a riding whip in her hand, but one did not go armed into the presence of the King of Kings. She was whisked into a carriage beside Dr Tholozan and Marcel. Their escort of royal footmen in red coats with ballet-dancer skirts, green knee breeches, white stockings and tall stiff hats rode ruthlessly through the crowd, their white horses swishing magenta-dyed tails. Artillery Square, so dark and deserted on the night of Jane's arrival, was a blur of gorgeous military uniforms and men in Western-style dress. Through an ornamented gateway the carriage entered a tree-lined street, at its end the turquoise domes of the citadel, the Arg, floating beyond a high wall. Then another gateway guarded by soldiers half asleep, where the fluttering royal standard, lion and sun in yellow on a green ground, proclaimed they had reached the Golistan Palace.

Jane had fleeting impressions of formal gardens and deep shade cast by white-stemmed plane trees marching in parallel lines. The scent of roses sweetened the air. Clear water bubbled from fountains and flowed gently in long pools lined with blue tiles. A white marble throne stood empty beneath a ceiling sparkling with mirror tiles high on a *talar* open to the garden. Yet another gateway, how many gateways? Jane lost count of the barriers ensuring the seclusion of the shah. Flashes of enamelled tiles on an encircling wall, fountains, trickling water, deep pools, roses on trellises, orange trees in tubs. An ornate palace façade reflected in a small lake. They passed through a reception room hung with tapestries and portraits of foreign kings, a blend of East and West that did not appeal, and entered an enclosed garden.

When Shah Nasr-al-Din appeared at the end of an alley not a single diamond glittered on his frock coat, only gold frogs and emerald buttons marching to the waist. Could this be the shah who had stunned the wild rebellious Kurds and Lurs into submission by appearing in a coat sewn from shoulder to boot with diamonds? When Nasr-al-Din stepped from his tent at dawn the low-angled sun had struck the jewels and the tough little man appeared as a huge and shining god, perhaps Ahura Mazda himself, the source of all light. The ignorant superstitious tribesmen had fallen on their faces and for a few years the ruinous taxes imposed on them flowed without complaint into the royal treasury.[8]

Jane had not seen the shah when he visited Europe in 1873, and she was still a provincial housewife in Toulouse when five years later he had been the toast of Paris for twenty-two days. She had seen the photographs, but this man was dark and swarthy, smaller, more 'tribal' than the newspaper image. The clothes were the same – the full-skirted coat gathered at the back, flaring from the waist, slim-legged white cotton trousers, a high black Persian lambskin hat, except there was no diamond aigrette and no sword with jewelled hilt and scabbard. He was what he was, the great, great nephew of a Turcoman tribesman who preferred the silk-hung tent of his hunting trips to palace immobility.

Dr Tholozan presented Colonel and Madame Dieulafoy.

'What! That sweet boy is a woman?' exclaimed the startled shah in Farsi. When Marcel claimed her as his dear wife, quickly in French the shah asked, 'Why, Madame, don't you wear women's clothes?' Then, his new-found European sophistication kicking in, he answered his own question, 'Sensible,' the shah commented in his staccato delivery, 'In my country a woman can't go about unveiled without exciting the population, but can

Shah Nasr-al-Din

you think what a sensation a veiled Persian woman would be on the Paris boulevards? And furthermore, the French don't have the same excuse as my subjects, many of whom have never seen any woman other than their mothers. Can you paint?'[9] he finished abruptly. No, but she could photograph. The unveiled foreign woman won his approval by obligingly photographing his sister's children.

As for Marcel, the shah told him he looked much older than his thirty-seven years, an instant aging Dr Tholozan attributed to his illness. As the audience proceeded Marcel gained entrée to royal favour through his service in the Franco–Prussian War. (Jane's does not seem to have been mentioned; perhaps that would have been going too far.) The shah sent his regards to their mutual friend, the general commanding the army of the Loire. Soon whispers of the royal affability would reach the bazaars and be their protection; on the road the royal approbation would be their insurance.

For the shah was a tyrant, with life and death dependent on his whim. There were no controls or restraints to his power such as a constitution or a body of law. There was no law, other than orally transmitted precedents administered by corrupt secular judges and shari'a law, based on the Koran, equally corruptly administered. The shah's ministers, having bought their offices, were nothing more than superior servants who carried out his orders. They had no security, a full year's tenure not guaranteed even by their *No Ruz* 'present'. Like *hadji* mirza Hosein Khan, they could be dismissed in an instant.

Appointees in the next rank were lesser men whose bribes had provided the wealth to the ministers. And as it went on down the scale, the ultimate source of the bribe money, the peasants, craftsmen and merchants, were squeezed dry. For a time, while Hosein Khan was grand vizier, they had hope. When that principled idealist fell, they lost it.

Consequently, the riches of the shah increased year by year. In a vast audience hall approached by a sweeping staircase of cream-coloured alabaster and set with chairs and tables overlaid with beaten gold, the shah's fabulous treasures, including many of the crown jewels, were laid out. 'Possibly,' sighed an astonished Isabella Bird, 'the accumulated splendours of pearls, diamonds, rubies, emeralds, sapphires . . . not arranged, but piled like tea or rice . . . basins and vessels of solid gold, ancient armour flashing with precious stones, shields studded with diamonds and rubies, scabbards and sword hilts incrusted with costly gems, helmets red with rubies, golden trays and vessels thick with diamonds, crowns of jewels, ornaments (masculine solely) of every description, jewelled coats of mail dating back to the reign of Shah Ismael, exquisite enamels of great antiquity, all in a profusion not to be described, have no counterpart on earth. They are a dream of splendour not to be forgotten.'[10] Perhaps old accounts of magnificence at ancient courts were true, Isabella thought, dazzled by the profusion. A jewel-studded throne, created from the Peacock Throne[11] stolen from Mughal Delhi by Nader Shah in 1739, fascinated George Curzon.

Unlike those British travellers empowered by their legation's prestige, the Dieulafoys were not taken to view the treasure. Lacking mighty diplomatic backing, they were dismissed with a wave of the hand. They were grateful for an audience in the garden and even more for the Shah's pass, the whole object of their visit, which supposedly would give them entree to any building of significant architectural merit.

'Ya Allah, Ya Ali. Allah has sent the plague to Mashhad. Kitab! It was written!'

The news spread fast in the bazaar, on to the palace, through the mosques, and flew into the foreign legations. When Jane heard it she thought first of the Aga and Ali and the eight excited wives due in Mashhad any day now, before realising it would prevent her and Marcel taking the Mashhad road to Damghan, where stood Persia's oldest surviving mosque.

Instead, the Dieulafoys turned their caravan towards the southern gate. Leaving behind the men in full-skirted frock-coats and tailored trousers churning about in Artillery Square, they rode through streets where the hems of men's baggy pants trailed beneath loose dark gowns falling open over brightly sashed robes. Tall black felt hats gave way to Persian lambskin and the colour-coded turbans of the clerics. Smart kidskin boots were replaced by heelless slippers with upturned pointed toes. An occasional donkey led by a servant crept along the edge of the street, on its back a woman bundled in a black sheet, a frail hand holding the material together at the throat, a white mesh mask inserted where a face might be. At the stirrup, a yellow shoe peeped from the gathered leg of voluminous purple pants. She was only a parcel, a property.

Once through the city walls, the scene changed again. Instead of crowded noisy streets shut between the high blank walls of Persian houses, a single rocky track stretched out across an arid desert, empty except for a few caravans wandering along and horsemen urging tired mounts towards the city or spurring away from it. Apart from a few birds lonely in the vast sky, nothing else moved.

Jane's response to Persia was about to be shaken by a few weeks rambling through the countryside near the towns of Varamin and Rayy. On her journey from the savage and desolate landscape of the northwest corner of Persia, through the beautiful but bitterly cold high plains surrounding Tabriz, along the rolling country at the foot of the Alburz Mountains, and from Qazvin to Tehran (which she barely saw as she scrambled to save Marcel), Jane's diary is at times condescending. Given the long, difficult days, her constant exhaustion and the exotic society for which even her extensive reading could not have fully prepared her, it is hardly surprising that beneath her careful, often humorous, account of people and places lies judgemental anger.

Despite later editing in Paris, after Tehran her journals display a clear change in narrative tone. Criticisms are still there, but their tone is more the exasperation of a parent irritated by a loved child behaving to its own disadvantage. Seeing the people as victims, from now on she rails against 'the system': the method of government, the supine, greedy shah and the venal clerics. Riding through the Tehran hinterland she developed a deep empathy with Persia which, despite later terrible experiences in the south, informed the rest of her life. In 1896 when Nasr-al-Din was assassinated she rallied to defend the country in the French press and she remained an advocate of its beauty and its past achievements until she died.

The drama of the landscape, angular mountains rising abruptly from the plain, their colours ranging from magenta through burnt umber to violet and even bright yellow depending on the sun and distance, the omnipresence of the shapely white volcanic cone of Mount Damavand and the huge ever-changing sky are constant themes in her diary during these weeks. She was a European accustomed to enclosed green fields, painted villages sheltered by copses, close-up hills and diminutive valleys, and her sensibility was shocked by the vastness of the Persian countryside. A prospect without fences or hedges, where distance hid walled towns the colour of the desert earth from which they were made, where only the irrigated fields near the villages produced crops, with nothing growing between, where the land stretched out brown, stony and parched to the horizon, required a different understanding, a new eye.

In the unlimited landscape Jane encountered a time scale to match. Persia's long history, reaching back through an endless cycle of invaders who smashed and created, and further into the old Zoroastrian communities, was revealed in the ravaged countryside. Architectural ruins and broken ceramics recorded ancient tragedies, making more poignant the realities of the contemporary struggle. She saw villages depleted of probably a quarter of their inhabitants by a decade of famine, an economy shattered by silk-worm disease and bled by extortionate taxation, yet Persian resilience was written in the fragments of the past.

Transience and immutability disputed the land; ignorance and achievement dwelt side by side in the villages; death and survival stalked the same territory.

The ancient towns of Varamin and Rayy are so close to Tehran that the twenty-first century has seen them engulfed by sprawling suburbs. In Jane's time Varamin was a long day's ride away, which in midsummer was better done in the cool of night. The route lay in the shadow of mountains where the *anderun*s of wealthy Tehranis lay sleeping in high-walled gardens. It skirted the hilltop where dead Zoroastrians were laid out behind a high wall for the birds to pick their bones clean – air, fire, water and the earth itself were elements too pure to be defiled by a corpse in the still-surviving pre-Islamic religion of Persia. It ignored the new golden domes and minarets rising above the remains of three of the venerated family of Ali entombed at the shrine of Shah Abdal Azim in Rayy.

Soon the caravan was passing villagers harvesting in the moonlight, cicadas harmonising the workers' songs. In the opium fields the first cut was being made. The caravan wandered on under a multitude of stars, the tcharvadar bachy fell asleep on his mule and they lost their way. Barking dogs led them to a village. When they beat at the gate, nightcapped heads peered over the walls. The headman, asleep under his trees, offered them shelter, as he was obliged to do if the village had no caravanserai, but at six next morning they left for Varamin, the heat already unbearable when they arrived at ten. The village headman assigned them a room in his compound and they immediately set out to explore. Marcel was determined to net the Sasanids, but Jane was soon walking through the Seljuk years.

The Ilkhanid Mongols, whom Jane first encountered in Tabriz, were not the first central Asian tribe to sweep into Persia. For thousands of years climate cycles had been squeezing bursts of horsemen out of central Asia. History records innumerable savage mounted invasions into adjoining territories such as China, the Russian steppe, Afghanistan, Persia and Anatolia, and occasional penetrations as far as India, Europe and Egypt.

The relative prosperity of Persia made it a magnet for covetous Asian raiders, its great central plateau of Fars having been occupied for millennia by a creative urban and agricultural population descended from Aryan tribes. And no part of the troubled frontier between settled Aryan and nomadic Turc has seen greater numbers of speedy, spindle-shanked ponies sweeping through than the area south of the Caspian Sea where Rayy and Varamin stand. The marauders riding in from central Asia in 1038 we call Seljuks.

World climate changed at the beginning of the eleventh century. A greenhouse event known as the Little Climate Optimum or the Medieval Warm Period produced a warmer, wetter climate. On the suddenly grass-green plains of the Asian steppe two generations of nomad Turcs watched their horses multiply and their sons survive into adulthood, while in the mountain valleys tribes who scratched crops into the earth and herded cattle and sheep saw bumper harvests and a population explosion. As increased numbers competed for constant acreage, warfare broke out. Whether the Seljuk Turcs were forced out or in an excess of wild health voluntarily adventured has not been determined. Whatever impelled them, the Seljuks galloped out of the steppe in 1038.

Within fifty years of their first ferocious rampage the Seljuks controlled an empire extending from the borders of China in the east to the Mediterranean in the west. They conquered Persia, Mesopotamia and Arabia to the south, and, in the eastern Mediterranean lands, along a deadly frontier they confronted the Byzantine Empire, descendant of the Greek and Roman Empires. When Alp Arslan defeated the Byzantines at Mantzikert in 1071, the Seljuk Turcs won most of Anatolia, which later took their name, becoming part of the state of Turkey.

The Seljuks ravaged and destroyed, and then, converted by Persian aesthetics, they began to commission incomparable, exquisitely decorated buildings. Once again Persia had tamed her conquerors, extracted their best and survived as distinctly Persian. Under the ex-barbarians, Persian architecture flourished, while itinerant Persian craftsmen carried its distinctive forms and decorations into all parts of the new empire, including Palestine and what Europe called The Holy Land.

Rayy was one of the first towns affected by the Seljuk whirlwind as it radiated from the central Asian heartland. Its men were slaughtered and its mosques destroyed, but later, when Isfahan became the capital of the Great Seljuk Empire, Rayy resurrected as an important provincial centre. From Rayy, artisans were sent to Qazvin to build the mosque which Jane and Marcel had inspected while the mullahs were breakfasting, and its beauty had inspired the Momine-Khatun mausoleum at Narchevan. Of the Seljuk achievement in Rayy little more than a roofless, fluted tomb tower remained. The onslaught of the Mongols in 1220 had taken care of the rest.

Rayy's Seljuk survivors had fled with their skills to Varamin, a village too insignificant for the Mongols to notice as they swept west, but in time those horsemen returned and settled, making the village into a town, then a city, where they built a great mosque. In 1881 the mosque stood apart in a field because, in the eternal Persian cycle, Varamin had shrunk to a village again. When the Dieulafoys rode towards it, the pungent aroma of herbs crushed underfoot filled the air. They were welcome to enter the mosque, the mullahs said, perhaps hoping its damaged walls would fall on the infidels. The mosque is long and from the entrance Jane had a sweeping view through the courtyard to the domed sanctuary, 'its façade ornamented with ravishing faience tile mosaics in two shades of blue,' Jane wrote joyfully. Within the sanctuary was a mihrab[12] 'enriched by admirable floral relief-carved panels, whose daring and sureness of hand struck us.'[13] Carved and painted stucco clung to the walls and filled the squinches.

Although the afternoon heat was unbearable and the structure dangerously unstable, Jane and Marcel climbed to the unrailed gallery around the dome and surveyed the country. They marked down for exploration a crumbling citadel to the north, felt the loneliness of the desert stretching out to the south, and descended, deciding they would keep village hours in future.

They rose in the pre-dawn light and at four joined the villagers streaming out to the fields. Examining the ruined citadel, Marcel at last found something tangible from Sasanid times, its solid aggregated brickwork confirming its Sasanid origins. In that era builders piled still-wet, unbaked bricks on top of each other, leaving them to dry into one fused unbreakable mass before laying further courses. The walls enclosed a huge space that had been, long before the Arabs came, a 'paradise garden' filled with flowers and captured animals for the chase.

Forced by the heat back to the village on a road crowded with returning workers, they breakfasted at eight on abundant village fruit – apricots, cherries, plums and peaches – and then retired, like the villagers, to sleep through the midday heat. Life, and work, began again with the evening cool and continued until late in the night. Then, Jane hung her black curtains across the door of her room. Before dawn the cycle would resume.

Europeans were particularly unwelcome at the imamzadde[14] Yaya, not only because an infidel foot defiled wherever it trod, but because a panel of the wall tiles had recently been stolen. In 1881 the market in antiquities was already hot. The complex was dilapidated, walls broken, the dome of the mosque almost bare of tiles. Before its rearing portico stood a white-tur-baned mullah with a guard of baton-armed peasants. The cleric examined the royal pass, frowned, and reluctantly dismissed the men who returned relieved to the fields. Marcel and the 'boy' walked into the rubble-filled courtyard. At the end stood the domed mosque and to the side a damaged tent-roofed tomb.

Its cross- and star-shaped lustre tiles were made in the Kashan potteries in the early thirteenth century during the Ilkhanid era. The tiles had first been glazed with opaque white (gazelle's milk again?) and fired. When cool, they were overpainted with silver and copper compounds and refired in a carefully controlled atmosphere which chemically reduced the compounds, stripping away the oxygen and leaving a thin lustrous veneer of silver and copper metal on the surface of the pale glaze. In places the lustre tiles had fallen away, exposing tiles from the earlier Seljuk period. Bursts of pure colour, 'brass, clear yellow and coppered bronze,'[15] wrote Jane, delighted by their brilliance. Some of these tiles, too, had fallen off, revealing the original painted stucco, and beneath that was yet another layer – the shrine was old even before the Seljuks had galloped in. It meant little to them, so why destroy it?

Though the Seljuks adopted Sunni Islam, their rule was secular. Religion ran second to the business of the state. They were the first dynasty after the Arab invasion who could not validate their rule by claiming descent from the Prophet. They had come in from the steppe and were not Arab, and in an empire that burned with Arab doctrine they needed another way to legitimate their power. They fell back on the old Zoroastrian precept: 'Only the virtuous should rule and if he go astray, obedience should be withdrawn from him.' For Seljuk shahs, virtue was indexed to happy citizens, not obeisance to the mosque. Political stability and general prosperity legitimated their rule. They allowed the caliph in Baghdad, leader of the faithful, to represent Islamic succession. The caliph to them was no more than a symbolic unifying figure, their secular state, based on purely ethical-legal tenets, was supreme.

That attitude invigorated intellectual life. Probably none of the original invading Seljuks could read, yet their reign is renowned for its intellectual brilliance. Especially under the great vizier Nizam al-Mulk the Persian mind grew fertile. Freed from religious constraint, philosophers and scientists produced works that have deeply influenced European thought. Through images of wine, drinking and physical love, the Sufi poets struggled to express their yearning and love for God. The ambiguous verse of the mathematician, Omar Khayyam, appeared. And with the sultan's encouragement one of the most important medieval scholars, Muhammad al-Ghazzali, began to integrate Sufism and mysticism into Islamic theology.

Under the Seljuks, generously endowed madrasas spread from Persia throughout the Islamic world. They no longer taught only the Koran. Students studied languages and literature as well as theology and jurisprudence. Libraries filled with volumes on natural sciences, mathematics and political science. It was an intellectual golden age, significant for the West as well as the East, for into this brilliant secular state, ornamented with its distinctive architecture, rode the Christian Crusaders, by contrast barbarians.

Perhaps the most important legacy of the Seljuk years is the Persian language, Farsi. For a time, after the Arabs conquered Iran in 637, Persian culture was completely eclipsed and Arabic became the official language. In the late tenth century, the Baghdad-based Abbasid caliphate in decline, Persian confidence recovered and a 'New Persian', Farsi, became the common tongue. It evolved from the 'Middle Persian' language of the Sasanids, but was written in arabic script, not in the old pahlavi characters. Persian scholars recovered their literary heritage and set it down in Farsi. *The Tales of Sinbad*, the love story of Shirin and Khusraw, the fable of Majnun's longing for the unattainable Layla and the life of Alexander the Great were retold in Persian poetry's distinctive rhythms. Rich patrons lured Persian-speaking poets to their courts to recite this verse, so spreading Persian literary culture throughout the entire Muslim world, with profound consequences for the development of Islamic literature.

From this time comes Firdauzi's *Shahname*, the Book of Kings, published in 1010, which recounted the old, almost lost, dynastic histories. The deeds of the great Sasanid hero Rustum, scarcely mentioned during the centuries under Arab hegemony, were told again in memorable verse. Translated for the Crusaders, Rustum entered European romance poetry. He lives on in every European literature, particularly in the tragic episode where he kills Sohrab his son.

When Jane first heard the *Shahname*, or part of it – it is enormously long – she missed its significance. Approaching Tabriz, frozen by sleeting snow, in pain from long days in the saddle and fearing another rebellion like that in Marand, she had been impatient when the muleteers halted, flung their prayer carpets on the ground, and sat enthralled by a wild recitation from a hairy dervish. She did not then understand what performance of the *Shahname* perpetuates in the Persian psyche. Later, at Nasr al-Din's court, when Marcel told the shah he had come to Persia to study the Sasanians, he was commanded by Nasr al-Din to 'read the *Shahname*. There you will find precious information.'[16] Judging from her many references to him, from then on Rustum rode with Jane.

After their siesta Jane and Marcel went shooting in the wheat fields, returning to the village with a bag of partridge and lark at five o'clock, so exhausted by the heat that they passed an octagonal Seljuk tower without a second look. The headman's compound was full of noise and business. Beds of roses and pomegranates were being splashed with water. A servant was washing down a wooden platform, more to cool it than to clean it, before laying a carpet and placing cushions. Villagers streamed into the garden. The headman and a scribe appeared and stepped onto the platform, where they sat on bent legs to convene the weekly village court.

The moon rose and still the cases of petty theft and broken contracts proceeded. A labourer who had signed for a year but decamped to a better-paying master when harvest time came was ordered to return to the man who had paid him through the winter or take five strokes of the bastinado. Someone had stolen a chicken; he could give back two or pay forty chais. (My cook is overcharging me, I must check his accounts more carefully, thought Jane.) There was unfinished business from the previous week; a gardener who had filled his donkey's panniers with fruit and cucumbers for the Tehran market had complained, 'I took the road home with Reza, Ali, Houssein, Ismael and Yaya. I slept while we rested the donkeys, and when I woke my beautiful coat was gone. Only one of them could have taken it.'

The headman had instructed his secretary to cut five pomegranate sticks of equal length and to give one each to Reza, Ali, Houssein, Ismael and Yaya. 'As everyone knows,' he said, 'the one held by the thief will grow longer. Bring your stick here next week.' So here they were and the villagers were waiting with great anticipation. The judge examined the sticks.

'Yaya, you wretch. You stole the coat.'

'Grace to Allah, it is not true.'

'Yaya, you have cut a piece off this twig. Go with the guard to your house and bring the coat here. And twenty strokes when you return.'[17]

The Dieulafoys dined outside their room. Their cook had marinated the game birds in verjus and served them as kebabs alongside a mound of rice. Barley soup and flat bread began the meal and mact, fermented milk, ended it. Across the garden the headman dined with his male household. Servants carried in a large brass tray and set it on the ground in front of the men squatting on their haunches. Then the two main dishes were brought, one a mountain of rice sprinkled with finely chopped herbs and streaked with saffron, the other lamb and chicken pieces swimming in sauce. Chopped cucumbers and flat bread were stacked between.

The meal began after water was poured over the hands. The left hand, the unclean hand of the East, held back the clothes against the chest, while the right took a scoop of rice, then some chicken or lamb, or both, perhaps adding a piece of cucumber before forming it into a ball with the fingers. The ball was flicked into the mouth and swallowed at a shot. No one chewed. If the ball stuck, the diner craned his neck and gobbled like a turkey until it went down.

There was no conversation and in ten minutes the matter was concluded. What was left was taken away to the *anderun*. Delicately carved wooden bowls filled with rosewater were passed around for hand washing and the *kalian*s brought. Before the moon shone on the bent backs of the men making the evening prayer and on the bedding being laid on the ground for the night's short sleep the Dieulafoys had retired behind their black curtain.

For a week the village graciously accepted them. Persian rural life, Jane concluded, was not so very different from peasant life in her own Languedoc. Only once were they afraid. As a hurricane raged out of the desert they crouched with the terrified villagers while the winds tore the fruit off the trees, a disaster for Varamin and for Tehran, 'a city dependent on its hinterland because the country lacks proper roads, canals and rail-ways.' Fortunately the wheat harvest was already in.

Jane was beginning to feel comfortable in Persia. She was dazzled by its tiles and monuments, although she regretted that everything was so dilapidated. She now knew how to deal with this country and these people, she had their measure, or so she thought. She was relaxed and happy, Marcel was completely recovered, the shah's royal pass authorised their entry to the religious monuments, everything was set for success. They would return to Tehran and when the weather was cooler they would head to the south.

But first she would inspect the Seljuk tower that dominated the village. The intricate geometric designs on its counterparts further west had inspired the Crusaders to beautify their dour European surroundings.

From 1096 battling Christian and Muslim armies pulverized the western parts of the Seljuk Empire: Syria, Palestine and Anatolia. Two hundred years later, when the last Crusaders withdrew, the Europeans had been entirely seduced by Seljuk architecture and its associated arts, with enormous consequences for Western urban development. Persian accomplishments had infiltrated the very soul of European culture.

By then the Seljuks had fallen, rotted from within. In 1090 the Assassins, a sect of the dissident Shi'a Ismailis, established themselves in the Alamut Mountains with an agenda so vicious it added a new word to European languages. They 'assassinated' the Seljuk sultans and viziers one by one, justifying their atrocities by distorted Islamic readings. The first to go was the learned, tolerant prime minister, Nizam al-Mulk in 1092. Later that year they murdered Malik Shah himself, setting off fratricidal warfare and compromising efforts to repulse the Crusaders in 1096. While Malik Shah's warring sons endangered their inheritance, provincial governors declared independence, excising princedoms on the edges of the Seljuk state. The Crusaders advanced into a diminishing empire, soon reduced to only Iran and Iraq.

With fanatical Ismaili terrorists stalking the country and beyond, the disempowered clerics saw an opportunity to regain their lost supremacy. Both Sunni and Shi'a lunged for power and the resulting internal dissension further weakened the regime. When population problems in central Asia squeezed out another mounted cavalry, the Seljuk hegemony was lost in a decisive battle at Rayy in 1220. The Mongols had arrived. Destructive madness was the new philosophy.

In Qajar Persia Jane sensed and analysed the tensions without realising that what was evident to her in 1881 was no more than a reprise of what had exercised the Persians during the Seljuk years – clerics and secular rulers vying for power, innate intellectual brilliance resisting the constraints of theological bigotry, terror ruthlessly and randomly applied, fanatical religious sects distorting the Islamic message. (Nor is it any different in Iran today.)

In late June, in its hollow in the plain, Tehran was stifling. July and August would be worse. Though anxious to be on their way south to search for the Sasanids, the Dieulafoys were daunted by the prospect of travelling in midsummer along a route that skirted the edge of the great Dasht-i Kavir desert. Postponing their journey, they accepted an invitation to stay at the summer residence of the French chargé d'affaires on the side of the Alburz Mountains. There, in a Persian garden, on 29 June Jane celebrated her thirtieth birthday. She was still enjoying the cool retreat on 13 July when a royal messenger delivered a letter in Persian script so flowery no one could read it. Eventually the Dieulafoys understood they had been recalled to Tehran by command of the shah's third son, Naib-es-Sultaneh, Governor of Tehran, Commander-in-Chief and Minister of War.

The road to the capital was crowded with carriages, horsemen and baggage-laden mules streaming out of the city. The shah was on his way to Soltanabad to raise his silk-hung tent in its cool pastures. Soldiers led the way, raising the dust and pushing oncoming traffic off the road. These were followed by the led horses and the suites of the ministers, in the middle of which was Tehran's jume mullah, married to the shah's daughter, bowling along in a six-horse carriage. When mules appeared carrying the paired baskets in which women crouched on quilts, Marcel and the 'boy' reined in, turned their backs and waited for the cavalcade to pass – mandatory court etiquette to prevent a man even glimpsing a royal wife. The panniers passed quickly. If the rumour were true that the shah had more than 140 wives, although who would know since only eunuchs were allowed to enter his *anderun*, they were certainly not all going to Soltanabad, said Jane.

In Tehran they went straight to the Naib-es-Sultaneh's palace and were led through a formal garden to the summer hall. Persia being a country of climatic extremes, all but the meanest houses had separate summer and winter quarters, sometimes merely rooms that received the sun in winter as opposed to almost windowless spaces on the south side of the courtyard. In the palaces of nobles, dignitaries and princes the distinction was much greater. The Naib's vast underground summer hall was a cool and brilliant space suffused by flashing light. The ceiling and deep cornice were decorated with the carved stucco work called muqarnas, receding clusters of distinct, arched niches, the 'exquisite design . . . taken from snow on the hillsides, which is often fashioned by a strong wind into the honeycomb pattern,' romanced Isabella Bird.[18] Each facet of the niches was pasted with mirror glass, each tiny piece reflecting the light coming from windows set high in the end walls. Glinting and sparkling, they turned the spray rising from fountains sunk in the marble floor to diamond arabesques.

'The 26-year-old prince is fat and looks forty,'[19] wrote Jane, describing the interview with brutal honesty. Diamonds glittered on his chest and winked in his gold epaulettes.

Knowing the Dieulafoys intended to travel via Isfahan, the prince asked Marcel if he would detour through Saveh to inspect a dam. Built in the reign of Shah Abbas, the dam was cracked at its base. Would Marcel advise on its repair? Would he go at once?

Chapter 6
On business for the shah's son

They had chosen not to travel south while the summer blazed but how could they deny the shah's third son? On magnificent black horses from the prince's own stables, magenta-dyed tails signifying royal ownership, Jane and Marcel left Tehran in the chill of night escorted by the prince's trusted aide, General Abbas Kouly Khan, and a troop of soldiers. When they stopped at midday the temperature was 45°C in the shade and the air quivered over the burning ground. Not a single tree was visible on the arid plain. Behind them the white peak of Damavand dazzled in the sunlight. At the town's best house Jane climbed down into a cool underground room. A badgir, a square box with movable shutters mounted above the roof, captured every passing breeze, sucking it down through a tall chimney. Bathed by the moving air, Jane slept in the darkness until the caravan moved off again at night.

The desert gave way to an old salt lake running east–west across the route, a band of deep murky pools where the horses had to pick their way along narrow strips of deeply cracked ground. On the third day, three hours after dawn, the town governor, his cavalry and a retinue of household functionaries escorted the Dieulafoys into Saveh. The populace peered suspiciously, fearing the general had come to extort more taxes when in fact he had come to intrigue with the mullahs against the governor.

After the official reception Jane hung her black curtains across the windowless windows and doorless door of the town's best house. On the edge of sleep she felt little feet crawling on her skin. She flung back the curtains to see light-allergic bedbugs fleeing to their homes in the cracked walls and spiders swinging away on their silk. But without the curtains, the temperature rose to 44 °C and mosquitoes and flies invaded the room. The honour of being the Naib-es-Sultaneh's representative did not bring parallel comfort, she concluded.

It was worse out at the dam. The Dieulafoys were housed in a plum orchard in earth huts used in winter by the pruners; their provisions ran short and the master mason used their drinking water. To escape the heat they abandoned the security of four walls to sleep under the stars, ordering their beds to be carried up to the roof and the bedstead's legs placed in basins of water. In a province notorious for deadly scorpions no one slept on the floor. Yet perhaps the servant let the bedding trail on the ground a moment because during the night Jane was stung. Her foot was already swelling when she went with Marcel to discuss his report with the general. The dam was fundamentally sound; it needed only a little repair at the base. Aha, said the general, I will take care of the costing – it will be . . . Despite Persian workers being paid a pittance and the materials little more than local stone, the figure was twice the cost in France. And of course there would be something in it for Marcel, added Kouly Khan.

The principled Colonel Dieulafoy drew himself up. The report was not quite ready after all, he said coldly, he would complete it in Isfahan and send it direct to the Naib-es-Sultaneh. As they rode away Jane decried Persia's corruption. Pragmatic Marcel recognised he could not change the system. Such an attempt had cost *hadji* mirza Hosein Khan his life, and that grand vizier had wielded more power than an infidel engineer could imagine.

Suddenly the general was struck by a convenient stomach complaint – he could not eat with them, in fact he could not accompany them on to Qom, indeed he would have to return at once to Tehran. When the Dieulafoys discovered the general had sent their baggage mules back to the capital, they raced for the prince's black riding horses, fortunately tethered in the orchard out of the general's reach, and fortunate too that he had no authority to dismiss their soldier escort.

Kashani scorpion bites are often fatal. 'May he be bitten by a Kashani scorpion,' Persians cursed their enemies, but Jane regarded her bite as a problem, not a restraint. She treated her foot from her medicine kit and began to organise a caravan. Ramadam had begun: muleteers and baggage animals were unavailable. Jane was offered an aged camel but settled on asses. The three-day trip was a nightmare. After four days in the orchard, their horses were too fresh to travel at the pace of 'little donkeys the size of dogs' and had to be constantly reined in. For Jane it was a horrible necessity since the Persian bit had a spur mounted in the centre which lacerated the roof of the mouth. The horses pulled up from a gallop with their muzzles buried in a foam of bloody saliva. Her foot throbbed and swelled inside her boot. Lost. Separated from the caravan.

After thirteen hours in the saddle, they found the Avah gate still closed and the guardians reluctant to open it.

When the military escort informed the gatekeepers that the foreigners had been at Saveh to advise the shah on the dam's repair, the villagers threw back the gate. Thinking Marcel would make their desperately needed irrigation water flow again, the impoverished Avah peasants offered their hospitality. If Marcel ever learned what happened to the dam, he would have been mortified by his memory of their generosity.

In 1882 the Naib-es-Sultaneh constructed a new road between Tehran and Qom – at least he cleared the stones and cut down the bushes along a route, and then built expensive caravanserais at the stages, expecting the revenue to roll in. When the travelling public stuck to the older, cheaper route a curious thing happened – the old salt lake across the original way began to fill with water. The shah rode out to inspect. Allah kerim! God is great! It is a miracle, mashallah! Praise to Allah! he said, ignoring how the flood submerged the old road. No one dared tell him that Naib-es-Sultaneh had cut the Saveh dam and diverted the waters through a gap in the hills. With the old route drowned, fees from his high-priced caravanserais over-flowed the Naib's coffers.

Their military escort revealed more to the Avah people than the Dieulafoys' business at Saveh – Jane's gender, an indiscretion which under other cir-cumstances could have had serious consequences. Only a few years earlier, another 'very handsome youth' was arrested in a coffee house in Tehran. The arresting officer said to the chief constable, "'A nice looking boy, is he not? ... and nicely dressed too ... look at the pretty Kurdish hand-kerchief he has wound round his [felt cap]," [then he] plucked it off, and the girl's hair ... fell down over her shoulders. When the Haji discovered that [the] prisoner was a girl dressed in man's clothes ... he reviled her in unmeasured terms, and ordered her to be locked up in a cupboard ... In the morning she was taken out, placed in a sack, and beaten all over ... after which her head was shaved.'[1]

Two things stood between Jane and a beating. One was the attitude of dignified authority assumed by all Europeans, though, as Jane learned later in Kashan, if even for a moment that aura was compromised the European became dangerously vulnerable.

Jane's second shield was the Avah women's interest in fashion. Hoping

Jane could advise them they invited her into the headman's *anderun*. It was her first opportunity to penetrate the quarters where wives were kept in seclusion; she would certainly not reject it. Each wife touched the tips of her fingers to Jane's, then withdrew them to her lips and wished Jane welcome. Fatma, the head wife, wasted no time. 'You've been at court,' she began, 'Since his last trip to Europe, is it true the shah has made his wives lengthen their skirts?' Fatma, wrote Jane, seemed distracted. 'Her head was covered by a square of white silk fastened under her chin with a turquoise; except for a short fringe across her forehead her thick hair fell in a multitude of little ringlets down her back; a thin gauze chemise, split at the front, left her breasts almost naked. Her Benares-silk skirt ended above her knee. The other wives were dressed similarly, only the older women chastely wearing calf-length tights of white cotton.' In this *anderun* metre-length skirts were going to be a revolution!

'I have also heard that the princesses are wearing European headbands made of artificial flowers.' If she would give her a garland, Jane could have 'one of my silver bracelets set with coral, pearls and turquoises.' Amazing enough that Jane was travelling without feminine baubles, but why was she travelling at all? The wives could not comprehend it, a woman's pleasure being to rest and adorn herself.

'Do you spend the whole day at your toilette?'

Certainly not, but making oneself beautiful took a lot of time. Finger and toenails must be coloured, palms and soles carefully hennaed, eyebrows painted to meet in the middle, eyes enhanced with kohl, hair perfumed. 'Do you think it's so easy that it's the thing of an instant?'

Asked what they did after their toilette, Fatma told Jane, 'We smoke, drink tea, visit our friends. They're happy to have company. We amuse ourselves,' she said, 'You are our entertainment today.'[2]

Jane's swollen foot was lanced before their departure on the following night. They were almost ready to mount when news arrived of nomad ambushes further on towards Qom. The donkey masters were terrified. If for Persians travelling in the heat was better than being robbed, for Europeans attempting to cross the Qom desert during daytime at donkey speed would be sure death. Trusting the caravan to follow, Marcel and Jane left at three in the morning, 'determined to kill the Naib's horses, if necessary, but to reach Qom before eight.'

Marcel set the regime: fifteen minutes galloping, five minutes walking across a desert where the legendary Kashani scorpions were the only living things. At five the escort said they were halfway, at six the heat became unbearable and the leather on their saddle bows began to crack. 'We were so sweaty that the bridle slipped through our fingers, our eyelids swelled and our pupils, blinded by the glare from the sand, refused to open, our temples throbbed so hard we thought our heads would burst.'[3]

At seven they saw the golden dome of Fatima's tomb shining in the distance; before eight they had crossed a long graceful bridge spanning a dry river bed and passed beneath the blue-tiled gate of Qom. The royal horses had survived.

Their horses' magenta tails, insignia of the royal stables, announced the Dieulafoys' status, prompting Qom's governor to invite them to stay in the palace. His Qajar princess wife had taken the children to the mountains for the summer. The Dieulafoys were shown into an empty *anderun* consisting of two buildings, one at each end of a garden courtyard. In the summer quarters at the southern end the reception rooms were backed by small dark spaces, tiny cool subterranean chambers where the women napped in the daytime. At night they spread their carpets on the flat roof where a high encircling wall ensured privacy from everything except the stars. The rooms were bare, the carpets, quilts and silk cushions now padding the baskets in which the princess's suite bumped along the mountain tracks. Jane thought them mean quarters for a shah's daughter.

The horses' brilliant tails also ensured that the infidels could ride safely in a place notorious for religious fanaticism. In the ruined town, 'mostly rubbish and litter with forlorn miserable houses . . . grouped near festering pools,'[4] only the Qajar tombs and Fatima's shrine were in good repair. The streets were crowded with corpses, mullahs, sayyids[5] and pilgrims, for the economy of Qom was based on importing the dead and exporting mullahs trained in its many madrasas. The corpses, destined to lie in graves alongside Fatima's tomb, arrived in varying stages of decomposition lashed to the sides of donkeys, and brought with them pilgrims to pray in the shrine. Because of Fatima, sister to the eighth Imam[6], Qom was the second most sacred city in Iran. Only her brother, Imam Reza lying dead at Mashhad, outranked her, most other Shi'a Imams' tombs, and even the knowledge of their location, having been lost during the centuries before the Shi'a faith was officially adopted by the Persian state. (Ali and his sons lie in Iraq; the tenth and eleventh Imams were buried at Samarra.) Even so, such reverence for Fatima was curious, thought Jane, in a population that held women in contempt.

Jane could only look from the gate at Fatima's copper dome, gold-plated and topped by an attenuated ornament made on Fath Ali Shah's order from fifty kilograms of pure gold. Canary-yellow, azure-blue and iridescent-green glazed tiles gleamed on its five minarets. Jane longed to get closer but the shrine was barred to infidels.

Qom's vaulted bazaar was dedicated to serving the dead and their mourners. Chisels for the tombstone engravers and shovels for the grave-diggers were sold in a narrow side alley, shoes and water containers for the pilgrims about to set off on their homeward journey were laid out in shops bordering the crowded central street, while the provisions Jane needed for the next stage of her journey to the south were close by the spice-sellers' market.

Jane rode out of Qom in the dark of night on the back of a very inferior hack. The superb Persian horse with its arched neck, haughty bearing and a gait 'as though the earth were too vulgar for [its] touch' that had carried her into Qom had been regretfully surrendered. Sure-footed and 'fine-legged though not at the expense of strength,' Isabella Bird wrote admiringly of a similar thoroughbred she rode from Tehran to Qom in 1890 along the Naib-es-Sultaneh's new road. Jane's desperate ride across the desert had proven the breed's hardiness and stamina and she regretted that she was unlikely ever again to be so well mounted.

When Jane and Marcel took up their long journey to the Persian Gulf, Tehran lay 160 kilometres behind them. Ahead were fabled cities strung out along a 1200-kilometre route. Their way lay across the great central plateau of Iran, the land bridge between the Mediterranean world and the Asian steppe, raised 900 to 1800 metres above sea level, sprinkled with unexpected mountains and haunted by deserts, exposed relentlessly to the sun and the winds. Jane and Marcel would skirt the deserts and climb the mountains that could not be avoided. Leaving the plateau, they would travel into the Zagros Mountains, parallel ranges running along an axis northwest to southeast, pushed up in the geological past by immense forces and shaken in the present by tectonic collisions. Dropping down through mountain passes onto the Khuzestan Plain, they would descend to sea level. There they hoped to enter Mesopotamia, where the Ottoman Turks ruled a troubled province and where the most sacred Shi'a shrines lay.

A daunting itinerary, but not to the Dieulafoys. Apart from the length of the planned route and its geographical difficulties, their mode of travel was circumscribed by its being self-funded and unofficial. The prince's soldier-escort left behind in Qom along with the haughty horses, their only protection now was the 'beautiful sheet of white paper on which a calligrapher of the third order' recommended them to the French Consuls, and they were found only in the major cities. With one of the travellers being a woman when even a masculine infidel travelled at great risk, it was an inherently dangerous proposition.

The Dieulafoys joined a caravan to Isfahan, marching at night, when temperatures often fell to the other extreme, to avoid the desert heat. The first nights were moonless, the path lit only by the brilliance of the stars, the spread of the caravan marked by electric sparks generated in the dry atmosphere as the horses swished their tails against the sand flies. It was impossible to see the great desert, the Dasht-i Kavir, whose edge they were skirting, or the range of mountains to the west. There was only the noise of the bells, the shouts of the muleteers, and the curses of the walkers when they stumbled.

Although Jane's foot had been cauterised twice more in Qom and was less swollen, it still pained in the stirrup. Along the early stages she was often hungry, unable to buy food in villages reduced to poverty by famine and misgovernment. After one night's long ride her meal was a single hard-boiled egg. Yet, however long the stage or inadequate the supplies, her travelling companions never complained. She admired their patience and fortitude, while they tolerated the two infidels with a careless contempt in accordance with the Persian saying, 'If you travel with stinking dogs, don't expect the scent of the rose.'[7]

Still visible across the flat desert, Damavand was flushed with the rose of dawn when Jane dismounted in Nasrabad thirty hours after leaving Qom, twenty-one of them spent in the saddle. She staggered to a steep ladder, dropped down into a cavern dug out five metres below lit only by the entrance shaft, and in its cool dimness fell instantly asleep.

In late afternoon the caravan left for Kashan. As they approached the city, arid desert gave way to fertile plain. Cotton and tobacco plantations stretched into the distance, mud villages hid among green orchards, cucumbers and watermelons filled gardens surrounding flat-roofed houses. Irrigation water alone was responsible for the changed scene.

On the Persian plateau rain is rare, on the mountains snow abundant. Meltwater tumbling down to the plain in springtime is lost almost immediately, sinking into the sand or sucked up by the sun. Only the springs in the mountain flanks, fed by slow melting snow, can provide a continuous supply. For thousands of years the Persians have built tiled subterranean aqueducts, *kanats*, to bring this water to towns and villages. Still in use today, the *kanat*'s course is indicated by long lines of piled earth heaped up around large manholes, access points for diggers and maintenance workers.

If its *kanats* collapse or the spring dries up, a village is doomed. It is slow, back-breaking work to replace them, so keeping them in good repair is vital. When the Mongols invaded Persia they deliberately destroyed the *kanats*, bringing slow agonising death to the villagers and starvation to the cities, and to this day they are cursed, while the Safavids are revered for constructing and maintaining *kanats*, which underpinned that dynasty's great prosperity. Yet everywhere Jane travelled in Persia she heard the Qajar dynasty being reviled for its neglect of the country's infrastructure, *kanats*, caravanserais, roads and bridges falling into ruin while the shah and his sons built opulent palaces.

Kashan irrigation depends on the snows of the Kuhrud Range, angular shapes rearing up from the plain. The summer heat reflected from them burned into the city at the foot of the mountains, where the caravan was promised five days to recover from the desert. When the keeper of the English telegraph station invited the Dieulafoys to stay in his house, just beyond Kashan's city walls, they accepted gratefully.

The station was one of a chain strung at about 100-kilometre intervals along the London to India telegraph line. Service was seldom disrupted but if the daily hook-up indicated a problem it was immediately repaired. The station was both office and residence for the Farsi-speaking European telegraphist. In the lonely life he and his family led European travellers were a welcome diversion. For Jane this interlude of European comfort must have been enjoyable, but her diary does not say so. Conversely, she rarely complained about the lack of amenities, though her careful descriptions of caravanserais and village houses are infused with discomfort and privation. Only once did she acknowledge that 'during the long stages of the caravan, I often woke from sleeping on the floor afraid I would never be able to get up on my horse again.'[8]

Such comfort did not seduce Jane from exploring the town. She set up her camera in the noisy Kashan bazaar. Merchants, customers, mullahs, laden asses and camels streamed between her lens and her target, the doorway of a thirteenth-century mosque. Probably hoping to get into the picture, nearby traders halted the traffic and Jane disappeared under her black cloth. She was about to take the cap off the lens when suddenly an unnerving silence fell. Throwing back the cloth she saw a drove of pannier-bearing mules approaching, a military escort aggressively clearing their path. Everyone except Jane had fallen back against the wall. Jane stood her ground, unaware the governor's favourite wife and her suite were inside the panniers. 'The *khanum* can pass safely in front of my apparatus, I won't photograph her,' she said. Contemptuously, the soldiers pushed her aside and knocked over her precious equipment. Jane's scream brought Marcel flying from the mosque where he had been measuring the mihrab. Too late. Jane had been publicly humiliated.

'In an imperious voice, Marcel ordered our servants to go immediately to the palace and complain to the governor; then, with the proud digni-fied air of people sure of receiving justice, we left the bazaar followed by a crowd of children. The naughty things, faithful interpreters of popular sentiment, somersaulted around us [calling us] dogs, sons of dogs, sons of a burnt father', the usual epithets for infidels.[9]

The governor called on the Dieulafoys at the telegraph station, a subtle acknowledgement of their protest yet not an apology. Glimpsing a little harmonium in the corner of the room he insisted Jane play for him. An accomplished pianist, her rendering of *La Fille de Madame Angot* was too slow for his taste. She must play it again, fast, faster, faster! Coarse and ignorant, he owed his office to his sister, the shah's current favourite, whose sparkling eyes and vivacious manner had captured Nasr-al-Din's attention when he came to Kashan on a hunting trip.

The governor's sister was made available to the shah in a 'temporary marriage', a common practice when notables arrived in a town. Not only travellers but any man – even youths studying in a madrasa or a festering mullah – could contract a 'temporary marriage', a year, a month, a day, the coupling recorded (for a price) by the mullah so that children could be recognised. Impoverished widows with children and divorcees were often forced to accept the arrangement. A feminist before the word was coined, attitudes prompted by injustice towards women, Jane was perplexed by a culture which enclosed some women in cells and turned others into mosque-legitimated prostitutes. Like *kanats*, temporary marriages are an enduring feature of Iranian life.

The governor's sister's temporary marriage had soon become permanent enclosure in the shah's *anderun*.

Next day the *khanum* inveigled Jane into the governor's *anderun* to take her photograph. Head buried under her black cloth and trying to focus the camera, Jane heard the *khanum* tell another wife, 'the daughter of the Russian Tsar commands a regiment and wears helmet and epaulettes, but the queen of England is worse! She has long moustaches!' Jane almost choked

Governor's wife, Kashan

with laughter when the *khanum* asked, 'The queen with moustaches, how many husbands does she have in her *anderun*?'[10]

From the parapet of a twelfth-century tower Jane looked down onto the rows of little half-domes roofing the bazaar and across to the enamelled cupolas of Kashan's mosques. Beyond the surrounding fertile fields, she glimpsed the glittering, terrifying Dasht-i Kavir and had a sudden attack of vertigo. Weak and trembling, she descended the spiral stair on Marcel's arm. Perhaps, thought Jane when told the tower's terrible history, she had been attacked by the ghosts of women thrown from the top by jealous husbands.

In the exquisite garden at Fin, on the mountain flank above Kashan, Jane saw the past reflected in the present. There in a Safavid palace Shah Nasr-al-Din's first significant murder took place, the victim, his close childhood friend and tutor whom he had appointed vizier in 1848, at the beginning of his reign. Determined to reduce corruption and consolidate the shah's power, mirza Taqi Khan challenged clerics and bureaucrats alike. Nasr-al-Din rewarded him with marriage to his sister, but the mullahs and administrators gave him only hatred. He might have survived their plots had he not reprimanded his mother-in-law for her dissolute behaviour. From that moment he was doomed. Banished to Fin, the wife who loved him watched night and day but etiquette barred her from the hammam. Taqi Khan was found in the bath swimming in his own blood, his veins cut. Nasr-al-Din's morose looks were said to date from that day in 1852; yet the life and death of mirza Taqi Khan set a pattern which the shah reprised in 1873 and would repeat once more before Jane left Persia.

Curzon considered Kashan to be 'one of the most dilapidated cities in Persia', perhaps being more than usually choleric when he reached it, but Jane, who was always positive, except when very ill later in the south, describes a 'city richer and more industrious than most Persian towns, as its prosperous aspect testifies.'[11] Jane recognised the city's resilience.

Razed to the ground by the Mongols, Kashan was later resurrected as a producer of exquisite ceramics. For centuries little donkeys streamed out of the city laden with the lustre tiles Jane had so admired at Varamin and the lustre water jugs that she already knew as collectors' items. The trade ceased abruptly in 1722 when furious Afghanis invading from the east killed the potters, broke the kilns, and tore up the recipes for the glazes. Though Kashan's silk industry was now threatened by silkworm disease, Jane found the bazaar still humming, the lanes crowded with cameleers who had brought their trains safely across the desert routes loaded with the riches of the Far East and India. The desert tracks converging in Kashan, the bales were rearranged and goods sold on while the drivers restocked their supplies for the final stages up to Tehran. Jane passed through alleys filled with exquisite silks and satins brought from China, velvets and brocades from Yazd, fine shawls from Kerman – and the deafening noise of coppersmiths. She was stocking up for the three-night journey to Isfahan.

It was now full moon. Riding at the head of a caravan setting off south in the moonlight was the slight 'boy' called Jane. After crossing a stony desert, the track began twisting up into shadowed mountain gorges. Suddenly at a turn in the road their faithful companion, Mount Damavand, disappeared. Curiously, as the Alburz peaks had sunk away with each day's travel from Tehran, Damavand had seemed to grow larger. Now they felt they had lost a friend, even a guardian.

Through dramatic scenery, along narrow rock ledges twisting and turning but always ascending, they climbed towards a 4000-metre pass. The ring of horseshoes on rock and the wheezing of pack animals joined the metallic jangling of bells and saucepans. They crossed a high, broken plateau where shepherds guarded flocks of fat-tailed sheep from wolves and the bitter wind before reaching a second pass at 3000 metres. Warnings of oncoming caravans were constantly thrown back by the leading riders, and after the melee of pack animals, horsemen and foot-travellers had struggled by, the muleteers shouted their farewells, cries of Ya Allah, Ya Ali echoing along the ridges.

Along this route goods imported through the Persian Gulf were brought up to Tehran. The shah's extravagant European furniture, whose purchase scandalised the clerics, was borne by pack animals along the winding track, pianos tinkled over the passes and through the deserts, and the weight of guns and ammunition had left broken-backed mules to die under a blazing sun.

At the second mountain caravanserai Jane and Marcel left their still-sleeping fellow travellers and set off at sunset down a steep descent. Dozing in the saddle at dawn, Jane was roused by a shout from Marcel to see the great plain of Isfahan spread out below.

At the foot of the mountains they hired fresh horses, 'determined to take the last seven farsakhs [35 kilometres] in style'. The setting sun silhouetted the minarets and cupolas of Isfahan as they approached the city gate.

Chapter 7
Isfahan, rose flower of paradise

If the word, 'Persia', evoked in the nineteenth-century European imagination images of exotic sensuality set among silks and sumptuous fabrics and called to mind the mutual hatred and devastating warfare between ancient Greeks and Persians recorded in Greek classics, the name, 'Isfahan', evoked a picture of a fabled city, its glory celebrated by poets, its people depicted in exquisite miniatures, where different races lived in harmony and Shah Abbas ruled benevolently over his Safavid world.

> Isfahan is the idea connoted by the word 'world';
> World is the word, and Isfahan is the meaning,[1]

said the Persians proudly. Seventeenth-century travellers and ambassadors, dazzled by the city's beauty, carried the boast to Europe.

In England the merchants Robert and Anthony Sherley regaled the court of Elizabeth I with stories of a polo field surrounded by wondrous buildings, while Herbert told Charles I of graceful palaces. The French were informed of its gorgeous embellishments by the jeweller Tavernier, and Chardin wrote of the 'Grand Sophy', their name for the Safavid shah. Though spies from other European nations spoke of treachery amid the Safavid grandeur and later visitors suggested that some of the splendour had dimmed, the Europeans hung on to their myth.

When Jane rode across the plain towards Isfahan she did not see the desert threatening on the east or the snow slipping off the Bakhtiari Ranges to the west, or even the lines of *kanats* converging on bright-green plantations outside the city wall. Her mind filled with expectation built on the old accounts of Isfahan, she rode through the city gate, 'looked quickly around and suddenly stopped. What bitter deception is mine! Am I in a sacked village taken by storm?'[2] Jane writes of ruins, abandoned bazaars, deserted streets, walls threatening to fall on the passersby, terraces dismantled so their supporting columns can be removed, sheets of tiles chiselled off leaving exposed earth walls to disintegrate in the rain. She describes peasants in a deserted quarter breaking and crushing the fallen bricks and shovelling the mineral-rich powder into baskets. Has the royal city, she asks, come to this? Has the *rose flower of paradise* become mere dust to spread on watermelons and cucumbers? In the great thoroughfare, the Chahar Bagh, she notes the plane trees being cut down, on the orders, she later learned, of the shah's eldest son to provide timber for his new palace in Tehran. Dismayed, she rode on through the fabled city, crossed the Ziyanda River and arrived distressed in New Julfa.

Jane entered the Christian city of New Julfa on 13 August 1881 in the middle of Ramadan, a time when Muslims fast from dawn until sunset and are forbidden the pleasures of their *anderuns* during the same hours. Consequently tempers are often short and passions inflamed. It would be very unwise to go into the city of Isfahan until Ramadan is finished, advised general mirza Taqi Khan, doctor and personal assistant to the city's governor, hurrying to head off the Dieulafoys the day after their arrival. Taqi Khan had received letters of recommendation from his former teacher, the French Dr Tholozan, the Dieulafoys' adviser in Tehran. Even then they would be unable to visit the mosques and religious establishments 'unless the governor issues a firman. Isfahan is a fanatical city and only he has the power to override the clergy. The clergy and the governor hate each other.'[3] It will be impossible, he shrugged, even to make the request until the end of August, in the last days of Ramadan.

'I live a thousand years in your visit,' Jane said, using the Persian phrase of farewell to acknowledge that she must wait patiently in New Julfa if she wished to see the wonders of Isfahan.

For Jane and other Europeans approaching from the north and so having to pass through Isfahan, the most striking thing about New Julfa was its cleanliness and order. Through the streets ran sparkling tree-fringed canals and even the labyrinthine lanes were swept and tree-shaded. Though massive closed doors separated the city quarters at night, in the daytime the inhabitants circulated freely, patronising the shops along the way, choosing from fruits and vegetables spilling from baskets, fingering fine fabrics. At certain hours the streets were filled with vermillion-uniformed children skipping home from school who greeted obvious newcomers with a slightly cheeky, 'good morning,' or a tentative 'bonjour monsieur,' exactly as Iranian children greet foreigners today.

Accommodated in the convent of the Roman Catholic community, the Dieulafoys had the use of a sitting room, cool by day though rather airless, which opened to the convent's large enclosed garden where nightingales sang. In their bedroom in the bell tower they had no trouble waking in time for morning mass, the great bell almost bouncing them out of bed as it tolled its call to the faithful. From the tower Jane could look longingly to the enamelled domes and minarets of Isfahan which she could not yet visit; she must be patient.

Patience did not come easily to Jane. While Marcel was occupied making scale drawings and costing his ultimately futile recommendations to the Naib-es-Sultaneh in Tehran for the repair of the Saveh dam, Jane was not idle. She made friends with the congenial monk Père Pascal, head of the Catholic community, who advised her in his deep bass voice on the intricacies of moving about Isfahan safely – should she gain the entree. He also heard her confession and gave her communion.

Jane was a staunch Catholic, a surprising dimension to her character, considering what an individualist she was and how she flouted so many of the conventions of the day. Many years later when she had become a 'public intellectual', almost an empress in Parisian cultural life, gliding through the salons in her perfectly tailored trousers, holding court in her elegant house at 12, rue Chardin, Passy, writing exotic libretti for Saint-Saëns operas, France was galvanised by a debate about divorce. The liberated women in Jane's circle saw divorce as redemption for wives locked in loveless or brutal marriages and were unforgiving when, after a metaphysical struggle, Jane publicly opposed it. It was one of the paradoxes of this intelligent, independent woman that church dogma could overrule her French rationalism.

She roamed the streets of New Julfa impatiently, watching the people, turning her camera on the women's colourful dress, noting their jewellery, and making friends. Whether in the bazaar or on the road, or when trying to get into a mosque, Jane always sought the best in people, welcomed their conversation and never condescended. People responded to her charm. Many secrets were confided.

And in the convent's austere library she read Isfahan's history.

The once-nomadic Mongol dynasty, the Ilkhanids, who became palace dwellers and monument builders, collapsed in 1335 when the Black Plague spreading from China depopulated whole cities and exacerbated power

Armenian woman, New Julfa

struggles within the clan. Once again Persia became a sorry battleground. Simultaneously, the Little Ice Age, which had begun in the late thirteenth century, shrank the grasslands and reduced grain crops, bringing famine and social unrest to add to the misery of plague and warfare.

In the central Asian steppe the shortened growing season prompted the tribes to renewed aggression. Deterioration of their pastures disastrously affected their horses, the basis of their economy and lifestyle. The sweet quick-grown grasses withered in the cold, leaving only the hardier coarser species, which the horses, lacking the ruminant's multiple stomachs, were unable to digest.[4] In search of better grazing, the Timurids under Tamerlane swept into Persia and around to Azerbaijan and another cycle of destruction and building began. Before new invaders pushed out the Timurids the Blue Mosque had been built in Tabriz and new tile techniques developed. In retreat, the Timurids took with them the Persian craftsmen who would create the architectural splendours of Samarkand, Bukhara and other central Asian cities.

Next came other Turcoman tribes from the east to confront the Ottoman Turks, now established in Anatolia and invading from the west. Azerbaijanis, Georgians, Armenians, Kurds and Persians alike were slaughtered or left destitute in a climate increasingly cold, their treasures stolen by marauders, their heritage ruined and their lands trampled by armies.

Mystical religious sects flourished in those hard years. Sufism consoled many a forlorn Persian. In Azerbaijan an order of Sunni Islam called Safaviya after its founder Sheikh Safi (1252–1334), an Azerbaijani of Turc descent, was taken up by those yearning for social and spiritual salvation. When its leaders converted from Sunni to Twelver Shi'a, so called because it recognised twelve caliphs, successors of the prophet, the order became militant. In 1499, Ismael, a violent, aggressive twelve-year-old, became its head and once again peasants and merchants, artisans and women were sacrificed in a struggle between competing power seekers. By 1512 Ismael Safavi ruled triumphant from the Amu Darya River in Central Asia to the Indian Ocean, from Afghanistan to Syria, and from the Caucasus to the Persian Gulf. His capital was Tabriz, his kingdom a theocracy and he its absolute monarch.

Rejecting the aspirations of his fellow Turcs to destroy the Persians and seize their heritage, Ismael came down on the side of the old Persian elite of officials and landowners, incorporating them and their talents into his administration. Although the cold had not relaxed, with increased political stability and less warfare population levels gradually returned to pre-plague numbers.

When Abbas I Safavi came to the throne in 1587, despite the edges of the empire having been chipped away in the age-old fight between nomadic Turc and settled Aryan, the still-extensive Safavid kingdom was ruled from a new capital at Qazvin. Through a brilliant combination of warfare and diplomacy Shah Abbas stabilised the empire's boundaries, then turned to domestic issues. The state, which in the glory days of the Seljuks had led the West, now lagged behind the intellectual and commercial development of Europe. Abbas modernised his realm by freeing foreign trade, domestic business dealings and the arts from religious restrictions, and in a new era of religious toleration encouraged Jews and Europeans to contribute to the wealth of the state. At the same time religious and racial minorities were incorporated into the political and administrative body without distinction. Painting, poetry and the decorative arts once again flourished. Not culturally, economically, or politically has any subsequent Persian regime outranked Shah Abbas's state.

He was, above all, a builder, a creator of material things of benefit to his subjects and his own lasting memorial. Beginning with *kanats* and dams to support and extend agriculture in a still unfavourable meteorological climate, Abbas filled the hands of his subjects with construction tools and set them to work. Although by the late nineteenth century his caravanserais and bridges were falling into disrepair through Qajar neglect, they filled Jane and Marcel with admiration.

His greatest project was building a new capital. His inherited capital, Qazvin, was tactically exposed to Ottoman Turks raiding from Anatolia and rampaging along his western border. Instead Abbas chose Isfahan, an old city in the geographical heart of the Safavid Empire, accessible from the Persian Gulf as well as the Caspian Sea, and to emphasise that Persia was a free and united country again after centuries of foreign domination he transformed it into a glorious city of mosques, madrasas and palaces.

Across the river, New Julfa, too, was built on Shah Abbas's orders. Abbas wanted his new capital to be more than an architectural marvel. Disappointed with its commercial management and dissatisfied with returns from the state-monopoly silk industry, he looked to Armenia for fiscal expertise. The Armenians, known for their industry and financial cleverness, had mercantile connections stretching from Italy to India. In 1604 Abbas selected several thousand Armenian families in Jolfa on the Araxes, the town where Jane entered Persia, to relocate to the southeast. When they were reluctant Abbas turned off the water. He destroyed *kanats* and dams, leaving the inhabitants of old Jolfa no choice but to leave their homes and contribute to Isfahan's commercial success.

Although Abbas was a tolerant man, not all his subjects were so enlightened. For their protection, Abbas settled the Christian Armenians on the south bank of the Ziyanda River, allowed them religious freedom and built them a cathedral. In their well-constructed New Julfa the reluctant immigrants thrived and Abbas was more than satisfied with their contribution to his exchequer. However, later Safavids and after them Nadir Shah and the Qajars were less tolerant, more hungry for taxes and infinitely more cruel. To escape the cycles of persecution, the Armenian men slipped away, many to India, sending for their families when they made good. The New Julfa where Jane stayed was only a shadow, and a frightened shadow, of its rich past, a closed fearful community of 3000 Christians neighboured by 70 000 fanatical Muslims.

'I am your sacrifice,' began the merchants and pedlars waiting outside the door of the convent, 'Your slave will be honoured by your glance.' News of the Europeans' arrival had spread quickly and all the temptations of fine carpets, Kermani shawls and exotic Eastern goods were laid out for Jane's inspection. One astute vendor, quickly discerning Jane's real interests, returned regularly with ceramics and tiles and pieces of ancient metalwork. Although it is impossible to know exactly what Jane bought, fifteen mules were needed to carry the Dieulafoy baggage when she and Marcel left Isfahan and, later, the oriental treasures and magnificent carpets in her home were the talk of Paris. Certainly they did not all come from Isfahan, yet something substantial must have filled those fifteen paired loads.

Anxiously awaiting the end of Ramadan, Jane investigated New Julfa. The long-established Persian silk industry was only just beginning to recover from silkworm disease, which had struck fifteen years earlier, and from drought that had brought famine and depopulation to most of Persia from 1869 to 1873. Opium cultivation was filling the economic void. In the Varamin area Jane had seen the milky fluid being harvested from the poppy capsules, and she had been vaguely aware of extensive poppy plantations when riding expectantly across the Isfahan plain. In New Julfa the Dutch colony was involved in the opium trade. At their factory Jane watched the fairly hygienic processing of pharmaceutical-quality opium. Later, she was amused to see bare feet trampling an oil and opium mixture to produce the smoking-grade product, which brought into her mind an image of feet pressing the grapes in her family's vineyard at château de Terride. The Dutch manager complained that, although medicinal opium, exported to England and Germany, and smoking opium, mostly destined for China and

India, had the potential to fill the Persian exchequer, taxes levied at every stage of production and distribution compromised the industry, as was the case, he said, with all local products.

Despite a centuries-old schism that separated the Catholic community from the Orthodox Christian Armenians, there was no animosity between Père Pascal and the Orthodox archbishop. As a friendly gesture the archbishop sent Jane some peaches, so large that six of them overflowed the basket, so lusciously scented that the boy carrying them to the convent succumbed and ate one. To Jane's distress he was punished with the bastinado, Persia's most common, though certainly not her most brutal, punishment. As he was soon running about bragging that his soles were hard as leather and he had only cried out to embarrass Père Pascal, presumably he was only lightly whipped. Usually the victim of a whipping crawled about on hands and knees for days – weeks if his toes fell off. Simple to administer and of simple construction, a bastinado is a long pole with a central cord noose, two wooden canes and four men. The target is thrown onto his back, his feet raised and tied in the noose, then, while two men hold the pole horizontal, the other two take turns caning the upturned soles. Rich and poor, humble and grand were subjected to the treatment.

Ramadan seemed interminable despite diversions such as an Armenian wedding that began at sunset and finished at noon the next day, a luncheon at the Orthodox archbishop's palace, and a tour, led by His Eminence, of Our Saviour's Cathedral, where Jane was struck by the frescoes and altar paintings. Executed long ago by minor Italian artists, the painted surfaces were little damaged by the years, there was no *crackleur*, only a delicate enhancing patina, their colours still bright. She wrote that she found the cathedral's interior beautiful and soothing.

Perhaps this response is the true indicator of how difficult the past six months had been. Many travellers entering this cathedral are shocked by the violence in those 'works of art', by their crude realism and discordant harsh colouring. Constant exposure to the harmony and subtle tonal qualities of the Muslim world's abstract geometric art often causes a shift in aesthetic values. Representational art then becomes confronting, especially when it incorporates the brutality of much Christian iconography. Gentle floral motifs do not have the savage impact of torsos shot through with arrows, elegant arabesques do not agitate as nailed hands do. Yet, far from being distressed, Jane applauded the cathedral's interior. Reflecting upon images that represented a familiar culture, she ignored its deficient aesthetic and was comforted.

In Jane's complex character there were many contradictions and this response was only one of them. For six months, while travelling very hard in an alien land, she had been fearless, polite and, in her record at least, cheerful. She admired the country's harsh beauty, respected the brilliance of Persian achievement and the resilience of its people, yet she had suffered physically and been abused emotionally. Now, for a time, she needed the security of her own kind and her own culture. There was still the south to be faced.

Towards the end of August, general mirza Taqi Khan, the governor's doctor and personal assistant, general being an honorary title, reappeared in New Julfa to advise the Dieulafoys that the time had come to request the governor's permission to visit the mosques. The governor of Isfahan, Fars and all the southern provinces of Persia was Zil-es-Sultan, Shadow of the Sultan, a man greatly feared for his cruelty and ruthless greed. At the moment absent in the mountains, when in Isfahan he lived in tremendous state, protected by his own army. Although the second most powerful man in Persia and the eldest living son of Shah Nasr-al-Din, the Zil-es-Sultan was not in line to the throne, his mother being only a beautiful Georgian slave, and the Qajar throne being reserved for the sons of Qajar princesses. Unmoved by the death of two eligible older brothers, he was enraged when their demise promoted to crown prince his younger brother Muzaffar-al-Din Mirza, whom he hated with passionate vindictiveness. The then twelve-year-old Zil-es-Sultan ordered his new sword to be engraved: 'With this weapon I will kill my brother the crown prince.'[5] When the shah heard of it he flew into a rage and with all the weight of Qajar tradition threatened to have him blinded.

Allah must have intervened because the short, very fat, now thirty-one-year-old prince still had two eyes, although one eyelid drooped considerably, and Shah Nasr-al-Din, appreciating his son's ability and intelligence, had honoured him with appointments. In return Zil-es-Sultan filled his father's treasury with ruthlessly extracted taxes. Until the mullahs' complaints forced the dismissal of the twenty-eight-year-old crown prince from the governorship of Azerbaijan province, the Zil's treacherous and rapacious ways were of no consequence to the shah, but with Muzaffar-al-Din Mirza now in disgrace the shah was growing uneasy about his eldest son's ambition.

The southern mullahs dared not complain about Zil-es-Sultan. He was for the moment untouchable. They fumed in silence, plotting and waiting. But such was his present power that even though he was extorting the taxes from the peasants at Borujerd, 400 kilometres away over fiendish mountain tracks, merely the knowledge of a letter being written decreased the level of risk sufficiently for the Dieulafoys to go into Isfahan, although only to the palaces and discreetly into the bazaar, certainly not the mosques.

In readiness Jane tucked her fair hair under her helmet and picked up her riding whip. Though looking smart in her usual trouser outfit, she was outshone by mirza Taqi Khan, luminous in white uniform and white lamb-skin hat, and hoping that Jane would photograph his dignity on horseback. Escorted by six cavalry soldiers, his splendid charger led the Dieulafoys out of Julfa and onto the Si-o-se Pol, one of Shah Abbas's bridges over the Ziyanda Rud. Little water flowed through the arches in the middle of summer, although crowds streamed across it. In the raised pedestrian side lanes women fully wrapped in dark-blue *chadors* slipped between Kermani-sashed merchants and Bakhtiari tribesman, their white felt hats swathed in shining striped silk, and sidestepped turbaned mullahs. Underneath the bridge, in the small rooms where the river washed past the windows, dreaming men lolled on bright cushions as smoke bubbled through their *kalians*.

Jane's party made its way through the crowded centre roadway, the mirza's splendidly furnished horses and aggressive escort earning a begrudged right of way from cameleers and muleteers. Reaching the wide neglected avenues of the Chahar Bagh, they wheeled right, passed through a dilapidated gateway and entered Shah Abbas's seven-hectare royal park.

The private walled estate of palaces and pavilions, small courtyards and enclosed gardens had housed Abbas's family, his courtiers, servants, and his *anderun*. Although seventeenth-century travellers had left accounts of its magnificence, Jane found the gardens a wilderness, made worse by Zil-es-Sultan's axes on the plane trees. The buildings were in a pitiful state, their architectural and decorative elements removed to adorn his new Tehran palace. Approaching the Chihil Sutun, the 'forty columns' palace, Jane saw an inverted image of twenty slender carved cedar pillars trembling in a long pool. Beyond the reflection the originals rested on stone lion bases to support a flat roof. Accustomed to the substance of European columns, the lightness and grace of the wooden structures impressed her Western eye, even more so than the tent makers using the pillared forecourt as a work-shop. In the mirrored *talar* where a throne had once stood, men squatting on their haunches forced long curved needles through canvas and silk.

Twice burned since Shah Abbas's day, each time precisely and exactly rebuilt, the palace interior revealed a heavy patina of dust. Light reflected from mirrored muqarnas in the vaults played on huge paintings – enchanting illustrations of Persian literary characters in the smaller rooms and in the hallways scenes of lissom youths picnicking, as they must once have done, in the walled garden outside. In the main reception room, Persian painters had experimented with European techniques. Jane saw ornately uniformed blacks riding white elephants into battle and in a further three panels Shah Abbas receiving foreign legations. The works brought to life the magnificence of Shah Abbas's ceremonial receptions for foreign ambassadors and the lavish banquets given to honour visiting dignitaries. The minute details of dress, weapons, carpets, fabrics, jewels and variously wound turbans confirmed written records of the grandeur of his court. Later, riding back to New Julfa, Jane took some of the sadness from the decaying Chahar Bagh by peopling it in imagination with figures from those paintings.

After Taqi Khan's vanity was satisfied by the infidel's lens, 'Come,' he said expansively, 'I will show you the university.' In another walled garden within the bounds of Abbas's seven hectares they found the Hasht Bihist, a palace of eight rooms on two levels opening from a central domed hall, where the garden seemed to float into the rooms and the rooms were part of the garden, an architect's depiction of the eight levels of Islamic paradise. The palace was 'expressly made for the delights of love ... The climate contributes much towards exciting this amorous disposition; but assuredly these places, although in some respects little more than cardboard castles, are nevertheless more smiling and agreeable than our most sumptuous palaces,' wrote Chardin in 1665 of the Hasht Bihist.[6] When told that Shah Abbas had kept his eight favourites here, Jane replied, 'The rest of his *anderun* must have been very jealous,' though she doubted he would have risked exposing his women to other men's eyes in such open chambers.

In the empty rooms of the Hasht Bihist Zil-es-Sultan was developing a university to provide an alternative to the madrasa's narrow curriculum. Physics, mathematics, history and foreign languages were supposedly taught by a young Persian who had been sent to Paris and London for his education, but, says Jane, 'instead of developing his intelligence, like most young Persians coming in contact with the Occident he grafted on to his existing oriental vices our most detestable faults.' The opium addicted teacher and his pupils on holiday, the only evidence of the palace's present use was the bastinado in a corner. 'A Persian scholar,' Jane tells us, 'writes very ingeniously on a piece of paper held in the palm of the hand, so his only need is a carpet to throw on the floor,' adding ironically, he may as well 'learn from infancy the beatings on the soles of his feet which will prepare him to bear future misfortune.'[7]

At last came the end of Ramadan. The deputy governor commanded the Dieulafoys' presence two hours after sunrise. Furious with the domestic who failed to call them in good time, Père Pascal led the Dieulafoys through the narrow lanes, spurring his horse out of New Julfa. At the Si-o-se Bridge a long camel caravan was already making its way along the central roadway, the cameleers slowly advancing the heavily laden beasts against the press of traffic. Impatient, the party launched into the river. Having viewed it from the bridge, Jane and Marcel knew it was less than a metre deep, but had not realised the strength of the current. Struggling up the far bank well downstream, they whipped their reluctant horses to a gallop and reached the royal gardens on the dot. Behind the Chihil Sutun in yet another semi-ruined palace the deputy governor received them with the polite Persian phrase, 'My house is purified by your presence.' Wearing a full-skirted, tight-waisted coat of violet silk brocade over slim-legged trousers, a camel-hair robe embroidered with gold thread thrown over his shoulders and a traditional high Persian lamb hat, he was an impressive sight.

Jane thought him erudite and charming, yet several years later his life was brought to an end by an 'obscure and rapidly fatal disease that defied the skills of the physicians . . . popular rumour ascribed his death to a cup of "Kajar [sic] coffee" which had disagreed with . . . him.'[8]

They spoke of Shah Abbas and the glory of his city. Jane was moved by the deputy governor's long theatrical account of the wretched last years of Abbas's reign. As his vigour declined and the crown prince's popularity grew, the crowned head had become increasingly uneasy. Fearing a coup, Shah Abbas ordered his son killed, his remorse turning to rage when his subjects turned their affections towards the next son. In turn he was seized, but before he could be put to death the prince's children, Abbas's dearly loved grandchildren, pleaded for his life. The death sentence was cancelled. Instead his son's eyes were put out.

Like Medea, the bitter angry prince took the only revenge he could, murdering his children and sending the bodies to his father before poisoning himself.

Jane thought it infinitely tragic that this great shah should have turned on his own family. The Safavid ruler had recreated the kingdom of Persia from a rabble of badly governed foreign-subjugated provinces and had defined the borders that, despite some fluctuations, delineate Iran to this day. Although of Turcoman ancestry, he had united Turcs and Aryans into one all-embracing Persian nationality and had set an example of tolerance by making other races and religions part of the demographic. He established a climate where literature and philosophy and even some science flourished, and the decorative arts, which had only surreptitiously developed under foreign rulers, reached a peak that has not been achieved since.

He built palaces, certainly, yet his pragmatism recognised that dams and bridges, *kanats*, caravanserais and roads were as necessary as mosques, realising that without them agriculture could not flourish and trade could not develop. He turned Persia's face, too long bent over its navel, to the outside world, encouraging his country to take a place in international mercantile, artistic and intellectual commerce. He built the beautiful city of Isfahan, but his greatest contribution to Persia was to complete the rout of the Arabs who had invaded Persia in 637 AD. In confirming Shi'a Islam with its elements of Zoroastrianism, Sufism and mysticism the official religion, he liberated his country from Sunni domination. After a thousand years Persia regained its independence.

Yet in the end Abbas proved himself just another bullying father, another murdering shah. Worse was the precedent he set for his successors who kept their sons under virtual house arrest, denying them education and any experience of governing. They came to the throne ill prepared, often psychologically impaired, always ignorant, and misgovernment was the consequence. As all the achievements, material, intellectual and social, withered away, the Safavid family tragedy became Persia's.

Surprised at how deeply Jane was affected by his recitation of Abbas's despotism, the deputy governor proposed a visit to Sar Puchideh palace. In the glittering reception space where Zil-es-Sultan received his supplicants, four octagonal mirrored columns supported a flashing muqarnas ceiling. Each pillar rested on the shoulders of four addorsed (back to back) nude female figures grasping lion heads, which spurted water into a central basin.[9] It amused the Zil to see the mullahs' dislike of the stone women. Behind the palace the Zil's *anderun* enclosed what the mullahs called 'the women, the vulgar human merchandise.'[10] Bored perhaps while their lord was absent in the provinces, his favourites had already been sent for. Soon a military detachment would take them over the terrible roads to Borujerd where, the Zil complained, the females were 'dull and very ugly'. Jane tried to inveigle an invitation to visit the women, but had to be satisfied with a visit to a slender pavilion whose fretwork had screened Shah Abbas's ladies as they watched his world move along the Chahar Bagh. Faience tiles on its interior walls presented a garden where slender women in silken robes feasted on cherries. Many were broken, smashed with a hammer on the orders of Abbas II after he killed his favourite there in a drunken rage. Their colours were still clear and bright, Jane noted.

While deploring the dark side of the Safavids, she understood how it had contributed to the fall of the dynasty. She hoped that the Qajar prince Zil-es-Sultan would not reject with equal violence her request to visit Isfahan's mosques.

The city was still burning under the relentless summer sun, and further south it would be intolerable. Impossible to think of leaving even if she were prepared to give up the chance of seeing Isfahan's greatest treasure, the medan complex. Its tiles, she was told, are incomparable. Impatiently awaiting the outcome of the letter to Zil-es-Sultan, Jane wasted no opportunity.

Previously she had been afraid to enter the arched portal of the Madar-i Shah madrasa, built by Shah Husain (1694–1722), the last of the Safavids. Though tantalised by the twisted blue ceramic ropes that defined the entrance and the tile mosaics reaching up to a sunburst of yellow muqarnas above the door, she had ridden on down the Chahar Bagh. Now, with her status publicly established by an audience with the deputy-governor and the fanatic's hand, if not his mouth, stayed by the letter to the governor, she crossed the threshold escorted by Père Pascal and Marcel.

Jane stepped through the portal into a domed octagonal hall, from which four large rectangular bays opened. Expecting students, she found merchants; instead of Korans there were baskets of peaches and raisins, jugs of yoghurt, kebabs threaded on sticks ready to be laid on the brazier. The clerics sat quietly smoking at the cell doors, their students on holiday. No one seemed at all disturbed when the infidel set up her camera and began photographing the dome's interior. Moving to an adjoining tree-filled courtyard, Jane found a dome standing upside down in a long reflecting pool. While she was charmed by the subtlety of yellow arabesques curling around its turquoise-blue shell, not everyone considered the Madar-i Shah madrasa so fine, one contemporary visitor noting, 'the effect of beauty passing into preventible [sic] decay is very mournful.'[11] Many judge its late Safavid tilework slightly decadent. Perhaps a perception of beauty reflects the observer's emotional state. Happy and relaxed by not having to contend with the usual abusive hostility, did Jane's aesthetic standards slip a little?

Looking around for Père Pascal, she found him enjoying a calm debate in a circle of senior mullahs, each speaker addressing the points raised rationally and without acrimony. Drawn by the discussion, some merchants had dropped their provisions and sat quietly listening until, suddenly, they remembered the midday prayer and thought of the lunch that would follow. Their interest vanished.

Before leaving the madrasa the foreigners briefly visited the other parts of the complex. Deserted and crumbling, it seemed inevitable that the caravanserai and bazaar would soon become a mere memory, at best remembered for Hajji Baba's raid after he was taken into slavery by the Turcomen. Although we know she carried a copy of *The Adventures of Hajji Baba of Isfahan* by J.J. Morier, Jane apparently did not connect the barber's son with this caravanserai, not mentioning him in the context.[12]

Too hot and too far to ride back to New Julfa for lunch, said Père Pascal, and suggested they try their luck in the bazaar. They rode into a long covered street, lofty and spacious, crowded with merchants and animals. A network of narrow passages ran off on either side and great metal-reinforced doors opened into caravanserais stacked high with bales of cotton goods from England, woollens from Germany, raw sugar from Mauritius, tea from China and glass from Austria. Wisps of steam rose from freshly dropped dung, the smell mingling with the acrid odour of sweat on hard-ridden saddles. Their soft pads soundless on the earth floor, camels swayed past laden with bales of tobacco and opium, brassware, pottery, tiles and painted pen boxes on their way to Bushire on the Persian Gulf to be loaded into ships and carried across the seas. Mules slipped by, their hard hooves clipping out a staccato beat, their panniers filled with vegetables, fruit and the humble necessities of life. Dealers wearing tall black lambskin hats negotiated over cups of tea with Bakhtiari chieftains in white felt skull caps encircled by twisted lengths of coarse striped linen. The turbans of sayyids and mullahs floated through the crowd and gathered in corners where *kalians* bubbled.

Second in value after Tabriz, Isfahan's trade was controlled by merchants with a reputation for thrift, epitomised in the saying, 'as mean as the merchants of Isfahan, who put their cheese in a bottle, and rub their bread on the outside to give it a flavour', and in the story of the Isfahani merchant who, catching his apprentice gazing at the cheese in the bottle while he ate his dry bread, accused him of greediness and asked, 'couldn't he eat plain bread for one day?'

The merchants were probably traduced by this sly humour. They lived within a system of extraordinary corruption and venal maladministration, at the mercy of arbitrary justice, in a country placed at the crossroads of aggressive national ambitions, yet somehow they and their culture survived. Of all the writers contemporaneous with Jane, not one had

anything but respect for the resilience of the ordinary Persian, their dia-
tribes being directed at 'the inherent rottenness of Persian administration,
an abyss of official corruption and infamy without a bottom or a shore, a
corruption of heredity and tradition, unchecked by public opinion or the
teachings of even an elementary education in morals and the rudiments
of justice.'[13]

Trying to move discreetly through the crowd while avoiding strands of
slobber drooling from camels' mouths and kicks from bad-tempered mules,
Jane did not fail to appreciate the Chinese porcelain and exquisite inlaid
metalwork set out in the shops. Perfume from bunches of roses and hya-
cinths tied above the shopfronts cut across the smell of sweating animals
and unwashed bodies. Antique jewellery encrusted with pearls and turquoise shone in the gloom.

In the Armenian caravanserai Père Pascal's parishioner, Kodja Youssouff,
offered them lunch. Soon jewellers, metalsmiths and carpet sellers had
enveloped the Dieulafoys. Beginning with the polite phrase, 'I am your
sacrifice,' the Muslim merchant *hadji* Houssein entreated, 'My best carpets
are too heavy to be easily brought here. Honour your slave and drink tea in
his house.' With customary hyperbole he enticed them with the wonder of
his carpets, the perfection of their patterns, the quality of the wool ('only
from the underneath of a lamb's throat'), the delicacy of the silk, the brilliance of their colours, the number of knots, 'that are unequalled in the
whole of Persia!' Jane remembered Youssouff *khanum* saying that *hadji*
Houssein's wife was the most beautiful woman in Isfahan and was about to
accept the offered tea, hoping she might get into his *anderun*.

Then *hadji* Houssein made it impossible. Flattering his potential customer, he offered Marcel the most delicate compliment a Persian man could
pay another. 'Your slave has seen immediately that the boy is your honour's
son,' he said, waving at Jane, 'God has given him such a perfect copy of your
own features that one is struck by the likeness.'[14] His words slammed shut
the *anderun* door in Jane's face.

As Jane wrote dryly, 'Persian men have so little confidence in their
women's virtue that a comment on the likeness of father and son is received
with the greatest pleasure.' Appreciating the intent, Marcel knew he could
not embarrass *hadji* Houssein by revealing his true relationship with Jane.
Causing him to lose face would be gross discourtesy. Nodding gravely,
Marcel thanked the merchant for the compliment, so turning the key in
hadji Houssein's *anderun* door.

Though Jane had come to Persia seeking evidence of its past, she found

Youssouf *khanum*, Isfahan

its present too intensely interesting to accept defeat. She was determined to see Isfahan's reigning beauty.

In New Julfa next morning, after Kodja Youssouff had gone to his shop in the bazaar and while Marcel was busy arranging a courier to take his dam plans to Tehran, Jane called on Youssouff *khanum* and asked would she take her to visit her friend Houssein *khanum*. Of course, with the greatest of pleasure! But it was complicated. It was forbidden for an unveiled woman to enter Isfahan and dangerous for a veiled woman to ride into Isfahan accompanied by a foreigner. Consequently Youssouff *khanum* set off alone, except for her servants, astride her magnificent black mare, a present to her husband from Zil-es-Sultan. Half an hour later Jane followed accompanied by an escort from the convent.

Hadji Houssein's door had the usual two knockers, one for the master and one for the *anderun*. Youssouff *khanum* had tactfully alerted Houssein *khanum* to Jane's gender. At her knock the trouser suit was swept through the entrance and hustled into the women's quarters. Jane realised immediately how different this woman was from the Kashan governor's wife who had assumed Queen Victoria would have an *anderun* stocked with husbands. Ziba *khanum*, the merchant's only legal wife, had once been in the shah's *anderun* and had brought with her all the civilities and elegance of court life. It was common practice for a shah to give a member of his extensive *anderun*, used or unused, as a sign of favour. How the merchant had earned the reward is not known, but this lovely woman, having no say in her exile to Isfahan, could only make the best of it and try not to long for the amusements of her former life. She wore a chemise of spangled gauze swinging open down the front to expose nipples and belly, and a short full skirt dropping from below her navel to mid-thigh. A square of expensive lace tossed over her long dark hair, her eyes rimmed with kohl, her eyebrows a black arabesque, her ears covered by fresh flowers fastened in her hair, she was sensuous and beautiful.

Intelligent and vivacious, Ziba *khanum* had been among the shah's favourites when he set off on his first journey to Europe, but the *anderun* saw nothing at all of the world on their journey. From the moment they left the Caspian shore, the women were shut in their cabin and never allowed on deck; in the railway carriage on the journey to Moscow the blinds were drawn and the door locked, and once there, they were sequestered in a lonely palace while Tsar Alexander entertained their husband. After several weeks they were sent home, the shah continuing into Europe with an all-male court.

Sitting now in a provincial *anderun*, in a courtyard cooled by fountains and shadowed by plane trees, jasmine and roses scenting the air, Ziba *khanum* trailed her fingers in an alabaster basin and sighed for the excitement of the royal household's summer visits to the country, for the court's elaborate New Year celebrations and for Tehran's fervid Moharram dramas.

Jane returned to New Julfa to find general mirza Taqi Khan holding a letter from Zil-es-Sultan, but it was not permission to enter the mosques. To save the clergy's face, Zil-es-Sultan had issued a firman instructing the clerics to find verses to sanction the infidels' entrance to the sacred places – the Dieulafoys must wait while the mullahs searched their Korans. The letter was unsettling, for while it asked the deputy governor to accord them all respect due to people 'whose fame has been known to me since they first entered Persia', and whom he invited to visit him in Borujerd, it also informed the Dieulafoys that he had issued instructions to all the governors in the south to ensure the safety of the foreigners or answer with their life, and to give a double number of strokes to any person who offended the foreigners. Hiding her horror of causing another bastinado, Jane laughed gaily that 'southern Persia, judging from the precautions taken to safeguard our precious selves, must be a very dangerous place',[15] not suspecting how true that would prove.

Assured of their standing with his master, Taqi Khan proposed a country outing. If they cared to ride out to see some of the sites on the Isfahan plain, Taqi Khan would have them brought home in the wheeled vehicles sent to carry the Zil's favourites across mountains and plains to join their impatient husband in Borujerd.

Jane and Marcel stood the next evening on an isolated rocky hill on the Isfahan plain watching the sun set. To the east the religions of two cities were held apart by the Ziyanda River, winding its way from the mountain slopes, under the three bridges and on to die in a useless swamp far out in the desert. Below them, encircling the cities in a flash of green, were plantations of maize and cotton, tobacco and sorghum. Jane could see the road running between the fields where she and Marcel had ridden west in the cool morning, when the only sounds had been the rustle of water in the irrigation channels and the cooing of pigeons in the high circular towers rising up among the crops. Valued more for their manure than their eggs, the clouds of pigeons now returning to their towers on the gentle evening breeze flew a fine line in the balance sheet between crop destruction and field fertilisation.

The mosaic brickwork of the pigeon towers was crumbling back to the mud from which it was made, like every other building they had seen that day, or indeed, had seen in all of Isfahan. Though still carrying tattered panels of fine faience tiles, the broken mosques in the villages dotted among the fields were nearly all roofless. Only in New Julfa, it seemed, did anyone fight decay.

Riding across the plain, the Dieulafoys had not seen the villages hidden by shade trees until they were right on them, a brocade of honeysuckle and wild roses disguising their mud walls. Now, looking down from the hill, Jane could see into their gardens. Lemons, peaches and walnuts flourished in the shade of taller mulberry and plane trees. Underneath the upper storeys, ramping about in the cool rich dark earth were purple aubergines and the yellow melons which slaked the Persian thirst during hot summer months. Raided and abused too often, the villagers had been wary of the riding party, unsure of their intent, smiles only appearing when the Dieulafoys paid for their melons.

Far to the west, the jagged crests of the Bakhtiari ranges stood against the sunset like a frieze cut with a fretsaw. In the southeast the loneliness of the desert began and to the south was the road they must take to Shiraz.

It seemed to Jane, on that little hill above the plain, that she was standing in the centre of Persian history. At her feet were the remains of an old Zoroastrian fire temple, its Sasanid brickwork dating from before the Arabs brought their fury into Persia. In the distance rose the minarets and domes of Shah Abbas's city, where nothing had been added and much lost since infuriated Afghanis in another religious rage had ridden in from the east and besieged it. The last Safavid ruler, Shah Husain, a weak man reared in the *anderun* and dominated by the Shi'a clergy, had ignored Abbas's precept of tolerance and waged an offensive against his Sunni subjects, who included at that time the Afghanis to Persia's northeast. The Afghanis retaliated, and for seven terrible months in 1722 indescribable acts of cannibalism occurred in besieged Isfahan, while corpses choked the Ziyanda River. When the city finally submitted to the primitive tribesmen, fifteen days of sack, pillage, rape and despoliation followed. To Jane on the little hill 160 years later, Isfahan's devastation was brutally obvious.

Jane understood there was no salvation. Nasr-al-Din Shah had not visited Isfahan for thirty years, and its governor, his eldest son, was interested only in ravaging it further to enhance his Tehran palaces. He exercised his unlimited power over his father's subjects solely for his own benefit. During the morning the Dieulafoys had ridden past a decaying manor house which had come to Zil-es-Sultan's covetous attention. Its owner, like many other property owners before him, was ordered to undertake a pilgrimage. Naturally, he died on the road and the estate was subsequently seized. So too was the pilgrim's wife, whom rumour said was the real object of the Zil's greed.

It was pointless to petition Tehran, since official corruption was of no interest to the shah, nor was extortionate taxation. The verdant crops on the plain below would be illegally taxed at every regional boundary on their way to the gulf ports so that the tax rate, supposedly fixed at 5 per cent, became 25 per cent, often more. Despite the richness of their plain, the villagers barely profited from their hard labour.

Dusk was approaching. Wreaths of smoke rose from the two cities and on the road below a great cloud of dust signified the approach of the Zil-es-Sultan's wheeled vehicles and their thirty-soldier escort.

Until 1598 only another stop on the caravan route, Isfahan became a remarkable city under the great Shah Abbas. His architects and artisans centred their major creations on a rectangle where he played polo. Goal posts stood at either end, one pair in front of a new mosque, another at the entrance to the old bazaar cleverly incorporated into the plan. Dusty or muddy, depending on the season, the field was enclosed by two arcaded storeys of shops, a palace façade breaking one long side, a second mosque the other. Although Jane preferred the simplicity of Seljuk, many consider this Safavid complex of palace and mosques, the Medan-i Nagsh-i Jahan, the pinnacle of Persian architecture and associated decorative arts. Since the 1979 revolution Medan-i Nagsh-i Jahan has been called Imam Khomeini square.

The Medan-i Nagsh-i Jahan was Shah Abbas's residence and playground, the religious, commercial, and power heart of his city, where he impressed foreign ambassadors, terrified his ministers and abused his sons. When polo matches were played or the troops paraded, the shah and his court watched from the Ali Qapu on the western side. Both palace and formal portico into the royal gardens, the Ali Qapu is a building of such lightness that it looks as though it would float away unless it were tied down. Above the portico an open *talar* shaded by a roof rearing up on impossibly slender columns gave the shah a clear view of events in the medan, of the tiled minarets and domes of his city and the ring of jagged snow-capped mountains surrounding it.

Almost opposite, on the eastern side, rose the Sheikh Lotfollah mosque. Without a central courtyard, its portico leads direct to a perfectly proportioned space, a single domed chamber empty of furniture, columns or any interruption except a discreet mihrab recessed into the wall. Descending from the top of the dome a giant sunburst of tile mosaic fills the chamber with flickering light. It has been said that 'this vast, glowing room is probably the most perfectly balanced interior in all Persian architecture.'[16] At the southern end, beyond the goal posts, a minaret-guarded portal leads into the Shah mosque (also renamed since the Islamic Revolution).

On a September morning in 1881, from balconies either side of the bazaar's entrance, trumpets and tambours saluted the dawn, their cacophony heard with pleasure by Jane and Marcel Dieulafoy and Père Pascal. The previous day the mullahs had found the verses to authorise the foreigners' visit to the religious places, though they banned the infidel foot from the floor of the prayer halls, limiting it solely to surrounding galleries.

Skirting a string of grazing camels, the three foreigners walked down the medan. Slanting dawn light reflected from slender mirrored columns shimmered on the gilded ceiling of the Ali Qapu's *talar*. The sun's early rays struck the great dome over the sanctuary of the Shah mosque and sparkled on its tiles. The face of the mosque's minaretted portal was still in darkness, but against a background of deeply shadowed mountains, its frame, banded by Koranic verses tiled in white calligraphy on a blue ground, was clearly visible. As they waited for the faithful to leave the mosque after their dawn prayer, the foreigners watched as the growing light set the portal's tile mosaic flashing and glinting. Twisted ceramic ropes rose from alabaster vases inset in a marble dado, vines climbed the walls in tiled arabesques. Above the muqarnas tenting the doorway, gold stars glowed in a deep-blue tiled sky. The clarity of the colours and the oriental richness of the designs delighted Jane.

In the long story of Persian tilework, if the Ilkhanids were the first to take the Seljuks' luminous monochromatic glazed tiles, cut them into precise little pieces and fit them together in complex polychrome mosaic patterns, a technique perfected by the Timurids, it was the Safavid artisans who took the tile mosaic concept in a new direction. They took an unglazed tile, cut out shapes in an intricate pattern, and then filled the spaces with matching shapes cut from coloured tiles. Finally, they set the composite tiles into panels.

As in the earlier tile mosaics, the inserts never lie absolutely flat, each plane reflecting light at a different angle, imparting a glittering brilliance to the panels. Tens of thousands of such compound mosaics were needed to cover the entire façade of the portal. But such meticulous work is expensive and time-consuming. Shah Abbas examined progress on the portal, counted the years left to him and realised this technique could never in his lifetime cover the vast interior surfaces of his beautiful mosque. Instead, he commissioned cuerda seca tiles. Onto a fired monochrome glazed tile artists painted a design in coloured glazes, each liquid colour contained within a dark outline which burnt away when the tiles were refired. Because the firing temperature was of necessity a compromise between the optimum firing temperature of each different glaze, the colours are less brilliant than in monochrome tiles. Even so, the mosque's interior glows with colour, reflected and refracted light pulsating and sparkling within it, a multitude of patterns enriching the walls. Sadly, Shah Abbas did not live to see its embellishment complete.

On alabaster benches in the portal's vestibule twenty turbaned figures waited – the mullahs appointed by Isfahan's grand mujtahid to guard the infidels against fanatics. Some wore the dark-blue cloth of the prophet's descendants wound round their heads, others plain white. None wore the bright green of the Sunnis, anathema to these fierce priests. They stood up, their high turbans towering above them, their long faces, thought Jane irreverently, reflecting the gravity of keeping such headgear upright.

Before the mullahs could take charge another figure appeared. Wearing a full-skirted grey coat and a lambskin hat, 'I am the Protector of Foreigners,' he claimed, 'specially charged by Zil-es-Sultan to watch the safety of travellers and to protect them in case of a popular uprising . . . Your Excellencies will praise my devotion and tell His Highness the Prince.'

Irritated by such pomposity and wondering why he had not appeared sooner, Marcel turned to the mullahs, who indicated they were ready to take the Dieulafoys into the mosque.

'By my sacred oath! You want to go into the mosque! Allah be praised that I am here to disabuse you of that idea!' gasped the Protector of Foreigners.

'What danger do we run?' returned Marcel. 'Are you not here to guard and watch over us?' But the Protector of Foreigners, not up to such responsibility, fled.[17]

Recognising the vanity of the mullahs, Jane turned it to her advantage and suggested a photograph. At first they recoiled in horror, then reconsidered. She unpacked her camera, fixed the tripod's legs and selected an appropriate lens. By the time each mullah had put his head under the black cloth and looked at the image of his fellow turbans, then retaken his place for the final shot, the infidel's eye had established friendly relations between the Dieulafoys and their mullah minders.

To ensure that the infidels had no opportunity to defile any sanctified floor, the clerics led them up a steep stair and across the roof, then descended to the upper gallery of a two-storey arcade encircling the huge courtyard at the heart of the many-chambered mosque. A network of passages connects this central arcade with similar arcades around the sanctuary, the winter prayer halls and the madrasas. The Dieulafoys began work, Marcel recording dimensions of madrasas, arcades, courts and halls, while Jane photographed the tilework rioting on every vertical surface. The mullahs settled to argue doctrinal points among themselves. Their discussion turned Jane's mind to the great mosques she and Marcel had visited in other countries. In Spain, she remembered, mosques such as that at Cordoba had been converted into churches four centuries earlier and were easily accessed, since churches are open to all. In Cairo and North Africa a formal request was necessary, but they had never been refused entrance nor been troubled in any way. In Constantinople the Turks were so proud of their mosques, particularly the converted Byzantine Christian cathedral of Hagia Sophia, they had encouraged leisurely study. Yet in Iran the only interiors the Dieulafoys had been allowed to see were decrepit structures at Varamin and Rayy, subterfuge had got them inside the Qazvin mosque, and here in Isfahan it had taken three weeks to gain access.

A mosque is a place where people come for shelter from the burning sun, where travellers can rest, where students are taught, where the ulama, the college of senior clerics, meets to debate issues of orthodoxy and law. When necessary it is a defensive fortress, but above all it is a centre for prayer and contemplation. Looking down from the upper gallery Jane considered the Shah mosque's plan. It was fundamentally different from the forest of columns in the hypostyle mosques of Cairo, North Africa and Spain, and clearly was not a copy of the great domed church of Hagia Sophia, the inspiration for all subsequent Turkish mosques. She saw that the essence of this Persian mosque was a central unroofed square, from which opened four cavernous vaulted halls, *iwans*, one on each side of the square. Porticos, madrasas, side courts were mere additions to the fundamental courtyard and four-*iwan* model.

She wondered about the origins of that plan. Being a late nineteenth-century woman with Eurocentric vision, she was deluded into thinking it derived from the Greek cross. Today, with more known about early Persian mosques, the courtyard and four-*iwan* model is recognised as uniquely Persian, a plan inspired by Sasanid temple antecedents.

Her mind filled with these comparisons, Jane had not noticed the faithful down in the courtyard preparing for the midday prayer. Now she saw men at the central pool making the prescribed ablutions, taking off their stockings to wash their feet, turning back the wide sleeves of their robes to clean their arms to the elbows. The head and face had to be washed, and ears too, so off came the felt or lambskin hat, or the turban, revealing a crown shaved in a wide swathe from forehead to nape, only two long henna-dyed ringlets spared on either side. Springing from above the ears, the ringlets were twisted and flattened to make a stable platform for the headgear.

Suddenly one of the washers looked up, saw the foreigners on the upper gallery and shouted. Others opened their eyes in disbelief. They raised their arms, shook their fists and screamed curses on the infidel dogs. Roaring their outrage and led by a blue turban, they massed and raced as one towards the stairs.

Only Père Pascal fully understood the danger. The mullahs had no idea that Jane was a woman, and this was the first time Marcel and Jane had seen unbridled fanatical fury. 'Go, some of you, and lock the connecting doors,' Pascal ordered the mullahs. 'Stand by them. The rest of you stand guard at the head of the stairs, you must stop them. Obviously your fellow clergy have not been informed of the governor's permission.' As the mullahs moved to obey, the angry crowd reached the first floor gallery and ran towards the second staircase. Père Pascal pushed Jane back behind the clerics. And waited. None of the visitors was armed. Although they always carried arms, out of respect for the mosque's sanctity they had left their weapons at home. If the crowd discovered that one of the infidel dogs was a woman, an unveiled unclean female, there was no way they could protect her. The outcome was unpredictable.

The blue turban could now be seen rising up the second staircase, behind him a file of panting, screaming fanatics. Scrambling up and up, suddenly the blue turban wavered, jerked, teetered and disappeared. Curses and thumps followed as the descendant of a glorious lineage, having caught his foot in his long robe, descended ingloriously, toppling the whole file of men behind him down the steep, narrow stair to its foot. Worse, his turban came off and rolled across the floor unwinding as it went, leaving a trail of dark-blue respect on the white marble.

A hush. All very still. Then suddenly . . . everyone burst out laughing. The faithful lying on the floor and those who had not yet reached the stair, the defenders standing fearful above, all of them saw what a foolish figure the mullah had become without his turban, and they roared with laughter.

Not long afterwards, having rewound his headpiece, the mullah reappeared on the stair and sheepishly asked, 'Am I too late to have my photograph taken?'[18]

The Dieulafoys agreed with Père Pascal that it would be diplomatic to retire. Grateful for being spared further embarrassment, their guardians led them through the passages to the clergy's dormitory gallery. A Persian bed being a bedroll flung on the carpet at night, strapped up and put in a corner during the day; a Persian table being a cloth spread on the carpet then shaken and folded away; and Persian seating being the same carpet as for sleeping and eating, with a few cushions, the cell of the most senior of the mosque's clergy was not overfurnished. Dressed all in white, the mullah invited the Dieulafoys onto his carpet, a mark of deep respect, as most Muslims considered the infidel defiled everything he touched. Once seated, he offered them tea and *kalians* and suggested they watch the service from the front of his cell where, unseen, they would not incite any passions.

The women who had visited the mosque during the morning had disappeared to make their prayers at home, their presence in the sanctuary believed to disturb the minds of the faithful 'leading to thoughts of love inappropriate in a place consecrated to the love of Allah.'

From the conversation that followed it seemed that what most disturbed the venerable elders' passions were not Christian dogs, not women, but Sunni sons of burnt fathers.

Despite the prince's firman and the latitude of the Koranic verses, the fierce hostility continued as the foreigners visited the monuments. At the jume mosque it was veiled, although the veiling slipped a little when a ladder broke under Père Pascal's foot, the mullahs smiling with satisfaction at his fall, doubtless remembering the unwinding blue turban. But even this incident, like most things in Persia, had another face. Concealing his gashed leg from the clergy, the infidel hurried to a good friend living nearby to have it bathed and bandaged. To Jane's astonishment his 'good friend' wore a blue turban. 'I love him with all my heart,' Père Pascal explained. 'Many years ago the sayyid saved a Christian from certain death.'[19] With ironic ambiguity, the death which the naïve proselytising French Catholic had avoided was threatened by the outraged Orthodox Christians of New Julfa's Armenian community.

Before Père Pascal's accident, Jane had climbed the perilous ladder to the roof of the jume mosque and stepped out among rows of small bubble domes marking out the galleries and halls beneath. Two huge decaying domes defined the north–south axis of the complex. From the edge of the void that was the central courtyard, ribbed and braced half-domes reared above the four *iwans*. Beyond the roofscape, Jane could see the bazaar and further still the medan.

Because she had 'the infidel foot', the only way to view anything of the southern chamber was via an aerial walk along planks bridging a line of broken bubble domes and, from the edge of its great dome, to peer down through holes where bricks had fallen out. The chamber was commissioned by the great vizier Nizam al-Mulk in 1088 when Isfahan was the Seljuk capital. It was designed to be seen from the floor, its lines intended to draw the eye up into the dome and to thoughts of paradise. Squinting from above, Jane was not aware that behind the cobwebs and beneath the centuries of desert dust was the Seljuk architecture that had inspired the Crusaders and which Marcel had come to Persia to record – the model that had radically transformed European building practice.

More tragic was that she and Marcel were not permitted to see what lay beneath the other dome: the north chamber, the Gunbad-i-Kharka, 'the masterpiece of medieval Persian architecture,'[20] the acme of Seljuk genius.

The Gunbad-i-Kharka is a celebration of the pointed arch of the East which enabled medieval Christendom to place elaborate stone vaulted roofs on top of high thin walls to create their gothic cathedrals. From a square at ground level, colonettes lead the eye up through arches and squinches and into an octagonal drum to 'perhaps the most perfect dome known.'[21] It is the circle set on a square, its load carried on pointed arches which thrust the weight directly down through slender columns. The thick walls and buttressing demanded by the Roman arch could be forgotten and within sixty years of the return of the First Crusaders to Europe the Romanesque was totally abandoned, replaced by Seljuk-inspired gothic.

The brickwork in the north sanctuary is exquisite, every surface uniquely ornamented. In every niche and every panel, in the dome and on the walls, the bricks are placed in a different design. Projecting bricks form the kufic lettering in an inscription encircling the drum. Decorative brickwork fills the blind panels between the supporting columns. In their buildings the Europeans would punch out the blind panels and fill the void with coloured glass in patterns inspired by the Seljuk brickwork. The dark interior would fill with light.

To the mathematically accomplished Seljuks proportions were all-important, ratios that bind parts into an aesthetically satisfying whole being their significant architectural legacy. And to achieve intense, continuous verticality to bear the spirit upwards, they aligned the repeating decorative elements – pillars, arches, panels, without any horizontal disruption, another technique the Europeans would fully exploit.

Such Seljuk architecture in Persia's eastern Mediterranean provinces (Syria, Palestine, Lebanon) inspired the Crusaders. They took home new ideas and skills, ingenious mechanical devices, new technology such as lifting machinery. In their train of prisoners were engineers and skilled craftsmen, in their memory visions of precious stones and metal ingeniously wrought. The spacious light-filled medieval churches were the realisation of their Eastern experience. Defined by graceful pointed arches, decorated with colourful wall painting and rich carving and furnished with precious, elaborately wrought plate, jewelled shrines, sumptuous hangings and vestments made from rare Eastern textiles, European gothic is the gift of the Persians.

The Seljuk and the Sasanid were what Marcel had come to see, and by unfortunate restrictions he missed the best of the first.

Though neglected, Isfahan's jume mosque outranked the Shah mosque in sanctity. Each town, city and village has a jume mosque where the faithful gather every Friday to mourn the prophet. In theory, the shah joined (jume means 'reunion') his subjects there; in reality he appointed jume mullahs to represent him, and in order to manipulate them he created an indebtedness, sometimes through marriage, as, for example, Tehran's jume mullah, or by raising them from obscurity, and always by chaining them with an official salary. Through them he hoped to keep control over mosque and subjects.

Conversely, independent mullahs and mujtahids living off endowments willed to the mosques and madrasas were a threat to the shah. The blue-turbaned sayyids, descendants of the prophet, supported by the five per cent of their income which even the most impoverished had to give, disdained the shah. Filled with ancestral pride, idle since they had no need to work, their Arab lineage made the sayyids a constant worry to a Turc dynasty. The Qajar Shah Nasr-al-Din lived in fear of a sayyid-fomented rebellion. As a bulwark against them he encouraged the jume mullahs, hoping they would at least forewarn him. And it was on Isfahan's jume mullah's ability to rein in their intense antipathy that the safety of the Dieulafoys depended.

To avoid a confrontation at the Imamzadde Jaffar, Père Pascal shepherded the Dieulafoys out of New Julfa in the middle of the night to enable them to reach the Ilkhanid tomb before the faithful left their beds.

Pushing open the door, the three foreigners felt their way into the shrine's dark courtyard. In the pre-dawn glow Jane set up her camera and waited impatiently until the eastern sky offered enough light to activate the chemicals on the glass plate. Back in the saddle and halfway down the street, she realised she had left behind a precious ruler. Persian bazaars being full of carpets and dates but not measuring instruments, the trio were turning back just as a blue turban closed his house door with a bang and turned the key on his wives. Screaming after the foreigners, his curses of 'sons of dogs' and 'sons of a burnt father' brought the merchants flying from the bazaar like a flock of angry crows. Jane and Marcel tossed their reins to Père Pascal, ran into the courtyard and swooped on the ruler, but the crowd arrived before they could leave. Seized by the arms, they were beaten on the shoulders and pushed into a street exuding hatred. Into the melee rode Père Pascal, leading their horses, afraid once again that Jane's gender would be discovered.

Colonel Dieulafoy saw Jane safely into her saddle, then mounted and turned his horse towards his tormentors. He upbraided them, the deep bass voice of Père Pascal adding the Persian equivalent of 'Here, here.' The indignant colonel cowed the crowd, a reprise of Soltaniyeh. The foreigners rode away, heads in the air, backs straight, while the merchants, having been manipulated to his satisfaction by the mullah, sheepishly turned to selling vegetables and lengths of cotton made in England.

The French party went straight to Isfahan's jume mullah and demanded an escort. Back at the shrine, they found a huge padlock hanging off the door. The escort tore it away. The blue turban had posted a watch and once more his call brought the faithful flooding from the bazaar, only to be brought up short by the mullahs and sayyids supporting the Dieulafoys. Again Colonel Dieulafoy harangued them and, to signify his control, haughtily ordered the lock replaced. As the team rode away the subdued merchants were turning their backs on their mullah and returning to their own affairs.

The Persians' extreme civility was only a superficial veneer. It hid such deep anger that the smallest incident could set off a furious storm. A carpet merchant, for instance, unfolding his rugs and throwing them on the ground for inspection, and beginning his pitch by humbly declaring, 'I am your slave, I am your sacrifice,' quickly became your violent assailant if he felt slighted. An argument immediately became physical if he thought himself cheated; he would strike – with a sword, his hands, a whip – as Isabella Bird witnessed: 'and there was a severe fight in the course of which the combatants fell over the end of my bed. So habituated does one become to scenes of violence in this country that I scarcely troubled myself to say . . . "Tell them to fight outside."'[22] The instantaneous switch from civil compliance to outraged aggression was the nightmare of governors, shahs and all in authority, not only of foreigners.

Although the violent intolerance at the Imamzadde Jaffar was undoubtedly very frightening, particularly with the ever-present danger of Jane's disguised gender, it is difficult not to feel uncomfortable with Marcel's autocratic response. More than a century later, when religious fanaticism and arrogant cultural superiority are equally deplored, our perspective is too different to accommodate this incident without embarrassment. Yet it deepens one's admiration for Jane's courage.

Deciding she had seen enough mosques, Jane summed up the battles this way, 'The Isfahan mosques are . . . very beautiful and very interesting, but accessing them is difficult. It has needed the peremptory orders of the prince, the energy of Père Pascal and also, I must admit, our tenacity, to overcome the resistance.'[23]

Chapter 8
Caravan to Pasargadae

'You know where we are?' Marcel said laughingly. Jane glowered and said nothing. 'At Ispahanec, the village we visited a few days ago. We march for five hours in the darkness, and we finish up here in this delightful hotel!' Marcel gestured to the ruined mosque with its fallen dome where they had spent a short uncomfortable night. 'At this rate we'll reach Shiraz at the same time the Jews find the promised land.'

'Nothing,' said Jane, in a rare display of temper, 'makes me more angry than your good humour when we have landed in a mess. And,' she continued, turning to the tcharvadar bachy who had walked up with Marcel, 'if you are thinking of keeping us sitting here for days, I warn you I'm going back to New Julfa.'

'Why are you fussing, Excellency?' he replied, 'You are unjust. Most of your fellow travellers have already been here three days waiting for the caravan to leave and they aren't complaining. It isn't possible to get a caravan of four hundred baggage animals and more than two hundred people ready to move in just twenty-four hours.' It was not an auspicious beginning to the fifteen-stage journey to Shiraz.

Around the ruined mosque lay a rich fertile plain. The morning sun struck the backs of the villagers, at seven o'clock already hard at work clearing out irrigation canals, cultivating and weeding their crops, and taking no apparent notice of the caravan spread along the sides of the road leading out of the village and into the distance. On the verges, laid out ready for loading, were piled crates full of opium and tobacco, bales of cotton goods wrapped in goatskin, heaps of carpets rolled in canvas, bundles of wood and wicker baskets. The mules that would bear all this to the Persian Gulf were hobbled and staked out to graze or being led to drink from the edge of the canal. Tethered fowls clucked and scratched near their opened crates, while a few sheep, unaware of their destiny, picked at the sparse dry forage.

Along the same length of dusty road, gossiping groups of muleteers watched their animals. Women sheltering behind the bales from the sun and the glances of passing men watched their children. Armed guards watched over the valuable merchandise. Over the whole extended camp hung pungent smoke from the fires where camp cooks were preparing the daily rice.

'A caravan can't be organised at a caravanserai. It has to be done at a place like this where the merchandise can be collected and sorted for loading, and where I can make sure all the travellers have arrived,' explained the tcharvadar. 'We'll leave tonight, I won't wait any longer for latecomers or for travellers still scattered along the road to Isfahan. They get here and remember their favourite *kalian* and go back for it,' he said with good humour, 'or they go to say goodbye again to their wives and children. And someone else goes off to buy a kilo of salt or maybe pepper, but if they are not here tonight I go without them.

'If you don't like the mosque, you can go to the Kala-i-Shur caravan-serai, two hours down the Shiraz road. I'll send someone to warn you an hour before we depart.'[1]

Without delay, Jane ordered the horses saddled.

Since their visit to the Imamzadde Jaffar Jane had been anxious to get on the road. The experience had turned her against Isfahan and refocused her reasons for visiting Persia. 'Sasanids and Seljuks are our objective,' she said, ignorant of what she had missed, 'not Safavid architecture, however glorious. We must go south.'

Daytime temperatures were still high but less testing than they had been and the nights were already very cold. Letters from Shiraz reported that the summer fevers had gone, and, most important, the tcharvadars had brought their horses and mules back to Isfahan. For four months they had been co-opted to transport Zil-es-Sultan and his entourage around the provinces, and only camel caravans had been able to leave Isfahan and New Julfa.

Père Pascal, dreading the return of loneliness to which his nationality and monkish vows committed him in a Christian Armenian city lying in the heart of Muslim Persia, enticed them with promises of daily excursions. Spend the winter here and go south in the spring, he cajoled, as they rode along the Zayanda River inspecting palaces ruined during the

Afghani invasion. Jane noted their recent pilfering by Zil-es-Sultan, photographed an Ilkhanid minaret and climbed Kuh Sofe. From that tabletop the crystal-clear atmosphere showed her the deserts lying beyond Isfahan and the lonely road winding off towards the south. It was the road she and Marcel must take.

Knowing a spring departure would see them entering Iraq in the extreme heat of summer, Jane insisted they must leave with the first caravan. Accepting her decision, Père Pascal helped her negotiate terms with an Armenian tcharvadar bachy. Paid one-half the cost of mules and horses, with the balance payable on arrival in Shiraz, the tcharvadar also agreed to a rest day at Abadeh, almost halfway. From Abadeh Jane planned to visit a nearby village with a reputedly interesting mosque and where she hoped to contact the Bakhtiari chieftain. She had no intention of wasting a day while mules rested.

Père Pascal invited the leading families of New Julfa to a farewell dinner. Youssouff *khanum*, who had taken Jane to visit the beautiful exile from the shah's *anderun*, arrived in the gown that had set the whole of New Julfa society talking. Imported from France, it was very décolleté. Her ample figure laced into the accompanying whalebone corset, the *khanum's* breasts overflowed as none had ever been seen to do in New Julfa. In Paris they would not have been noticed, but this was not Paris. As the guests set about the roast venison, which until the day before had been a gazelle bounding about the convent's garden eating the new rose shoots, the men shot indiscreet lustful glances at her melon-like breasts while their wives pouted with displeasure. When Père Pascal complained afterwards, 'There is too much gossip and envy here in this society,' Jane reminded him of the parochial feuds and limited perspectives in a French provincial town. No doubt she was thinking of the Toulousiennes' advice to kill silver fish and inspect her pantry but not, not go to Persia.

Many of the dinner guests were among the crowd who rode out of New Julfa with the Dieulafoys the following day. This was the first time that Jane and Marcel had experienced the Persian tradition of travellers setting out on a long journey being accompanied for a short distance by their friends; it was the first time they were leaving friends behind. Last-minute gifts of sweets and fruits expressed the warmth of the relationship that had developed between Jane and the New Julfans during her five-week stay. Curious, people-oriented, open and without Marcel's haughty reserve, she had made many friends.

Afraid of being locked out when the gates closed for the night, the friends turned and hurried back to the city before the sun set. The mule-teers called, 'Ya Allah, Ya Ali,' and fifteen laden mules swished their tails and stepped out around the lower slopes of Kuh Sofe. The cook steadied his clashing saucepans. Arabat, their new Armenian servant working his way to Bombay, waved a last goodbye to his weeping wife and children, wondering when he would see them again. The Dieulafoys turned in their saddles for a last glimpse of Isfahan, like Curzon, seeing 'the cupolas and minars, the pigeon towers and terraced bridges, the long avenues and strag-gling suburbs of the fallen capital. From this distance the pitiless handiwork of decay is blurred and imperceptible, and a certain majesty seems still to hover over the wreck of departed grandeur. I know of no city . . . with a greater pathos.'[2]

Without a warning twilight, night fell abruptly. There was no moon. In lonely darkness the little caravan continued on. Jane and Marcel were fully armed, but even so they doubted they could defend their goods against robbers. Jane did a mental inventory of what the fifteen mules carried. She had spent hours packing fragile glass plates and her purchases from the bazaars, particularly her collection of lustre tiles, which she had slid between wads of cotton wrapped around her precious notebooks. The real difficulty came in allocating the individual parcels to the crates and saddle bags. Each mule could carry up to sixty-five kilograms on either side, but the loads had to be perfectly balanced. Jane had been reluctant to leave her ruler in the shrine because she could not replace it in Persia; similarly she had been unable to buy a weighing scale, finally begging the tcharvadar bachy to lend her his. As she suspected, her crates were uneven. It took her three days to take everything out, resort, repack, and get the balance right.

Despite the darkness the Dieulafoys sensed they had turned off the main road. Soon the side road became a track. Why, they asked, are we going off into the fields? This is not the road to Shiraz. The encampment came as a surprise and they were not pleased when told that the caravan was not ready to depart, even less so when it was assumed the 'two masters' would join the blanket-wrapped muleteers snoring on top of the bales. They had insisted on being taken to a village – a crumbling mosque was a better lodging than the open air on this freezing night and safer for Jane. In the shell of a prayer hall they had lit a fire and soon lamb kebabs were roasting on the spit and water boiling for tea. Before she unrolled her swag and prepared for a night on the bare ground, Jane took a new notebook, entered the date 18 September 1881, and began the account of her journey into the south.

The accommodation down the road was much superior. Jane describes the Kala-i-Shur caravanserai as magnificent. It had only recently been seized by Zil-es-Sultan, along with the wife and the manor house, from the man ordered to make a one-way pilgrimage to Mecca, but by the time Browne came riding down the road to Shiraz eight years of neglect prompted him to describe it as 'dilapidated'.

Near midnight Jane and Marcel sat by the roadside holding the reins of their horses, nibbling the herbage around them. This, Jane knew, was the real beginning of the journey that Père Pascal had described as 'fifteen punishing stages', but which would be longer for the Dieulafoys, who planned to leave the caravan at Pasargadae, three stages short of Shiraz, and visit Persepolis on horses which the tcharvadar bachy agreed to lend them with their baggage as surety. Jane expected to be in Shiraz in three weeks, Shiraz the 'city of wine, of roses and of poets', five-hundred kilometres from Isfahan.

Over the plain came a muffled noise. Beginning as only a gentle wind, it swelled to a rumble like a chapel organ played with the stops full out, unlocking Jane's memories of the road from Tabriz to Qazvin, recalling the pilgrims and the dust and the Armenian girl caring for her master's wives. Jane recognised the noise of a large caravan, a very large caravan, twice the size of the pilgrims' caravan. The curses of the muleteers, the tinkle of bells, the clash of cooking pots, the crack of wooden tent pegs swaying in their goatskin thongs, and the crying of children came separately through the darkness. For the next few weeks this would be her world.

The prospect of being on the road again had restored Jane's good humour. Wanting to spare her legs from being crushed between crates in the melee at the centre, she leapt into the saddle and fell in at the head of the multitude. 'The caravan is safe now with two brave champions to guard it,' she joked to Marcel. 'Arms at the ready!' she laughed, easing the rifle across her back and feeling for the revolvers in her belt.

Soon the track left the plain and ascended the mountains through a steep rocky defile, the sure-footed mules bearing their loads up the narrow pathways in complete darkness, never missing a tread. On the chiselled ledges suspended above deep gorges, it was critical that the 130-kilogram loads be balanced – a sway and the animal would be gone. They reached 'a ladder hewn in the mountain,'[3] the pitch so steep Jane could only loose the rein and trust her horse to get her safely to the top. With each traveller intent on his own safety, there was little conversation, only the voices of the muleteers encouraging their charges.

When dawn came the caravan was strung out on the descent to a plain stretching out eastwards into lonely desert. An elongated grey shape moving slowly in the south resolved as it approached to become a caravan of corpses and pilgrims taking the Isfahan route to Karbala. Greetings, then farewells, rebounded from the mountain peaks.

They crossed a glaring stony plain and in mid-morning reached Mayan, a town of crumbling walls encircled by plantations. In its neglected Shah Abbas caravanserai, the loads were lifted off and stacked in the courtyard or in open-fronted rooms. While the muleteers brought water and fodder and groomed their animals, the cooks lit fires and unpacked their saucepans. The noise of 200 people and 400 animals reverberated around the walls, until gradually a silence fell as people and animals settled to sleep during the heat of the day behind the caravanserai's locked door.

Called at 10 pm, the caravan slowly assembled. Loads were replaced on sore backs, children tied on donkeys, horses saddled, and they were on the road by midnight, although a few stragglers scrambled after the last of the mules. The night was freezing cold; on the Kumishah plain rolling south-wards at 2300 metres above sea level between parallel mountain ranges daily temperature changes were extreme.

The stage was long and dawn found them still on the plain, separated from the desert by a range of mountains, Jane still riding at the head of the caravan. Tracking a chain of verdant villages, each encircled by *kanat*-irrigated plantations, Jane felt the sun begin to warm her. The route was busy, horsemen galloping past and pilgrims plodding north. In the clear light it was difficult to judge the distance of the approaching camel trains when they first came into view, or the mountains whose jagged purple out-lines peaked into a clear blue sky. The plain seemed vast and the ranges somewhere on the edge of the world. The space and openness was what Jane most loved about Persia. She was exhilarated, filled with a sense of boundless freedom.

And so the caravan continued on, sleepy hot days interspersed by cold night marches, and along the way the people came to know each other.

The merchants kept together. In the caravanserais, they secured their goods, spread their carpets and ate together, kneeling and squatting back on their haunches as Persians did – even the shah, with his back to a bolster on the Peacock Throne. Long flowing robes belted at the waist by several tightly wrapped shawls and loose baggy pants caused no difficulties. Short, tailored European-style coats worn over narrow-legged trousers, the new fashion among the city rich, made squatting uncomfortable and European chairs had become necessary, but in the provinces and among the merchants the dress that had suited them for centuries was unchanged. Two hennaed ringlets beside each ear, plaited and twisted into place by the barber when he gave them their weekly head shave and beard trim, still supported their tall black lambskin hats.

While the caravan was assembling, the merchants pulled on a pair of dark-coloured voluminous pants, gathered at waist and ankle and similar in cut to the purple ones women wore in the street. Next they picked up the ends of their robes and pushed them inside the pants. If it was cold they shrugged into a thick cloak with holes for the arms. They were then ready to mount.

Perhaps because of the accumulation of clothes worn, Persian men squat to pee, a habit that saved Jane from having her gender discovered while travelling on the long stages. Lady Hester Stanhope, confronting the same problem informed a friend, 'Imagine, madam, a plain which never seems to end, where you travel eight or nine hours together. It will be in vain to seek a bush or tree for any little purpose. Pitch up your tent . . . saying you wish to repose or eat.' Isabella Bird, usually travelling without European companions, her caravan comprised of muleteers and sometimes a soldier escort – all male and no help – regularly pitched her tent at noon.

On the road the merchants kept a watchful eye on the muleteers and a vigilant one on their goods, and, much to Jane's disappointment, held the infidels at a distance while they entertained each other with poetry and stories. But Jane heard snatches and understood how stories shortened the interminable hours of a long stage. Some were send-ups of the mullahs or of an avaricious tax agent, others were morally instructive, humorous illustrations of a maxim such as 'A wise enemy is better than a foolish friend', and many contained encoded information. One dangerous story prompted by howling jackals and barking dogs hid a message that all the listeners understood: scorn for the Qajar dynasty, tribal Turcs ruling over Aryan Persians. To the Persians, a dog was much more unclean than a jackal, 'sons of dogs' being a piece of invective Jane knew only too well.

One merchant, old, sick and determined to die among his family, turned toward Mecca five times a day, praying Allah to give him the strength to reach Shiraz. 'Inshallah. May it please Allah.' At the end of each stage his servant spread his carpet beside his goods, and each day his frailty became more pronounced.

Twenty angora cats accompanied the cat merchant. The fluffy bad-tempered creatures, which he expected to bring a fortune in India, meowed and shrieked in their sacks all night and slept in the sun all day, pegged out on a running line. When their food appeared, they turned into growling, threatening lions swallowing the diced raw lamb at a gulp. As the caravan prepared to leave, their owner put them back in their sacks and hung them off his mule. Having become accustomed to his noisy cargo, the mule ignored the struggles going on inside unless their claws scratched his flanks.

The mule was the joint property of the cat merchant and a musician, the two owners taking turns riding behind the cats until one day they fell out. When the musician appealed to the tcharvadar bachy for justice, the Dieulafoys somehow found themselves part of the solution, the musician appearing the next night perched on top of one of their baggage mules. For the remainder of the journey he was their troubadour, entertaining them during dinner with his single-stringed harp, although from Jane's description the mewling cats may have sounded better.

The Armenian women rode astride donkeys, their children on the pommel, their faces unveiled, only a white cotton strap binding their chin, a high bonnet covering their hair. Their husbands, long departed from New Julfa, had found fortune in Bombay and sent for the family. Selling all their possessions, the women and children set off undismayed on the difficult sixty-day journey to Bushire and thirty-day sea voyage to India, happy to leave behind all they had ever known and the centuries of persecution. Although Zil-es-Sultan, governor of Isfahan, held the fanatics in check, no one knew how long his reign would last or when the cruelty and killing would begin again. The women swaddled themselves in layers of cloaks and shawls on the cold nights and kept apart in a locked room during the day, but were happy to talk to Jane around the cooking fires.

A fierce-looking dervish remained aloof during the stages and at the caravanserais no one was his friend. Like his mind and his tormented soul, his body was in constant motion; his wild, jet-black mane blew in the wind and his black eyes darted from the deep pools where they lived, visiting the present only briefly, returning to the contemplation of eternity. His tattered clothes fluttered like flags as he strode first left, then right, muttering and sometimes singing. A tiger skin was slung across his back and a torn shawl swathed his waist. In the towns he pulled an axe out of the leather belt worn over the shawl and set off with a metal bowl, daring anyone to pass without giving alms, his terrifying appearance enabling him to live comfortably. Superstitious Persians provided the chicken on his pilaf, while gullible women bought a powder to make her the favourite among her husband's wives or a charm to make her son brave and strong. Pathetic old men purchased aphrodisiacs, and the sick asked for a talisman to restore their health. Jane gave him a wide berth.

In the villages the tcharvadar bachy bought fodder, when he could, and the travellers trawled the bazaars for fresh foodstuffs. Each place had its own character, sometimes friendly, sometimes not. At Kumishah, beside the blue dome rising above the imamzadde of Imam Reza's brother, Jane looked at the sour faces of the inhabitants and shivered. The numerous relations and descendants of Imam Reza, himself tucked away in Mashhad, were scattered all over Persia, each shrine being the centre of a bigoted, dangerous coterie. The Kumishah imamzadde, restored by the Safavids, had somehow survived the Afghanis' destructive rampage, although the Safavid glory of Kumishah itself had not.

Cantering ahead of the caravan across a flat plain, the Dieulafoys saw a huddle of low flat houses strangely lacking a town wall, and had almost reached it before they were brought up short on the edge of a gigantic rift where mighty sub-terrestrial forces had torn the land apart and left a great open gash. Jane looked down into a dark chasm, perhaps forty metres deep and five hundred wide. Sailing off from its western end into the middle of the gash was a long narrow rock. Stacked on it, a collection of houses piled on top of one another gave the appearance of a ship overburdened with superstructure. The sides of the rock-ship rose up sheer on port and starboard and the prow was even steeper, only the thin strip of rock at the western end linking it with the plain. A wooden bridge thrown across the void could be drawn up to make the ship impregnable. Yazd-i Khvast had no need of a wall.

Needing provisions, the Dieulafoys crossed the bridge into the only street. It followed the line of the 'ship', piercing through the central axis rendered pitch dark by the houses built above it. People hurried confidently along, calling 'Ya Allah,' as warning, then disappeared into small vaulted side passages or bounded up staircases to the upper levels. Relieved to reach a shop without having a collision, Jane bought a melon.

'Do you want it with dust, or without dust?' asked the shopkeeper.

'Without dust.'

Taking off his slipper he carefully wiped the melon. Jane recoiled. In revenge the merchant bit her coins and rejected two, a common practice in Persia, where a great deal of questionable coinage circulated.

Back on the plain, hurrying to rejoin the troupe at the caravanserai beyond the chasm, Jane glanced across at the village-topped rock and saw brown stalactites hanging off the sides. The villagers had solved the sewage problem – it all went out the window. When told that these arabesques were gathered in the winter and used as fertiliser on the fields she was even less certain about her melon. Anything that slipped into the river winding along the bottom of the ravine also ended up on the irrigated fields. The surrounding wheat plantations looked very rich.

Yazd-i Khvast was famous for the lightness and flavour of its bread. As a popular saying went: 'Nothing compares with the wine of Shiraz, the bread of Yazd-i Khvast or the women of Kerman.' Jane could be sensitive and starve, or accept and enjoy. Hunger won. Jane found the bread excellent and was glad she had taken the advice of experienced travellers who convinced her that even when a week old the bread would be delicious and advised her to stock up before leaving the town.

There was nothing to indicate when they had crossed the unmarked border of the province of Isfahan, known to the Persians as Irak, and entered the province of Fars. To Europeans the high mountain plateau of Fars was synonymous with Persia, but to the Persians who had taken their name from it, Fars being Pars until the Arabs came with an alphabet with no letter 'P', it was only one part of the empire of Iran. Pars was home to the Aryans who had come in millennia before from the central Asian steppe. Although some of the Aryan tribes pushing westward had decided Irak was far enough, settling there and becoming known as the Medes, the Persians continued south to Pars, where, despite innumerable wars and invasions, they have remained ever since. They wrote their history on clay tablets, carved it on sheer mountain sides and later inked it on parchment. During a roll call of dynasties worshipping a variety of gods, they built great cities and glorious palaces, saw them destroyed and their people driven off into slavery, yet always the Aryans of Pars survived to build new cities and bow to new rulers. In September 1881 when Jane and Marcel entered Fars, its capital was Shiraz, Nasr-al-Din its shah, but its governor, Zil-es-Sultan, held the real power.

'My mules are very springy, they're travelling well, they don't need a rest, I want to push on,' the tcharvadar bachy said when the caravan reached Abadeh.

'I am your slave,' Jane replied with Persian politeness, 'but our contract stipulates a day-long stop at Abadeh.' Jane's agenda to visit the mosque with the interesting mihrab at Eqlid was threatened, as was her chance to contact the chieftain of the Bakhtiari tribes who held the mountain passes beyond Shiraz through which the Dieulafoys hoped to reach Susiane province.

In September 1881 Susiane held only archaeological interest for Jane and Marcel. Although they did not know it, in fact it held their future fame.

Jane insisted. She sent a present to the town's governor and asked for an audience. The governor read the contract and upheld her right to a day's halt. The reluctant tcharvadar bachy insisted he must go on; he was afraid of running out of fodder, he said, to delay would put the caravan at risk. He had barely finished speaking before the governor growled, 'I hope you know how to swim,' and ordered his soldiers to throw him into the deep water tank at the centre of the courtyard. He was halfway to the drink when Jane, shocked, cried out that the punishment was too harsh.

In the rapprochement that followed it was agreed the caravan would go on its way, while the governor's son would escort the Dieulafoys west to Eqlid and then across country to rejoin the travellers at Surmaq. Except that the governor's sixteen-year-old son (who in Jane's photo looks a mere child) was late leaving his newly acquired *anderun* and the Dieulafoys were diverted by two hours of partridge shooting, all went according to plan until the first of the Bakhtiari ranges loomed up ahead. Shots rained down from a group of men standing on the heights. 'Sons of dogs,' cursed the governor's son, 'I'll burn your fathers.' The cowardly cook said nothing – he turned his mule about and spurred off back towards Abadeh, saucepans clashing. Jane and Marcel levelled their rifles. 'Stay here,' the boy ordered, 'I'll go and find out who they are, but whatever you do don't wound any of them. If you draw blood, they'll fall on you and kill you.'

As he rode forward the armed men came down from the peaks and after a brief parley signalled the Dieulafoys to come up. Black felt hats atop their coils of black hair, the tribesmen were fierce looking, dark-skinned, with black eyes that flashed as they talked. Ammunition belts crossed their chests, daggers and pistols were tucked into waist belts, swords hung under the saddle flaps.

Wary of strangers and well prepared to defend themselves, when the Eqlidians, one of the tribes of the nomadic Bakhtiari clan, understood the reason for the visit they abandoned their hostility and invited the foreigners into the village. But there was the problem of the cook: he had taken the pots, the tea kettle and all the food with him. As a sign of trust Jane and Marcel dismounted, passed the reins to two of the strangers and said, 'Get him. You can scare him, but don't hurt him,' and watched calmly as they galloped away on the tcharvadar bachy's horses.

With dinner retrieved, the Dieulafoys were led up over the lip of the mountains to a long, wide upland plain irrigated by small streams curling down from higher slopes. Pathways connected a patchwork of wheat and vegetables, tobacco and maize. Further down the plain the black tents of shepherds were pitched among flocks of grazing sheep and goats. To the Dieulafoys it seemed a rich paradise – until the villagers explained their misery. Even at the height of the Shiraz famine three years earlier, they complained, they could not sell their surplus produce. Setting off with sacks of wheat and barley, they were set upon by brigands near Abadeh. On the next occasion they were not only robbed, some of the villagers were killed. The robbers eventually became so daring they lay in wait at the foot of the pass, and the villagers gave up all thought of trade, while the Shirazis continued to starve. All over the country it was the same, poor and unsafe roads preventing a local abundance from relieving a shortage elsewhere.

'And the taxes!' they said. 'They think we're rich. Last year the tax gatherers beat our headman – we had nothing more to give, we couldn't save him from the bastinado, they'd already taken everything.' When the villagers sent a deputation to the governor to protest the cruelty, he dismissed them. The villagers knew he pocketed his cut from the farmers' tax. Away from the ears of the governor's son, they told Jane, 'We have to look after ourselves, Excellency, that's why we held you at the pass.'

The vaunted mosque was a forlorn structure made of dried mud, its dome as dented as an old cooking pot. 'We've drowned our tcharvadar, frightened our cook to death, and added an extra seventy kilometres to our road for this!'[4] Jane cursed.

Their attempt to contact the Bakhtiari chieftain was equally fruitless. Soon the Eqlidians would harvest their crops and set off with their flocks to the warmer lowland valleys, leaving only a small group to guard the village through the winter.[5] Although the Eqlidians alone were unable to hold the road to Abadeh, together with other Bakhtiari tribes they controlled the mountain roads into Susiane. For the Dieulafoys to travel the Bakhtiari route without their permission would be extremely dangerous. No one passed through that territory without their leave, even the emperor Darius having to pay tribute, as had Alexander the Great. For decades the Qajar shahs had been trying to break their power. Much blood had been spilled in the struggle, the dealings marked by characteristic Qajar treachery and Bakhtiari subterfuge.

While Jane visited Eqlid in late September, in the northern part of his territory the Bakhtiari leader, the Ilkhani Husein Kuli Khan, was receiving a visit from Zil-es-Sultan. Torn between the proud Bakhtiari tradition of generous hospitality and the knowledge that any show of wealth would result in increased taxation on his already oppressed tribes and seizure of their property, Husein Kuli Khan walked a tightrope, which the Zil-es-Sultan was already planning to cut. In June 1882 the Zil invited him to Isfahan where he was either strangled or given 'a cup of Qajar coffee.'[6]

'Is there a way to get in touch with the Ilkhani for permission to cross into Susiane?' Jane asked.

'None. And without his word . . . you would risk your life.'

'So that is where you learnt your manners,' she teased, confident now of the Eqlidians' goodwill.

'Excellency, our guns wouldn't reach halfway to where you were standing.'

'What would you have done if I'd returned your fire?' Then with newly acquired oriental exaggeration she boasted, 'My rifle has a range of several kilometres.'[7]

The owner of the house where they were accommodated was absent, attending on the Ilkhani. Jane was dismayed by the neglected exterior, but when she saw the interior she realised he was avoiding the tax gatherers' attention. It was clean and comfortable, its parquet floors and solid wooden shutters witness to the valley's wealth, trees being rare and highly valued in Persia. Scenes painted on the insides of the shutters illustrated a *Shahname* story of the Sasanian king, Bahram. The incident had occurred in their own valley, the villagers proudly claimed.

Word of the strangers spread overnight. Country-dwelling Persians assumed that all foreigners were doctors, many travellers using medicine chests as passports, so Jane was not surprised when she stepped out the following morning into a street crowded with the sick. Among them were two beautiful Bakhtiari women who had set off the moment they heard of the foreigners' arrival, riding through the night to bring a sick child. Proud women with strong features, their faces were not veiled, their heads covered with an elegantly draped, loosely woven cloth that fell in graceful folds over dark waist-length ringlets. Their full cotton trousers, gathered at the ankle, floated out from beneath a short woollen tunic.

Jane did what she could for the sick, but already the governor's son was urging them on. 'It's a six hour ride, Excellency,' he warned, 'we must leave if you want to reach Surmaq before nightfall.'

Surmaq also claimed the legendary Sasanian King Bahram. Its crumbling fortress on the edge of town was built during his reign, though its provenance did not prevent the farmers from smashing and grinding its walls into fertiliser for their melon fields. Marcel had barely time to count its broken towers and roughly estimate its dimensions before their escort swept them along to the caravanserai. Outside its walls a row of kneeling camels was being fed, the bales they had brought from the east along the desert road through Kerman and Yazd already piled in the courtyard. Soon the train would be on its way, perhaps north to Tehran and the goods on to northern Europe by the Black Sea ports, perhaps south through Shiraz to Bushire on the Persian Gulf, where the merchandise would be shipped to Arabia or the Mediterranean lands. Surmaq was a junction town on the east–west trade routes, a strand in the ancient Silk Road. The onselling of goods made Surmaq's caravanserai a busy place and brought considerable wealth to the town.

After a few hours sleep the Dieulafoys were again on the road, climbing towards the highest point of the route, a bleak and lonely upland plain 2400 metres above sea level. The track on the two next stages was stony and steep, and swept by a bitter wind from the great desert to the east. The plateau was not only the high point of the route, it was also the high point of Jane's health, which from there on declined, at first gradually along with the general elevation, until it reached its nadir at sea level on the Persian Gulf. After the restful regime of convent life and a diet that included the best fruit and vegetables from the surrounding gardens, Jane had left New Julfa in excellent health. If her tiny frame was carrying a few extra pounds they were soon jolted off and her muscles toned by the long stages. Her slide into ill health began during a night of intense cold on the Kumishah plain. Despite the helmet completely covering her head, her ears froze and her nose became numb; the metal stirrup chilled her instep and her toes felt like stubs of ice. She was so disabled by a sudden attack of acute arthritis that she had to be lifted out of the saddle at the caravanserai. She could not straighten her back. Bent double, she hobbled into the room over the gateway and lay all day in the heat. The pain gradually diminished and her joints became mobile again. When night came she pulled a heavy woollen greatcoat over her new woollen trouser suit tailored in New Julfa, rolled herself in a blanket like a parcel and was lifted into the saddle. Being so small she had insufficient core heat to survive extreme cold, so she suffered more than most on the long cold nights.

Crossing the upland plain her world became a flat and empty place stretching away to the mountains, always the mountains. There were no cities to fill the space or trees to soften its harshness, only the road going on ahead, the one road, no side roads to reduce the monotony, only travellers' footprints leading on into loneliness. Of these two long, punishing stages Jane wrote, 'I have never known such tiredness . . . and can only dream of a time when I will no longer be condemned to ride my mule all through the night.'[8]

The whole caravan suffered. The Armenian women were grey with fatigue and their children's cries splintered the darkness. Querulous moaning came from the women in paired baskets. The voices of the muleteers in their sheepskin coats became mere croaks. The exhausted mules lost their sure-footedness and fell; their loads were taken off, the animals helped to their feet and the pitiless packs replaced.

The tcharvadar bachy knew the state of his caravan. 'I would give you a rest day,' he said when they reached Deh Bid, one of the coldest, loneliest places in Persia, 'but I can't. There's no fodder here for the horses. On the far side of those mountains,' he continued, pointing southwest, 'at Madar-i Sulaiman there is hay. We leave at eight tonight. Given the state of our beasts we'll be lucky to get there by ten tomorrow.'

It was a night of misery and tiredness and penetrating cold. The moon shone silver on the Polvar River as they crossed by the stone bridge to climb the next range of hills. On the far side they met the river again and followed it down into a glen along a track that lurched from rock to rock. Crossing a desolate valley, a sudden call to halt startled the caravan. Sleep-walking beasts collided with those ahead and dozing riders woke in fright, believing the Kashquia nomads were making a raid. Only the cat merchant, comfortable in the warmth of his charges, continued to snore.

The sick old merchant who had begged Allah to allow him to die in his own city had failed by four stages. Kitab! It was written! The tcharvadar bachy rode down the flank of the caravan calling for the dervish and found him sleeping like a log in the saddle. Only the dervish could determine the direction of Mecca from this lonely spot on the Fars plateau. Alongside the rock where the donkey carrying the corpse had come to a halt, muleteers began digging a shallow trench. That it was in the middle of the road made no difference. Others prepared the body, stripped it of its clothing, then laid it out in an undershirt and aligned the head with Mecca. Soil was thrown onto the grave and trampled a little, and the signal for departure given. Looking back at the slightly raised oval shape, Jane realised the significance of all those other small hillocks she had thought so curious along the way. Dead camels, decaying horses and broken mules were left to litter the route, dinner for the vultures. When a traveller died, a hasty unceremonious burial only briefly interrupted the inexorable progress of the caravan.

In what seemed an endless night there were more hills to cross. Streams gushed out of the rocks, wild fowl flew out of thickets and plovers called from the plain, and then, when the morning was already hot, another stop at the crest of a pass. Two mules were missing. The merchant who owned their load was inconsolable. An angry tcharvadar bachy sent back a search party, while the caravan waited, too exhausted to complain.

Deciding only breakfast would keep her alive, Jane located her cook and servant and set off to search for shade. As they unpacked the cooking gear in a little dell Marcel suddenly shouted, 'Put up your weapons, we're being attacked.'

Four felt hats appeared above a crest of rock and the barrels of four rifles glinted in the sunshine. Marcel aimed towards them. 'Stand to!' he called. Jane levelled her rifle.

'Bismillah! In the name of Allah! Stop! Are you going to kill the soldiers sent out to guard the pass? Are you the foreigners the governor of Shiraz is expecting? We've been watching you for some time. We thought you were dervishes – people of importance could not look so bedraggled.'

'We carry letters of introduction to the governor,' Marcel replied pompously, although Jane laughed.

'Peace to you. Your excellency's health is good by the grace of God?' saluted the leader, accepting his mistake, 'Our orders are to escort you to Shiraz.'

If the soldiers were misled by appearances, theirs made Marcel deeply suspicious. 'They're not a military escort,' he whispered to Jane. 'Look at those worn-out felt hats, every coat is different and their cloaks don't match. Soldiers would be in uniform.' Not realising that the only 'uniform' of a Fars soldier was the brown felt hat and a belt with a metal clasp, Colonel Dieulafoy replied stiffly that their escort was unnecessary: in broad daylight they would come to no harm. The leader of the troop assured him that these mountains were very dangerous, the scene of many crimes. Caravans had been attacked and robbed, he said, as you may have been if the governor had not sent out his brave soldiers as soon as he heard of your approach.

Unconvinced, keeping their weapons to hand and without taking their eyes off the men, Marcel and Jane continued with their breakfast. The troop's leader, edging in towards the breakfast cloth, asked to examine their arms. The apprehensive colonel refused brusquely. The soldier turned towards Jane. She reached for her revolver. Loosing his rifle he offered it to her butt first, saying, 'If you won't let me touch your weapon, at least cure me of this sickness that's killing me. I'm all right today, but yesterday I had the fever and tomorrow it will come back and I'll be sick as a dog again.'

In this way Jane learnt that malaria was still rife in Shiraz. She had hoped the annual epidemic would be over before they arrived. Now they would be exposed to its unpredictability. And it was as she feared. From Shiraz she was in its grip until she left Persia five months later.

Still suspicious of their 'escort', the Dieulafoys kept their weapons cocked. When at last a great shambling noise came rolling down the slope, Jane cried out, 'Allah kerim! God is great! Never has a marching caravan sounded so melodious.'[9]

At one o'clock, under a burning sun and after seventeen hours in the saddle, the caravan reached a village where there was hay for the animals, but no caravanserai for the people. Jane inspected the houses willing to offer lodging to unclean infidels, chose one and immediately lay down to sleep. Marcel, waiting like a zombie for the baggage to arrive, too tired even to dismount, raised his eyes and surveyed the horizon. Suddenly his back straightened, his face came to life, he grabbed the saddlebag with the photographic equipment and shook the reins of his poor exhausted mount.

The tcharvadar bachy shouted after him, calling him a madman. 'Infidel dog! You'll kill my horse. For the love of Allah, give it rest, give it water,' but Marcel was intent on a hill where a whitish square shape stood against the skyline. 'Curses on your beard,' the Persian stormed ineffectually. Jane lay on the floor, a battle raging between weariness and a desire to see what had excited Marcel. Curiosity won and her fatigued body was once more in the saddle and on the road, though at a greatly reduced pace.

Across the valley and over the hill was Pasargadae. They had reached the Achaemenids.

Chapter 9
The Achaemenids

The ancient nomadic tribes of central Asia were artistic people who believed in an afterlife. Burying a tribal chieftain in 2300 BC, they stitched a diadem of gold rosettes onto a felt band and tied it around his head before lowering him into a grave.[1] When Aryan nomads began pushing their cattle into Iran in about 1500 BC they may not have brought similar diadems with them, but in their cultural baggage they brought the rosette motif, which remained with them always. When they came to power as the Achaemenid dynasty a thousand years later they embellished their creations with a stylised, sophisticated version, using it almost as a signature. A garland of rosettes lies in the shadow of the dark curling beard of a stone head at Persepolis, another decorates the chest of a bull at Susa and rosettes stud the volutes on towering columns in both. Rosettes appear on golden jewellery, at the centre of silver bowls and on bronze harness fittings. Six-twelve- or twenty-petalled, they link the Achaemenids to their forefathers in central Asia.

Rosettes were hard to find at Pasargadae, a severely damaged early Achaemenid site, on the day Jane and Marcel lay on the grass surveying the limestone platform that had caught Marcel's eye. Pasargadae's rosettes had mostly been removed, along with columns and ashlars (cut stone building blocks), to be incorporated into village housing and local mosques.

As Marcel clambered onto the constructed platform on the summit, Jane continued to lie on the sweet-smelling herbs; it was some time before she found the energy to follow and gaze out over the Polvar Plain. Ringed by high mountains, the open space was a vast theatre, a few shepherds with their flocks giving the site of a great battle a strangely peaceful look. The remains of several buildings lay along the old course of the river; in the west the water in its new bed shone silver beside the Shiraz road snaking out towards the dark Polvar Gorges. A curious square building, twice as high as it was wide, marked the track leading down from the eminence. In the field two tall columns stood erect, distant from each other, one rising from a black basalt base and each crowned by the nest of an irreverent stork. Flat among the grasses were the remains of several low terraces, platforms for large buildings, now bearing nothing more than a few broken column stumps as witness to what once had stood there. Only the very large, too heavy to be carried off, and the very small, small enough to be overlooked, remained, spread out and flung about. Donkeys grazed where kings once walked.

Standing separate and dominating the southern half of the plain, a large white stone monument seemed strangely forlorn. Marcel failed to recognise it. When Alexander the Great had inspected it, it carried an inscription, long since obliterated, that asked the visitor:

'O man, whosoever thou art and whencesoever thou comest, for I know that thou wilt come, I am Cyrus, and I won for the Persians their empire. Do not, therefore, begrudge me this little earth which covers my body.'[2]

It was the tomb of Cyrus the Great.

When it was only a place where shepherds tended their sheep, Cyrus, son of Cambyses, King of the Persians, fought a battle on this plain. With his victory he became King of the Persians and the Medes, uniting the Aryan cousins in a powerful state that would quickly conscript an empire and make Cyrus King of Kings and King of Asia.

The nomadic Persians had stepped into a power vacuum created by the mutual destruction of the Elamites, Babylonians and Assyrians, whose complicated alliances and bitter rivalries had destroyed cities and fields, forced tribes into nomadism and reduced city dwellers to villagers. High on the great central plateau of Fars, Persian King Cambyses had married the only child of Astyages, king of the Medes. While their son Cyrus was growing into an ambitious and capable youth, his Medean grandfather was foolishly adopting the Assyrian practice of elevating himself to a god-king role, a concept his subjects rejected, especially when taxation was increased to fund megamaniacal symbols. When young Cyrus challenged his grandfather in 550 BC, many of the Medean tribesmen joined him on the Plain of Polvar. King Astyages was humbled.

But not killed. This single graceful act set the tone of the future Achaemenid Empire. As states were conquered, they were incorporated into a Persian-led federation, their kings retaining their positions as long as they swore fealty and paid tribute, their beaten armies given increased privileges to ensure their loyalty. Cyrus was not foolish enough to trust absolutely; he placed the armies under new commanders and set up a political commissariat that reported only to him.

Within fourteen years Cyrus, King of Pars and Medea, became Cyrus, King of Kings, King of all Lands, his empire extending across Mesopotamia, northern Syria and into Anatolia, and eastwards into the Aryan homeland of central Asia. Perhaps poetically, that is where he died in 530 BC in a battle against the amazon queen of the Sogdians. By then, he had banished the sheep from the Plain of Polvar and created Pasargadae, the first architectural monument of the first Persian Empire.

Marcel scratched around in the grass and found six column bases, while Jane gazed down from the citadel, absorbing the grandeur of the setting, then together they struggled down a collapsed double stairway, grabbing at thyme plants growing in the cracks to steady themselves. Back in the village of Deh-i-No, the tcharvadar bachy grumbled about his horses but Marcel and Jane were too exhausted to care, or even to eat the kebabs and rice their cook had prepared.

'After riding a horse through fourteen nights, it was wonderful to spend the fifteenth lying on the beaten earth floor of a room with a door that closes . . . Discouragement, fatigue, bad temper have vanished; my energy renewed I am returning to work on the ruins,'[3] Jane wrote next morning before she and Marcel went off to search the plain and measure what remained of Pasargadae. They found column bases and a fragment of black stone carrying a raised rosette, but nothing of the tableau that once regularly filled the Polvar Plain with noise and dust and colour.

It was here that the Persian tribes had assembled in the spring to pitch their tents by the river and meet their king in ceremonial stone reception halls dotted about a wide shady park. Here the lesser kings had come, accompanied by soldiers and nobles, administrators and followers, and here they resided, but never for very long. Here the supreme figure, Cyrus, King of Kings, received his subjects in two columned audience halls large enough to awe them, magnificent enough to furnish the tribute bearers with reports of majesty to carry back to the mountains and valleys of the conquered tribes and nations, accounts that contained fear, but also pride in being part of a mighty realm. The shining, brightly painted buildings were set in gardens where water flowed in rills and the spreading leaves of plane trees created an inviting green shade. The splendour of the halls and pavilions and the delights of the gardens were an integral part of the Achaemenid attempt to ensure loyalty and admiration from their subjects, while the provision of palatial and luxuriant surroundings reinforced the legitimacy of the judgements which the king handed down on transgressors and rebels, and gave dignity to the worship of their god Ahura Mazda, the supreme being.

A shepherd gazing down at Cyrus's Pasargadae from one of the hills would have seen the king's silk-hung tents pitched among the flowers, with guards standing alert nearby. Within call of the king was the bivouacked army. At a distance, outside the royal park, were the smaller tents of lesser courtiers amid a chaotic jumble of people. On the fringes, horsemen wheeled their mounts and tethered mules and hobbled donkeys grazed. And out on the encircling hills the flocks foraged.

There was never a city at Pasargadae. The powerful then were nomads of necessity and almost certainly by choice. Just as Nasr-al-Din, Shah of Shahs, two-and-a-half millennia later delighted in pitching his tent in the pastures of Soltaniyeh or in his preserved hunting grounds elsewhere, so the habit and pleasures of nomadism drew the Achaemenid king away from any fixed abode. His large tents, hung with carpets and lined with silk as described in the Bible, could be quickly erected or dismantled. The tents of his followers, their size reflecting the status of the owner, though less comfortable, were easily transported on the back of a mule. The meanest of the tribe rolled themselves in lengths of felt and slept close to their lord's tent and had little to carry.

When the surrounding villages had been eaten out and the camp become full of dung, flies and disease, the king moved on. A ruler could not stay long anywhere, no matter how delightful the encampment. The hard hand of authority and the glamour of the monarch had to be displayed in all parts of the kingdom in order to perpetuate the myth and substantiate the reality of power. Until the next visit, the grass could grow again on the trampled plain.

Approaching these Achaemenid ruins with their heads full of classical Greek perfection and the bias of the Greek historians, Marcel and Jane failed to appreciate their indigenous nature. Several decades of excavation in Mesopotamia had revealed the achievements of the Sumerians and Assyrians, but Europe at that time knew almost nothing of ancient Persia's architectural attainments. Since then, and largely due to the ground-breaking work undertaken by the Dieulafoys at Susa, archaeologists have systematically explored many Persian sites. Built on a scale that relates to the massive mountains that form their backdrop, the megalithic Achaemenid structures scattered about southern Iran proclaim their originality. There is nothing puny or mean in their conception, and the Dieulafoys were mistaken in seeing them as derivative.

The tcharvadar bachy allowed his tired animals and weary travellers only one full day's rest. In the middle of her second night at Deh-i-No Jane was woken by the 'infernal din' of an assembling caravan. Luxuriating on a freshly filled straw palliasse she turned over, grateful she did not have to join it. Earlier in the evening the tcharvadar bachy had farewelled the Dieulafoys with great ceremony, warning them to stay close to the governor's escort and telling them to be especially watchful in the defiles along the Polvar, but, he said, before everything they must look after his horses and remember to cover them with a rug after the foreign saddles were removed.

The caravan had departed, taking with it Jane's fifteen mule loads of baggage as surety for the tcharvadar's horses, when the Dieulafoys stepped out at dawn to ride to Cyrus's tomb. Sometime after the Achaemenid dynasty had been defeated and Alexander the Great had marched on to Afghanistan, the tomb had been raided and the golden treasures stolen, the golden casket smashed and Cyrus's bones thrown out in the dust. Alexander was appalled when he returned from his Indian adventures and ordered the tomb repaired and sealed, but the contents were lost forever. Since then, like many other ancient structures in Iran, the name of Solomon had been attached to it by the local people, perhaps long ago when the Arabs first arrived with their new religion and destructive rage towards anything predating Islam. A spurious connection to Solomon, the great king and writer of Songs, honoured by all three 'religions of the Book', may have safeguarded the tomb. The villagers named it the Tomb of the Mother of Solomon, installed a crude mihrab and handed it to the women. Men could not enter. So when Jane in her trouser suit was caught asleep inside it was a major incident in the village.

While recording measurements for Marcel, Jane had been seized by a chill. She put down her pencil and sat in the sun. Still she shook with cold. Exasperated, she set up her camera but after four attempts with shaking hands the lens cover was still in place. Then, as suddenly as it had come on, the chill turned to fever and sweat poured out. She knew she must lie down or fall down. Where? On the burning ground? In the nearby village? Why not inside the empty tomb?

Not unnaturally, when the village women discovered a young man lying full length in their mosque they were incensed. They screamed abuse,

Cyrus's tomb, Pasargadae

pelted pebbles. In the throes of malaria Jane could only fling her boots to
defend herself.

She lay in the tomb for several hours. Raised up on a six-level pediment
made of huge precisely cut limestone blocks, the gabled tomb reached up
a further six metres, its roof grotesquely crowned by a flourish of bushes
growing out of the cracks. Carved in relief on a pointed disc over the door
was the Achaemenid signature: two concentric rosettes, one twenty-four-
petalled, another twelve-petalled.[4]

Laid out prostrate and defenseless in the royal sepulchre was surely one
of Jane's most bizarre Persian experiences. When the fever subsided she
mounted her horse, rode back to the village and dosed herself with quinine.

The Dieulafoys rode at the head of the caravan through the Polvar Gorges,
their weapons ready to hand. Snorting wild boar smashed an escape through
the undergrowth when they heard the party approaching. Behind them the
cook and their servant walked along together, followed by the two muleteers whom the tcharvadar bachy had insisted on sending to look after his
horses, taking turns riding the mule loaded with kitchen gear and bedding.
The mounted government guards brought up the rear.

The two-day descent from Pasargadae to the Marv Dasht plain was steep and difficult. The tcharvadar bachy had warned that robbers haunted the dark defiles but had not mentioned the wild beauty of these narrow trails or the roses and geraniums that scented the air where the cliffs briefly parted and meadows filled the space between. Trees hung down from broken rock-faces and at their base the river raced along, crashing against the boulders and flinging spray high in the air.

Emerging from the last gorge their escort suddenly charged ahead and galloped towards a cluster of goatskin tents. Recognising the insignia of brown felt hats and metal-clasped belts Jane was not alarmed at the sight of the governor's soldiers, but she was amused by their enormous trousers. Ballooning out below their fitted coats, they had to be tucked into their belts before the soldiers could walk without tripping. They seemed curious garb for men supposedly guarding the passes.

If the mosquitoes had been a nuisance at Deh-i-No, on the plain they were relentless. During the night Jane and Marcel were tormented by a silent tiny species. With swollen lips and spotted nose, Jane approached Naqsh-i Rustam, where the bones of later Achaemenid kings had lain in mausoleums more secure and elaborate than Cyrus's simple tomb. Through puffy eyelids she stared up at funeral chambers deeply incised into a sheer rockface and at monumental pictures carved in high relief below them. The scale of the works dwarfed a shepherd standing at the base of the cliff and gave his sheep the appearance of ants. Yet even built high in the cliff the tombs had been plundered. Of the four interred Achaemenid kings, only Darius the Great is recognised by an inscription; the identity of the others remains the subject of academic debate.

In the eight tableaux carved on the lower part of the cliff Marcel found the Sasanids, his inspiration for visiting Persia. Although overwhelmed by the position and size of the austere Achaemenid work, the Sasanid reliefs are more detailed and human, triumphal gestures memorialising the heroic deeds of the later dynasty. In one, a pictorial record of a Persian victory later described in Firduzi's *Shahname*, the captured Roman emperor Valerian cringes before Shah Shapur.

After sketching the reliefs, Marcel looked upwards to the Achaemenids. Not content with inspecting the façades through binoculars, he sent the soldiers to climb up behind the rock and let down a rope. Before long Marcel was swinging in the air, and then scrambling onto the terrace at the front of Darius's tomb before disappearing inside. When Marcel descended Jane assumed it was her turn, but no.

'Why do you want to go up there?' he asked, dismissing the vaulted chamber and the hewn coffin within as unimpressive. She had slept in Cyrus's tomb, she could at least inspect Darius's sepulchre, Jane insisted.

'I want to see Darius's face. And besides, the view out over the plain must be spectacular.'

'I won't let you do anything so foolish. It's no use going on. You have no idea how it feels to be swinging fifteen metres above the ground at the end of a rope . . . You're not going to the tomb.' To terminate the argument Marcel ordered the soldiers to come down.[5]

It was the first time in their eleven years of marriage that Marcel had imposed what Jane called his 'lord and master' role on her; certainly it was the first time he had forbidden her to do anything. She met it with a temper tantrum. She resented his condescension and was extremely angry, which more probably indicates how ill she was feeling, despite the quinine, rather than any serious rift in the marriage – they were to live together in complete harmony for another thirty-five years, dependent on each other while pursuing independent public lives, devoted until the day she died. Finally Jane capitulated, realising that in the strangeness and hostility of Persia they needed each other too much to allow an elaborately decorated mountain to come between them.

Persepolis appeared quite suddenly. Having ridden down a valley enclosed by hills, the Dieulafoys entered the Marv Dasht plain and there it was, jutting out from the mountain behind, a huge stone platform rising above a mud-brick village fringed by palm trees. Thirteen towering, damaged columns proclaimed it. As they approached, they could see the fabled double stair case up which soldiers had marched ten abreast and up which Alexander the Great had ridden in the footsteps of Darius III, whom he had defeated in battle and whose palaces he looted and destroyed. It is impossible to look at the ruins without thinking of those two men, the king whose military skill was not as great as his empire and the ruthless treasure-hungry Macedonian who came seeking Greek vengeance. Together they brought tragedy to what was the most amazing assembly of the Achaemenid Empire, the most dazzling structure of their era.

From the top of the platform the view over the plain to the encircling ranges could not be ignored. Through the crystal-clear air Jane saw scarps and gorges slashed like carmine shadows across the purple mountains. Small prosperous-looking villages surrounded by irrigated fields dotted the plain. She looked down on the nearest village, fifteen metres below the level of the platform, and saw flat-roofed houses, fruit trees and water tanks in their central courtyards. Behind her on the platform stood two six-metre-high bulls. That one stone bull was completely headless and the other mutilated made them pathetically grotesque. Their legs were braced forward as though the weight of the ceremonial doorway they guarded was overwhelming and each thick neck wore a garland of central Asian rosettes.

To the right, fifty metres away across a sea of litter, the forlorn remnants of a once-majestic columned hall rose from an elevated stone terrace faced with sculpted stone slabs. Four flights of stairs reared from the shadows to climb the terrace's northern wall, one at either end and a projecting pair placed in the centre. Ignoring the stone reliefs, Jane and Marcel hurried up the central pair, pausing on the landing where the stairs came together to survey the desolation of the *apadana*, the audience hall of the Achaemenid Kings of Kings. Most of the erect columns, slender, fluted, almost twenty metres tall, had lost their capitals, their shattered fragments lying around them. The fallen drums of other columns lay at strange angles in heaps around the damaged bases, ants hurrying in and out of the holes where dowels had once held the drums in vertical alignment.

Seventy-two columns had once stood on the terrace. Six rows of six supported the roof of the central hall, with the remainder carrying the roof across three surrounding porticos. The forelegs and heads of paired bulls arranged back to back formed the capitals of the columns, the saddle between them once a cradle for the cedar roof beams. Cross beams of ebony and teak had carried a lattice of dried palm fronds covered by a thin layer of earth, perfectly insulating the hall from the fierce sun.

The *apadana*'s magnificence derived from its proportions and overall dimensions, which not even time could destroy, but the glamour of its glittering decoration had gone. The bullheads on the capitals had once boasted golden horns; the beams had been gold-plated and inlaid with ivory and silver patterning. Red, yellow and blue glazed terracotta tiles had shone on the cornices, and plaster and paint had enlivened the walls. With the aid of bright pigment, the elongated stone leaves encircling the column bases became inverted palm hearts, and colour had filled the fluting of the columns. The sway of rich textiles augmented the brilliance: heavy gold-lace curtains to keep out draughts and shimmering silk hangings as the backdrop to the dais where the King of Kings presented himself to his subjects. If the effect was overwhelming, it was meant to be.

The simple dignity of Cyrus's halls at Pasargadae was insufficient for his successors. Opulence and splendour must attach to an empire that now included Egypt and extended from Thrace, which jostled the border of Macedonia, across Anatolia, Mesopotamia and central Asia and into the Indus valley, the largest empire the world had yet known. The first Darius, Darius the Great, who ruled 522–486 BC, two generations down from Cyrus, built (or perhaps only completed) the spacious platform, but certainly he raised the *apadana* on it – an inscribed golden tablet housed in a stone box under a corner of its terrace tells us so. For good measure he placed its silver twin under another corner.

Better than any inscription is a pictorial record of ceremonies on the *apadana* that explains the purpose of its magnificence and how it was funded. Jane and Marcel, retreating down the broad staircase from the scorching sun on the now roofless *apadana*, found the record carved on the high terrace wall beside them. They lingered in the wall's shade to read the sculpted reliefs, the full document extending along the entire seventy-metre façade.

With exemplary detail, the carved record depicts the celebration of *No Ruz*, New Year. At the spring equinox, 21 March, a delegation from each of the subject nations brought gifts to the King of Kings. Lithic symbols encode dates and rituals. A ferocious lion biting into the back of a garlanded bull warns that when the constellation Leo rides the zenith of the night sky and Taurus disappears below the southern horizon it is time for the ceremonies to begin. Easily read fertility symbols denoting vigour, life, fecundity fill borders and separate segments, but the panels showing Medean and Persian noblemen leading delegations into the King of Kings' presence are the sculptors' triumph.

Hats played a signature role in Achaemenid times. Footwear and clothing were regionally distinct, but the hat was the truly defining symbol. The Persians can be recognised by their 'tiaras', hats made from long erect leaf-like pieces of probably stiffened felt stuck into a headband, while the Medes wear a round fur helmet with a tie, perhaps a lamb's tail, dangling behind. Although they were much fairer than the Turcs in the north or the Elamites in the south, both are hirsute people with curling beards and ringletted hair. Moustaches twirl in arabesques along the upper lip.

Recorded, too, is each delegation's tribute. The Bactrians lead in their double-humped camels, the Sogdians push their sheep forward and the Armenians from near Mount Ararat hold the reins of their famed horses. The Elamites from Susiane had snared a lioness and cubs and offer them to the king to stock his hunting park. Several nations bring gold jewellery and vases studded with semiprecious stones. Before they were stabled or slaughtered, stored or sent to the treasury, scribes recorded each gift, redeemable in times of need. When Alexander burst in, in 331 BC, the treasury was bulging with silver and gold, the stables were full of horses, the kitchen stores overflowed with honey and grains.

The carved ranks of gift bearers, the nobles and the guards are not stylised figures. Each is a sculpted stone portrait of a contemporary member of the Persian federation, suggesting that even in their hierarchical society the individual was recognised and his dignity respected. Carved in tiers on the grand staircase, their grouping into larger units reflects the harmony and integrity of the kingdom, the resolution of conflict within it and the individual's pride in being part of such a magnificent conglomerate. Persepolis's artistic unity mirrors the confidence of a mighty, prosperous empire.

The ritual of the spring ceremonies has been inferred from these carvings and other evidence. Given that the setting was undeniably gorgeous, some on-site interpreters present today's tourist with a scenario in the style of a Hollywood epic with a remote king and legions of intermediaries restricting access to him, the final scene being the king's ritual deflowering of virgins in the palace beyond the *apadana*. Scholars see a more accessible king enthroned on the *apadana*, who encourages his subjects to bring their grievances and present their petitions directly to him, a practice which enabled him to monitor the state of his kingdom more realistically than having to rely solely on reports from his political commissariat and satraps. This less theatrical interpretation of the spring rites accords with the dignity of the figures marching up the staircases and with the homily recorded in the Zendavesta, 'From your labours we receive our subsistence; you derive your tranquillity from our vigilance; since we are mutually [dependent], let us live together like brothers in concord and love.'[6]

Without their roofs, the various halls and palaces elevated on the great platform are fully exposed to the sun, fierce even in October, and with the heat, the flies. Waving away insects buzzing around her head as she inspected Xerxes's Palace, when Jane saw the carving on a stone doorway she laughed out loud. Caught in mid-stride, the imperious King Xerxes is accompanied by two stone attendants, one sheltering the king with a parasol, the other brandishing a fly whisk. Xerxes, son and successor of Darius the Great, burned the first temple on the Athens Acropolis after 'the Athenians [had] crossed the sea and sacked and burned the city of Sardis with its Lydian sanctuaries,'[7] an appalling affront to the Persian king's policy of religious toleration and protection of minorities. So began the Greco–Persian Wars, culminating a century and a half later in Alexander's rampage. For hundreds

Doorway, Persepolis

of years the men from barren Greece had lusted after the riches of oriental Persia, and at Persepolis they found them in abundance.

By midday Jane was exhausted. She retreated to Darius's small palace beyond the *apadana*. It suggested more intimate although still formal occasions. It is unlikely that he lived there. Where were his women, she wondered? There is no space for them in these few rooms, yet he was known to have a vast *anderun*, the size of the harem being an index of a monarch's greatness, a symbol as subtle as the volume of the trumpeters who welcomed delegations at the bull-guarded gate.

She wandered out again onto the platform littered with debris, piles of sand and mounds of rubble, and remembered the governor of Azerbaijan, Ferhad Mirza, whom she met in Tabriz, telling her that when governor of Shiraz he had excavated a central area of the site. He was, he said, seeking the truth of Persepolis, but others said it was the whiff of treasure that brought his spades to work. In the Hall of a Hundred Columns he had uncovered some column stumps, carved gateways and mysterious religious symbols. Finding no gold and not recognising the unique stonework as more valuable than gold, he sacked the workers and for some unrecorded reason hanged one of them from the parapet.

It was fortunate that Ferhad Merza had not dug in the space between the Hall of a Hundred Columns and the *apadana*, because his brutal excavation technique would surely have damaged what was hidden under the rubble. Three months after Alexander first rode up the great staircase the palaces and halls of Persepolis were burned 'to the ground'. Yet Persepolis was a stone city made primarily of white limestone, dug from the mountain behind. Certainly the hangings would have burned, hangings made from cloth woven with gold thread imported from the corners of the empire. The cedarwood beams, tribute of the Spardans (Syrians), that spanned the vast halls, would have come flaming down, the ebony and teak crossbeams flaring, the painted ceilings smoking. Vestments and carpets would have burned just as quickly, although they had probably already been looted. The treasury was empty, the contents already on the way north to Alexander's new strongroom at Ecbatana, according to Plutarch on the backs of 10 000 mules and 5000 camels.

When the embers cooled there would have been a last hunt through the ashes for any overlooked jewels or coins. Luckily 30 000 sun-baked clay tablets were considered worthless and so postal records, administrative details, the wages paid to the men who built Persepolis, and sacred observance rituals remained safely buried in the debris until the twentieth century, together with ledger entries of the *No Ruz* tribute.

After the site was abandoned, many of the remaining walls were demolished, primarily for the smaller ashlars, which were carried away to be recycled in village houses and in the keeps of desert chieftains. Only the monumental, too heavy for easy transport, remained.

And so Persepolis continued for another thousand years, the carved stonework and grand staircases ever more deeply buried as desert storms deposited tonnes of sand on the ash. As the baked bricks forming the walls of the palaces decayed, their earth contributed to the protection of what lay below. Then came the Arabs with Mohammad's message of one God: Allah, who forbade representation of living things. The column capitals were smashed and the bull heads defaced, exposed carvings of man and beast chiselled off. Plants, lotus flowers and leaves, pomegranates and palm hearts, not seen as living things, were spared. And, because they were hidden low in Alexander's ash, saved from desecration were inimitable carved reliefs, images similar to those on the north front – when the *apadana* roof collapsed it fell to the east, preserving the main eastern stairway. To Alexander's fire we owe the pleasure of seeing the stairway's train of tribute bearers intact, almost as they were in 330 BC. In destroying Persepolis, perversely Alexander saved its greatest pictorial record.

The eastern façade was excavated in 1932, fifty-one years after Jane's visit. Jane saw only a sea of sand and had no inkling of the treasures hidden below. It was fortunate the reliefs were not exposed at that time for the site was subject to vandalism. The Turcoman Qajar dynasty did nothing to protect it, having contempt for the ancient Aryan dynasty that had constructed it. The Achaemenids were not related to them, they said dismissively – and the Persians of Fars province returned their contempt.

Nor did the common people appreciate its significance. The headman of a village not far from Persepolis advised one visitor, 'You have come from afar to see our country; do not, like the majority of the Firangis [foreigners], occupy yourself with nothing but dumb stones, vessels of brass, tiles and fabrics; contemplate the world of ideas rather than the world of form, and seek for truth rather than for curiosities ... It would be a pity that you should come here at so much trouble and expense and take nothing back with you but a collection of those curiosities and antiquities with which your people seem ... to be so strangely infatuated.' Instead the visitor should visit Karbala and Najaf, a suggestion he declined, saying, 'the imams ... would drive me from their shrines like a dog if I attempted to approach,'[8] a prediction which Jane was to find absolutely true.

Deploring the neglect of the ancient site, the same visitor wished that some of the money 'spent in building new palaces in the capital ... were devoted to the glorious relics of a past age! That ... is the last thing an oriental monarch cares about. To construct edifices which may perpetuate his own name is of far more importance in his own eyes than to protect from injury those built by his predecessors'.[9] More recently, following the Islamic Revolution of 1979 a proposal to obliterate the whole of Persepolis, together with other pre-Islamic sites, threatened its survival.

'There are probably many more interesting discoveries to be made at Persepolis, but the air is so insalubrious, the heat so fierce, the mosquitoes so punishing and the inn near the ruins so squalid that after a single day the visitor has only one idea, to flee as fast as possible,' Jane wrote. The Dieulafoys fled to a village two farsakhs [ten kilometres] from the ruins, and stayed another three days. The village headman's house had an upper room, 'a palliasse of straw and a metal amphora constituting the only furnishings.' An easterly breeze bringing cool fresh air straight from the mountains kept the mosquitoes away while the Dieulafoys dined in the moonlight on the adjoining rooftop, watched by village women peering from their flat roofs.

Each working day at Persepolis began and ended for Jane with a ten-kilometre ride across the Marv Dasht plain. In the cool morning following the line of the *kanats*, skirting the plantations where men were already at work building up and breaking down mud walls to direct the flow of water in the irrigation channels, it was very enjoyable. Veiled women with wicker baskets flitted into the orchards, while others bent from the waist to weed the gardens. Wherever there was water the rich soil produced an abundance, but where the *kanats* had been neglected the ground was barren and the mudbrick houses deserted. Since the Achaemenids had first built the subterranean channels that brought water to the Marv Dasht plain, the battle between destruction and repair, creation and neglect had determined the fate of the villagers.

Returning in the afternoon was more challenging. Fearing robbers, their soldier escort insisted on travelling while the sun still burned the plain. 'Six living brigands are buried there,' they said, pointing to six piles of earth. The robbers had been forced to dig a deep pit and were then hanged by the feet from a bar placed across its opening. Head down in the hole, plaster was poured in around them. Mounds of soil piled over their feet were left as a warning to others. When Jane murmured, 'How terrible', 'Yes,' the soldier replied, 'it's a terrible waste of plaster when the earth would have done as well.'[10]

The villagers were not unfriendly. Simple people, uneducated, malnourished and living in squalor, they were true Aryans in colouring, most fair-haired and blue-eyed, some, like their muleteer who came from a nearby village, green-eyed redheads. The boys who had survived their bleeding on day three of their little lives, to rid them of the mother's impure blood, ran about naked with their sisters until the age of three, strings of glass beads jangling around neck and ankle. They were filthy, their noses snotty and their eyes infected. Child mortality was very high, two out of every three succumbing to 'fever', almost certainly malaria. Little was known about the disease at the time. Laveran was already working in France to reveal its parasitic cause and earn himself a Nobel Prize[11] but it would be the next decade before Ross linked its transmission to the mosquito. In the meantime everyone blamed the air, the *mal* air, for the sickness. Jane took a large stock of quinine to Persia because people saw that the drug cured the symptoms, although no one understood how it did so.

Jane did not realise the consequences of overdosing on quinine, so in dangerous ignorance she took huge doses and kept on riding and working. In the eight days between suffering her first devastating attack near Cyrus's tomb and leaving Persepolis, she had made the difficult descent through the Polvar Gorges, inspected Achaemenid tombs at Naqsh-i Rustam (though only from the plain), ridden at least another 100 kilometres over the Marv Dasht plain and spent four days photographing and recording in debilitating heat on the exposed Persepolis platform. In the evenings she had developed her photographic plates, written up her diary in the moon light and listened to Marcel's theories about Persepolis.

Marcel's and Jane's classical education blinded them to seeing Achaemenid Persia with an unbiased eye. Europeans knew only the Greek version of what they called 'The Persian Wars', the long centuries in antiquity when Achaemenids and Greeks were mortal enemies. The Greek sources were readily accessible to Europeans since Greeks and Europeans use the same alphabet, but the Achaemenid accounts, written in cuneiform syllabic characters, had only begun to be translated in the mid-nineteenth century, primarily due to the work of Englishman Henry Rawlinson. Without knowledge of what was inscribed on baked clay tablets the Dieulafoys had no alternative perspective to balance the Greek's biased history.

Jane had been transfixed by her first view of the Parthenon on her way into Persia. All her life it had been the benchmark of perfection against which everything was judged. When she first saw its miraculous beauty her preconceptions were confirmed. Inevitably, when she reached Persia she interpreted Persepolis through a veil of European assumptions. She thought its columns and capitals derivative and did not recognise the originality and power of the architecture or the artistic strength of the spectacular bull- and lion-headed capitals.

The relationship between the art of Persepolis and ancestral central Asian forms is much better understood since the discoveries in 'greater Persia' of metalwork and jewellery buried with Lurs, Scythians, Cimmerians, and other Achaemenid 'cousins' descended from their central Asian cultural forebears, but in 1881 that material was not available to offset Jane's Greek mindset. Most significantly, the inscribed silver, gold and baked clay tablets proclaiming Darius's creation of the Persepolis *apadana* still awaited excavation. Europeans assumed that Darius's son, Xerxes, had built Persepolis after he had penetrated the Athenian homeland and seen and destroyed the embryo temple on the Acropolis. But Persepolis already existed at that time, and had not been inspired by anything seen in Greece. Darius had begun construction at Persepolis forty years before Xerxes set foot in Greece and more than seventy years – three generations – before the first Pentelic marble block of the Parthenon was laid.

What especially led Jane and her contemporaries astray was the blazing inscription on the Gate of All Nations, where she had confronted the two six-metre-high defaced limestone bulls guarding the ceremonial entrance as she first stepped onto the platform. More than a gateway, it was a roofed entrance hall whose elaborately painted walls enclosed black marble benches. While the decoration had become nothing more than an occasional paint flake or speck of gilded plaster, the trilingual inscription above the bulls remained, and it had been deciphered before Jane's visit. She knew it declared, in Persian, Babylonian and Elamite:

> A great god is Ahura Mazda, who has created the earth, who has created the heaven, who has created man, who has created good things for man . . . I am Xerxes, Great King, King of Kings, King of Lands, King of many races . . . son of Darius the King, the Achaemenid . . . By the grace of Ahura Mazda I constructed this Gateway of All Nations. Many other beautiful things were constructed in Persia. I constructed them and my father constructed them. Everything we have constructed looks beautiful . . . King Xerxes says: May Ahura Mazda protect me and my kingdom and whatever is constructed by me as well as what has been constructed by my father.

Xerxes was responsible for adding the Gate of All Nations, but not for creating the Persepolis platform. Today it is well established that Darius the Great ordered the platform in 520 BC, and when it had been completed he began to adorn it with palaces and audience halls of great magnificence. We know that his son Xerxes (486–465 BC) continued the task, and his successor Artaxerxes I (465–424 BC) added his flourishes. When Alexander arrived, it was still being embellished. But fifty years before its proper archaeological excavation began, Jane must be forgiven for not seeing it as a miracle of indigenous achievement.

Besides, she was far from well. Seeing her become paler and thinner in the relentless sun and brutal heat as day followed day, Marcel cut short his work on the platform and ordered the horses. Descending the monumental staircase for the last time, Jane paused long enough to look out over the plain and consider how busy it must have been when covered by the tents of the tribute bearers from 'All Nations', the encampments of the soldiers, and the chaos of the retinue who followed the king for the spring festival. Behind her a single mountain guarded the east, but across the plain, beyond the memory, was a complete ring of stone.

Returning to the village they found pitched tents outside the walls and the bazaar full of fair-skinned, blue-eyed people. Asked who they were one replied, *Zardushti, Kiyani* (Zoroastrian, Achaemenian). Although the men wore more clothes than their forebears and a colour patch on the shoulder it seemed to Jane that the Persepolis stone reliefs had sprung to life and the Achaemenids had stepped off the staircase. The dress of the unveiled women, baggy pantaloons and knee-length tunics, a loose silk turban on their fair hair, appeared more a replica of the Sasanids carved into the hard cliff at Naqsh-i Rustam. What Achaemenian and Sasanian women had worn, Jane could only speculate since there were no carved females at either site.

Energy surged through her. She forgot she was tired and ill. She was in among them, talking, asking questions. Yes, at home in Yazd, they complained, they had to wear a yellow robe and turban. No, their religion did not allow polygamy or seclude their women or force them to veil. They only veiled for protection in unfriendly places, the women explained. Their answers would soon appear in Jane's little notebook.

Each wore a sacred cord made from many fibres twisted into three strands and twisted again into one to represent the three principles of Zoroastrianism: good thoughts, good words and good deeds, for which they would be judged, they believed, three days after death. Only the soul having

Zoroastrian family from Yazd (Yazidis)

significance, their inconsequential body would be exposed after death in a high place for the birds to pick the bones clean. The sacred elements of earth, water and air must not be contaminated by a corpse, and to burn a corpse was unthinkable – fire was the most sacred element of all.

'Ride with us to Naqsh-i Rustam,' they invited.

They had come from Yazd on a pilgrimage to worship their god Ahura Mazda in his dedicated places, they told her. The claim was only partly true, since the 15 000 Zoroastrians of Yazd and Kerman dominated the commerce of Iran's south-east, and soon the carpets and cashmere shawls, lengths of silk and pieces of inlaid metalwork in their baggage would find their way into the Shiraz bazaar.

More than 2300 years after Zoroastrian rites had been celebrated at Persepolis, the Yazdis had brought a flame, lit from the sacred fire burning since 470 AD in their temple at Yazd, to burn in the two rock-cut fire altars near the Achaemenid tombs at Naqsh-i Rustam.[12] The sacred fire, symbolising purity and the need for constant vigilance against evil, burned symbolically in the beehive-like structures carved on the walls of the staircases at Persepolis, which Jane had caught with her camera that morning. Above them the Zoroastrian god Ahura Mazda, represented by a complex winged circle, had watched her shaking hands erect tripods, insert glass plates and open shutters.

The Zoroastrian god Ahura Mazda arrived in Persia with the central Asian tribes after speaking through the prophet Zarathustra (Zoroaster to the Greeks) in the seventh century BC, the conversation recorded centuries later in the Avesta. He has remained ever since, despite his followers and his priests, the magi, being killed and his books burned with the arrival of the Arabs. Ostensibly surviving only in small communities, the teachings of the Zoroastrian faith transformed the religion of its conquerors, converting Sunni concepts into the more mystical Shi'a doctrine. As on so many occasions in Persian history, the cultural thread stretched the mind of the powerful invader, adding new fabric to its make-up.

In Yerevan on her way into Persia Jane had seen the Muslims celebrating *No Ruz*, their bazaars full of spring decorations, festive good wishes flying between merchants and customers. Talking now with the Yazdis, she realised how the ancient Achaemenid New Year rituals celebrated at Persepolis had been incorporated into modern Persian ceremonies.[13]

Zoroastrianism teaches that not only is humanity locked in an eternal struggle between good and evil, but also that a ruler's first duty is to provide enlightened leadership in the struggle for social justice. The precept that

'Only the virtuous should rule and if he go astray, obedience should be withdrawn from him,' has haunted dynasty after dynasty, down to the present day.

Darius said, 'I am one who loves righteousness and hates iniquity . . . It is not my will that the strong should oppress the weak . . . God's plan for the earth is not turmoil but peace, prosperity and good government.'[14] Tribute, not domination, was the Achaemenid aim. In their empire the pride of each nation, the sincerity of different faiths, and the dignity of the individual were respected. Conquered nations, accustomed to oppression and cease-less wars, were happy to buy the Achaemenid peace.

Marcel had filled a 200-page notebook with notes and drawings and Jane had taken dozens of photographs, but now it was time to roll the bed swags and fasten the packs. Shiraz lay two stages away across the Marv Dasht plain. Tired of Persepolis, the servants set off early and the soldiers accom-panied them. Riding out alone into the darkness at ten o'clock Jane and Marcel were soon lost. They groped their way back to the village, where their landlord set them in the right direction, but once more the track disappeared among stones. Literally going round in circles, Marcel heard the English telegraph wires singing in the wind. Following the poles, they caught up with the soldiers at dawn, who assured them, 'The care of your precious lives is the single happiness of your slaves.'[15]

The village where they planned to lodge was abandoned: so many people had died of fever that the survivors had taken to the mountains. There was no other village, no hay for the horses, no food or beds for the caravan, and the water was foul. Frail and sick, Jane had to ride on into the day, across the parched plain, under the burning sun, along the stony track. After thirteen hours and seventy-two kilometres, she was jolted awake in the saddle and saw through a gap between the hills the fabled city of Shiraz lying at the centre of a large upland valley surrounded by snow-topped mountains. Tiled domes peered over a city wall, ranks of black cypress marched across the encircling gardens. 'Allahu akbar,' exclaimed the mule-teers, 'God is great'.

Chapter 10
Shiraz, city of wine, of roses and of poets

A few kilometres west of the city of Shiraz, on the slope of a hill over-looked by the dazzling summit of Kuh-i-Barf (Snow Mountain), Jane and Marcel found refuge in a garden, the Bagh-i-Sheykh, home to the English members of the telegraph staff. From the barred gate, lines of judas trees led away into the depths of the garden, each row ending with a dwelling, or a pavilion, or a terrace shaded by the autumn-gold leaves of hornbeams.

When they arrived the widowed director who had offered the Dieulafoys hospitality was lying ill with malaria. A wooden airing horse draped with bedding and clothes of the sweating sick stood at the foot of the staircase to catch the breeze blowing in from the courtyard. The deputy director appeared, but almost unable to stand after a brief welcome he tottered back to his sick bed. The gardener was ill, too, as were all the servants except the cook. Within days Marcel also lay on a straw mattress. As he recovered, Jane succumbed, and until they left the city they took turns fighting the vicious Shirazi strain of malaria. Accompanied by delirium, hallucinations, high temperature and rapid pulse, it forced sweat from every pore and was totally debilitating. After an attack, Jane wrote, 'I passed my apprenticeship in the mountains, but this fever has left me a past master.'[1]

They were attended by Dr Olding, who occupied one of the houses in the garden, a kind man with a stone of grief in his heart. His wife had died three weeks earlier and he begged Jane to visit his children.

Oranges, lemons and cumquats swelled from the trees and ripe plums littered the ground near Dr Olding's house. In the *talar* Jane found a Shirazi wetnurse feeding the doctor's five-month-old daughter while the older sister played sadly on the floor. In Jane's photograph the nurse's short gathered

Wetnurse, Shiraz

skirt puffs over broad hips and hennaed curls fall to the waist. The child's tiny hand scrunches the nurse's silk gauze blouse, drawing it tight across milk-filled breasts. Behind stands a servant bearing her mistress's *kalian*.

She would rather feed a monkey or a dog than a Christian child,[2] the wetnurse had told the senior clerics who were anxious not to lose the European doctor. Scornfully rejecting a large payment and a silk robe, the nurse capitulated to the prestige of having her own servant to light her *kalian*, tobacco being a recognised way to fill Shirazi breasts.

The recuperating superintendent also shared his grief with Jane. As he stared at goldfish darting in the stagnant water of a rectangular pool, he told how his wife had lost her battle a year before. 'She tried to keep her health, but this garden', he said, waving towards geraniums and roses growing in the shade of tall trees, 'wasn't big enough for the vigorous exercise she needed. She longed to ride over the hills to let the fresh air fill her lungs, but when she went out unveiled she was attacked by fanatics and when she veiled I was attacked for being with a Muslim woman.'

Jane was sitting alone in a columned pavilion noting in her diary a rare moment of contemplation and idleness when the garden gate was thrown open and two soldiers rode in ahead of a veiled woman mounted on a white donkey. Jane saw the silver-inlaid saddle, the Kermani wool saddlecloth and the servants who followed and was astonished that a Shi'ite woman should enter a Christian compound; more astonished when the woman dropped from the saddle, put out her hand and greeted Jane in perfect French. She had just returned from the mountains, she said, and couldn't wait to welcome a compatriot.

Child of a French father who had come to Persia and married an Armenian Christian, homesick for a country she had never known, the woman begged Jane to visit her and her two daughters.

One midday Shiraz's city governor rode unannounced through the gate in the garden's mud wall. His rich brocade coat spread over the back of his saddle, one of his coiled hennaed ringlets escaping from under a high Persian lambskin hat, his High Excellency the Governor was a nine-year-old child with large sad eyes. He was a puppet of his father, Zil-es-Sultan, whose influence dominated two-fifths of Persia, so when the Zil said the child must go to the mountains to escape the fever his tutors hurriedly packed the little governor's bags. But perhaps the child was his father's son: he outwitted his tutors and rode down to the valley to satisfy his curiosity about the foreigners. Before he mounted his grey Arab pony to ride away, Jane photographed him, a dignified little person and already willful.

Marcel was invited to lunch by the deputy governor's Persian doctor and his doctor son. The younger man, a former pupil of the French Dr Tholozan in Tehran, was attempting to introduce European medical concepts to his orthodox father. He asked Marcel's opinion of using arsenic to treat the deputy governor. 'He's very ill,' the father agreed, 'the quinine we've given him has done nothing. How much of this rat poison is it safe to give?'[3]

Recognising how worried they were if they deigned to consult a foreigner, Marcel asked why they didn't confer with Dr Olding, a real doctor. A circuitous answer revealed it was a matter of saving face: a resident foreigner could not treat his High Excellency, the deputy governor. While Marcel would soon be gone, they hoped Dr Olding would stay.

During Marcel's consultation, Jane was entertained in the *anderun* by both men's wives. Unable to decide who belonged to the doctor and who to the doctor's son, Jane shrugged. Did it matter? Their lives would be equally narrow whoever owned them. The Shirazi ladies' only conversation was: how much money do you have, how many wives does your husband have, and how long are the skirts in Tehran?

The deputy governor's health deteriorated and Marcel was commanded to the Arg, the citadel, the residence of his High Excellency. Although guarded by four towers, the fortress was completely vulnerable. The sentries lay on the ground in the grip of malaria, their rifles propped against the wall of the portal. When Marcel and his escort entered the courtyard a recumbent soldier opened his eyes, then with a great sigh rolled over and returned to fevered sleep. In the *talar* Marcel found the deputy governor, Sahib Divan, stretched out on a pile of quilts and cushions, surrounded by clerics, clerks and his Muslim doctors. His violet satin robe did not flatter his flushed cheeks or jaundiced eyeballs, nor match his hennaed beard – only its silver regrowth harmonised with the violet. When he struggled to rise from the carpet his legs refused. His conversation was more powerful – Marcel thought him very astute and wondered why the Shirazis hated him.

Over the bubbling sounds of the *kalians*, Marcel advised, in his most dignified manner, on arsenic treatment. The clerks were appalled, and recommended tincture of Koran. The clerics quoted the holy writings, then weakened – they would accept arsenic but only if it was put into little stitched sachets and rubbed on the stomach twice daily accompanied by tincture of Koran. The Protector of Foreigners hiccupped and suggested six bottles of good Shirazi wine with tincture of Koran. Marcel shrugged at the

H.H.E. The Governor of Shiraz

hopelessness of medical practice that had not moved on since Avicenna, and said, yes, the little sachets would suffice, if Sahib Divan would go at once to the mountains.

Although the Zil-es-Sultan had ordered that Jane and Marcel were to be admitted to mosques and madrasas, no invitations had yet arrived from the reigning clergy. Lethargic from intermittent attacks of fever, the Dieulafoys waited in the garden, receiving visitors when they could, accepting invitations if enticed.

'Go,' advised the Superintendent when the Protector of Foreigners invited them to breakfast, 'dinner will be too late.' The Protector had spent several years with a Persian delegation in London, where he never learned English yet became proficient in French, skipping over the Channel whenever possible to take cooking lesson with a noted French chef.

When the Dieulafoys arrived at his house it was obvious he had already taken pre-breakfast sustenance. The only other guest was a frightened old sayyid who was losing his sight. Giggling and sitting down abruptly on his blue and white Na'in carpet, the Protector plunged straight to the matter of the knife. 'Can the foreign doctor, Dr Olding, cut out the sayyid's cataracts and give him back his eyes?'

'Certainly,' said Marcel, 'but not yet, they are not quite ready to be operated.'

The Protector turned to the blue turban and told him, 'It is as I said, they will lie you on a table and they will take out your eyes and lie them on the table beside you, first one and then the other, and they will slice your eyes, and then they will put them back in your head.'[4] He giggled hysterically.

The sayyid turned green, then white, then excused himself, 'I am your Excellencies' slave, for the love of Allah permit your slave to depart.'

The sayyid's stricken face removed Jane's appetite for the French food laid out on a white cloth. Bitterly regretful, she reproached herself, 'For eight months I have been in this country of kebabs and rice. When will I taste the French cuisine again?'

While the Protector lay on his carpet and snored, Marcel did justice to the feast.

Being curious about the Shirazi world outside the Bagh-i-Sheykh, Jane happily accepted a picnic invitation. Early one morning, when the sun was barely above the horizon and the jasmine just beginning to release its scent, she and Marcel rode down onto the plain and continued eastward, bypassing the city, to the far end of the valley, where the ruins of a palace perched high on a ridge. Its view swept across the upland plain it had once dominated and leapt up to the snow-topped mountains beyond. The upper ruins were too despoiled to identify, but were probably Achaemenid. On a lower terrace the deliberately disfigured faces of undoubtedly Sasanid carvings gave no clues as to who they might have represented, but looked inscrutably into the shade of walnut trees, where servants were spreading a white cloth among the geraniums and setting it with crystal glasses and monogrammed table silver. How different, Jane thought, from her meals laid on the dusty ground along the caravan routes. On the plain below, mudbrick walls defined the many private gardens scattered extravagantly about.

Only a traveller who has crossed a Persian desert on camel, horse or mule as Jane had done, and arrived at a stand of shady trees, heard the music of running water and the song of birds can fully understand why the Persian word for garden is Paradise. A Persian garden represents escape from the heat and flies of the plain, from the dust and noise of the bazaar and, especially, flight from the prosaic to the spiritual. While European gardens are a continuation of the landscape and an elaboration of its admired features, the Persian garden is an interruption, an interjection in its harsh environment. It differs as much from the Occidental notion of a garden as Persian domestic architecture differs from the Western suburban style. Both garden and dwelling are based on a different premise in the East. Western houses embrace the outlook, the view, and sit confidently within their surroundings, but the introverted Eastern house turns its back on the hostility of its world and puts a pool and flowers in its central courtyard to counter what is outside.

A Persian garden contrives a fantasy to overcome reality. Magnificent though the Iranian landscape is, it is not comforting in the way of even the smallest green hill. Stark treeless mountains rearing up from a desertscape have a spiritual dimension but never a domestic appeal; their grandeur is on a different scale. A garden's mudbrick wall stops the searing wind; the bubbling of fountains and the sound of water trickling down a tile-lined course replace its scream. Inside the wall the glaring, burning sun is rejected by a canopy of trees, and in their shade, instead of rocks, there are the fruits of apricots and oranges and pomegranates; instead of sand studded with camelthorn, irises and roses rise from the ground. Small pavilions provide the comfort that is never available in the uninhabited desert. To enter a Persian garden is to intrude on a dream.

Her host indicated the gardens where the poets Sa'adi and Hafiz slumber. 'If the Shirazis love their gardens, they love their poets more,' he said.

True, thought Jane, knowing that even the illiterate could quote a stanza appropriate to a moment of joy or sorrow or despair. Sa'adi, author of the *Gulistan* (Flower Garden), the *Bustan* (Fruit Garden), and the more accessible *Divan*, lay buried behind high walls in a forlorn, neglected garden east of the city. Born in Shiraz in about 1209, Sa'adi took to the road, visiting many countries before returning to his native city to transform the fruits of his wanderings into proverbs and homilies. After thirty years of literary moralising he died, respected for the purity of his style and the richness of his vocabulary, yet his memory was tainted by a suspicion of Sunni sympathies. When his headstone was destroyed by a fanatical mujtahid it posed a conundrum for his followers: dare they replace it?

Black cypress tower above the walls of the garden perfumed by orange trees where Hafiz lies among rose bushes. Jane found his tomb[5] covered by a slab of 'yellow Yazdi marble' – alabaster – the encircling headstones of his admirers perhaps discouraging those whom he advised:

> Sit on my tomb, friends, with mirth of minstrel and flagon,
> so shall I rise from the grave dancing, aglow with desire.
> To the rose garden take the cushion, so that of the lovely one you
> can take the lip and kiss the cheek. Wine you may drink and the
> rose, smell.

Hafiz's more than 6000 Sufi poems are filled with images of roses and wine, of sex and drunkenness, of sensual pleasures and the release of drugs. Combining joyfulness and mysticism, they celebrate nature's beauty, music and lovers' grief, flowers and nightingales, 'all of which are but metaphors for God and God's immortal beauty,' suggested her host. Perhaps they are, thought Jane, but they certainly mirror the pleasures of the young Shirazi nobles and their friends partying in the gardens below.

Riding past their gates, Jane had seen elegantly dressed men going in. Now the songs of minstrels and the strains of the rebeck drifted up to the ridge where she sat. Laughter escaped over the high walls. She saw servants slipping through the gates with dishes of cooked food, baskets of fruit, and flagons of wine and she smelled the aroma of roasting lamb. She imagined the food being spread on a cloth in a pavilion, the *kalians* being lit, perhaps a dancing boy adding a frisson to the late afternoon before the men called for their horses and galloped off to reach the city before the gates closed.

Jane knew women were not invited to the parties despite the poet's serenades to their charms. They rarely visited the gardens, although a contemporary recorded seeing in the Dilgusha, the deputy governor's garden a little below Sa'adi's on the hillside, 'a large party of closely veiled ladies, waddling along like bales of blue cotton set up on end.'[6] Always enclosed by walls and veils, the women lacked vitamin D and suffered from rickets, they aged quickly and lost their beauty early. Every foreigner fortunate enough to glimpse them remarked how lovely the Persian girls were at puberty, particularly Shirazi girls, and regretted how soon they became 'ugly old crones'. Worse, their inactive lifestyle prevented them developing the muscles needed to deliver their babies quickly and safely. They suffered agonies in childbirth and death in childbed was tragically frequent.

That evening Jane reclined in her garden, where the golden leaves of the plane trees glowed in the moonlight against an indigo velvet sky like a medallion at the centre of a carpet. Everyone else being too ill to dine, the cook had served her dinner of chicken steeped in pomegranate juice in a small pavilion. She opened her book of Hafiz poetry, wondering whether its mingling of gaiety and mysticism was an inspirational allegory or a celebration of the pleasures of a sensuous, sybaritic life. She recognised that the significance of the two Shirazi poets was greater than the beauty of their verses – they had consolidated and locked in the Persian language at a critical time. When Firdauzi wrote his *Shahname* in the eleventh century, the language of their Arab conquerors had almost obliterated Persian. *The Shahname* resurrected the old pahlavi Persian as 'new Persian', Farsi, but it was the appeal of Hafiz's verses that made Farsi the language of ordinary people, not only of scholars. Its musical cadenzas formed their speech patterns.

The poets' influence in their home city makes Shirazi speech the purest and most melodious in Iran. Hearing it spoken all around her, Jane realised how much her Farsi differed, fluent though it was. Getting out her Persian grammar, she struggled with the difficulty of choosing a verb appropriate to the addressed person's status. 'The Persian,' she concluded, 'is very punctilious on the question of etiquette, attaching the greatest importance to details such as judging whether to address a stranger as an equal, a superior or an inferior.' Not wanting to offend 'a governor or a person of importance,' with her usual ingenuity she solved the problem by 'adopting the simplest diplomatic formula. As soon as we meet . . . I begin by declaring that I have not mastered the subtlety and elegance of their tongue, having only the muleteers met along the way for my tutors.'[7]

Impatiently waiting for an invitation to visit the city, Jane closed Hafiz and put away her Farsi primer to read history.

For much of its past Shiraz was an unimportant country town, a mere staging post on the Silk Route to the port of Bushire on the Persian Gulf. Ironically, it was the two dynasties that most ravaged Persia that brought Shiraz to a peak of beauty, enlightenment, and influence – the Mongols (1220–1380) and Tamerlane's terrifying Timurids (1380–1502). During the thirteenth and fourteenth centuries Shiraz was one of the greatest cities in the Islamic world, home to scholars and brilliant artists. Illuminated manuscripts and exquisite painted miniatures poured from its studios, its calligraphers set the scriptorial standards for Korans, while the verses of Sa'adi and Hafiz spread throughout the world and at home consoled the Shirazis through subsequent defeats. In the fifteenth century its architects and designers took the creative Persian genius as far as central Asia, where they built the Registan in Tamerlane's city of Samarkand, and into India, where its artists and craftsmen created the beauty of the Mughal cities. A Shirazi architect designed the Taj Mahal.

According to the Shirazis, when Tamerlane came to their city he sent for Hafiz to chastise him for his verse, 'I would give Tamerlane's great cities of Bukhara and Samarkand, if I could kiss the black beauty spot on my beloved's cheek.'

'Yes, Sire, and it is by such acts of generosity that your slave has been reduced to the poverty which you see,' the poet replied.

The long-awaited invitation received at last, the Dieulafoys were shocked by the shattered buildings, the dusty unpaved streets of the capital of Fars province, a city ranked third in commerce and population after Tehran and Tabriz. Eclipsed by Isfahan when the Safavids came to power, its architectural treasures lost through earthquake and civil war, Shiraz was a vista of neglect and decay. Perversely, the great Persian city lying in the very heart of ancient Fars, surrounded by the archaeological jewels of its two great dynasties, the Achaemenids and the Sasanids, had almost nothing older than the eighteenth century, when during a third period of glory Shiraz was rebuilt by a new dynasty, the Zands.

The Zands came out of the Zagros Mountains, the tumbled chains of geological upheaval that define the western edge of the Fars plateau, and rode into a power vacuum created by the murder of Nadir Shah in 1747. Despite ridding Persia of the Afghanis, who had destroyed Isfahan and ruined Shiraz, the tyrant Nadir Shah brought disaster to his country and his neighbours, bankruptcy to the Persian people, misery to his family and outrage to the clerics in his attempt to integrate Sunni theology into Shi'a Islamic doctrine. No cruelty, no extortion, no territorial ambition was beyond him. Glad to be rid of him, the Persians welcomed the compassionate Karim Khan Zand and his renewal of their country.

As Jane toured the city it became obvious that the Shirazi heart was still held by the Zands and particularly by Karim Khan, the dynasty's founder. The main street was called the Zand and the main bazaar was the Bazaar-i-Vekil, Vekil al-dawla, Guardian of the people, being the name Karim Khan adopted when he declined the title of shah. Mosques and madrasas, city walls and the Arg, she was told, had all been either built or restored by the Zands during their short moment of power in the second half of the eighteenth century (1747–96). But however strong the Zand memory, the Qajar reality of cracked walls, broken minarets and collapsed caravanserais was not being addressed by the present malaria-ridden inhabitants of the Zands' former capital.

With boots well polished and trousers freshly pressed, Jane strode along beside Marcel, absently flicking her riding whip as the mullah led through a narrow passageway into the jume mosque. Shirazis prided themselves on being more intellectually sophisticated and open-minded than other Persians, and more aware of the outside world through their trade initiatives. Consequently, the few faithful gossiping between the pillars were unconcerned as the foreigners inspected the mosque. At the tomb of yet another of Imam Reza's family, this one his brother Mir Ahmad, known as Shah Cheragh, King of the Lamp, Jane photographed its details without comment from the friendly, unconcerned mullah. Jane inspected the New mosque, which despite its name contains some remains of the pre-Mongol original, and then asked to see the Madrasa i-Khan located in the vegetable market at the far end of the Bazaar-i-Vekil.

The mullah climbed into the mosque's galleries and led her out onto the roof, assuring her, 'This is the shortest route, Excellency. All good Shirazis find their way as easily on the terraces as they do in the streets and bazaars. Up here they don't have to swallow the dust kicked up by the horses or leave when the sun sets.' Jane's camera captured the sleepy Persians in high lambskin hats lolling against the madrasa's shallow pudding-like domes, taking time out from the noise and crush below, and the attenuated dome of the Vekil mosque rising from a narrow neck to stab the sky. Descending into the bazaar, she was charmed by its spaciousness and its elegant arches reaching up to the light-giving bubble domes. If, in the cultural decline that followed the death of Shah Abbas, 'Persia ceased to live,'[8] the vaulted Bazaar-i-Vekil, the most beautiful bazaar in all Iran, must represent a little after-death flutter, Jane thought. But the vibrant cuerda seca tiles in the Madrasa i-Khan she dismissed as excessively pretty.

Zand glory came crashing down, quite literally, at the hands of their centuries-long rivals, the Qajar tribe, its leader an enormously fat eunuch, Aga Mohammad, who carried the deepest, most bitter hatred for the Zands – in a game of tit for tat played as atrocity for atrocity the Zands had castrated him. After a decade of subversion in northern Iran, Aga Mohammad besieged Shiraz in 1796. The city walls were strong and the Shirazis resolute, but it seemed to the trusted Zand vizier, *hadji* Ibrahim Khan, that defeat was inevitable and his head would be among the first to go. Consequently, the trusted vizier opened secret negotiations with the Qajars. If, as long as he lived, Aga Mohammad would guarantee to honour and protect *hadji* Ibrahim Khan, the gates of Shiraz would be opened.

And so it came to pass that one dark night the Qajars flooded through an undefended unlocked gate and set about looting, raping and destroying with a ferocity almost matching that of the Mongols. The bureaucracy was slaughtered, but not the trusted Zand vizier, *hadji* Ibrahim Khan, who was loaded with honours. Aga Mohammad Shah kept his word. As long as he lived, he honoured and protected *hadji* Ibrahim Khan. Sadly for Aga Mohammad his reign was short; sadly for *hadji* Ibrahim Khan, the shah had instructed his nephew and heir, Fath Ali Shah, 'as soon as I am dead . . . be rid of the traitor and all his brood, for one who did not scruple to betray a master who had shown him nothing but kindness will certainly not hesitate to do the same should opportunity offer. Let not one of that accursed family remain.'[9]

Aga Mohammad's headstone was barely in place before the bloodshed began. *Hadji* Ibrahim Khan was thrown into a vat of boiling oil and everywhere his relations were hunted out and killed, though a few were merely castrated and blinded. Only one was untouched, a boy child, who for some reason, perhaps pity, perhaps negligence, escaped the vengeance. That child's grandson, Sahib Divan, became the deputy governor of Shiraz in 1880, and in that story Marcel found the answer to why the deputy governor was reviled. The city that could never forgive his ancestor's treachery heaped its hatred on Sahib Divan.

With treachery bringing the Qajars to power and Tehran becoming their capital, Shiraz was once again a backwater. A severe earthquake in 1824, in which, according to the Qajar chronicler Hasan-e-Fasa'i', 'only a few thousand people perished', brought down buildings both old and new. Another in 1852 increased the devastation. Plague, famine, riots, heavy taxation, even a deputy governor who 'died . . . from the illness of lethargy'[10] added to the Shirazis' misery. Seeking solace in courtyards and gardens, they never realised their pools were another source of their distress.

Delightful as some aspects of Jane's Shiraz sojourn were, malaria was forcing her back to the road. Far from recovering after the rigours of travel, each day saw one or the other of the Dieulafoys ill. Some days it was Marcel shivering and sweating, on other days it was Jane delirious and fevered. The deputy governor had gone to the mountains, but in Shiraz the telegraph office staff and all their acquaintances were still suffering intermittent bouts. Even the gardener, most importantly the gardener, was too ill to work, so the ponds became more and more stagnant, the goldfish suffocated, and the wrigglers hatched into mosquitoes. Taking their meals of human blood, the mosquitoes spread the malaria parasite among their victims. Jane did not know the parasites' life cycle but she knew the city was dangerous and that they must get away.

The Dieulafoys had telegraphed to France for funds for the next part of their journey and until the money arrived they were anchored. Impatient but not willing to waste a chance, Jane continued to explore the city – when she was well enough – and, discreetly, its people.

When she recognised some women by their dress as Babi, she approached carefully. Having met Babis in Zendjan, she knew the women were veiled only to escape notice: enclosure and a restrictive dress code were not part of the Babi ethic, which also forebad polygamy and professed respect and dignity for women, a view that accorded with Jane's sympathies but aroused the ire of the traditionalists, women's freedom being irrevocably linked in the oriental mind to profligacy and immorality.

The sect was founded by a sayyid, mirza Ali Mohammad, born in 1820. He returned from a pilgrimage to Mecca and long study in Karbala and declared himself the Bab, the Gateway to spiritual truth, which would lead to universal justice and peace. Deploring the mullahs' venality and the corruption associated with the religious foundations, he demanded new ethical standards. His message fell like rain on the parched Persian ground and by 1845 the Bab had too many followers, many of them mullahs, mujtahids and *hadjis*, for the Qajar power holders to ignore. Imprisoned, the Bab filled his days refining his beliefs and codifying doctrines to sustain his persecuted, yet ever-growing number of adherents, who eventually had to be dealt with. The massacres at Zendjan and Yazd were horrendous, but nothing compared with the Shirazi slaughter.

In New Julfa Jane had learned of the atrocities committed in Isfahan only four years before against the Babis. She did not want to compromise the Shirazi women, but she did want to meet them. They told her about the only woman given heroine status in Persia. Persian poets celebrate women's erotic charms, but to honour a Persian woman for her actions was a new phenomenon.

The Kazvini poet, known as the Eyes' Solace for her beauty, threw off her veil and preached the Bab's message. Not a political message, it was a religious and ethical perspective only, but for it she was hideously tortured. After her cruel death, she was renamed Zerin Taj, Crown of Gold, and celebrated for her courage.

It seemed to Jane in 1881 that Persian women had little chance of ever living an open, free life.

Jane quickly understood that Shiraz was a complex society with many strands. While most mullahs were ignorant and fanatical, venal and corrupt, there were some learned and truly devout clerics and mujtahids who interpreted their role as guardians of the people. Appalled by Nasr-al-Din's extravagance, they considered the shah's arbitrary power a tyranny and deplored that civil law was a matter of personal caprice, not an impartial code. They knew the clerics' corruption had made Shari'a law a subject of bitter humour and were embarrassed by the clergy's betrayal of simple people who trusted them as their last refuge against injustice.

Some radical, some reactionary, yet all considered their Islamic duty of 'enjoining the good and forbidding the evil' committed them to struggle for 'just' government. 'Just' government, they considered, was honest government by an uncorrupt ruler, a very Persian entwining of Islamic thought with the haunting Zoroastrian tradition: only the virtuous should rule and if he go astray, obedience should be withdrawn from him.

Many lay Shirazis also wanted reform. Renowned for their subtlety and intellectual sharpness, more open to change than other Persians, Shirazis recognised that Persia was in many ways medieval and that corruption and intrigue were constraining constitutional development. They were stimulated by the intellectual currents entering Persia in the baggage of returning diplomats and wealthy travellers, by merchants trading ideas with their export/import goods, and by the elixir of the Islamic modernist movement seeping in from more advanced Muslim countries. A whisper of support from a most unexpected direction encouraged them. The grand vizier who had accompanied the shah to Europe in 1878 had returned with dreams of a better educated population and with pragmatic views on the benefits of improved roads and a system of railways. Haunted by his predecessors' fate, he played a difficult hand, balancing the shah's confidence against self-interested critics plotting to bring him down.

Nasr-al-Din Shah saw the reforming clerics as potential leaders of a popular uprising, the daily nightmare of every despot. Especially in the bigger cities, the balance between order and disorder was precarious and the shah knew it could be tipped as easily by a religious fanatic as by a food riot.

Only a weak boy of seventeen when he began his reign, Nasr-al-Din had for thirty-three years concentrated on centralising power in Tehran, restraining the independence of local warlords such as the Khan of the Bakhtiari tribes, and battling the ulama to assert temporal power over spiritual power in the tradition of the Seljuks. He knew the clerics and sayyids despised him as a Turcoman, unable to claim religious legitimacy through descent from the prophet. Aware that the people of Fars thought themselves superior to Turcoman newcomers, he would never condescend to visit them.

Previous shahs feared only foreign invaders and popular uprisings, but Nasr-al Din was unsettled by two vague concepts creeping into his country like mist across a lake. Blown in by the wind of incoming foreigners and travelling Persians, the concepts were individual freedom and the supremacy of an impartial written law, chilling ideas to a Muslim despot.

Fearing there was something beyond his grasp he took himself to Europe in 1873, despite the resistance of the clergy to such a totally unprecedented venture, shahs having formerly gone abroad only at the head of an army. Even his visit to the Shi'a holy places in Mesopotamia in 1870, the first royal pilgrimage outside the country, had been criticised by the mullahs. The shah had wept beside the tomb of Hussein at Karbala, gone as a penitent to the shrine of Ali, the first Shi'a Imam, at Najaf, and had visited the tombs of the tenth and eleventh Imams at Samarra. Although the visit's second purpose was diplomatic: to reinforce peaceful co-existence with Iraq's Ottoman rulers, it pleased neither clergy nor lay people.

When he set off to Russia in 1873 Nasr-al-Din's tour faced great problems, not least the *anderun*, as Ziba *khanum* had told Jane in Isfahan. From Russia the shah went on womanless to France and England. All three countries, jockeying for influence in the strategic area straddled by Persia, offered extravagant hospitality and flattered Nasr-al Din's ego. On the homeward journey his baggage overflowed with gifts.

On a second visit in 1878 the tsar and all the princes turned out for him in Moscow, and in Europe the foreign press welcomed him exuberantly. He was present for two days at the Congress of Berlin, which so unsatisfactorily settled the Russo–Turkish War, and for twenty-two days he triumphed in Paris. He brought home more than the camel loads of florid European furniture whose cost upset his subjects. Filled with an exaggerated sense of his importance in the world, he reinforced the Persians' certainty of their superiority to the despised foreigners. Worse, Europe's apparent adulation convinced him that Persia did not need change. Industrialisation, roads and railways, written laws and especially constitutional government were unnecessary. The misconceptions the shah brought home did not match his grand vizier's dreams.

Sitting by the pond in the garden of the English telegraph station, Jane turned from Persia's tribulations to self-examination and laughed at what she found. 'How I have changed,' she wrote, 'I don't get upset when I hear of someone given the bastinado, I'm not appalled at the governor's venality or the cupidity of wives preparing for widowhood. I am late to my appointments and now I find that somewhere between Tehran and Shiraz I have lost three days!'[11] What did three days matter in a journey of fourteen months?

Jane Dieulafoy aged 20, veteran of the Franco–Prussian War, wearing the grey blouse and trousers, uniform of a *franc-tireur*. Artist unknown. ROSSITER 2005

The enamelled-brick Frieze of the Archers excavated by Jane Dieulafoy in 1886. The Dieulafoy expedition retrieved the beautiful facades of Susa's palace, revealing that its walls and staircases were finished with colourful, shining enamelled bricks.

Top left: A visitor is
diminished by the great
Frieze of Lions, Musée du
Louvre, Paris. Excavated
1885 by Jane Dieulafoy, it
once decorated a wall of
Darius I's 2500-year-old
palace at Susa. ROSSITER 2005

Top right: Two details
from Frieze of the Lions.
ROSSITER 2005

Left: Detail, 2500-year-old
enamelled bricks from Susa.
ROSSITER 2005

Top: Detail of an Archer's tunic showing the cloisons that were filled with coloured enamel before the siliceous brick was refired. Excavated by Jane Dieulafoy 1886. ROSSITER 2005

Centre: A parapet built by the Sasanians from recycled Achaemenid enamelled bricks: 'panels with a whirling, spinning circular motif in apple green, dark green and yellow', wrote Jane in 1885. ROSSITER 2005

Bottom: Staircase adjacent to the parapet shown above, also made from recycled Achaemenid enamelled bricks, the spinning motif delimited by upper and lower rows of triangles and chains of rosettes. ROSSITER 2005

Top: A bullhead capital which capped one of the 36 huge columns on Susa's apadana. It held the wooden beams (shown in section) that supported the roof. Its huge size diminishes the door of the Dieulafoy gallery, musée du Louvre, Paris. PHOTO © RMN-GRAND PALAIS (MUSÉE DU LOUVRE) / HERVÉ LEWANDOWSKI / FRANCK RAUX

Bottom: Damaged bull-head capital at Susa 2004. Note the 'saddle' which carried the wooden roof beams, and the Achaemenid rosettes banding its neck. ROSSITER 2004

Top: Twelfth-century Seljuk tomb, its eight sides patterned with turquoise-blue enamelled bricks inserted into a background of soft-red unglazed bricks. 'The marriage of turquoise blue enamel and the rose tint of bricks is of exquisite delicacy', Marcel wrote.
ROSSITER 2004

Bottom: Detail of Seljuk tomb. Unglazed bricks projecting from the plane form intricate laced designs, their shadows accentuating the textural effect. Beneath a muqarnas cornice is an inscription frieze: 'Everything passes. May this remain'.
ROSSITER 2004

Top: Oil painting of the Blue Mosque, Tabriz, by Frenchman Jules Laurens, 1872. In 1881 Jane was shocked by its derelict state. Musée Fabre de Montpellier Agglomération – photograph by Frédéric Jaulmes

Bottom: The cable moulding spiralling around the portal arch of the Blue Mosque, Tabriz, had lost many more of its turquoise blue tiles by 2001. Much of the mosaic tiling had also fallen. Rossiter 2001

Top: Moulded faience tile with dragon and cloud scroll enamelling, dated 1275 AD, Il Khanid era. A hexagonal tile of the same era with similar dragon-decoration inspired Jane's passion for enamelled tiles and bricks. © Victoria and Albert Museum, London

Bottom left: Moulded enamelled cornice corner tile, Qazvin. Cobalt blue kufic lettering is raised on a lustre ground with white leaves and tendrils and Koran verses in nakshi script. Made in Kashan. Rossiter 2013

Bottom right: Glazed ceramic tiles decorated with metallic lustre from the imamzadde Yaya, Varamin. Each design is surrounded by Koranic quotations. Made in Kashan 1262 AD. Much of the bright silver and copper lustre had lost its shine; Jane admired their subtle delicacy. © Victoria and Albert Museum, London

Top left: Portico, Shah Mosque, Isfahan, a riot of patterns and techniques. Turquoise cable moulding separates (left) mosaic-tiled muqarnas inside the half dome from (right) cuerda seca tiles on the flat facade. JOHN TIDMARSH

Top right: Tile mosaic with floral design, Iran (probably Isfahan), 1450–1500 AD. The stylised lotus flowers were made as composite tiles like that on the next page (bottom), then embedded in the plaster matrix alongside the simpler shapes.
© VICTORIA AND ALBERT MUSEUM, LONDON

Bottom: Cuerda seca tiles, Shiraz, which Jane thought 'excessively pretty'. ROSSITER 2001

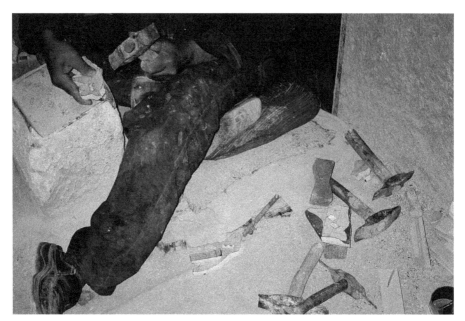

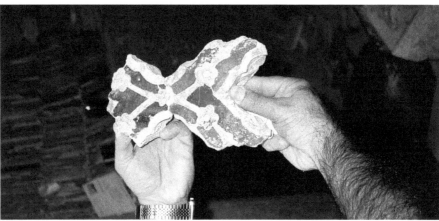

Top: Craftsman at work in Isfahan 2004 repairing damaged mosaic tile panels. ROSSITER 2004

Centre: Damaged mosaic tile section to be repaired or replicated. ROSSITER 2004

Bottom: A composite tile made in Isfahan 2004. Various holes were cut out of a cobalt blue tile, then the spaces filled with complementary shapes cut from other coloured tiles. Such a flower would then be included in a tile mosaic like that on the previous page (top right). ROSSITER 2004

Top left: Wall painting, Ali Qapu, Isfahan. Painting and other arts flourished under the tolerant Shah Abbas 1642–1660. The opulent fabrics shown reflect the buoyant economy. ROSSITER 2001

Top right: Riding down the pass. ROSSITER 2001

Bottom: Wall painting in Chihil Sutun, Isfahan, built ca. 1644 during the reign of Safavid Shah Abbas. Shah Ismael is shown defeating the Uzbeks in 1511 AD. JOHN TIDMARSH

North chamber, jume mosque, Isfahan, 'the masterpiece of medieval Persian architecture',
Seljuk dynasty, 1088. Tri-lobed squinches support the dome, colonettes lead the eye
upwards, the brickwork is exquisite. JOHN TIDMARSH

Top: Persepolis at dusk, 2004. Few of the apadana's mighty columns remain.
ROSSITER 2004

Bottom: Relief carving at Persepolis, a stone catalogue of Achaemenid footwear.
ROSSITER 2004

Top: Remains of a fifth century AD Sasanian palace at Sarvistan, which Marcel, ill and delirious, labelled Achaemenid. Rounded arches springing from short round columns were unknown to the earlier dynasty. JOHN TIDMARSH

Bottom: Sasanian palace, Sarvistan. Squinches, semicircular scallop-shell shapes, bridge the corners of a square room to support the circular base of the dome, an architectural legacy of the Sasanians. JOHN TIDMARSH

Top: Darius I's palace, Susa, 2001. Excavated stubs of the apadana's huge columns diminish the figure on the far side. The modern brick wall is to stabilise the site. ROSSITER 2001

Bottom: Column base 'among the spiny bushes', Susa 2004. ROSSITER 2004

Top: Stone billboard, Sakavand 500 BC. A Zoroastrian priest prays at a fire altar above an empty tomb. The author accessed the carving, 350 m up a steep cliff, wearing full hijab. ANON 2001

Bottom: The landscape that captivated Jane, 'angular mountains rising abruptly from the plain, colours ranging from magenta through burnt umber to violet and even bright yellow'. ROSSITER 2004

Chapter 11
South to the Sasanids

Susa was still Jane's inspiration. It had long ago sparked her imagination and from Marcel's first mention of a Persian tour she was determined Susa would be included, even though she knew there was almost nothing to see except a huge earthen mound. It was the site of ancient Shushan, the winter capital of Achaemenids and Sasanids, identified by the Englishman Loftus in 1852 when his excavator's spade made a few productive hits. Before any significant revelations could be made, however, he was driven away by troubled tribesmen.

Jane's vision of the city had sustained her through hardship and illness and was still propelling her onwards, despite an increasing fascination with enamelled tiles and bricks. Since the revelatory moment in Tabriz, Jane had hunted them out in mosques and ruins, yet ceramics had not displaced Susa and she did not expect to find them in that long-destroyed city.

Marcel was equally committed to the Sasanids, believing their achievements were seminal to both Seljuk and European architecture. Although Sasanid hegemony had extended over a far greater area, the southern part of Iran was the dynasty's homeland.

The Dieulafoys consulted the map specially prepared in France 'to inform the journey of Mme Dieulafoy from Tiflis to Baghdad, Susa and Mohammerah.'

Their plan to reach Susa by travelling northwest from Shiraz through the Bakhtiari-held mountains had been aborted at Eqlid when they were unable to contact the Ilkhani, so they looked for an alternative that would meet both their objectives. If they were to drop down to the Persian Gulf, sail up its waters into the Shatt al Arab, then follow the Karun River up into Susiane province as far as Ahwaz, they could slip across the plains to Susa and Jane would be content. And if they used a circuitous southwesterly route to reach the Gulf, one leading through the ancient Sasanid heartland and old Achaemenid territories, Marcel would be satisfied. It seemed very simple, the black and white lines on the page showing nothing of the terrible passes, the primitive villagers and hostile tribespeople they would encounter.

They knew the route was dangerous. The governor of Fars, the shah's uncle Ferhad Mirza, had extinguished rebellions in the southern parts of Fars and along the Persian Gulf in 1877, 1878 and 1879 with such forcefulness and brutality that the rebels had not dared raise their heads in 1880. Though Ferhad Mirza had since been transferred to Tabriz and Zil-es-Sultan was now governor, 1881 had so far been undisturbed. The Dieulafoys weighed the risks. Putting their trust in the instruction Zil-es-Sultan had issued to all the southern governors – to ensure the safety of the foreigners or answer with their life and to apply a double number of strokes from the bastinado to any person who offended them – they decided to chance it. Their courage was never in question.

Travel arrangements for the Dieulafoy enterprise were Jane's responsibility. The three independent caravans she had already run had taken them safely from the Persian border to Tabriz, around the Tehran hinterland, and from Saveh to Qom. Those journeys had traversed well-garrisoned territories, where the roads were busy and the risk of attack relatively low. Striking out on a lonely track through the south required more caution. To avoid attracting robbers she addressed their cumbersome fifteen mule loads of baggage, now increased by additions from the Shiraz bazaars, to the governor of Bushire, entrusting their delivery to a tcharvadar bachy assembling a large caravan for the shorter well-frequented westerly route which dropped off the plateau through four terrible passes. Although the Dieulafoys' chosen route descended more gradually to the coast through less dramatic passes, it was 100 kilometres longer and would take an extra three weeks even with minimal baggage. Jane packed only her photographic equipment, a change of clothes, kitchen items and bedding.

Her biggest worry was money. Their finance, telegraphed from France and received by a Shirazi merchant, presented as an enormous bulk of Persia's coinage. Jane knew that the sleeping Dieulafoy heads would always have to rest on bags of hard silver kran, and while they travelled their revolvers must always be at the ready to defend saddle bags and waistbelts.

Engaging a highly recommended tcharvadar bachy, Jane paid him half the agreed price of the mules, the remainder to be settled in Bushire. For some obscure reason, Marcel paid in full for two beautiful saddle horses paraded in front of him. Jane shrugged, sent her servant off with last-minute messages and took the cook shopping in the bazaar. As night fell she joyfully anticipated being on the road to Susa early next morning.

She was not. She paced up and down, flicking her boots with her riding whip, cursing the Persian attitude to time and the unreliability of the East. At nine there was no sign of the muleteer, at midday a messenger sent to the bazaar reported the horses were on their way, at three they arrived. But not the horses Marcel had paid for. Instead, outside the door were two broken down bags of bones, one wall-eyed, the other lame, and each had a deep sore where poorly padded and heavily loaded pack saddles had rubbed almost to the bone. Refusing to let their saddles be put on, Jane cursed the tcharvadar bachy, 'son of a burnt father', until he cried.

Discovering that Arabat, the Armenian servant so highly recommended by Père Pascal, was behind the scam Jane cursed his chicanery, but as no other horses were available the situation was irremediable. Did they want to spend another night feeding the Shiraz mosquitoes? With the tcharvadar bachy swearing to Allah and his prophet he would exchange the horses as soon as they got into the country, Jane and Marcel bowed to Persian venality and mounted. A farewell wave to the English telegraph officers and a lingering glance towards the sad little girls, and Jane led the caravan through the gates of the lovely but deadly Bagh-i-Sheykh. Two soldiers assigned by the governor brought up the rear, for without them the infidel dogs would be turned away from the villages when they looked for lodgings and would find the shutters down when they shopped for food in the bazaars.

Beyond the city's eastern gate the road passed through an avenue of rough cement cubes – the tombs of living malefactors when Ferhad Mirza governed Shiraz. For the offenders, piled one on top of another and mortar poured over their backs, leaving only heads and feet free to express remorse or ask forgiveness, death came too slowly, their family's anguish sometimes extending to days. Instructed on appointment to 'end depravity and punish criminals, to restore order and make the roads safe,'[1] for the prince no method had been too cruel. Jane could only hope the terrible message had been understood where she was going.

When night fell they stopped to sleep in a small pavilion inside the gate of Sahib Divan's lush Dilgusha garden. Although Jane ordered a midnight start, it was six before the caravan was assembled. Not wanting to cast any shadow on Marcel's happiness at heading at last into the Sasanid heartland, she shrugged off her anger and signalled the tcharvadar bachy to move off. It was a bad start and became worse. Within 300 metres of the gate her decrepit horse collapsed, throwing her to the ground. The rifle slung over her shoulder discharged and shot a hole in her jacket, missing her body by only a wisp of charred cloth. Her loaded revolvers were, fortunately, not cocked. 'Son of a dog,' swore the tcharvadar, and beat the poor horse until it staggered to its feet. Covered in dust and very shaken, Jane refused to remount. Instead she commandeered Arabat's mount, waving aside his protests that a saddle mule was unworthy of the little master, and ordered its wooden saddle removed and her own put on.

Cresting a pass they saw lying below a shining white expanse broken by scattered patches of mysterious pale blue. On its far side a range of pearl-grey mountains looked down at their reflection in open water, on the nearside a crust of dried salt marked the road meandering around the shore. Leaving the lake behind, they slipped through steep deep-grey mountains into an irrigated valley, which explained the squares of cotton, corn, barley and melons growing in the desert. There was no sign of villages, although rough guardhouses punctuated the gardens, and nothing to suggest the ruins that had tempted them to take the route.

Suddenly Arabat was lying in the dust, the tormented horse dead under him. Although Jane had steeled herself against the Persian attitude to animals, she was deeply grateful the beast's suffering was ended. The muleteers salvaged the horseshoes and redistributed the loads while she and Marcel rode on, but their meat had gone off and the bazaar was empty before they reached Kerabad at seven. The Dieulafoys dined forlornly on cucumbers and yoghurt and rolled out their bedding in a rat-infested room, where spiders stalked the ceiling and the earthen floor was 'like the back of a camel'. The intrepid Jane admitted in her diary she wanted to weep.

Fearing another malaria attack Marcel swallowed more than a gram of quinine before they set off at dawn – too much, yet not enough. As quinine and disease gripped, he slid semiconscious from his horse. At ten o'clock, with Marcel stretched on the ground in the burning sun and the soldiers warning against staying in the increasing heat without shelter, water for the horses, or wood to make a cooking fire, the tcharvadar bachy remembered a nearby ruin. Marcel was tied onto a mule and the caravan moved off toward a distant mud wall that suggested a village but revealed only a few wild, ragged nomads camped behind it. Placed in the shade of a doorway, Marcel continued to shiver, and the hours went by. Desperate to break the fever Jane ordered a fire, heated her saucepans and resorted to the old-fashioned therapy of 'blistering'. Whether that treatment on the skin of his stomach and the soles of his feet brought about a feeble recovery is doubtful; however, by nightfall Marcel was able to continue.

But to where? Sarvistan, said the guide, is four farsakhs distant, there is nowhere else. Jane knew the Persian farsakh meant anything from four to eight kilometres, so she guessed the distance to be about twenty kilometres, a long ride for a sick man, but they could not stay camped behind the wall. With Marcel disabled, Jane would have to stand watch all night. The muleteers knew very well what the saddlebags and money belts contained, the fierce nomads were on the move, and she had no confidence in the two soldiers. Pushing her helmet down firmly, she told the tcharvadars to pack and ordered one of the escort to ride on ahead to ensure the town gate would stay open.

For two days Marcel lay in the windowless, smoke-blackened hovel which the village headman assigned to the Dieulafoys. The least movement made his head explode, and he could swallow only the ricewater and pomegranate juice Jane forced on him. For herself, she starved. In a village without a caravanserai, etiquette demanded that when a party arrived too late to negotiate independent lodgings the headman must provide shelter, food and basic needs. The travellers, in effect, became his guests; at departure the 'guests' would make him an appropriate present. When Marcel was carried into his house in the middle of the night, Sarvistan's headman concluded the big foreigner was going to die. A living infidel was bad enough, a dead one polluting his village was not to be permitted. Fear of the Sahib Divan's vengeance prevented him from sending the foreigners packing directly – he knew more subtle ways to get rid of them.

Calling on Jane in the morning, 'I am your slave,' he said, 'Sarvistan is an unhealthy place with a poor climate, full of fever, and our water is polluted. The next village has good water. You will be much better off there. It is not far, only three farsakhs.'

She could not think of moving the older sahib until his complete recovery, Jane replied. Disregarding her vulnerability, she thanked him for his concern and waited for the usual provisions to be sent. None came. When the shifty-eyed, hard-featured headman returned with the same suggestion, which Jane again declined, she indicated that while Marcel was unable to eat she was rather hungry. Still nothing appeared. Realising she was being starved out, Jane called one of the soldiers to take her to the bazaar. He was appalled. 'Excellency, you cannot buy your own food! It would shame the headman. Besides, none of the merchants would dare to deal with you.'

At the pitiless headman's fourth empty-handed call, Jane lost her temper. 'If moving to another village would rid me of your visits and your counsel, be sure I would make the effort if it were possible. However, I will be staying here until the Sahib is fully recovered. Please do not honour me with such frequent calls.' She turned away to sponge Marcel's forehead. The headman showed no sign of leaving. 'And on your way out would you please shut the door,' she added.

On the second day Jane escaped the hovel and foiled the headman's plot. Sarvistan, at the centre of a rich plain and surrounded by gardens and orchards, was a prosperous town. In the bazaar the townspeople succumbed to her friendliness. They not only sold her provisions but proudly showed her a ruined Ilkhanid imamzadde. The tiles peeling from its walls could not compare with those at Kashan or Varamin, Jane considered, and did not linger but hurried back to cheer Marcel with the news that an ancient domed building lay not far from Sarvistan.

On the third morning Marcel woke feverless. Their host was stunned. 'Banquo's ghost sitting down at Macbeth's table did not frighten the thane nearly as much as the sight of my husband has terrified the whole entourage. The headman, the escort, the servants threw themselves flat on their faces before us and in no time the little pies, the eggs, the meat began to flow into our lodging,' Jane reported. Still angry, the little master drew herself up to her full height, looked straight into the hypocritical headman's shifty eyes and said to him, 'I pray to Allah that when you find yourself ill, far from your country, far from your family, you will receive the same hospitality you have given us.'

Paling, he turned away without a word, yet later had the audacity to ask Jane to photograph him. She would not be able to develop the plates before they left, she prevaricated. 'Bismillah,' he said, 'I'll send a servant with you to bring back the pictures when you wash them off.'

She let him pose and went through the motions, vowing, 'This servant boy is destined to see the country. I will make it my business that he does.'[2]

They rode for three hours down the valley, redolent with the scent of crushed herbs. Long before they reached the ruin they could see a domed silhouette standing alone on the plain without tree, fence or village. Closer, inside a ring of tumbled stone an old palace took shape, its outer walls crumbling, its doorways doorless, its rooms and galleries open to the winds and wild animals.

The muleteers drove the pack animals into the courtyard and lifted off the loads, hobbled them and turned them out to graze, then stretched out in one of the long lateral galleries where massive high-reaching arches supported the vaults. In the shade of a baked-brick dome rising above a square central room Jane and Marcel set up their equipment. Holed at one side, the circular dome was set on squinches. Carved and painted stucco dripped from broken walls. While Jane photographed, Marcel measured and made a careful sketch plan. The palace's architectural harmony, he concluded, was mathematical, the dimensions of the central chamber, main dome, and adjacent spaces all being simple multiples of the width of a single arch.

Why Marcel, who had come to Persia seeking the Sasanids, did not recognise the old palace as belonging to that dynasty is impossible to explain. 'It's Achaemenid,' he said. What was it about the architecture that misled him? At Persepolis and on the engraved Achaemenid tomb facades at Naqsh-i-Rustam he had seen their flat roofs supported by great wooden beams and had measured their high narrow pillars. Dome and squinch technology was unknown to Achaemenids. Yet here near Sarvistan Marcel looked at the thick rectangular columns set on short round stubs, saw how the springing of the vaults depended on their strength, and did not recognise Sasanid achievements. One can only assume three days of delirium had blunted his faculties.

The man who yesterday had been so ill worked on through the afternoon until it was too late to reach the next town before nightfall. Looking for a place to camp, the soldiers found a group of hairy, dirty dervishes inside a ruined imamzadde and evicted them. The 'holy ones' left behind more than their curses. Jane had barely closed her eyes before she was covered in vermin. She had become well acquainted with the Persian bedbug, but never an infestation such as this. When her shriek of disgust woke one of the soldiers, he burrowed out of his bedroll, examined the creatures dancing on his hennaed beard and told her, 'They will bring you good luck, they come from Mecca,' and burrowed in again.

In a lonely valley hedged by high mountains Marcel collapsed. They were heading for Darab, where carved stone monarchs that identify a ruined city as unmistakably Sasanid might have helped Marcel sort out his dynasties. After a day and a half of intense anxiety Jane turned the caravan round, back towards Shiraz. Accepting defeat was bitter, the risk of death worse. But Marcel soon became too ill to travel, even towards Shiraz.

The village where Jane nursed Marcel back to health lies in one of the upland valleys of the Zagros Mountains, an enormously long and very wide system of rock furrows. Between that village and the blue waters of the Persian Gulf lie many parallel mountain ranges, each pair separated by a long narrow valley. From below the Caucasus, through northwest Iran and around to the southeastern desert towards Afghanistan the ranges hang like curved wavefronts on a beach. Pushed up by massive subterrestrial forces, they are the result of tectonic plate collisions and are still rising. When Marcel's purpose returned with his health, he convinced Jane to renege on Shiraz and instead aim for the Gulf via Firuzabad. The Dieulafoys set off to cross the lithic chains and descend to the coastal plains.

Although the Persians had transported their cannon westward down this route to Bushire in 1857 during an argument about territory far to the east, the road was no more than the usual plaited dirt tracks in the valleys and, on the rocky slopes, a mere suggestion from piled stone cairns. Each steep climb led to a pass where the view across a fertile valley led the eye to the next range. A traveller explained, 'Imagine that you have ridden . . . across a plain; that you have then come to a barrier of snow-mountains and ridden up the pass; that from the top of the pass you have seen a second plain, with a second barrier of mountains in the distance, a hundred miles away; that you know that beyond these mountains lies yet another plain, and another, and another; and that for days, even weeks, you must ride, with no shade, and the sun overhead, and nothing but the bleached bones of dead animals strewing the track.'[3]

Having seen only the stark, bare mountains that rise dramatically from the Persian desert, Jane was surprised by the forests of elm and low-growing oak on the west-facing slopes of these mountains. Creeks and rivers tumbled along between stands of walnut, pistachio and maples, and in the damper gullies the rich colours of autumn blazed on poplars, willows, alder and ash, and the bitter juicy fruit of junipers and wild raspberries hung in the underbrush.

In the valleys patches of emerald green flashed amid the stubble, and partridge whirred from their hides. Wheat and rice had already been harvested and now, in November, the women and children were busy repairing and redirecting the irrigation channels. Men opened the ground in furrows, while others spread the seed for the next crop with open-handed largesse. Little had changed since the days when southern agriculture underpinned the wealth of the Achaemenids and the Sasanids. Both dynasties had implemented Zoroastra's advice to his followers, recorded in the Avesta, to beget children, plant useful trees, convey water to the drylands and practise agriculture. A paragraph asserts, 'He who sows the ground with care and diligence, acquires a greater stock of religious merit than he could gain by the repetition of ten thousand prayers.'[4] Although in 1881 the domed mosque had long replaced the Zoroastrian fire temple at the heart of every village, the husbandry was timeless.

Security in the passes and narrow defiles was a constant concern for the ancient dynasties travelling between their dispersed capitals, and it was a major problem for the Qajars. Only a few years before Jane crossed its shadow, the Fortress of Tebr had been a stronghold of robbers who terrorised travellers on the lonely roads, almost closing the route to traffic until Ferhad Mirza subjugated them in 1877, murdering the whole nest in one brutal summer operation.[5] Jane's escort assured her that the present governor sent out regular patrols to prevent a new lot of brigands from seeing an opportunity, information she found reassuring when tackling a narrow descent overlooked by crags, a likely place for robbers to lie in wait.

Through it all the Sarvistan servant stuck like a leech, even pestering the sick Marcel on the road back from Darab, 'I am your humble slave, Excellency. When will my master's photograph be ready?' Marcel finally detached him in a small village.

As the caravan made its way through the village gates, nothing about the scraggy mules or Marcel's bony horse indicated wealth or prestige. The village headman saw only two weary dusty infidels, the older one gaunt, the younger apparently no more than a smiling lad, and curtly dismissed their request for lodgings.

'You are misled,' the escort protested, 'Their Excellencies are under the protection of the Sahib Divan at the particular request of the Zil-es-Sultan.'

Blood drained from the headman's cheeks. Although Sahib Divan was not as cruel as Ferhad Mirza, his taxes were extortionate. The village could not afford the deputy governor's wrath. Suddenly the headman was kissing the hem of their dirty greatcoats. 'Peace be to you. Your Excellency's health is good by the grace of God?'

The muezzin was calling the faithful to evening prayer when the Sarvistan servant approached once more. 'Excellency, I am your humble slave, when will my master's photograph be ready?'

Already irritated, this was too much for Marcel. 'Go to the devil, you, your master, your ancestors and your descendants. If you bother me again, I'll give you a hundred strokes.'

'Excellency, my master will give me two hundred if I return empty handed.'

'In that case, I will fill them.'

Marcel quickly dashed off a note. 'Take this to your master.'[6]

The servant did not wait for morning to set off.

Warming her hands at a shepherd's fire one chilly morning, Jane looked ahead and saw the track stop at the foot of a wall of rock. How, she wondered, can we get over this? The shepherds laughed, 'From here it is all downhill to the plain.' One of the escort rode towards the rockface and seemed to disappear inside it. When Jane followed she found herself inside a diagonal cleft between two rearing rockfaces, 'as though the mountain had been cloven by an axe, and would fit together again if pushed.'[7] The eerie passageway led into a long gorge, where a river raced downhill, smashing against piled boulders, and a narrow pathway wound through the spray.

The defile was filled with the scent of roses. Looking around Jane could see only an old fortified palace perched on top of a sheer rock wall, but no roses. Later, catching up with a caravan of shiny-coated donkeys tripping along in an aroma redolent of a Hafiz garden, she realised the defile had been too narrow for some of the loads of bottled rosewater packed in straw and strapped to the donkeys' flanks.

When the track became precipitous Jane dismounted. Within minutes her mule had slipped off the edge of the path and somersaulted in a flurry of harness into the river below. Where the gorge briefly levelled out, the mule washed up against a patch of geraniums and guilder roses and was recovered almost unhurt. Further on, where the path again pitched steeply beside the tumbling waters and sunlight fell into the gorge, Jane glanced up to see an immense carved relief, more than twenty metres long, high on the rockface, and recognised Marcel's Sasanids. The rock relief recounts the origin of the Sasanid dynasty.

The Sasanids elevated the art of the billboard to new heights, although the tradition was old. Wherever a cliff reared beside a frequented route the ruler of the day sent his chisellers to spread his message. The carvings, and there are many of them, especially in the southwest, speak of worldly power, divine authorisation and dynastic achievement.

Near the present Iran–Iraq border in the town of Sar Pol-i-Zohab the oldest known Iranian rock carving was cut into the cliff more than 4100 years ago. With curious contemporary resonance, it shows a female figure leading a naked male by a leash around his neck. Behind him another sweats in fear. An aggressive male facing the wrathful goddess stomps upon a nude prisoner, while in an underground cell six shackled figures, stark naked except for their hats, are wide-eyed in terror. The carving is interpreted as the goddess Ishtar offering kingship to the successful warrior, Anubanini. When learning was restricted to a small educated caste, rock advertising brought a readable message to an illiterate populace.

The gorge's pageant was carved much later. In the shadowed light Marcel struggled to decipher a sequence of three pairs of mounted fighters. They tell the passerby that Ardashir, the first Sasanid king, was supported by all levels of society in the battle to take the kingdom from the Parthians. The first clashing pair shows Ardashir unseating the Parthian king, whose horse falls under him; the second shows Ardashir's son Shapur defeating the Parthian grand vizier; then, to represent popular support, a Sasanid page leans from his horse to choke a Parthian soldier.

It is a concise lithic account of real events. When Alexander rampaged through the Achaemenid kingdom, the people of Fars controlled territory spread from Libya and Egypt, through central Asia, to the Indus River. After Alexander's death in Babylon in 323 BC, the Macedonian general Seleucus and his descendants took over Fars and the eastern part of the Persian kingdom, while the western part was split among various claimants. A century later an obscure horde, the Parthians, displaced the Seleucids, quickly establishing hegemony from India across to the edge of Syria. They are mostly remembered for their Parthian shot. Almost two millennia before the great physicist, they understood Newton's Third Law. Seated on stirrup-less saddles the archers shot their arrows backwards, the rebound from the bow throwing them back onto the neck of the galloping horse and not off over the tail.

For all the Parthian cleverness, the people of Fars resented four centuries of their dominance. When Ardashir Sasanides in 224 AD claimed Achaemenid descent they were happy to believe him. After his successful rebellion they crowned him king, renaming him Artaxerxes.

With dramatic suddenness the gorge opened onto a wide fertile plain and there, beyond the palms on the far bank of the river, was Ardashir's palace.

The palace was built before Ardashir defeated the Parthian king. Representing his defiance, huge and massive-walled, it is one of the most important buildings in Persian architectural history, for it shows how the Sasanids solved the roofing problem. The wealthy Achaemenids had imported cedar beams from Lebanon and teak from India to support their flat roofs, but neither the Parthians nor the Sasanids controlled those tree-bearing territories and Persia's sparse trees were of no architectural usefulness. Relative poverty forced the Sasanids to find a different solution to cover angular space. A dome could keep out the weather just as well as a flat roof, but the question was: how could a round dome be raised above a square room.

Using technology known in Persia since the second millennium BC, the Parthians had built *iwan*s, narrow barrel-vaulted chambers, the weight of their arched roofs carried on the sidewalls. Those first *iwan*s were long dark tunnels, lit only from one end. Wanting light, the Sasanids inserted load-bearing piers along the sidewalls and bridged the aerial space with transverse arches to carry the weight of the roof. Between the piers, the side walls were pierced and filled with coloured glass. From these vaulted rectangular halls sprang the naves of Westminster Abbey and Chartres cathedral.

In the old Firuzabad palace, long barrel-vaulted *iwan*s lead toward three square halls, where Ardashir's builders used newly developed technology to place a squinch, an arch back-filled by a scallop-shell shape, across each corner at ceiling level. This simple concept distributes the weight of a superstructure, resting on the arches, to the side walls of the chamber. Repeated to bridge the now eight sides to produce sixteen, and again repeated, thirty-two load-bearing members provide enough support to carry the circular base of a large dome.

Both concepts, the transverse arch between piers and the squinch solution to support round domes over square spaces, spread from Firuzabad throughout the Sasanid Empire. The Romans rampaging across the banks of the Euphrates and into Armenia saw in replicas of Ardashir's little domes the blueprints for the magnificent domes of later Christian churches. They already knew how to put a dome on a round chamber; now with the squinch the Romans could put domes on square structures. The technique changed the appearance of Europe.

Sasanid technological developments provided the formula for all subsequent Persian architecture. The god whom Ardashir celebrated in his domed halls, which he entered through barrel-vaulted *iwan*s, may not be the same god in whose honour the Isfahanis bend their backs, but they do so beneath a direct descendant of Ardashir's dome, and they enter their mosques through related barrel-vaulted *iwan*s.

There was trouble with lodgings again. Part of the reason the deputy governor had insisted that the Dieulafoys have an escort was to ensure the villagers would rent them accommodation, but perhaps the soldiers, high-handed and representing a hated governor, were part of the problem. When Jane tried to mollify a widow whom the soldiers had evicted, the outraged woman threw Jane's money back in her face.

The village where the Dieulafoys stayed that night was built inside, on top of, and from the materials of Ardashir's city. If that represents historical continuity, the scale is descending. The city had a diameter of two kilometres, the village comprised only a few mudbrick houses, a bazaar and a mosque. The nearby remains of a thirty-metre-high square tower, made from stones and mortar with an external staircase spiralling its way to the top, confused Marcel into thinking it a mini-ziggurat. It was in fact a Zoroastrian fire temple. When its sides were covered with carved and painted stucco and the sacred fire burned aloft, it brought religious inspiration to the Sasanians.

In the five centuries between the collapse of the Achaemenid dynasty and the rise of Ardashir, the Zoroastrian religion had been corrupted by the randy Greek gods carried into Persia in Alexander's baggage. With them came altars and images and also tolerance. Ardashir of the strong arm and brilliant mind understood religion: it was a social phenomenon which he could manipulate to express the spirit and aims of the society he was forging, and he recognised its power to unify his growing empire. Immediately he was crowned Artaxerxes, he set about refining and purifying his people's worship.

He reinstated the mighty Ahura Mazda as the only god, and ordered the destruction of temples and the gods they housed. Since the essence of the beneficent creator was everywhere and the high mountains, symbolically represented by fire temples, were his sacrificial places, altars were unnecessary and were destroyed. Earth, water, fire and the sun were reinstated as the symbols of divine purity and statues were smashed. Because the fight between light and darkness, good and evil could be won only by constant vigilance and only the triumph of virtue could bring eternal peace and harmony, he encouraged priests to be zealous guardians of public behaviour. Rituals were systematised to combine the many competing sects into one, and the priestly caste, the magi, empowered to cleanse intransigent elements from the old observances.

Artaxerxes's approach established a unified nation and under his successors it inspired the re-conquest of former Persian territories, but in the longer term it contributed to the destruction of the Sasanids. As with all authorised and monotheist religions, its priests became too powerful, doctrinaire and, inevitably, corrupt and oppressive. They tithed the people, restricted education to their own sons and became a closed heritable caste of bigots. As they distorted the essence of Zoroastrianism, they lost the respect of the populace and their support fell away.

Jane's immediate problem was food. Because of the days wasted when Marcel had been too ill to travel, the journey had already lasted longer than planned and Bushire was still many stages away. The soldier sent on a shopping trip to New Firuzabad returned with the town governor's offer of hospitality, but the invitation was only a formality, he advised, and should not be accepted. The soldier, a tribal Lur, recognised the governor's financial embarrassment. The governorship of Firuzabad was the prerogative of the Ilkhani of the nomadic Kashquai tribes, but in the previous year the tribal leadership had changed heads, a process assisted by the Qajar government – in an attempt to centralise power, the government played off tribal leaders against each other, appointing the highest bidder to office. The new Ilkhani, having connived to have his predecessor deposed and hanged, was still paying off the deputy governor of Fars, Sahib Divan, as well as his tribal allies. To do so, he was squeezing his local governors. He was also beseeching Allah to safeguard his eldest son, held hostage in Tehran to ensure his father's loyalty.

If the greedy Qajars accepted the bribes and appointed to office those who had made gifts, it was always the ordinary people who paid. The Ilkhani imposed a tax on the Kashquai's flocks and herds, sending part of the revenue to Sahib Divan in Shiraz, who in turn transmitted less than the whole to Zil-es-Sultan, who bankrolled Nasr-al-Din in Tehran. Artaxerxes, who codified civil as well as religious law, understood that taxes are a necessary part of maintaining the public and social structures of a nation. 'The authority of the Prince,' he wrote, 'must be defended by a military force; that force can only be maintained by taxes; all taxes must, at last, fall upon agriculture.' But then he added a codicil that distinguished his governance from the Qajars, the recognition that 'agriculture can never flourish except under the protection of justice and moderation.'[8]

The Kashquai and their animals streamed through the defile. Goats and sheep driven on by wild dirty children brought dust and chaos; a pathetic bleating accompanied a string of horses whose bulging saddlebags carried new-born lambs and long-legged foals still too unsteady to stagger along the rocky path. The tribe was returning to spend the winter in the warm lowlands.

The southern valleys were the home territories of the Kashquai nomads, ethnic Turcoman tribes from near Kashgar in central Asia who, reputedly, were forcibly resettled there centuries before by the Mongols. When the autumn chill checked the growth of the sweet grasses in their summer pastures in the high mountains, they rolled up their felt tents, loaded them on the back of mules, and hung their cooking pans from the saddles. They caught the chickens and tied their feet together and now the birds swayed along on top of the loads, clucking and fretting. The men had loaded the cereal grinders and the equipment for dehusking rice onto the back of the cows and saddled their horses while the women were picking up their carpet looms and their bright wools and loading them, too, and fastening the little children to the baggage. After they counted their metal bracelets and amber necklaces and checked their turquoise nostril studs the women had tied headscarves over the long ringlets falling around their shoulders, for the tribe did not veil although they were Muslim. Fastening the wrappings tight around their babies they laid the little bodies flat among cloth-wrapped parcels. Now, after weeks of travel they were approaching their winter haunts in the coastal plains and lowland valleys. There they would dig out the cereals, buried by the few men who had remained to guard the crop during the burning hot summer, and resume their struggle to outwit the tax gatherers while taking advantage of every opportunity to plunder.

Struggling through the gorge on the last stages of their journey to Bushire, the Dieulafoys' small caravan followed the tide of Kashquai nomads in the narrow defiles, overtook them where the pass widened, and after two hours emerged onto a vast plain to find another Kashquai tribe resting their animals before tackling the next strenuous descent. In the shade of rectangular brown felt tents, women wearing calf-length red skirts and low-necked blouses were busy at their carpet looms. Wild dark hair, flashing eyes and strong features made them beautiful, but what impressed Jane at this first meeting with tribal women was their self-assurance. As she, apparently a young man, approached, they waited with dignified self-confidence. When she asked to see their work they unrolled their treasures with pride. They were quite unlike the idle, jealous creatures she had met locked away in *anderuns*.

Riding cheerfully away after the encounter, her money belt lighter, her mule's load heavier, and her saddle bags flush with yoghurt and goat's cheese, Jane reflected on the difference between the two groups of women and concluded that the confidence of a Kashquai woman was a consequence of her husband having only one wife, while her self-assurance came from knowing her work, whether knotting carpets or chasing recalcitrant cattle, made a vital contribution to the tribal economy.

Beyond the next pass, palm-fringed oases appeared and that night Jane slept in a conical hut made entirely from palm fronds. It was clear they were nearing the coast, though not yet on the plain where the great palm forests began. They rode past villagers adjusting water flow in the canals and women carrying date-filled baskets. As the caravan negotiated tortuous gorges and crossed hot palm-filled valleys, the river water became bitter, while the well water, tasting of petrol, purged the horses, who became so weak they could manage only three kilometres an hour. Jane and Marcel suffered cruelly from thirst, for several days drinking only lemon juice, or goats' milk when they could buy it. Thirst was the lesser evil. Apart from its purging effect, virulent fevers lurked in the dirty brown liquid stored in cisterns and the Dieulafoys knew their physical resistance was compromised. Exhausted and dehydrated, they longed to reach the gulf.

When at last they emerged from a gorge and saw through a gap between the ranges the bright blue waters far in the distance, Jane was filled with emotion. The Persian Gulf represented the link to France and family and home. 'All the wonders I have seen in Persia are nothing compared with this,' she exclaimed. Weakened by months of arduous travel and weeks of recurrent sickness, she was overwhelmed by an attack of acute homesickness.

What a temptation to return to France that thin blue line lying between the sky and the golden sands must have been. It offered emotional and physical comfort, a relaxation of constant wariness. 'Since March,' she wrote, 'I have ridden 91 stages, 4000 kilometres, across a country without roads and without any comforts. Except in the big cities I have slept in mean caravanserais and terrible lodgings. God be praised! In eight months over difficult paths He has brought me from the glaciers of the Caucasus to tropical skies, from desolate plains to oases, and at last He has brought me to the port.'[9]

Perhaps it was less an inventory of achievement than a way to encourage herself. Yes, she had done all that. As well, she had survived sickness, thirst, weariness, unreliable tcharvadars and hostile mullahs. She had reached the Persian Gulf. Did she need to go on? Her reputation as a distinguished traveller had been established. The articles she had sent back to France were already appearing in *le Tour du monde*, the French journal that had published the writings of great explorers. Although Amundsen and Shackleton had yet to appear in its pages, Dr Livingstone and Richard Burton had described Africa and Arabia for its readers, and Charles Darwin had recounted the voyage of the *Beagle*. The editor's acceptance of her reports might not place her in the first rank of such names, but certainly implied that she was something more than a provincial housewife, a recognition that endorsed her decision to leave the listing of saucepans to confront a challenge in a far away country. Why insist on Susa? Had she not done enough? Perhaps she might slip aboard a ship and sail home to France, home to her much-loved family.

Chapter 12
Smuggled into Babylonia, Iraq

On board the *Pendjab*, Jane gloried in idleness. 'A whole day,' she exulted, watching the low yellow coast of Persia slip behind, 'to be a sybarite.'

Susa had won. Easily. The temptation had lasted only an instant. Having reached the Persian Gulf, she could not turn away from Susa, she could not evade the enigmatic mound. The *Pendjab*, a British India Company ship, was heading not south to the Arabian Sea and Europe, but upstream to where the waters of two great rivers, the Tigris and Euphrates, emptied into the gulf through the Shatt al Arab.

Bushire lay astern. Resting in a deck chair, Jane recalled the last two terrible days of the long journey from Shiraz. Tantalised by the sight of the ocean, she had been filled with despair when she found there was still a wilderness of sand dunes and marshes to negotiate before she could dip her fingers into its waters. Tormented by thirst, she and Marcel had struggled on through villages full of dirty brown-skinned children and thin yellow dogs, and past parties hunting gazelle with hooded falcons on their gloved wrists. Ignoring the stares of silk-turbaned village chiefs, the caravan made its slow way along the goat tracks, urged on by the prospect of clean, sweet drinking water.

But the water in the wells and cisterns of Bushire was also undrinkable, inhabited by guinea worm, skinny parasites that burrowed out of the gut, through the muscle tissues and materialised as large itchy lumps beneath the skin. Dr Ross, first secretary of the English Consulate, warned there was only one treatment – slash the skin, seize the worm and wind it out on a bobbin. Jane was saved from the worm and from cholera, diphtheria and other diseases by two large carafes of Tigris River water, sent by Bushire's governor.

Alerted to the powerful provincial deputy governor's regard for the Dieulafoys and hoping to acquire status and prestige, the town governor invited them to dinner, but Jane had other matters to attend to first. She was lousy. Since the night spent in the ruined imamzadde near Sarvistan where the evicted dervishes had left their 'little *hadjis*', Jane had itched and scratched. Her hair was full of lice and her legs and arms covered with raised, red bedbug bites. After luxuriating in a hot saltwater bath, she asked Marcel to shave her head. Persian men might keep a ringlet over each ear but Jane wanted every blonde curl off and until she returned to France she kept her head shaved. She would not provide free lodging for head lice, she said.

The baggage sent on ahead from Shiraz had not arrived. It was three weeks since the Dieulafoys rode through the gates of the lovely Bagh-i-Sheykh and a caravan should complete the journey through the four passes on the 250-kilometre direct route in eight days. Jane regretted her carefully packed tiles, the exquisite Kermani silk brocades and her collection of carpets, but the possible loss of her notebooks and glass-plate negatives caused deeper distress.

The soldiers sent to escort the Dieulafoys to the palace found Jane wearing a clean lightweight suit and a new white helmet bought in the bazaar. In the streets the smell was nauseating, the roadway slippery with sewage flung from the windows of multi-storey dwellings, a central drain the only sanitation. Thin, almost naked children and lethargic men stared at the party. When her horse's hoof struck a dog's carcass rats ran from inside.

At the palace a long white cloth spread with food lay on the carpet. After the meagre rations of the last few weeks the aroma from little savoury pies and the sight of glistening legs of lamb, their juices seeping into beds of fluffy boiled rice, overwhelmed Jane. Bowls of pickles and yoghurt, steaming pilau and chicken steeped in pomegranate juice stood beside dishes piled with pastry-wrapped fish. Fried aubergine and pickled cucumber emphasised the colour of fresh-cut melon and shining fleshy dates. Delicate almond cakes and nougat squares filled any empty spaces.

Later, Jane recorded the feast in her new notebook. How could such luxury exist, she asked, in a town so decayed and so lacking in hygiene? The only medical care for the townspeople, who were constantly ill with fevers and infectious disease, came from Mrs Ross in her charitable dispensary. In the bazaar she had seen rich goods traded by Arab and Persian merchants and yet there was no evidence of wealth in the town, she wrote. She appreciated the ingenuity of the badgirs, which wafted cool air down to subterranean rooms where residents escaped the crushing heat, but why, she asked, did such cleverness not extend to proper sanitation and clean wells. Such poverty and misery tormented Jane.

Their baggage appeared at last. The caravan had been held back in Shiraz because the deputy governor had commandeered all the baggage animals to take his household into the mountains to escape the fever. A telegram from a fully recovered Sahib Divan thanked Marcel for his advice.

While Jane was sorting, repacking and arranging for most of her goods to be shipped straight to France, another telegram arrived telling of the death of the grand vizier, the third to pay with his life for attempting to reform the government. The dreams he had brought from Europe of a new modern Persia, of a reformed administration, of a better educated populace travelling on improved roads, of surplus foodstuffs transported by railways to famine-affected areas had cost him his head. Accused of being too much influenced by Western notions, intrigue in the shah's *anderun* brought him down. Dismissed as prime minister and appointed governor of Khorasan, he died on his way into exile 'from the fatigues of the road,' proclaimed the official announcement, but everyone knew it was 'a cup of Qajar coffee' that killed him.

When the English Consul's motor launch had arrived to take them out to the *Pendjab*, Jane closed the door of their Bushire lodging without regret. As the launch threaded its way between the sandy shoals that held the *Pendjab* almost five kilometres out at sea, a fleet of small boats was bringing off cargo and passengers. Their sails catching the wind, the boats danced over the crests, making better progress across the choppy water than the consul's motorboat. Bushire's harbour was shallow and treacherous, yet it was Persia's main port. The Caspian Sea in the north was landlocked, the southern fringe was inaccessible, and so Persia's only connection to the world's oceans was through the Persian Gulf.

Out through Bushire flowed carpets from the famed cities, brocaded silks and Kermani shawls from the east, tobacco and opium from the rich valleys, dried grapes and wine from Shiraz. And in flowed European manufactured goods, British printed cottons, Austrian glass, pharmaceuticals and metal pans from France, teakwood tables from India, the mundane and practical in exchange for oriental luxury. From the *Pendjab* Jane could see the ranges rising tier after tier behind the coastal plain up to the great plateau of Fars. Except for dates from the palmerais[1] along the rivers, all the exports had come down through the treacherous passes, the 'rock ladders' that connected the Persian plateau to the coast. The imports would climb those same impossible passes on the backs of pack mules and camels. Fifty days later they would brighten the eyes of the merchants in the Tehran bazaars.

The wind rose and rocked the *Pendjab*, threatening to blow her onto the land, and it was two in the morning before the captain dared to weigh anchor. Now, as Jane sheltered from the sun behind the stack, the prevailing northwest wind blowing in her face tasted of salt, fresh and delightful after days of Bushire's humid, fetid air. It promised a way into Susiane province, where both Achaemenids and Sasanids had reigned and expired. Susa lay ahead. France would wait.

Weeks before in Shiraz, when the Dieulafoys had informed Sahib Divan of their plan to travel up the Karun River to Shushtar and slip across the plain to Susa, the deputy governor, propped up on cushions and sweating with fever, had turned to the scribe squatting on the floor behind him and dictated a letter. 'Present this to Sheikh *hadji* Jabir Khan, governor of Mohammerah,' he told Marcel, 'he will arrange your journey on the Karun. You will find him at his residence at Fallahiyah in [Khuzestan][2] province, another fiefdom of his Highness, the Zil-es-Sultan.'

The scribe's exquisite calligraphy and the deputy governor's seal made the document so impressive that Marcel presented it almost with regret in Fallahiyah, a village on the bank of the Shatt al Arab, a little beyond the dark whirlpools where the waters of the Karun glide in.

Ordinarily a sheikh would not have dared ignore an instruction from the deputy governor of Fars province, but *hadji* Jabir Khan had been dead for fifteen days. His son Sheikh Mizal Khan was out hunting when the Dieulafoys arrived at the riverside residence, a fort smelling of war and coffee. A group of men lounged in the shade of its deep vaulted entrance, their bodies enfolded in the brown Arab cloak, the *abba*, although beneath it were the Persian tunic and baggy pantaloons. Their head covering, a large square of striped cotton or silk held in place by two bands of twisted camel's hair, proclaimed the Muhaisen tribe had fought its way in from Arabia.

Unlike most tribes in Khuzestan province the Muhaisen Ka'b Arabs were a settled tribe, who for several generations had held rich palm groves in Persian territory on the right bank of the Shatt al Arab and along both sides of the Karun River. Fishing and horse breeding supplemented their income. There were several fishermen among the soldiers and household dependents lounging at the entrance. Under the arch, a coffee pot, the height of a seven-year-old child and much fatter, sat on a bed of charcoal.

Sheik Mizal's coffeepot

A servant with loaded rifle on his shoulder and dagger in his belt brought the Dieulafoys cups of blackness tasting of mocha, the Yemeni bean the Arabs love.

Late in the day a fierce-looking middle-aged man rode through the entrance on a splendid Arab mare, its head and neck hung with red silk tassels and silver ornaments, its saddle richly decorated. He was followed by a slim seventeen-year-old boy astride another distinguished animal, and a large mounted retinue. Fishermen, servants, loungers, soldiers rushed to form two lines and bow their heads. The sheikh and his young brother had returned.

In the evening Sheikh Mizal Khan called the Dieulafoys to his *talar*. Astute and handsome, his moustache and beard henna-dyed, the sheikh was a troubled man. Though the Persian government had proclaimed him head of the tribe and governor of Mohammerah in his father's place, they demanded he send his young brother to Tehran as hostage for his loyalty. When the son-less sheikh confided his affection for the boy and his dread of losing him, Jane looked at his splendid *abba*, embroidered on the chest and around the neck with gold thread, its edges held together by frog-fastenings flashing with gemstones, saw that his tunic was silk brocade, and felt sympathy for him. So grand, so sad and without a son. She and Marcel, too, longed for a son. They understood his pain.

Jane realised the sheikh was vulnerable. Never reticent when it came to an opportunity to investigate an *anderun*, she enquired, 'How many wives do you have, your Excellency?'

Jane laughingly recommended he increase the number to twenty-four.

'My neighbour, Sheikh Kara, has 140 wives of all ages and from many different countries, but my small *anderun* is much more tranquil,' he replied and, of course, gave her permission to visit.

Led across terraces, past deserted suites and empty *talars* to a tiny courtyard surrounded by mean rooms, Jane found a woman dressed in black lying on a bed of palm fronds in a bare chamber. The dead sheikh's favourite wife, Torkhan *khanum*, had deserted her more elaborate airy quarters to grieve in darkness and solitude. With poignant dignity she conducted Jane upstairs to a marbled *talar* spread with rich carpets. Silk cushions decorated the room, hanging glass lamps lit up arrangements of artificial flowers under glass domes, the latest thing from Europe. A clap of the widow's hands brought servants running, a softly spoken order brought women gliding into the room. Their long black wool chemises dropped to gathered pantaloons frothing about the ankle; black gauze veiling thrown over the head and swept up across face and throat fell like Grecian drapery around their bodies. Each wife had three empty holes in her nose, the gems that usually filled the piercings removed as a sign of mourning. The blue tattoos covering feet, hands and cheek could never be removed.

The grieving favourite, a Circassian who covered her head but did not veil, had neither piercings nor tattoos. The deference and formality with which the other wives greeted her reminded Jane, incongruously, of the nuns at her convent school greeting the mother superior. The widow's position in the *anderun* was undisputed, her tact giving it the 'tranquillity' that the new sheikh enjoyed. Dominating the conversation, she translated Jane's Persian into Arabic for the wives, but shook her head sadly when Jane answered that, no, she could not speak Russian, her native tongue. Nor could Jane speak Turkish, another language in which the *khanum* was fluent. Jane was struck by the quick intelligence and exquisite manners of this woman bought by the old sheikh in Istanbul's slave market fifteen years before. Becoming his much beloved, she was given every token of affection, but, sadly, not a child.

Sheikh Mizal Khan offered his steam launch to transport the Dieulafoys up the river. Except that it needed repair. He would have a mechanic come from Mohammerah. In the meantime, 'I am your slave, my humble house is yours.'

Marcel settled to long discussions with one of the many house guests, a renowned Tehran theologian, while Jane returned to the *anderun*. Received most graciously by Torkhan *khanum*, she was admiring a moiré silk dress tailored in European style in Baghdad when she felt a warm breath on her neck and turned to find herself nose to nose with a panther.

'Here, Little Rose, here,' called Torkhan *khanum*, patting the floor beside her. The feline padded across and installed herself on the widow's carpet, from which she glared and snarled at Jane. Captured along the Karun, where they were common, the panther had been the devoted slave of the late sheikh, accompanying him everywhere, even to the distant horse pasture where he died. Grieving for its master, the cat refused to eat until brought back and reunited with the *anderun*'s mistress.

When Torkhan *khanum* offered to show her the gardens, Jane put on a dark robe and covered her head. The shah's Arab subjects did not practise the extreme enclosure of the Persians, but the way to the garden led through the village and to be seen walking with a strange 'man' would compromise the widow. The villagers ran towards Torkhan *khanum*, surrounding her, greeting her, kissing the edge of her robe. She was 'like a queen at the centre of her court . . . walking with the bearing of a sovereign receiving the homage of her subjects.' The tribe respected the clever Circassian woman, knowing the old sheikh had valued her counsel and trusted her advice. Her literacy had been invaluable to the rough tribal sheikh who could neither read nor write.

Stretched along the river bank, the orchard was filled with banana and date palms and many varieties of citrus weighed down with fruit. In deep cool tunnels beneath its abundant foliage the two women walked together, talking and laughing. Both being spirited strong women who refused to be overwhelmed by fate, they shared a view of the world. Jane appreciated the *khanum*'s quick mind, so unlike the 'ignorant silly creatures' met in other *anderun*s; while for the *khanum* Jane rekindled memories of life before the raid when she was captured and sold into slavery.

Visiting the 'queen' of the Muhaisen tribe was a pleasant diversion for Jane, despite the panther's jealous growls, while disputing with the Tehrani mujtahid was challenging for Marcel, but what both wanted was to be on the way to Susa. 'When,' Marcel asked the sheikh, after his frustrating daily visit to the river bank, 'will the launch be repaired?'

Torkhan khanum

The sheikh was used to his guests finding excuses to linger; hospitality was a matter of pride to the Arab, and the sheikh was very proud. Surely Marcel was not in a hurry to leave? But he was, answered Marcel, insisting that if the repairs presented a difficulty he would hire horses and arrange a caravan.

'I will never allow it,' said the sheikh sternly. 'You would be stripped and robbed by the nomads. Those tribes raid with absolute impunity. When they make a *razzia* in [Khuzestan], they slip away across the frontier. When they rob a caravan in Turkey, they come back into Persia. Their fleetness makes them impossible to capture. Be patient a little longer. I'll write to Basra for a mechanic. My launch will soon be at your disposal.'[3]

Jane returned to the *anderun*, Marcel to the courtyard. What else could they do?

For a once and only time Jane was present in a mosque during a religious event. The Muhaisen tribe, despite its Arab origin, was Shi'a in practice, proclaiming Ali the rightful heir of the prophet Mohammad and commemorating the martyrdom of Hassan and Hussein. The other women had already gone to the remembrance service, and the *khanum* would take Jane if she wished. 'It's very long and boring,' she warned, but Jane found the fervour with which they remembered the dead fascinating. Led by a shrill instructress, the wives had pulled their *abba*s over their heads, exposed their left breast and shoulder and were beating them with their palms, calling the names of the lost when Jane walked in. Instantly, the weeping and crying ceased and a scandalised silence fell. The *khanum* ignored it, settling Jane beside her on the carpet in the place of honour, calmly nodding to the celebrant to continue. The beating began again, one old woman striking the sole of her foot and a very fat dark lady thumping her upper thigh so hard her whole body quivered like jelly.

Despite the apparent grief, the *kalian*s were circulating and an old black woman was bringing cups of coffee to the distraught. 'It's cold,' screamed one worshipper, flinging the cup's contents at the servant. Such behaviour was unacceptable to Torkhan *khanum*. She brought the service to a halt and reprimanded the rude girl. Oh, thought Jane, the *khanum* must be very sure of her power.

After the lamentation Jane expected to see doleful, tear-streaked faces outside the mosque. To her surprise the women chatted and smiled as though they had been to a party, not a teardrop visible.

Torkhan *khanum* was very sad to lose Jane's companionship, her distraction from genuine grief and deep anxiety about her future. Would she be sold again or perhaps given away? To Jane their farewell signified that she was at last on the way to Susa. Or so she thought. In late afternoon she and Marcel went aboard the sheikh's launch and let the rush of Tigris and Euphrates waters carry them downstream to Mohammerah. Before a brilliant sunset turned the waters scarlet they had slipped into the canal – cut so long ago that its origins are unknown – that transports the waters of the Karun directly into the marriage of the great rivers Euphrates and Tigris. Night fell with oriental suddenness. Midnight found them travelling along a wide waterway fringed with palmerais. Happy and relaxed, Jane fell asleep. When she woke at dawn the boat had stopped, the mechanic was struggling with the engine, the captain was angry, the four armed guards were nervous and the servants were ashore building a fire to make flat bread for breakfast.

A week later Jane arrived back at Mohammerah under tow from a grain boat that had responded to their distress signal. In the meantime she had seen the banks of the river, a fertile neglected plain that stretched out into the distance, many of the Sheikh's flocks of goats and sheep, and some of the horses that were making him rich through the price they brought in Bombay. She had also seen, tucked away on a mooring, his two small ships that carried the mounts to India and could bear him to safety if necessary. She had not seen or shot any of the lions, lynx or wild boar that were said to lie in the long grass, nor any raiding parties of Arab nomads. She had once gone ashore to inspect a tomb whose pyramidal spire was made from blocks of blinding white plaster stacked up in thirteen decreasing layers. And she had not seen Susa, nor been anywhere near it.

Bitterly disappointed, Jane and Marcel left the Karun without regret, believing they were done with it, unaware that they would follow its devious course again, Jane not suspecting how close to death she would be when again on its dark waters.

But Susa. How were they to reach it? Having come so far Jane would not give up; difficulties only made her more determined. Once more the map prepared in France 'to inform the journey of Mme Dieulafoy from Tiflis to Baghdad, Susa and Mohammerah' came out. Though becoming tattered, it suggested a third possibility. If they were to continue up the Tigris into Turkish territory they could strike out eastwards across the plains, ascend the mountains and reach Susa from Dizful. In Fallahiyah they had been warned against travelling alone in that wild part of the country, yet there might be a caravan they could join. If they went up to Basra or even Baghdad perhaps someone would know of one, and they could obtain official permission to travel.

Either way it would mean going into the Ottoman Empire. What today we call Iraq was then Babylonia, a Mesopotamian province of the declining Turkish Empire, which it had been, off and on, for centuries, when not held by the Persians. Before the Arabs overflowed from their wild deserts bringing Mohammad's message, it had been Sasanid, when not Roman. Indeed the Sasanids had built a capital, Ctesiphon, alongside the Tigris. For millennia the question of whose land it was and where the boundaries lay had fertilised its alluvial plains with enough blood to fill the entire Persian Gulf.

The most recent border dispute, settled by an international convention in 1853, had made Mohammerah Persian but had given Basra, eight hours upstream by native boat, to the Turks. Jane's problem of how to reach that town lay not with transport – there was a plenitude of boats plying up and down the great rivers – but with the quarantine camp where incomers were held for ten days to prevent, said the Turkish authorities, the spread of plague. Jane argued that plague was not a Persian sickness; it was endemic in Baghdad and entered Persia with Shi'a pilgrims returning from Najaf and Karbala. The real reason for enforcing an unnecessary edict, she said, was that the corrupt Turkish border bureaucrats held the contracts for the supply of food and bedding in the camps. She refused absolutely to be detained for ten days in the marshes in boiling heat and in close proximity to all kinds of infections. She would not wait in the humid fetid air for fever to strike her down, she said. The Dieulafoys would find a smuggler to run them into Basra, two kilometres above the aquatic border where the Turkish navy lay in wait.

And so on the following night the Dieulafoys lay in the swill at the bottom of a native boat hidden by packets of dates and sacks of melons. It was a slow trip, the captain going ashore on business at midnight, the customs agents coming on board not long after. Only when customs cleared the boat were they able to emerge from their hiding place. Wet and smelly, Jane stood in the prow as the boat was poled down a back canal. The moonlight revealed white houses, some appearing to rise straight out of the water, others set back among dense stands of date palms, their rustling fronds reaching up to the gentle breeze. In front of the larger houses watchmen slept beside light elegant boats drawn up at quays. Orchards came into view, bananas and oranges gleamed in the silver light. Overhead was a sky filled with a myriad of stars. A tropical Venice, Jane called Basra.[4]

Before dawn the Dieulafoys and their escort were knocking at the door of the French consulate.

In Basra's bazaar it was very obvious she was in another country. Details of dress, not language, defined the many races and creeds going noisily about their affairs. Turks swaggered about in crimson leather slippers with upturned toes, their silk cloaks shimmering with gold or silver thread, jewelled belt buckles flashing when the cloak fell open. The Arabs wore rough leather sandals and long white tunics beneath woollen *abbas*. Jewel-hilted daggers and inlaid-revolvers sparkled in their belts; brilliant striped silk squares thrown over the head and stabilised by elaborate ranks of plaited wool held apart by brackets of silver and sometimes gold expressed their pride. Bright cotton *keffiyehs*[5] proclaimed the Syrians, while resident Europeans adopted oriental elements and dressed more casually than in their native cities. Women hid their faces behind thick black veils or coloured silk squares, but always managed to display their showy jewellery at wrist, chest and in the hair.

A vital charming town when the tide filled the palm-fringed canals, twice a day Basra became a mass of buildings separated by stinking slime-filled channels. Sixty years before, an upstream dam had broken and flooded the plain, isolating the city in an encircling fever-fed swamp, its only outlet the river. The Turks had neither drained the swamp nor repaired the dam, and every visitor damned them for their apathy. The people were enervated by the hot humid climate and constantly laid low by infectious diseases, making Basra 'one of the least desirable places to which Europeans are exiled by the exigencies of commerce.'[6]

Basra was an entrepôt: goods flowed in from India and Europe, while cotton, wheat, sugar cane and other agricultural products of the rich Mesopotamian soil were shipped away. Its main trade was in dates. Harvested in October, dates were still flowing through the port in early December boxed in imported timber or packed in wrappings made from palm leaves. After investigating the bazaar, Jane watched little native boats carrying the crates out to the ships lying in the anchorage, but after only one day in the 'date capital' fever struck her down and the energetic woman became a limp rag doll. Told that the plains between the Tigris and the foothills of the Zagros Mountains where Susa was tucked away would become an impassable marsh when the rains began, she raged at the delay. Fifteen days had already been wasted trying to get up the Karun, now they were held back by illness and, since Basra could not provide the information or permission they needed, they must continue to Baghdad. She was in despair.

Before she had fully recovered she and Marcel were aboard a Turkish ship, along with one other first-class passenger, many steerage class, much cargo and a great many chickens. Captain Dominici was unable to say how long the *Mosul* would take to reach Baghdad: it was a question of how often they ran aground in the Tigris. 'I've sailed on that capricious river for many years and I've never found the channel in the same place twice. The rushing current destroys one sand bank only to dump it where there was deep water eight days before. Often we can only proceed by sounding.' When pushed, his estimate was eight or ten days.

'If I'd known, I would never have stepped off the bank. I'd have waited for the summer,' said Jane, forlornly gazing out across a low plain losing itself in a possibility of mountains, its only relief an occasional forest of date palms.

Dominici spread his hands. 'It's worse in the summer when the water is low, then we do nothing but run aground, refloat the ship and run aground again.'[7]

Convoys of small boats speeding downstream on the current emphasised the *Mosul*'s slow progress up the Shatt al Arab. Some were only a raft of inflated animal skins and a dirty sail powered by the northeasterly, some dug-out palm trunks paddled with boards. The most intriguing were the perfectly round gophers, nothing more than a large woven basket waterproofed with bitumen. Behind their incurved top passengers could be seen drawing back from the splash of the single paddle. Hog-tied animals sometimes lay in the bottom among a jumble of cargo. The age-old design appears in Assyrian carved reliefs dated to 800 BC. The river bed had changed, flood waters and collapsed dams had gouged out new channels over the millennia, but the native boats sailing on the Tigris were timeless.

After some hours they reached the junction where the waters of Tigris and Euphrates meet to form the Shatt al Arab. Here, claim the Arabs, who share the stories of the Old Testament with Jews and Christians, all three being 'peoples of the Book', was the Garden of Eden. The Eves of the late nineteenth century wore red and white, the Adams covered their heads with brown turbans, and the garden, which stretched to the water's edge where boats were moored, was filled with palms, not an apple or serpent in sight, though the village was adorned by a leaning minaret.

As the captain had warned, the Tigris waters were treacherous. When the *Mosul* moved gently forward and began to settle on a sand bank, the sailors flung cargo into the boats and pulled away for the shore. Gophers came flying across the water from a nearby village to take off the passengers, for a price, and even the chickens. The captain gave loud orders and the waters frothed astern as he struggled to reverse, then, when that proved futile, to push the now-lightened ship forward over the sand. After hard work with a kedge anchor, the ship rolled off the bank and the passengers, cargo and chickens returned on board. And on each of the many occasions they ran aground the procedure was repeated.

Edging the river were buff-coloured plains sprinkled with bright-green palmerais and emerald patches of winter wheat. Mud villages and sometimes the black tents of the Arabs rose above the bank; herds of cattle and strings of camels radiated from them, flocks of dark-brown sheep grazed in the distance, but the real inhabitants of the plain were myths and legends and history filled with hatred and wars.

The *Mosul* drew alongside a quay where an enamel-tiled dome floated above a flat-roofed mud village. The venerable village tomb, domed and renovated after Shah Abbas's soldiers added Babylonia to his Safavid Empire, was ascribed to Ezra, who led the Jews out of captivity when Cyrus overran Babylon, which, though now dust like Ezra himself, was only a few days march away. As Jane dashed ashore to photograph the monument she was jostled by Jewish pilgrims hurrying aboard. She remarked caustically, 'Their English and Turkish shareholders would make a loss if one were to remove from the shipping companies' budgets the income from the transport of pious pilgrims of all religions visiting the tombs of prophets and imams.'[8]

Under a sky filled with stars the *Mosul* sailed away, making its slow way up the Tigris, servicing the villages, and attempting to avoid the shoals. It tied up for several hours at Amarah, as chickens and dates taken on at the last stop on the right bank were taken off, and chickens and dates destined for the next stop on the left bank were brought aboard. 'The boat traffic consists of transporting from right to left and from left to right the same items as taken on at the last stop,' Jane commented flippantly, ignoring the rest of its considerable trade. No one told her of the newly established port's trade link to Dizful. In Amarah she did not recognise her gateway to Susa.

Frustrated by the delays and increasingly impatient, Jane nonetheless took advantage of each opportunity. At Kout al Amarah, an Arab town of sun-dried brick, seeing Arab goatskin tents pitched a little way along the bank, Jane impetuously set off towards them, hoping to buy tribal rugs. As she approached, wild-looking men, some wearing long red cotton shifts, some blue, leant aggressively on their lances. Brown-skinned women, silver jewellery at neck and wrist tinkling with apprehension, chased their chickens and herded the goats. The fierce horse-stealing Beni La'am, whose greatest pleasure was pillaging the Turks, were no doubt surprised to see such a lamb walking into their den. Later, when she came to know them better, Jane was appalled at her rashness.

Early one morning a grey cliff pierced by a giant arch appeared across the plain. 'It's the great arch of Ctesiphon,' Captain Dominici told her. Having succumbed to Jane's charm, he continued, 'It's on a narrow peninsula. It takes four hours to get around, but you can walk across the isthmus in twenty minutes. If you'd like to go ashore and have a look, we'll pick you up on the other side.'[9] As he spoke the *Mosul* settled on a sand bank, aground again. Leaving the captain struggling to refloat his ship, the Dieulafoys set off towards the old Sasanid capital. Roars of anger followed them across the plain.

At Firuzabad they had seen the palace of Ardashir, founder of the Sasanid dynasty, who was crowned King Artaxerxes. When his son Shapur came to power in 240 AD the state had expanded almost to the reach of the old Achaemenid Empire. Stretching from the Euphrates River to the Indus, from the Caspian Sea to the Persian Gulf, it included Central Asia up to the Araxes and the Oxus. To proclaim their new power and reflect the character of an empire that had defeated the Roman emperor Valerian and made him their slave, the Sasanids needed heroic architecture and magnificent decoration.

On the Mesopotamian plain, in a loop of the Tigris River, Shapur built a palace vast enough to impress leaders of vassal states and fill foreign envoys with awe. Its outer wall rose thirty-seven metres above a crowded forecourt, its façade was bright with coloured stucco and patterned by shadows in its four ranks of shallow recessed arcades. A huge arch spanning twenty-four metres and reaching thirty metres at the high point, pierced the wall. The arch was the entrance to a classic barrel-vaulted *iwan* forty-five metres deep. At the far end hung a gold-embroidered curtain.

The Persian memory of what the parted curtain revealed is recorded in Firdauzi's *Shahname*. Visitors gasped in wonder at the huge domed hall, glittering and sumptuous, where The King of Kings, in blue and gold lamé robes, sat on an ivory throne. Above his head a crown blazing with jewels was suspended by golden chains from the dome. Ranked around him was the court, nobles and warriors dressed in splendour, and in the side galleries the magi, the priests of Ahura Mazda, carried gold symbols.

Masters of the dramatic, Sasanid kings granted audience at dawn and the throne was arranged so that the first rays of the sun struck the jewels that adorned his ears, his robe, his throat and his hands, and flashed upon the crown pendant above his head. A dazzling, awesome figure, personifying the wealth of the kingdom and signifying its power, he stunned the beholder, a performance imitated by Nasr-al-Din shah millennia later when he stepped from his tent at dawn wearing his diamond-sewn robe to subdue rebellious tribes.

As shah succeeded shah, the setting became ever more rich, more embellished. During the last days of the Sasanids a wondrous carpet covered the floor. Made of silk interwoven with gold and silver thread and encrusted with thousands of gems, *Spring in Paradise* was a large part of the state treasure.

In winter, when the shah was in residence he led hunting parties out onto the plain. Although repairing canals and maintaining a thriving agriculture occupied the villagers, the royal guard had to be exercised and young nobles trained. Hunting presented an education in riding, shooting and, most importantly, obedience. In summer, cavalry skills were practised in the mountains, where the hunting was more challenging and the training more arduous. Shapur mounted them on the best horses in Asia, armed them, dressed them in rich apparel, and did not hesitate to lead them into battle.

Mesopotamia, the land between the two great rivers, succumbed early to Sasanid ambition, but beyond the Euphrates was the voracious Roman Empire which had displaced the Greeks, the Persians' old enemy. At the head of light and heavy cavalry and followed by foot soldiers, Shapur crossed the Euphrates and marched westward, in 260 AD conquering Syria and Silicia and parts of Anatolia. Shapur had no wish to hold the conquered territories: his aim was solely to create a barrier against the aggressive Romans, so he laid the lands waste and retreated with their treasures, bringing Emperor Valerian in chains into Persia for seven years of humiliation. With him came thousands of captured Roman soldiers and civilians, who were put to work building palaces and bridges.

The Romans were not permanently deterred by this defeat, and so began a long series of destructive wars and reciprocal calamities. Mesopotamia became a battlefield, with Persian incursions west beyond the Euphrates and Roman towards the East. The rich irrigated plains have never fully recovered from the destruction those armies wrought.

The two battling superpowers not only destroyed the agricultural lands and the lives of their subjects, they also exhausted themselves. At the beginning of the sixth century AD, when a significant change in world climate occurred, both were debilitated. Global cooling brought drier years and reduced crop yield. In 535 AD a massive volcanic eruption at Krakatoa, Indonesia, exaggerated the climate shift. Dust trapped in the upper atmosphere shadowed the earth. In the following year Rabaul in New Guinea erupted and brought years of relative darkness, the filtered sunlight reaching the earth too weak to sustain effective plant growth. Crop failure brought famine and with famine came disease. Hunger stalked both empires. Weakened by starvation, in the bitterly cold weather people dropped dead from hypothermia. Population numbers declined and in Europe the Dark Ages began.

The arrival of bubonic plague from Ethiopia in 512 AD was the death knell for entire cities already challenged by failed agriculture in their hinterland. In parts of Syria to this day hillsides covered with the remains of abandoned villages are ghostly monuments to a disease that flourished among large aggregations of people and wiped from the record those whose immune systems were compromised by malnutrition.

The changed conditions demanded a different set of survival skills. With agriculture non-productive, farmers abandoned their ploughs and reverted to grazing and hunting, metalsmiths dropped their hammers and became weavers of thick cloth. Social stress brought lawlessness; learning and intellectual pursuits were no longer respected. While civilisation ran backwards, both Roman and Persian power holders responded to the crisis with increased warfare, which could only be supported by increased taxation. The people were literally and metaphorically bled dry.

The nomadic herding and grazing population in the Arabian Peninsula was less severely affected by climate change, and because they were dispersed the tribes were largely spared the plague. As had occurred many times in the past, Arabia experienced a population boom. In the seventh century, explosive emigration pressures coincided with a new religious doctrine based on truths revealed to Mohammad. When the prophet-inspired Arabs swirled out of Arabia like a giant dust cloud, neither of the battling empires had the strength to resist the onslaught. The Eastern Roman Empire, driven out of Syria and walled off in Anatolia, was not destroyed, but Persia succumbed completely and for centuries could not raise her head.

The triumphant Arabs sacked Ctesiphon, smashed its dome and stripped its treasures. The fabled carpet was cut into pieces and sent to Mecca; the masonry and embellishments were transported to the new capital emerging further up the river at Baghdad. Not a single jewel or piece of gold work escaped their plunder. When Jane walked across the isthmus towards Ctesiphon, part of the huge façade and the great arch remained standing; the reception hall, although a ghostly shell, still had an 'imposing majesty'. Part of its dome had survived and in its under-surface were the hooks from which lamps had swung. The king's private apartments and his *anderun* had become dust that lay about in forlorn heaps, searched and sieved many times for any crumb of the past. Jane picked at pottery sherds and broken tiles and tiny pieces of painted stucco. As the disturbed rooks flew out of the ruins, she sat down to read Firdauzi's lament for Ctesiphon.

In her saddlebags Jane carried parts of the seven-volume French translation of the *Shahname* published in Paris 1876–78, and knew by heart some stanzas of the epic poem, including the lament. In that shattered palace she was deeply moved by the poignancy of the verses.

Suspended twenty metres above the ground Jane ignored the admiring shouts of her sailor guard standing below and the dumbfounded Arabs staring up from their nearby camp, and looked out triumphantly over the plain. At Naqsh-i Rustam she had felt cheated when Marcel prevented her ascending to the ledge before Darius's tomb, but by the time they came to Ctesiphon there was no question that she would make her own risk assessments. Her endurance during the long stages had proved her indomitability, her courage when he lay ill and helpless and she directed and guarded the caravan alone had convinced Marcel his protectiveness was unnecessary. He now treated with an equal. When Jane added a length of cable to the kit they were taking from the *Mosul*, aground again near the head of the peninsula, Marcel merely lifted an eyebrow. What was she planning, he wondered.

The 'young master' swinging on a rope attached to a hook in the broken dome of Ctesiphon saw black goatskin tents pitched on the plain where the king had drilled his troops and a party hunting gazelles where Shapur had galloped after lion. Where there had been streets was a patch of newly sprung emerald-green winter wheat, where houses had stood was the lonely domed tomb of Mohammad's barber. Jane focused her binoculars on the far side of the blue Tigris where the city of Seleucia had stood. Like Ctesiphon, more than Ctesiphon, the Greek general's city had suffered history's revenge. Only a single low mound suggested it had ever existed.

Chapter 13
With the Shi'a to the Holy Places

For a short while in Baghdad Jane lost her direction and Susa lost its allure. Embraced by the French Consul's family, Jane's homesickness became intense. She yearned for her mother, her sister Anne and her adored niece, and she ached for France. Whatever had evoked tantalising images of château de Terride and the remembered comforts of her mother's Toulouse home, it was certainly not the consulate. Not in any way European, it was high-walled, its solid iron-studded door opening through a vestibule into a large courtyard where archways led off into stables, cellars, kitchens and official reception rooms. A door at the left, opened to a smaller courtyard which led to the family's private apartments.

The Péretiés passed the summer days in cool deep cellars, escaping at night like all Baghdadis to the roof, but the family had recently moved themselves and their furniture into the winter quarters on the first floor. A European bed dominated the room assigned to the Dieulafoys. Hung with embroidered cotton, sheeted with linen and piled with down quilts, it delighted Jane. She had not slept in a bed since Tehran, the slotted boards offered by Père Pascal at New Julfa and the equally spartan structure in the Shiraz telegraph station not worth the name.

Jane's sybaritic expectations were dashed. Tossing and turning during the night, Jane found the room airless, the bed uncomfortable, the quilts stifling, and the feather-filled pillows smothered her. Trying not to disturb Marcel she slipped out of bed, flung a quilt on the floor and slept soundly until dawn.

Action was Jane's panacea for almost any adverse circumstance. When the first morning rays touched the window she eased open the door, mounted to the roof and surveyed Baghdad. A blood-red disc rising into an orange sky revealed a city divided by a swirling highway already awash with a myriad of boats. On the Tigris's right bank, palaces, tiled domes and slender minarets pierced a high canopy of palm fronds, and substantial flat-roofed houses interrupted the many orange groves. On the left bank, the imposing British consulate set in magnificent gardens bowed to its trembling reflection. A bridge of boats, joining the two halves of the city, swayed beneath the traffic of camel trains and caravans, men on horseback and heavily laden mules. The city was awake, the business day had begun.

Knowing from his previous day's experience at the customs house that the dignitaries and bureaucrats would expect a bribe, Marcel began a cautious search for information about a route to Susa and how to obtain permission to travel. Jane, still not fully recovered from the Basra fever and haunted by images of France, gathered the consul's sleepy daughters and a flush of consular attendants and set off to explore Baghdad. Thinking it unlikely she would ever return, she was determined not to waste a moment. Baghdad must be investigated, discussed, analysed and recorded in her journal. In seven days her camera recorded all the major monuments and took portraits of the Armenian, Jewish, and Chaldean women who besieged her with invitations to visit their houses. Jane explored Baghdad's bazaars, discussed religion and politics with anyone who would converse, interrogated her guides on the difference between Sunni and Shi'a rites, and

Chaldean girl, Baghdad

Jewish woman, Baghdad

described in her usual piquant style everything she saw and learned. With intelligence and charm, energy and discipline, Jane laid out Baghdad like a filleted fish on a plate.

Jostled in the streets by heavily mustachioed soldiers on foot and on horse, she quickly realised why Baghdad, a provincial capital of the Ottoman Turk Empire, was so heavily garrisoned. Though called Dar es-Salam, Abode of Peace, by its founder, its many madrasas made it perhaps a city of religious learning, but never of peace. Preaching sedition and rebellion against their Turkish masters, its four Sunni sects despised and betrayed each other. They were united only in their dislike of infidels and hatred of Shi'as. Early one morning Jane watched Shi'a pilgrims from Persia streaming in through the city's eastern gate on their way to the holy city of Karbala. Waiting in the medan, which the pilgrims had to cross, were several gangs of almost nude young boys. Launching themselves like a flight of arrows, the boys attacked the caravan, stealing a saucepan hanging from a flank, shoving a dirty hand into a carelessly closed saddle bag, pulling at the robes of the old and tired bringing up the rear. They screamed with joy when a fusillade of stones caused a mule to break from the train, half its load crashing to the ground as it swerved and bucked. Darting forward, the little robbers seized whatever they could before disappearing into the mosque. The Arabs in their *abba*s, the Turks with their turned-up toes, the Armenians and Jews – none of them moved to catch the thieves. The red-capped Turkish soldiers turned their backs. 'It's not the infidels who live most dangerously in Baghdad,' Jane concluded, 'it's the Shi'a.'[1]

Walking alongside the crumbling city wall, Jane looked up at its fortified towers and recognised the similarities to medieval keeps in old European towns such as Carcassonne and Avignon, but was simultaneously struck by a singular difference. 'The crumbling Talism Tower[2] does not look out of place in its surroundings, Persian architecture not having changed in 800 years,' she writes, 'whereas the ramparts of Carcassonne and Avignon, although slightly younger than Talism and well restored, are so obviously from a distant epoch because our construction methods and ideas of architectural form have so profoundly altered since the thirteenth century. Only this single difference distinguishes the medieval military architecture of Muslim and Christian,'[3] she concludes. Considering what had brought Marcel to the Orient, it is strange that neither Jane nor Marcel recognised that one was the father of the other, European medieval military architecture having been built from master plans brought from the East by the Crusaders.

Jane was searching for a monument rare in the East – one that memori-alised a woman. She knew it existed, but the tomb of Sitt Zubaida, thought to be the mother of an Abbasid caliph,[4] was not easy to find. Eventually Jane located a green-draped coffin enclosed within a decaying octagonal tomb topped by a muqarnas dome rising in tiers of ever-smaller niches. Looking at it later across ranks of encircling graves, Jane realised that this, like everything else of architectural consequence in Baghdad, was Persian.

During the twelfth and thirteenth centuries, when the secular Seljuks dominated Mesopotamia, the Abbasid family held the caliphate, their address Baghdad. Very little remains of their city. Few of the monuments escaped the Mongol madness, and more perished during Tamerlane's tantrum, but in those that had survived Jane recognised the Seljuk architec-ture now so familiar to her. The intricate brickwork of the Souk al-Gazali minaret[5] was the epitome of Seljuk style.

In 1623 the Safavid Shah Abbas captured an empty and ravaged Baghdad from the Ottoman Turks. During the fourteen years they held it, the Safavids built, repaired and imposed another layer of Persian style. At al-Gailani mosque they added an exquisite tiled dome alongside the orig-inal tomb, although when the Turks took power again, not to be outdone by the loathed Persians, they covered the older dome with gold sheet. The Customs House, the site of a struggle between Marcel and a venal bureau-cracy, had once been a Safavid madrasa, as a band of superb tiles, white calligraphy on a blue ground, proclaimed.

In the late nineteenth century, the city the Safavids had embellished was once again decaying. Since 1637 when the Turks recovered Baghdad, little of consequence had been added and much of importance had been lost. Jane attributed the Turks' lethargy to the fatalism inherent in their reading of the Koran. 'Why bother to fight an epidemic?' a health official asked her, spreading his hands wide. 'Some will die, others will live. *Kitab*. It is written.' Another told her, 'What good is it to struggle against adversity? Man's destiny hangs around his neck,'[6] a concept very foreign to a determined daughter of the European Enlightenment. To their passivity Jane attributed the steep decline of that corrupt sultanate, the Ottoman Turk Empire.

After negotiating travel permits with Turkish functionaries and arranging finances through local bankers, Marcel returned each evening in a white-hot rage. 'Why should their corruption shock you?' asked Jane with a touch of the Eastern fatalism she so deplored, 'You know that every petty official supports four wives and each has to have her own apartment.

Besides, look at the gold on their wrists when their robe slips up their arm! The women have an insatiable desire for finery. Haven't you heard their bracelets and anklets clunking, even above the street noise?'

When Marcel learned they could reach Susa through Amarah, the trading port down the Tigris, Jane was invigorated. Feeling her homesickness betrayed her dream, she dismissed it and made plans for the week, or more, that the authorities in Istanbul would take to issue passes. To Jane it was insupportable to wait in idleness. Each moment, each opportunity must be grasped.

The Dieulafoys considered the archaeological sites of Khorsabad and Nineveh but these were far from Baghdad and had been reclaimed by the desert, they were told. Instead, they turned to the holy Shi'a shrine at Karbala, only fifty kilometres south of Baghdad. From the Karbala road they could reach the site of ancient Babylon, perhaps less interesting than the northern sites since little had been found there, but more accessible.

Before leaving Baghdad Jane and Marcel wanted to visit the Safavid shrine of al-Kadhimain. The shrine stood in a village outside Baghdad's walls, but its two golden domes and four minarets floated above the palm fronds and were enticingly visible from every part of Baghdad. Sightseeing at Jane's pace had exhausted the consul's daughters, so a party of only three processed through the Kadhimain bazaar. Their soldier escort, sheathed sword in hand, shouted to clear a way through lanes crowded with nomad women bringing in poultry and eggs, and used his baton to beat a path through a colourful vegetable market crammed with pyramids of watermelons, green melons, piled beans and figs, little green cabbages, and cucumbers still glistening with dew. The noise was deafening. The customers were mostly men – only poor widows did not have a servant to shop for them – and they bargained at the tops of their voices.

The shrine lay at the far end of the bazaar. As Jane approached, a gang of workmen emerged. She had been permitted to enter Shi'a shrines in Baghdad, so impulsively she moved towards the door. Realising what she intended, the merchants raced from their stalls to head her off, cucumbers and watermelons crashing behind them. Firmly but politely, 'Christians are banned from entering the tomb,' they said, then turned and cursed the escort. Suddenly the bewildered soldier was the centre of a crowd hurling abuse. Affronted, he drew his sword and waved it above the swarm. Marcel, a little way behind Jane, pushed towards him, grabbed his arm and forced it down. 'One drop of blood and we're all dead,' he said, 'Follow me.'

The trio filed out of the market, Jane desperately trying to appear tall as she led the way, the red-capped soldier, sword in its scabbard, bringing up the rear. Little boys shied stones at their legs and danced around the 'sons of dogs'. Well clear of the bazaar, Marcel stopped, put his hand on Jane's shoulder, spun her round and said angrily, 'What did you think you were doing? Don't you remember what happened in Isfahan? Did you want them to beat you again?'[7]

The 'sweet boy's' rashness had transformed Marcel's fear for his dear wife into rage, yet one look at her open, confident face and he knew his argument was with the closed, fanatical society that reviled her.

Marcel was determined there would be no risk-taking at Karbala. Departing Baghdad in the early morning, the Dieulafoys carried letters of recommendation to the religious, civil and military authorities, as well as a permit to view Hussein's shrine signed by the Pasha of Baghdad. Alarmed by the incident at Kadhimain, the French Consul had pressed the pasha to provide a proper escort. Preceding the Dieulafoy caravan as it crossed the Tigris by the bridge of boats were four handsomely uniformed soldiers on fine Arab mounts, saddles and bridles emblazoned with silver, weapons inset with flashing stones. On the west bank the guards executed a fantasia, wildly wheeling their horses, waving unsheathed swords in the air, firing off rounds of ammunition, raising dust and making a great noise. The crowd heading towards the bridge scattered to right and left, while Jane laughed at their absurd pretension.

Leaving the crowded lanes behind, they passed through the city gate and immediately entered a great empty plain, a blue sky overhead, and set off due south across Mesopotamia, their target Hillah on a loop of the Euphrates, near the ruins of Babylon. Wheat fields had given way to desert when the escort halted unexpectedly in mid-morning at a dilapidated caravanserai. When nothing could entice them back on the road, Jane shrugged angrily and ordered lunch prepared.

A whirling cloud of dust resolved into two soldiers, 'badly dressed, poorly armed and so ugly they would frighten the devil himself.'

'You don't expect soldiers like us to waste ourselves in the desert?' the leader of the recalcitrant escort asked Jane haughtily. Gesturing towards the newcomers, he told her, 'Those chaps will look after you. Everyone who saw you leaving Baghdad knows you're foreigners of rank and under the governor's protection – you won't be attacked.' Suddenly Jane understood the display at the bridge. 'Now pay us for the ammunition and uniform hire, and may Allah go with you,'[8] he concluded.

They shared the route with the dead, many travelling horizontally wrapped in cloth and slung two a side on little donkeys, others in make-shift coffins, their dry blackened skin visible between the wooden planks. Weary pilgrims stumbled along, full of joy that only two stages separated them from the martyred Hussein. The caravan's slow pace allowed Jane to read as she rode. Putting aside Herodotus as too modern, she turned to Old Testament accounts of the ancient city-states that had filled the plain. 'What has happened to the rich alluvium of Mesopotamia?' she exclaimed despairingly, pointing towards the flat desert, featureless except for a few broken canals and pieces of old inscribed brick puncturing the uncultivated soil. 'Wherever the Turk or Arab has put his foot Earth's fertility is destroyed,' she said, forgetting that centuries of ceaseless struggle between Romans and Sasanids had irreparably devastated the province long before Islam.

Refusing to share a caravanserai with the putrid stench of cadavers, they camped in the sweet desert air outside its walls. Next morning's ride brought them to a junction where the faithful, living or dead, went on to Karbala, while the infidel Dieulafoys turned towards Hillah and Babylon. In the afternoon, as they rode between lush palm plantations, a sudden heavy downpour began. Jane's despair became paeans of praise. 'The rain has brought new life . . . the green of the trees is most brilliant; sunbeams play on specks of crystal suspended from the ends of the leaves; doves hopping from branch to branch . . . impertinently shower the passerby with rain-drops.'[9] Jane had not seen rain since March and it was now December.

Built from the rubble of Babylon, Hillah was a gateway to the great mounds strung along the banks of the Euphrates where British excavators[10] were searching for Nebuchadnezzar's capital, but Babylon had yielded few secrets. Christmas day in 1881 was filled with speculation and homesickness. Babylon seemed to Jane very grey and mournful, despite the colourful robes of the Arab workers and the red fezzes of the Turks, singing as they attacked a huge mound. She was oppressed by the desolation of the once great city. What has become of the Tower of Babel and the Hanging Gardens, she wondered, and concluded that God's wrath had indeed fallen on the mighty civilisation as He had promised: 'I will come in my rage to the Kings of Babylon and their people . . . I will judge their iniquities and I will condemn the Chaldean earth to an eternal solitude.'[11]

Rich walled gardens, citrus orchards and luxuriant palm forests filled the Karbala plain, the battlefield where Hussein had fought and lost against Yazid in 680 AD. Riding across it on 27 December 1881, Jane was prophetically apprehensive about their reception in the city that had grown up around Hussein's tomb. Entering through the monumental town gate, the Dieulafoys found themselves in a square filled with masons cutting tombstones. Immediately, curses and hate-filled epithets rained on the infidels, 'Sons of burnt fathers' being the least unkind. The faithful pushed them out, screaming that the gate on the far side was reserved for Christian dogs.

Like Qom, Karbala was a city living off the dead. The corpses of people who wanted to lie in death beside Hussein and the pilgrims who came to pray at his tomb paid the salaries of mullahs and of bureaucrats jealous of the mullahs' power. The air was thick with grievance and revenge, rancid with hatred for Sunnis, acrid with detestation of the Wahhabis who in 1802 had attacked Karbala, desecrated Hussein's tomb and stolen its jewel-encrusted grill.

The tomb stood within a walled complex. The saga of Marcel's attempt to gain the mullahs' permission to view the complex from the roof of a nearby house – not to enter, merely to view it from above – was long, convoluted and bitter. Filled with prevarication and mendacious duplicity on one side, inflexible hauteur on the other, there was no chance of a happy ending. Marcel's letters of recommendation and the pasha's instruction were wasted paper, and the outcome acrimonious. The Dieulafoys rode away 'cursing the lot of them, a habit acquired in Persia.'[12]

Jane's experiences in Babylonia confirmed her already ambivalent response to Persia. 'During my stay in Persia I never ceased to rail against their administration and customs, while at the same time recognising the high intellectual accomplishments and artistic genius of the Iranians. "Allah, in creating the Turks, has wanted to make me regret the Persians," I said yesterday to Marcel, "Since the day I put foot in [Turkish territory] it seems to me I have been transported from Heaven to Hell."

'The clever European politicians are deluding themselves with the idea that by imposing our institutions on the Orient we will introduce them at the same time to our civilisation. To me, that is nothing more than an illusion; the administrative mechanisms of the Occident are much too complex . . . for inexperienced hands. It is not by enforcing them to copy . . . European customs that Muslim nations will progress, but by adopting the [philosophy] and political methods characteristic of the great Oriental dynasties. How I would like to reform the Turkish Empire into the old satrapies.'[13]

Did Jane really want to impose Sasanid rule on the Turks or to restore this former satrapy to the Achaemenid Empire? No. In her characteristic mix of irreverent amusing remarks and shrewd analysis she shows an understanding of Mesopotamian realities, which in the early twenty-first century seems curiously prescient.

Chapter 14
The deadly price of Susa

The dreaded robbers, the Beni La'am, were an Arab tribe with a fearful reputation, who haunted the plains and marshes between the Tigris River and the Zagros Mountains. The Bakhtiari were Lur tribespeople who at the time of Marco Polo's travels, had 'already vindicated for themselves the unenviable reputation as thieves and bandits, which their successors have diligently maintained.'[1] Jane gave her mule a whack on the rump and in January 1882 rode into their lairs.

In Baghdad the French Consul had not been encouraging. 'It is possible to take the caravan route from Amarah to Dizful, and it's true Susa is only a few hours ride from there across the plain. It can be done, but it's dangerous. Are you sure you want to go? Susa has nothing of interest except a great tumulus.' Then, recognising Jane's determination, M. Péretié gave a Gaelic shrug and set about helping her. 'The rains,' he said, 'look like starting early this year. If you're going, you'd better not waste any time.'

Jane's homesickness was still acute. Every night she dreamed of her family and increasingly she longed for the comfort she had left almost a year before, yet Susa still beckoned. Flandin's and Coste's drawings of Susa had captured Jane's imagination, despite Marcel and Viollet-le-Duc finding them inadequate. The few deciphered inscriptions increased her fascination. Little enough, but together they spawned the dream that was carrying her towards this place the consul dismissed as 'only a great tumulus'.

A compromise to their conflicting desires saw the Dieulafoys book two passages – one on the *Escombrera* sailing at the end of January for Europe and the other on the *Caliph*, which would take them down the Tigris River to Amarah at the end of the week.

With permission from the Pasha of Baghdad to travel through Ottoman territory and Zil-es-Sultan's letter to the Persians in a waterproof carrier, their holsters filled with bags of small-denomination Turkish and Persian coins, new panniers bought in the bazaar, and an introduction to Jesus, Jane and Marcel arrived at Amarah on 1 January 1882. A crowd of Turks, Arabs, Greeks and Jews rushed aboard, their nationality more recognisable by their dress than their tongue. Some came to do business, many to load the wheat and indigo brought down by caravan from Dizful and Kermanshah, others to take off merchandise sent from Baghdad. Hoping to stay out of the melee, Shi'a pilgrims returning to Persia from the holy places withdrew to the foredeck, while in the captain's cabin Jane and Marcel waited for Jesus.

When Jesus, a member of Amarah's Christian community, read the consul's letter he immediately set about arranging for the Dieulafoys to join a returning Dizful caravan, but without success. He had no luck hiring horses. Although there were some fine mounts in Amarah, a town where the Arab studbook was recited more often than the Koran and the owners knew the blood lines of every horse in their string, both Turk and Arab valued their mounts too highly to allow a foreigner on its back. 'An infidel will never defile my horse,' they said. If an increased fee overcame that objection, all deals were off at the mention of the route. No one would risk their animals in Beni La'am territory. 'Those sons of burnt fathers would steal a horse while the rider was hot on its back,' they declared. Days later, still unable to hire horses, Jane applied to the town governor, who explained, 'Even I can't get one. When I asked a tribal chief he said, "Do you want my daughter? She is yours. I would rather give you her, and with a large dowry to boot, than let you have my mare."'[2]

They would settle for mules, the Dieulafoys conceded – two good riding mules and four pack mules – but even these were unavailable. Light rain fell, an ominous reminder of the season and the risk of being cut off from the mountains by an inundated plain. The pressure to start became urgent. Jane paced streets narrowed by overhanging lattice-windowed upper storeys, breathed the humid air and thought of the uplands. Deafened by shouting merchants in the dark, covered bazaar, she longed for the silence of the road and the open sky. She feared the unhealthy town would bring another attack of fever. The restless, wasted days made her anxious and she knew time was running out for visiting Susa and still catching the boat to France.

News came of an indigo caravan making its way to Amarah, expected in two days. Hopeful they could hire its mules, Jesus contracted a guide who

Beggarwoman, Amarah

knew the route to Dizful, Jane organised their supplies and Marcel applied to the governor for a soldier escort.

'Certainly not. If anything happened to you, it would be on my head.'

On the eve of the caravan's arrival, Jesus took the Dieulafoys to his church, where a Chaldean priest celebrated mass in the tiny low-ceilinged room. Humbled by the poverty and piety of the small congregation and aware of the Christians' precarious existence in Amarah, Jane recognised that her frustration at being trapped in the town for a week was self-indulgent.

At midday on 7 January 1882 the Dieulafoys' small caravan left steaming Amarah and rode out onto a plain greened by the early showers. Rolling away east towards the Zagros Mountains, it was a part of the great Mesopotamian plain, narrowed at Amarah by an incurve of the Tigris River, and crossable in a few days. Divided north to south by the border between the empire of the Ottoman Turks and the realm of the Persian shah, a political nicety mostly ignored by animals, nomads and soldiers, the plain's rich alluvial soil became a stoneless desert in the burning heat, but quickly transformed into a quagmire when rain fell. Marshes lurked in its hollows, the cracked mud and beds of limp reeds a refuge for birds and desert animals in the summer. In winter they became impassable swamps. It was the territory of the wandering Beni La'am. Straddling the border and subject to two governments, the tribe hated Turkish pashas even more than the Persian tax gatherers. With the mobility of their famed horses, they mostly managed to avoid both, living by selling on the horses they stole from their neighbours and relentless pillage of caravans.

From Amarah, when the air is clear – though not on the threatening, overcast day when Jane set out – the Bakhtiari ranges of the Zagros Mountains can be seen rising in snow-topped tiers on the eastern horizon. Great rivers rush through its dramatic gorges. In the fertile valleys between the ranges nomadic Bakhtiaris pitched their tents and indulged their favourite occupations of raiding and feuding.

Beni La'am and Bakhtiari were sworn enemies. Both could be described as rough, ignorant and fierce, and both lived by plunder and thievery, but they also lived according to an inviolable law that decreed anyone coming to their tents must be given protection and hospitality, in line with Mohommad's instruction, 'Honour the guest, even though he be an infidel.' But should a caravan, such as the Dieulafoys', set up camp alone in the open they were anyone's game. The traveller was only safe if he reached the tribe's tents before night fell.

So it was a night of terror for Jane and Marcel, their muleteers and cook when they became lost in a swamp. As rain poured down, they were trapped on a shrinking piece of high ground. Using their new coffin-like trunks Marcel built a wall, spread their groundsheets behind it and rigged their mackintoshes as protection. Crouched underneath, he and Jane wrapped themselves in their bedrolls and prayed for the storm to pass. The muleteers pulled their sheepskin coats above their heads and huddled down; the cook 'crouched like a monkey on top of his biggest saucepan' and pulled his scarlet fez down to his eyebrows; the mules lowered their heads and turned their rumps to the gale. Everyone was hungry, their minds filled with thoughts of steaming rice and how it would warm them, but even if a fire had been possible in the rain, they would not have dared. 'No light, no fire, sahib, and do not make any noise or the marsh Arabs will find us,' the guide warned. 'We haven't paid to cross their land; they won't treat us kindly.'

Jane doubted any human noise could be heard above the violence of the storm. She could hear nothing except the wind thrashing the reeds and the rain pelting onto the mackintoshes. Nonetheless, she and Marcel loaded their revolvers and propped their rifles within reach.

The storm worsened during the night. As the wind raged and the rain drove in sheets, Jane fell asleep exhausted. Waking at dawn, she found Marcel had piled his bedding over her and she was fairly dry except for her feet and legs which, anyway, had been wet since the rain started in the afternoon. Urgently, the caravan sprang to life and prepared to leave. Grudgingly, the guide admitted that in the darkness he had led them westwards. He had his bearings now, he said, even though there was no sun in the brooding sky. Stiff and aching, Jane struggled into the saddle.

As they beat their way out of the reeds Jane began shivering uncontrollably. She told herself it was only the cold, but feared it was the fever. When the rain began again, a racing pulse and violent trembling left her in no doubt, but the caravan could not stop. They could not risk another night defenseless in the open, and the wasted hours when they travelled in the wrong direction had to be retrieved. Before darkness fell they must reach the tents of the nomads. She closed her eyes and clung to the pommel.

Young lambs, when they are dry, smell of milk and wild thyme. Their muzzles are moist and their little tongues rough and rasping. Waking in the night, Jane wasn't sure what was scratching her shorn head and moistly nuzzling her neck. She was aware that something very warm was lying along her back and across her legs, but her bedding was too soft to do anything other than sigh and go back to sleep. Waking again hours later, she saw that she was in a goatskin tent, lying on a pile of sheepskins among a fall of baby lambs. Beyond black felt strips corralling the lambs in the corner she could see women's heads moving about. The women were talking and laughing, tossing back their long wild curls, silver bangles clattering on their wrists.

Glancing in, one of the women met Jane's fevered eyes and called out something in Arabic. Marcel came and sat beside her; Jane then remembered riding up to the tents and being 'lifted off like a piece of baggage and carried into the big tent and laid down among the lambs. Only their warmth saved my life,'[3] she wrote.

Two days later Jane woke to sunshine streaming through the tent entrance. During the night she had burned with fever, but with the sunlight willpower and optimism returned. She could hear Marcel and the muleteers talking outside and caught the muleteers' impatience. 'We can't count on this weather holding,' they said, 'the winter rains have begun. We must get away while we can. We can't waste another day.'

Marcel came and asked her, 'Will we go on? Are you well enough? Should we give up and go back and wait for the boat in Baghdad?'

'We're not going back. We must go on,' she insisted, 'we've come too far to give up Susa now.'

Jane thanked the women who had shown such rough, generous kindness while she lay with the lambs. Their sour milk and yoghurt had given her back her strength, she said, walking unsteadily towards her mule. With the sun warming her face, she set off towards a large tumulus on the far side of the emerald-green plain. She pondered on the city whose achievement had crumbled away to leave such a large pile of earth. Behind it, like a theatre backdrop, rose shining snow-crested mountains. In their lower ranges lay the town of Dizful, gateway to Susa. Flicking the reins, Jane rode forward.

Anxious when they lost the track after crossing a flooded river, the party was reassured by the sight of a camel train plodding across the plain. The train swayed by, bells ringing, bright metalwork shining on embroidered harness. But before too long fever again gripped Jane, violently shaking her frail body. She clung to the pommel, her heart pounding against her ribs, then, almost unconscious, she slipped sideways and fell from the saddle onto the wet ground. Marcel rushed to help her, yet even with his arm around her she could not stand. 'Dear wife,' he begged, 'we can't stay here. You must get up, please try,' but she could not, her legs would not support her, they were jelly.

The muleteers gathered round and peered down at her. There was no wood and no food or water. 'Out in the open like this, the Arabs will murder us,' they pleaded, 'we can't defend ourselves.'

I can't go on, she thought. Is it my fate to die here of misery or will the Arabs kill me first?

Seven hours later, the setting sun was striking a group of black tents. Strings of camels and flocks of sheep and goats were being herded into brushwood corrals for the night, men in dark *abbas* hurrying on the stragglers. Women in bright red dresses were milking the cows and bringing water to the animals. Horses waited while their saddles were taken off, then, groomed and hobbled, they put their heads down to graze. Children swooped after clucking chickens. The Beni La'am, noisy and purposeful, did not notice the Dieulafoys' approaching caravan.

Marcel walked beside Jane's mule, holding in place a bundle lying along its back. Marching on the far side to stop the package from slipping his way, a muleteer guided the animal forward. Reaching the tents, Marcel asked for asylum; he and the muleteer unbuckled the straps holding the bundle on the mule's back, carried it into the tent and placed it near the fire. Inside the parcel, wrapped in bedding, lay Jane.

The muleteers were impatient with the delay. Another wasted day. Again Marcel said they should return to the Tigris, again Jane would not hear of it. Warily, Marcel negotiated with the Beni La'am for safe passage through their territory. For a substantial payment per baggage animal, the tribe famous for horse stealing and caravan plundering guaranteed the Dieulafoys' safety as far as Dizful, overgenerous of them since the Dieulafoys would be in Bakhtiari territory once they crossed the Kerkhah River.

The tribe left before dawn to take the animals out to the pastures, only a few old men remaining to guard the tents. Women with small children and babies stayed to do the tent chores, to squeeze and toss a bladder filled with milk to make curds, to bake bread. Jane knew the tribe's fearsome reputation and terrible history; she dosed herself with quinine and began a conversation. Few Europeans having crossed their plain the women were extremely curious about the 'young man', and happy to talk as they fed the lambs too young to go out with the flock.

Although the Beni La'am were polygamous, the wives led relatively free lives and were proudly independent. Jane thought them handsome, their bodies lithe and elegant. Supposedly Muslim, they wore their religion lightly. They did not veil, merely wrapped a fine wool turban loosely

Beni La'am woman

around the head. Heavy silver bracelets encrusted with turquoise and glass necklaces were prized possessions. In the afternoon they pulled forward colourful storage bags filled with dyed wool and set up their carpet looms. The conversation turned to how they resolved disputes within the tribe and how they thwarted Ottoman soldiers and Persian tax gatherers. They boasted about their fleetness. They escaped into the marshes, they proudly explained, where their pursuers became lost. Sometimes they hid their valuables in the reeds and galloped away, they said, but Jane knew they were not always successful. Tribal power was being broken, the pashas had taken many of their best horses and Zil-es-Sultan's extortionate taxation was impoverishing them.

In order to reach Dizful before nightfall, the caravan set off early. Parcelled up, strapped in place along the mule's back, once the sunshine warmed her Jane stopped shivering and her pounding pulse slowed. By midday she felt well enough to throw off her wrappings and investigate an imamzadde standing deserted and unlocked on the plain. Soon after the ascent into the mountains began, they came on a ruined Sasanid castle, defiant on a hilltop. Using its fallen blocks as a stairway, Jane leapt up towards broken arches at the top of a wall that had once supported a soaring vault. From there she had a sweeping view of the countryside. Large mounds suggested that other buildings had once stood nearby. A white streak tumbling from a gash in the mountains was the Kerkhah River. Susa lay downstream, inaccessible to the party through the wild gorges, their only route the longer, safer way through Dizful. But her effort had been too great, too soon, and she began to shake. Once more she was wrapped and strapped for travel.

The Kerkhah was the tribal frontier. In antiquity an Achaemenid bridge had carried the Royal Road across the river and its pure water had filled crystal jugs to slake the royal thirst in Susa. Now there was no bridge, and the waters of the river, augmented by recent rain, rushed fiercely over a ford, impossible to cross while lying flat on a mule's back. Sheer will power got Jane out of her bedding and upright in the saddle. Crossing her feet on the pommel to keep them out of the water, she brought her whip down on the flanks of a reluctant mule, shouting 'Ho, ho, son of a burnt father, son of a dog, get on.'

Carried down river by a strong current, eventually the caravan climbed the bank on the far side, all except one baggage mule bowled over by the torrent.

'Forget the sugar,' the guide admonished Jane who was bemoaning the lost load, 'we're on an island. We still have to get through the other branch of the river.'

Nothing would induce the mules back into the white water. Suddenly on the opposite bank riders appeared, their horses prancing and rearing. Heads turbaned in striped cloth and hung about with arms, the riders were not slow to grasp the Dieulafoys' predicament. Gathering up the reins they spurred their horses into the water. Jane had survived the Beni La'am. Plunging towards her were the Bakhtiari.

When the Dieulafoys had met a troupe of Bakhtiari at Eqlid some months before, they had the protection of the local governor's son. Here on the river bank they had only their own rifles and revolvers; the muleteers, despite the nasty looking knives in their belts were sure to abandon them in any confrontation. But, as with the Arabs, Jane's encounter with these tribesmen proved less terrifying in reality than in expectation. They were a hunting party led by a chieftain's son. 'Another week and you'd never get across. You'd be stuck for three months,' the youth said, forcing the mules into the water. Once across the river, shaking water from his saddle, he insisted they visit his father, Kerim Khan.

An Englishman who spent some time with the Bakhtiaris described them as 'individually brave, but of a cruel and savage character; they pursue their blood feuds with the most inveterate and exterminating spirit, and they consider no oath . . . binding when it interferes with their thirst of revenge; indeed the dreadful stories of domestic tragedy . . . in which whole families have fallen at each others' hands . . . are enough to freeze the blood with horror . . . the most wild and barbarous of all the inhabitants of Persia.'[4] Knowing their reputation and filled with trepidation, the Dieulafoys held their heads high as they walked past the tall fierce men standing guard at the tent's entrance. Kerim Khan, a handsome dark-eyed man with a commanding presence, welcomed them courteously and to Jane's intense relief offered tea instead of savagery.

The black tent was full of colour. Leaping flames rose from a fire burning in a ring of stones. Rich carpets lay in front of the fire, their bright borders framing gardens of abstract flowers. It was a pity, she thought as she sat down, it was not she who was the robber – she would like one of these beautiful rugs. Women spread an eating mat over one of the carpets, covering it with freshly made flat bread and yoghurt. Sour milk and *chai* appeared, then *kalians* were brought. Days of fever had left Jane very weak and her head was swimming. To appear vulnerable would endanger the whole party. She struggled to hide her weakness. When the sheikh's son hooked his index fingers together and vowed, 'From now on we are brothers,' Jane entwined her fingers and responded clearly, 'I am obliged to you, my dear Mohammad. In life as in death,'[5] having no idea how that vow would resonate in the future.

Heartened by the cordiality of the encounter and also perhaps by the hot tea, Jane took the saddle to ride up through the chain of oases leading to Dizful. Fields of wheat and indigo and substantial flocks and herds grazing the pastures testified to the rich soil of the Bakhtiaris' winter home. Horsemen and caravans streamed past on the busy route as it climbed slowly into the hills. The sun had set before they reached the old Sasanid bridge leading across the river to Dizful's town gates.

Which had already been locked for the night. Although Marcel shouted and beat on the gate with his riflestock, the watchman refused to let them in. Marcel felt in his saddlebag and produced Zil-es-Sultan's letter. That quickly brought the key to the town and admission to a room with a door that locked, windows that closed and a fire that warmed.

The anticipated four-day journey from Amarah had taken a week and severely compromised Jane's health. The flooded marshes, days of rain and constantly wet clothes, nights without privacy in the nomads' tents and persistent fever constituted a nightmare which only the dream of Susa could dispel. Yet still it seemed unreachable, closed off for two days by rain that fell in sheets, making travel inconceivable. In fact the delay was fortunate – Jane had almost reached her physical limits and, though her spirit was willing, the enforced idleness gave her body a chance to recover.

The deputy governor's invitation to visit his wives broke the monotony. During her previous visits to *anderun*s no man had been present and the women had talked and laughed quite freely. When the deputy governor's ten-year-old son escorted her to his father's *anderun* the ladies behaved very differently. The male child's actions and the women's response reflected the husband's absolute power over his wives and revealed to Jane his way of dominating and controlling them.

Each wife had her own suite in accord with Koranic instruction. Jane's guide arranged the visits in order of rank. The most senior was a Persian who had some education, although not in geography. To her all foreign countries were one, Britain and Russia existing side by side; France she had never heard of. Her friends laughingly chorused, 'They're all filled with infidels,' but the ten-year-old raised his hand, only slightly, and the women instantly fell silent. Trying on her white helmet and amazed at Jane's shorn hair, they pressed around her. Again the boy made an authoritative gesture. Back on their carpets, they exclaimed from a respectful distance, 'You comb your hair every day? It's enough at our weekly bath.' A raised eyebrow stopped their chatter. Tea was served, but only to Jane and the child. After several cups Jane reclaimed her white helmet.

In the next suite a submissive, tiny brown-skinned Arab woman, the mother of the only son, astonished Jane by her deference to her own child. Conversation was halting, yet even with the best intent how could these two women expect to reach across the divide of culture and experience to find common ground? There was no intellectual meeting point between Jane, a true daughter of the eighteenth-century Enlightenment, devoted to science, reason and classical moderation, and an uneducated tribal woman who believed in charms and talismans.

The Frenchwoman saw an open-fronted transparent silk chemise exposing the second wife's breasts and stomach, saw bare legs visible almost to the crutch under the flounces of a very full short skirt and judged the dress immodest. The woman's life, limited to personal care and the making of a few sweetmeats, appalled Jane.

On her side, the tribeswoman, pulling at her tinselled silk veil and stroking the luxuriant coarse dark curls falling loosely over her shoulders, looked with wonder and distaste at Jane's shorn head. Since her fine silky curls had tumbled to the floor in Bushire, Jane had kept her head shaven, and the Arab saw only a faint blonde fuzz. Was such unnatural hair the work of a sorceress? What terrible need, she wondered, forced this foreign woman to leave the shelter of her home and endure the rigours of travel to a far country. The poor thing was bone-thin, her face gaunt; there were dark shadows under her eyes. She looked ill. Why did her husband not take proper care of her? Was he so poor that his wife had to work, she asked, for she understood Jane's part in the expedition, recording and photographing, as something imposed. Though she felt desperately sorry for a woman who had to endure such a hard life, dialogue was impossible.

While Jane drank more cups of diplomatic tea they pursued a conversation that had no meaning for either. Only Jane's words of praise for the beautiful Arab mares stabled in the courtyard touched the heart of the second wife and filled her eyes with wistfulness. Did the tribal woman mourn the freedom of life under the black tents which she had lost when the deputy governor acquired her? The question could never be asked.

The son raised his hand. The visit was terminated.

In the rooms of the master's favourite a dark-eyed Arab woman longed for the status that a son would bring. Eight months pregnant and already the mother of five daughters, it was evident that a sea of jealousy washed between Bibi Dordoun and the mother of the only son. More cups of tea brought a request to predict the baby's gender. Put on the spot Jane foretold a son, justifying it later to Marcel, 'I will be far away when the baby is born and if I am wrong the mother will at least have had several weeks of happy expectation.'

After so much tea Jane was very uncomfortable, but etiquette demanded she contain herself, and there was still the fourth wife.

On the way back to her lodging Jane saw a patch of blue in the southwest corner of the sky. Thirty-five kilometres away in that direction lay Susa.

The track was treacherous after the rain. The horses slipped and slithered their way down to the plain. In the distance a great tumulus rose like a flat-topped mountain against a leaden sky.

For tens of centuries people had built their city on the ruins of the one they had destroyed, successive palaces commanding the plain from an ever-increasing height. As each was sacked and levelled, the pile of crumbled sun-dried bricks grew larger, until one day, one century, power moved elsewhere. With the heap of past achievement left to the mercy of seeds blown by the wind, grasses and spindly dry bushes appeared on its rain-riven slopes. Searching for plants came goats to climb the tumulus, their sharp hoofs cutting twisting pathways around its flanks and loosening the compressed dust. Sometimes a pile of crumbled earth fell away in a desert storm and revealed a part of the past, an inscribed stone perhaps, or a brass vessel, or an ashlar that a villager could use in building a new house.

Foreigners came and poked about the ruins. The news of what they found spread among Europeans curious about past civilisations and drew them to the tumulus. Rawlinson, an English officer then employed by the Qajars to convert straggling troops into an army, came in 1836 and 'was particularly struck with the extraordinary height of this mound,' and found, lying exposed on its western face, 'a slab with a cuneiform inscription of thirty-three lines in length engraved on it ... part of an obelisk, which existed not many years ago, erect upon the summit of the mound, and the broken fragments of the other parts of it are seen in the plain below.' He was not the first; in fact Rawlinson was lured to the site by an earlier description of a triangular stone inscribed on two faces in cuneiform. On the third were

Bibi Dordoun, Dizful

Egyptian hieroglyphs, which he hoped would help him decipher the cuneiform script. He was too late. The 'famous black stone with the bilingual inscription,' he lamented, 'was blown to shivers a short time ago by a fanatical Arab in hope of discovering a treasure; and thus perished all the fond hopes that archaeologists have built upon this precious relic.'[6] (Despite this loss Rawlinson did succeed in unlocking cuneiform.)

Another Englishman, Layard, who lived for a year with the Bakhtiaris, came in 1842 full of grief for his friend, the Ilkhani Mohammad Taki Khan, betrayed into the hands of the treacherous Qajars, and found inscribed stones re-used in a stair descending to the river. Others came, including the French artists Flandin and Coste in 1841. In 1852 William Kennet Loftus, a surveyor working with an international team to define a border between Turk and Persian following their recent war, moonlighted for a time as an archaeologist and put the first scientific spade into the tumulus. His finds confirmed that the mountain was indeed the grave of ancient Susa.

The lovely plain of Susiana, geographically a southeasterly sweep of the Mesopotamian plain but set apart by a history of interlocked plain and mountain peoples, appeared quite deserted. Only the extraordinary mound, which seemed to grow larger as they rode towards it, rose above the flatness. Like something turned out of a giant jelly mould, the flat-topped tumulus stood silhouetted against a mass of threatening grey cloud, its fluted flanks defined by violet shadows.

When they came closer they saw Daniel's Tomb standing apart and long-legged storks searching the bank of the Shaur River, a wandering stream, shallow and marshy, which guarded the western side of the mound. Splashing through the water Jane drew rein before the huge mass, the magnet that had drawn her from France. Its steep sides rearing thirty-six metres above the river, it overwhelmed Daniel's Tomb, reducing its spire to little more than a stack of sugar cubes. The Dieulafoys dismounted and followed the goat tracks winding to the top.

If the tumulus had seemed huge when sighted from the plain, looking along its summit magnified the impression. Before them lay a vast riven plateau formed from the tops of three distinct piles, each at a different level, connected by narrow isthmuses, with a total circumference of ten kilometres. Pushing through the woody shrubs on one crest they found an exposed broken doorway surrounded by enormous blocks of masonry, on another pottery sherds poked from the earth and on the third was an overturned column base inscribed in cuneiform characters.

Jane had reached Susa and found a mountain. What was hidden beneath its crust she longed to know, but not today, not this night. The ride had consumed all her strength and she was forced to leave the tumulus and seek a bed at Daniel's Tomb.

From the mound Jane had a view of the plain. In the clear morning light it swept away uninterrupted in three directions, to the north lay the snow-covered Bakhtiari ranges. It was impossible to stand looking out and not imagine the plain populated by the oncoming troops of Alexander the Great. How must the residents of the Achaemenid city have felt, she wondered, when they saw the Greek army marching towards them on that December day in 331 BC. King Darius III, defeated at Issus and Gaugamela, was somewhere in the mountains near Ecbatana; the people knew he would not come to save them. The city's governor had gone out to the bridge over the Kerkhah where he waited with twelve Indian elephants and a herd of camels as a symbol of the city's submission. If the offerings were not accepted, devastation and pillage would be the Susians' lot.

In the city that Darius the Great had built two hundred years before, the watching Persians would have seen the dust and heard the noise as the sweltering troops came on towards them, the Greek host disguising greed as revenge for the destruction of their temple on the Athens Acropolis. What form would their retribution take? Did the Susians prepare themselves for death? Did they stand frozen in acceptance of whatever Ahura Mazda had foreordained? Or did some flee with their treasures?

Jane knew that Alexander had accepted the governor's surrender and the city was not destroyed, not then. Instead, Alexander left the satrap in his palace, garrisoned a Macedonian general in the citadel and married off 5000 of the women from the moated walled city to his Greek troops. What a night of bacchanalia, she thought, must have followed the mass wedding, but better than destruction. Afterwards, Alexander trucked away the city's fabulous riches, exotic jewellery and gold rhitons in mule carts and piled its gold lace curtains and silk hangings onto the backs of asses.

Alexander was not the first king to cross the Susiana plain vowing vengeance. When capital of the earlier Elamite kingdom, Susa sometimes dominated the whole Mesopotamian region, sometimes trembled before its enemies. The Elamites' sacking of Babylon made King Nebuchadnezzar their sworn enemy. Carrying off rich booty from conquests in Assyria in 646 BC brought King Ashurbanipal screaming across the plain to recover Nineveh's treasure. When the Elamite king fled naked into the mountains,

Ashurbanipal axed the forests and destroyed the city, giving the *coup de grâce* to a dynasty already weakened by internal factions. Cyrus the Great, marching down through the mountain passes from Pasargadae in Fars, easily attached the shattered Elamite kingdom to his Achaemenid Empire. Cyrus's price for allowing the Elamites to remain a distinct people within his empire was a *No Ruz* offering. On Persepolis's staircase Jane had seen stone Elamites bringing a lioness and cubs to stock the king's hunting park.

The patched-up ruins of Elamite Susa soon became Cyrus's administrative centre and winter capital, but for Darius the Great, King of Kings, a battered town was not enough to reflect his power or the might of his empire. Twenty years before he ordered the construction of Persepolis, Darius called in the tribute from his many lands to create a splendid city.

Jane had read of Susa's magnificence in her Bible. The Book of Esther Chapter 1 describes Shushan (Susa) at the time of King Ahasuerus (Xerxes):

> Now it came to pass in the days of Ahasuerus . . . which reigned from India even unto Ethiopia . . . when the King Ahasuerus sat on the throne of his kingdom, which was in Shushan the palace.
>
> In the third year of his reign, he made a feast unto all his princes and his servants; the power of Persia and Medea, the nobles and the princes of the provinces being before him:
>
> When he showed the riches of his glorious kingdom . . . unto all the people that were present in Shushan the palace . . .
>
> Where were white, green, and blue hangings, fastened with cords of fine linen and purple to silver rings and pillars of marble; the beds[7] were of gold and silver upon a pavement of red, and blue, and white, and black marble.
>
> And they gave them drink in vessels of gold, (the vessels being diverse one from another) and royal wine in abundance.

On the Athens Acropolis Jane's thoughts had turned to Susa. Now at Susa her thoughts returned to Athens. The Parthenon had survived the centuries, mutilated and marred perhaps, but its beauty still dazzled the beholder. What of Susa? At first glance it appeared to have turned to dust, a bitter fate for a city once so proud. Yet, she wondered, does any part of its glory remain? Is there something buried in the heart of the mound that will reveal the life of the Achaemenid court and the minds of the people who lived here? If she could look down into the tumulus, would she see more than crumbled clay and rotted wood? Something intangible seemed to well up from the heart of the mound, something she could not define. What is it, she asked.

If only she could think clearly, but her head was swimming. All night, while the sayyid and his followers partied, she had lain awake astounded by their revelry at the sacred tomb, and now she was too tired for rational thought. When she had stood on the Athens Acropolis, she had been fit and strong, exhilarated by the dream of Persia, determined to reach Susa. Now, she thought, look at me! In less than a year I've become an old woman, thin and ugly, I've lost my strength, my health has gone, too much quinine has seriously damaged my eyes, and if I don't go and lie down I will faint and fall off this tumulus that I have struggled so hard to reach.

For a second time she was forced to leave the mound and return to the tomb, unsatisfied and unhappy.

In the courtyard at Daniel's Tomb a terrified child's screams beat at Jane's already splitting head. Pushing forward to the centre of the raucous crowd she found the arrogant sayyid who had arrived the previous night after the doors were shut. Beating down the door, he had burst into the courtyard with a ragtag of followers, blazing into a rage of hatred when he discovered the Dieulafoys lodged in a black closet under the tomb's peristyle.

'Get them out, the sons of dogs,' he frothed. 'An animal byre is too good for them, even cows and buffaloes would protest if they had to lie near them.'[8]

When the trembling tomb guardian brought him the letter from the chief mullah in Dizful that authorised the Dieulafoys' accommodation, the sayyid wrathfully installed himself in the arcade beneath the tomb's vestibule. Though doorless and exposed to wind and rain, from it he could guard the chamber against the foreigners. Having sung and prayed, argued and smoked until the early hours of the morning, he and his retinue were sound asleep when Jane and Marcel slipped away to the tumulus at first light.

Now in the courtyard, the sayyid was having an epileptic fit. In his arms an almost naked two-year-old screamed with fear as the sayyid's face contorted and his body shook. Not thinking of consequences, Jane was about to pull the child away when her cook grabbed her arm. 'Don't touch them. The sayyid is curing him of the sickness that the big sahib could not.'

The previous afternoon when some women had brought children with symptoms of acute juvenile arthritis to him, Marcel's impatient advice had been to unwind the huge turbans from their little heads and dress their shivering bodies with the cloth. 'Keep them warm,' he said. 'What do you expect when your children go naked in winter?'

Jane realised the cook had saved her from a very rash act and withdrew to the black closet. She was asleep when the sayyid recovered from his fit and set off with his entourage, no doubt to bully a tomb guardian elsewhere. Waking to silence, she peered out her door into a deserted courtyard. Knowing the guardian was at the tumulus with Marcel, she slipped inside the mosque. In a glass case protected by an elaborate silver grill lay a coffin draped with gold-embroidered cloth. Candlelight flickered on coins and jewelled offerings slipped in between the glass and the grill. A mirror-tiled ceiling flashed overhead.

The story of Daniel, a Jewish prisoner brought in chains to Babylon when King Nebuchadnezzar captured Jerusalem, is related in the Old Testament against a background of dynasties that ruled the Mesopotamian and Susiana plains long ago. Daniel witnessed Nebuchadnezzar's senile madness and lived through the reign of his son, Belshazzar, during which he dreamt, 'I saw in a vision . . . that I was at [Susa] in the palace . . . and I was by the river of Ulai [Shaur].'[9]

All three 'peoples of the Book' honour Daniel as a prophet. The bones in this Muslim shrine, a twelfth-century mosque topped by a conical white sugar-loaf spire, the fashion in Khuzestan, are very unlikely to be Daniel's. Even so, Jane ran a huge risk in entering the tomb. Had the fanatics discovered the infidel she would have been set upon, worse if their vengeance revealed her gender, but how could a woman as curious as Jane ignore such an opportunity, even when beset by illness? When a bundle of black rags in the corner of the room resolved into a sleeping woman, Jane fled.

During the night the rain returned. Afraid of being cut off by rising river levels, which would prevent their rendezvous with the *Escombrera* at the end of the month, the Dieulafoys packed up early next morning and left Susa for Dizful. To avoid running the gauntlet of the tribes when returning to the Tigris, they planned instead to go on to Shushtar and from there to Ahwaz, where, they had been told, they would find a boat to take them down the Karun River to Mohammerah, only a short distance from the Shatt al Arab and the ship that would return them to France.

The track had become a sea of mud. The rain fell out of the sky with a sad hopelessness, a match for Jane's thoughts. Behind her the tumulus had disappeared under a curtain of mist and cloud. Over her own ebullient personality hung a veil of disappointment, a web of regret that her inspection had been inadequate, had added nothing to the revealed secrets of Susa. She felt there was something not finished, something she had missed, but she was too ill to think what it might be.

Jane no longer had the stamina to survive long rides and rough camps, even when the weather was fine. That night a fearful storm arose. The party crouched beneath a broken stairway, the only shelter in an abandoned roofless caravanserai, while the cook struggled to light a fire and cook some rice. In the morning the clouds had rolled back, and the thunder, lightning and raging wind had vanished. The sun appeared above snow-crested Zagros peaks to reveal a rich green valley, where flocks of sheep and goats grazed, and a track winding south between the hills towards Shushtar. At four o'clock, drooping with tiredness, Jane rode over a rocky crest and raised her head. Suddenly she was revitalised. The beautiful Karun River lay like a huge aquamarine lake, its edges defined by golden sand on the west and rocks to the east, and only a misty indecision where the sky dipped into it.

To the south the lake terminated at a structure that was both dam and weir, a sequence of forty-one Sasanid stone arches wavering and looping across the river. Sluices set between the arches controlled the outflow, which raced away, translucent green beneath white spray. A wide cobbled roadway running along the top connected the palmerais and gardens on the fertile western bank to the town built on the rocks half a kilometre away. Enamelled domes gleamed in the slanting late-afternoon light, white sugar-cube cones towered above imamzaddes and a broken minaret pointed to paradise. Surmounting a sheer black rockface rising straight from the water's edge was the citadel, a fortress draped in bloody history. Here, records the *Shahname*, the Roman emperor Valerian served his seven-year imprisonment, while twenty thousand of his captured subjects laboured to build the meandering bridge, to dig canals and construct watermills.

Passing beneath the tiled gateway at the far end of the bridge, the Dieulafoys' caravan entered a wide street. Merchants left their baskets of dates and lemons inside the arcaded shops and came out to stare at the foreigners, sayyids under towering green turbans stood back waiting to denounce the foreign dogs, only the women, pulling their blue and black checked robes across their faces, hurried away. The street led into a maze of alleyways, which quickly revealed the ruined state of Shushtar and its appalling sanitary arrangements. Dropped into chutes within the masonry walls of the houses, wastes of all kinds spilled from openings at street level and slopped towards an open drain in the centre of the roadway. The stench was nauseating, the contrast with the dignity of the great bridge pathetic. The crumbling, half-abandoned houses, more shocking even than the dilapidation of fabled Isfahan, revealed the degraded and depopulated condition of Khuzestan province's capital city.

Prisoners lay in chains against the walls of the vestibule through which the Dieulafoys entered the citadel, and soldiers encumbered the hall. A short flight of stairs led up to a garden courtyard and through a vault-covered *talar* to an elevated terrace. The view was spectacular. Spread out below was the lake-river; the gold of oranges glowed beneath palm fronds in the verdant plantations on the far bank; upstream the river emerged from a pink sandstone ridge standing like an altar in front of the high Zagros Mountains which cut off the sky to the north.

Again malaria struck. Jane lay shivering in their rooms, unable to leave her bed, too ill to eat. Recurrent bouts had split open too many red blood cells and made her severely anaemic, fever was burning up what little was left on her bones. Her clothes hanging off her tiny frame, she looked like a limp, white-faced rag doll. On their first day in Shushtar she resented being too sick to go with Marcel when he called again on the governor and inspected the blocked canals and watermills that once had irrigated the plain. On the second day she began to worry about when she would be well enough to leave and on the third day she despaired at her trembling hands which could hold nothing, not even the pencil with which she was marking off the days on the calendar until the *Escombrera* would take them home. The provincial governor had asked for the little infidel to take his photograph, but it was impossible. Marcel, although also feverish, fulfilled the command and captured on a glass plate negative the hauteur of the shah's uncle at the head of his troops.

Marcel called on the mullahs, but the town had been a greenhouse for Shi'a fervour since the fourteenth century and not even the Zil-es-Sultan's letter could open Shushtar's mosque to an infidel. Yet mullahs and sayyids were among the callers who besieged Jane as she lay ill in the mean lodging, begging her to intercede for them with the shah, to bring their troubles to his notice. Like all Persians, they saw the shah as a father figure ignorant of their oppression by greedy governors and unaware that his subjects were sucked dry by rabid tax farmers. If only he knew, he would correct the iniquities, they said. Please, would the Dieulafoys tell the shah how the Shushtaris were reduced to starvation, how the roads and bridges were neglected, how the irrigation systems had fallen into disrepair? The only things still working in the town were the old Sasanid watermills which ground their wheat into flour.

But what could Jane do? She knew that the shah was the cornerstone of the corrupt system that abused his subjects, that he, a Turcoman, despised these Shushtaris of mixed Arab and Persian blood. In his thirty-year reign he had never come to visit his southern provinces and he never would. Even if she were mad enough to inform him of his subjects' condition he would do nothing to alleviate it. In this town, created by a Sasanid monarch whose public works had brought huge rewards and abundant food to his people, it was bitter to listen to their lamentations, pathetic to hear their complaints and know that the broken, neglected systems could so easily be repaired and the fertile soil made to yield as richly as it had in the past. Yet the year travelling through his kingdom had taught her, even if she did not phrase it as succinctly as Curzon, that the shah 'is as likely to undertake a genuinely great public work as he is to turn Protestant.'[10]

The only thing possible for a desperately ill 'young excellency' was to listen and regret. And count off the days. The *Escombrera* would sail at the end of the month. They had to get away from Shushtar.

With cook, muleteers and soldier escort, the Dieulafoys left Shushtar on 22 January. Although she could barely stand without support, Jane was determined to catch the ship to France. Driven by more than dreams of her country and a great longing to see her family, she feared she would not survive a further month of recurrent malaria. She knew how ill she was, how little margin she had.

Their immediate destination was Ahwaz, lower down the twisting, turning Karun River. Since there was no shipping on the upper reaches, their mounted cavalcade set off in pouring rain, past a hill crowned by a decrepit imamzadde, to follow a track across a plain, bare except for a few stands of leafless poplars. There were no villages and few black tents. When the horses tripped on fragments of broken canals or Sasanian stonework, Jane gripped the pommel and tightened her knees about her horse's flanks, but mostly she swayed in the saddle only half aware of where she was. They kept on all day, the horses finding the mud heavy going. When dusk approached they looked around for a lodging. The country was insecure and lions sometimes wandered up from the banks of the river.

They rode towards smoke in the distance and were greeted by barking yellow dogs. Inside a large tent a troop of wild-eyed Arabs knelt before a fire, behind them some women, and further back, divided from each other by strips of felt and thorn barricades were the tribe's sheep and lambs, goats, horses, and poultry. Leaving the cook to negotiate the killing of a sheep for their dinner, Marcel wrapped Jane in her bedding and laid her down away from the smoke and noise. He covered her with a carpet and brought her water. Her teeth chattered against the rim as she tried to drink. In the grip of malaria, violently shaken by chills, she was only semi-conscious.

When Marcel returned to the fire, dinner had not appeared. The sheikh was stroking his henna-dyed beard and declaring his poverty. A sequence of blind-alley prevarications culminated at 11 o'clock in a dinner of yoghurt, despite their having paid for a sheep. The cook was embarrassed and the soldiers furious that the slippery old sheikh had outsmarted them. Marcel simply laid out his bedding beside Jane, set the money chest as he always did under his head, and fell asleep.

In feverish half-sleep Jane was startled by neighing and stomping, and a dark shape leaping high above her. Then a large animal tore through the tent entrance and men began rushing about. In the light from the dying fire she could see tribesmen running off into the darkness, while others grasped the halters of a trembling mare and filly, steadying them, soothing them, calming them. Marcel sat up and saw his money chest crushed and broken. A stallion had broken its hobbles to get at the filly. Repulsed and kicked by the mare, it had jumped over the Dieulafoys to make its escape, its hoof striking the end of the chest sticking out beyond Marcel's ear. It was a matter of centimetres whether Marcel's head or the money chest had taken the hoof.

Not long afterwards, the tribe shooed the animals out of the tent and drove them to pasture, children carried out the chickens, horsemen galloped off to hunt or raid. All was movement and noise. The Dieulafoys' caravan set off again into the rain, Jane once more swaying in the saddle. The plain was a quagmire and the horses made little headway. The rich alluvial soil that during Sasanid times and even up to the thirteenth century had supported villages and produced rich crops, had now become a bleak and lonely place. The soldiers kept their arms primed and the muleteers scanned the horizon. It was ten at night before barking dogs once more proclaimed a resting place. By then Jane was distraught, dreading another night out in the rain. The night in the marshes when she was exposed to the storm and at risk from the Arabs was a still vivid memory.

The third day took them across historical rubble and ruined canals to the town of Weiss, on the Karun river bank, a town of mud brick houses graced by an imamzadde and palm trees, the upper limit of their friend Sheikh Mizal's land, but which his steam launch with Marcel and Jane aboard had failed to reach some months earlier. Dressed in their best clothes, the townspeople were celebrating the wedding of the headman's eldest son. Sadly, Jane declined their invitation. She, who loved to be part of local activities, whether following a mujtahid's coffin in Tabriz or watching the weekly court at Varamin, at Weiss could only lie limp on the floor of their lodging and send her compliments, though expressed with all the verbal flourish of polite Persian discourse.

Her courtesy was appreciated and soon sweetmeats were borne in, followed by the dancer hired for the occasion, 'a charming boy wearing a floating robe whose long sleeves streaming like butterfly wings when he pirouetted, long curly hair, jewels and languid poses made him seem more like a girl than a boy.'[11] The entertainment in the mud hut seemed bizarre, more so when a dervish brought in two grey monkeys which somersaulted and leapt about among the people crammed into the room, less to see the monkeys than to stare at the Europeans. Jane played her part graciously and patiently, though barely able to sit up and all the time thinking it was a surreal dream.

Floods inundated the plain around Ahwaz. The horses struggled through rising water, the sure-footed mules and their stoical drivers splashing along behind. They reached the town on the evening of the fourth day and the caravan could go no further. Marcel paid off the muleteers and Jane said goodbye with sincere regret, believing they represented all that was best in the oriental character, enduring, brave and honest. Only Seropa, the servant who had been with them since Amarah, and the cook would accompany them on the boat they planned to hire for the trip down the Karun.

Though the lands either side of the Karun from Weiss to Mohammerah were held by the Ka'b Arabs of Sheikh Mizal's tribe, the town of Ahwaz was governed by a deputy of the provincial governor. Even among his fellow venal administrators, the voracious mirza Akbar Ali was renowned for his skill at extracting the last kran from his townsmen and from anyone else who fell into his clutches. When his greedy eyes saw the pitiful state of the two sahibs, the little one apparently close to death, he read an opportunity. So they had dismissed their muleteers? So they wished to hire a boat to take them to Mohammerah? So they were in haste to rendezvous with a ship leaving in a few days? Right. Immediately he forbade anyone else to deal with them. Only he, mirza Akbar Ali could find them a *bellam* or a *mehala* (native boats).

'Yes,' he told Marcel, 'we will arrange it in the morning.' When Marcel called soon after dawn on 26 January and knelt on the mat, he gasped at the outrageous price the mirza asked. Having settled with the muleteers, the money chest was almost empty. Marcel could not meet the price. They would have nothing left. He showed the mirza Zil-es-Sultan's letter, and indicated the paragraph asking local governors to give every possible assistance to the French couple, but the Zil was far away and meant nothing to the mirza. He would not negotiate. He had named his price, that was it.

Marcel retired to look for another boat. Ten *bellams* and six *mehalas* lay in the water just below the rapids, but none was available. When he learned that the mirza had warned off their owners, he was enraged but hid his fury. As for Jane, she was aware of Marcel coming and going and that she was still lying in a mud hut, but in her fevered state she was too ill to understand they were being held to ransom and she was too ill to know the date or to count off the days until the *Escombrera* sailed.

For two days the battle raged between the mirza and Marcel. To the mirza Marcel was a chicken waiting to be plucked. He sensed the French couple's desperation and recognised how seriously ill the 'young sahib' was. On the twenty-eighth he tightened the screws, forbidding the people to sell food to the Dieulafoys. When their servant Seropa returned from the bazaar crestfallen and ashamed, Marcel looked at Jane lapsing in and out of consciousness and knew he must get her away at whatever price. He counted his money again. No, he could not pay what the mirza demanded. If he did, there would be nothing to get them from Mohammerah across the Shatt al Arab to pick up the *Escombrera* at Basra. His choice was between Jane dying here caught in the net of a rapacious old Arab or wasting away on the shore at Mohammerah.

He walked out of the hut and was immediately surrounded by locals wanting to sell him pottery sherds and ancient seals which, they said, had been washed out of old tombs on the sandstone ridge above the town. Bitterly he rejected them. If they would not sell him food, why would he want to buy Achaemenid trinkets? He continued along the river bank to where the remains of the Sasanian dam that had once controlled the irrigation of the fertile plain were being washed away into oblivion. How could a great historical city have been reduced to this collection of mud huts and stone ruins? How could the just law of former dynasties have been replaced by the capricious rule of a person so contemptible he would see them die rather than allow a single coin to escape his clutches?

Hungry and distraught, Marcel returned to his dear wife. The sight of her sweet face, fever-flushed, drawn, filled him with despair. During the night she grew delirious. At dawn on the twenty-ninth he was bathing her forehead when a messenger arrived from the mirza. A *bellam* was waiting to take them to Mohammerah. Yes, at the price Marcel had offered, but they must leave at once.

The long narrow craft, an oarsman at either end, was launched into the river. Caught by the current, it quickly left Ahwaz behind. Jane lay insensible in the bottom of the boat. Marcel made himself a place among the piled baggage where he could make sure her waterproof covering did not slip and expose her to the falling rain. Seropa, astonished at how quickly things had changed, interrogated the sailors. Before dawn a messenger had come to warn the deputy governor of the imminent arrival of a grand personage, an emissary of the Zil-es-Sultan, on his way to Shushtar with messages for the Khuzestan governor. The mirza had thought immediately of Marcel's letter from the Zil. The Dieulafoys' presence represented a danger to him. They had to be got away.

'Who is the emissary?' Marcel asked on hearing this.

'General mirza Taqi Khan, a good servant of Zil-es-Sultan.'

The name brought blood racing to Marcel's face. Taqi Khan, the Zil's doctor and personal assistant, former pupil of the French doctor Tholozan, who had befriended the Dieulafoys in Isfahan. If only Marcel had been able to meet him and tell him how the mirza had treated them. A worse thought occurred to Marcel.

'How was he arriving? Was he coming up the river?'

'In Sheikh Mizal Khan's steam launch.'[12]

That was the second blow. The launch would be returning to Mohammerah. And here were the Dieulafoys in a native craft so unstable that it threatened to capsize whenever anyone moved and it would take days to get down the Karun.

It was Marcel's lowest moment. Jane was spared. She was unconscious, understanding nothing.

During the two days and nights she lay at the bottom of the boat she roused only once, when the storm became so violent that the sailors edged into the bank, tied the *bellam* to some overhanging bushes and went to sleep nearby. Lying beneath her mackintosh, Jane suddenly became aware of the sailors returning urgently to the boat and pushing off. 'A lion,' they said, 'a huge lion.' Marcel grabbed his rifle and Jane somehow managed to get to her knees and level her revolver. A magnificent beast, its head maned with gold, stalked imperiously through the bushes, swishing its tail and growling deep in its throat. The storm cleared and the lion moved away. It was the thirtieth of January.

At Mohammerah Marcel carried his wife onto a *mehala*, a craft larger than a *bellam*, capable of crossing the Shatt al Arab and reaching Basra thirty kilometres upstream on the opposite shore. He had no idea how long it would take against the current. He settled Jane in the bottom of the boat, covered her with bedding and gave the order to cast off. It was the morning of the thirty-first. When the Dieulafoys had left Baghdad a month before, the shipping clerk could only tell them the *Escombrera* was sailing 'at the end of January'; he could not be more specific, since it depended on cargo and tides and currents. Had the ship got away early, Marcel wondered. Were they on the edge of time? He looked at his dear wife, so desperately ill, racked by chills, burnt up by fever, her body gaunt, her face bloodless. It was five days since she had eaten and even to get her to take a few sips of water was difficult. Without proper treatment she could not live much longer. If the *Escombrera* had sailed there was little hope.

Swollen with rainwater coming down from further up the country, the muddy Karun carried them rapidly towards the junction with the Shatt al Arab. The two streams met violently, the Karun in its canal and the merged waters of the Euphrates and Tigris pelting down from Turkey. The *mehala* rocked from side to side and the chop tossed it mercilessly. As they cleared the entrance to the Shatt, the little craft was lifted high on the crest of a wave, high enough to see the stern of a ship flying the tricolor going downstream. They had missed it.

The Persian sailors dropped their oars and stood in the prow screaming at the ship. Seropa snatched off his red felt fez and waved wildly. Marcel stood frozen, numb at the prospect. Roused by the noise and realising what it meant, Jane clutched the mast and pulled herself upright. Tears streamed down her face. They had missed it, missed the *Escombrera*.

A miracle happened. The ship slowed. It slewed broadside to the current. Its gangway was being lowered. The Persian sailors took up their oars and rowed like argonauts. In twenty minutes Jane was lying on the scrubbed white deck of the French ship. She could not stand or even speak, but she had a chance of living.

Chapter 15
Return to Susa: The cast assembles

In Sheikh Mizal Khan's *anderun* the ladies were playing cards. Only a dim light penetrated the fretted wooden screen at the window. Their faces and the cards were lit by an enormous lantern placed in the centre of the carpet. When Golag *khanum* invited Jane to take a hand she declined, not understanding the rules of a game obviously being taken very seriously. The sheikh's sister, Fatima *khanum*, welcomed Jane graciously. 'I live a thousand years in your visit,' she said, and turned back immediately to take the trick, triumphantly placing the cards beneath a tattooed foot loaded with rings. She was a pretty woman, tall and slim, but lifeless, placid, not like the vivacious Golab *khanum*, a widow of the old sheikh and new head of the Fallahiyah *anderun*. Both were heavily jewelled and richly robed in the Baghdad mode, Fatima in red lamé brocade pantaloons and emerald silk chemise, Golab in a long tunic of violet brocade over blue satin pantaloons, the ensemble topped by a gauze floor-length coat buttoned with rubies. The clashing colours, the flash of goldthread embroidery, the fall of transparent veiling from sequinned toques seemed to Jane to be the epitome of oriental exoticism, the brilliance of their dress a contrast to their restricted lives. Her friend Torkhan *khanum* and the pet panther, Little Rose, were not with the ladies. When Jane had asked after them, the sheikh replied, 'She's not here,'[1] in a tone which closed off discussion absolutely. Jane could not ask whether she had died or been sent to the Basra *anderun* to replace Golab *khanum* but she sincerely hoped she had not been given to another sheikh, perhaps to settle a debt.

There were more wives than on her first visit but there was still no son among the children playing in the shadows. (When Curzon visited Sheikh Mizal a few years later there were fifteen wives and still no son.)

Jane's freedom to come and go confounded the ladies permanently enclosed in the dark rooms of the riverside fort.

'Don't go to Susa, it will be misery. Stay with us. I'll teach you Arabic,' urged Golab *khanum*, who spoke that language as fluently as Persian and her native Kurdish. Jane wondered if the old sheikh had bought her in the same Istanbul slave market as Torkhan *khanum*. Although Jane had written in 1882,

> Despite the great pleasure I derived from examining Persia's remarkable monuments, and from warming myself under its sun and dreaming under a starlit sky arching overhead like a silver dome, and though admiring its groves of plane trees, its orange plantations, its palm forests and plum orchards, its savage deserts and fertile plains, I would not wish it on my worst enemy . . . I would allow an unfortunate adventurer to travel beside the English telegraph line from Tehran to Shiraz, but not permit his evil star to lead him out of Fars into [Khuzestan] or onto the vile rivers of the Karun system, those breeding grounds of terrible fever'[2]

in 1884 she answered Golab *khanum*, 'I want to reach Susa as soon as possible, but while we are waiting for the boat into the Karun I would be most grateful for an Arabic lesson.'

The woman who had been a waif close to death when she left the Karun, who had returned to Paris looking like a stricken elf, whose shaking hands and gaunt face had made her mother-in-law weep, now seemed almost robust in contrast, although 200 grams of self-administered quinine had permanently affected her sight. Smartly dressed in a cream trouser suit, a white shirt and silk cravat, Jane looked incongruous sitting among the sheikh's women. Beside their voluptuous dark, hennaed heads, her blonde curls, again cut short, although not shaved, seemed bizarre.

On their return to France in March 1882 the Dieulafoys became celebrities, Jane's articles appearing serially in le *Tour du monde* having captured the public imagination. They busied themselves organising and communicating their Persian material. Jane had engravings made from her photographs, Marcel addressed the learned societies, wrote reports on Seljuk and Sasanid architecture for Viollet-le-Duc and drafted architectural interpretations of the measurements he and Jane had made at the important sites, although his Greek cataracts detracted from their truth. One who read and listened was M. de Ronchaud, elevated to director of the French national museums. He was particularly struck by their account of the great mound at Susa. It was the biggest in Persia, antique and untouched, the English had merely scratched the surface and gone away, Marcel informed him. Archaeologically mysterious, it was exactly what the influential de Ronchaud was looking for, something that could restore French national pride.

From the mid-1800s many unknown Mesopotamian civilisations had emerged from oblivion and penetrated European consciousness. The nineteenth-century public's excitement at these finds was much like the thrill a century later when space exploration sent Sputnik, dogs, manned flights and Mars landers into space. Each era opened a completely new dimension in the understanding of our place in history and geography and both engendered intense national competition. Although the French had made the first successful foray into pre-Biblical history in Mesopotamia, it was the English who dominated archaeological exploration. Worse, the decipherment of Old Persian and Babylonian cuneiform, which had unlocked unsuspected secrets of that distant past, was also largely the province of the English, where the splendid figure of Henry Rawlinson set the pace. As the English bounded ahead with revelations from antiquity, French national pride suffered.

Until the 1840s the Old Testament of the Hebrews and the writings of a handful of Greeks and Romans defined the ancient Orient. The few stamped bricks and cylinder seals collected by early travellers added nothing to that sum of knowledge because, like the huge rock inscriptions at Persepolis, Naqsh-i-Rustam and Hamadan, no one could read the cuneiform writing, least of all the local inhabitants. That changed dramatically when Henry Rawlinson, an English military officer training the shah's troops, attacked Bisitun in southwest Persia. With nerves of steel and magnificent athletic skill, Rawlinson repeatedly climbed a sheer rockface to reach a narrow, perilous ledge sixty metres above the valley floor. There he meticulously copied the inscriptions carved in three unknown languages into the stone of fourteen immense panels. A central sculptured relief of the Achaemenid king, Darius, dated the inscriptions to the fifth century BC.

Later, appointed British Political Agent in Turkish Arabia and based at Baghdad, Rawlinson, soldier, playboy and famous horseman, used his spare time and linguistic genius to resolve the secrets of those inscriptions. He first tackled the five panels carved in Old Persian and by 1845 had deciphered a statement of Darius's antecedents and the events of his reign, analysed Old Persian grammar and published a vocabulary of the lost language. The events recorded on Bisitun's rockface were not mentioned in Greek histories.

When Jane was born in 1851, Rawlinson and fellow scholars were investigating the other nine panels, thought to be Elamite and Babylonian translations of the Old Persian inscription. By the time of Jane's marriage in 1870, Babylonian was deciphered. Elamite still remains very much an open field for scholars.

Scientific archaeological excavation was initiated early in the nineteenth century by another Englishman, James Rich, the East India Company's Resident in Baghdad, who was intrigued by the many large mounds lying about the flat landscape of Mesopotamia and by small hints of what lay beneath that sometimes, after rain, protruded from the piled clay. He employed workmen and dug systematically until a cholera epidemic in 1821 closed his trenches and ended his life. Inspired by Rich's reports, French scholars pressured their government and before long Paul Botta, a cultured career diplomat, was appointed French Consul in Mosul. By the time Rawlinson took up his appointment at Baghdad in 1843, the Frenchman's trenches at Khorsabad, twenty kilometres northeast of Mosul, had already revealed the astonishing palace of an Assyrian King. Embellished by colossal statues of human-headed bulls, its mudbrick walls were lined with stone panels on which dynastic history and religious beliefs were recorded in sculptured reliefs and cuneiform inscriptions.

Soon another Englishman, Layard, was digging by the Tigris and being urged by an Arab workman: 'Hasten, O Bey, hasten to the diggers, for they have found Nimrod himself. Wallah, it is wonderful, but it is true! We have seen him with our eyes. There is no God but God.'[3] As ancient Nineveh and Nimrud, Ashur and Babylon left the pages of the Old Testament and entered nineteenth-century reality, newspapers heralded the discoveries and scholars worked to decipher the inscriptions: 'Sargon II, King of Assyria, founded this city [in 713 BC], King Ashurnasirpal II built this palace [in the ninth century BC], this is the throne of king Shalmaneser III', and struggled to fit the pieces into a history they had never contemplated. The British Museum became London's most popular destination, the public flooding in to see colossal winged human-headed lions, inscribed black obelisks, and relief-carved stone slabs from Nimrud, which recorded 'the history, theology, language, arts, manners, military skill, political relations of one of the most illustrious nations of antiquity . . . filling up an enormous blank in our knowledge of the early history of the world.'[4]

But was the Louvre filling up with treasures? Though Botta and his opium habit had drifted back to France with a collection of small pieces and inscriptions, the huge Khorsabad finds and smaller pieces from other Mesopotamian sites languished in Basra, to which they had been floated on huge rafts. The English generously added a winged bull, since they had so many, deeply regretting their largesse in 1855 when the rafts broke apart and everything sank to the bottom of the Tigris. The French were chagrined and the Louvre remained deserted.

During the 1870s the dialogue changed and the conversation became more complex. By then Jane was a married woman and listening.

On clay tablets from the Royal Library at Nineveh were inscribed not only king lists, marriage records, gods and their rituals, but also medical texts, astronomical data, mathematical tables, and literature, including the Deluge story, testimony to the intellectual sophistication of these early civilisations. As Layard commented, 'A stranger laying open monuments buried for more than twenty centuries, and thus proving to those who dwelt around them that much of the civilisation and knowledge of which we now boast existed amongst their forefathers when our "ancestors were yet unborn", was, in a manner, an acknowledgement of the debt which the West owes the East.'[5]

While cuneiform inscriptions carved on panels and incised into clay tablets turned the proper nouns in the Old Testament into real people and local places and confirmed some of the Bible's historical events, although shifting the timeframe, they negated the Hebrew claim that the Old Testament had been handed to them by God. Adam and Eve were much older than the Bible, and in 1872, when the Great Flood story was found on clay tablets in the pre-semitic Sumerian language, it was very unsettling for temples, churches and historians. Some of them, including Rawlinson's clergyman brother George, called for decipherment to be banned.

In France, there was an unfortunate undercurrent among the very scholars who established Sumerian as the oldest written language. Predating Babylonian and Assyrian, and being neither Aryan nor Semitic, Sumerian precedence demolished the Hebrew claim to be the civilisation fundamental to all Indo-European cultures. The suggestion that the people 'who spoke [the Sumerian language] were the first civilizers of Western Asia, the inventors and perfecters of a system of writing which was destined to be one of the chief humanizing agents of the ancient world'[6] divided the academic world. Jane was aware of the bitter racist argument that broke out in 1872, and of the associated hostile exchanges during the early 1880s, when formerly respected Semitic scholars questioned the accuracy of decipherment, reluctant to 'reconcile themselves to the subordinate position of the Semite to the [Sumerian] in laying the foundations of all modern culture.'[7]

Jane left the argument behind when she went to Persia in 1881, together with the statues which the Louvre had recently bought from the French Vice-Consul at Basra, Ernest de Sarzec, who in 1877 had excavated a nearby mound and found Lagash, an old Sumerian city, which surrendered the earliest known historical document and vigorous, extremely beautiful, diorite sculpture. Although the Louvre scored ahead of the English with these first examples of Sumerian art, it still could not match the richness of the British acquisitions.

Because of such traditional French–English rivalry, de Ronchaud was able to obtain 41 000 francs of government funding, official recognition and military and naval support for an expedition to Susa. There was no question of who should undertake the excavation – Jane and Marcel. At first Jane was appalled at the thought of returning to a country where she had suffered so much and been so despised. But regret that she had been unable to penetrate Susa's mystery still lingered. Ill and exhausted, in 1882 she had felt unable to explore its meaning or to delve into its ambiguity. As her health recovered, so did her spirit. To return and excavate would be a brilliant coup. The challenge fuelled her ambition and by December 1883 Jane and Marcel, despite their stated 'desire to live with their feet on their own hearthstone,'[8] had accepted the commission.

The real difficulty was the Persian government. Negotiations through diplomatic channels in 1883 were tricky and twice refused before Dr Tholozan was brought into negotiations in 1884. Once more in favour at court, the doctor cynically suggested to his royal patient that illuminating a great ancestral dynasty could reflect gloriously on his own Qajar house while winning Nasr-al-Din himself the esteem of scholars and the public in promoting an activity to increase knowledge. The egoistic autocrat authorised the excavation, conditional on the finds being equally shared and the Persians retaining all precious metals. The royal firman acknowledged but absolved the regime from any consequences of Susian fanaticism and Khuzestan's marauding tribes, and stipulated respect for the Tomb of Daniel.

Confident of ultimately winning the shah's approval, de Ronchaud had arranged for the expedition's departure on 17 December 1884. Although the good news reached France by telegram in late November, the Persian document could not arrive before the sailing date. It would await the Dieulafoys in Bushire. So without permission in hand, the party went aboard the naval ship *Tonkin*, Jane in such a state of anxiety that she left her ticket at home and lost the keys to her luggage.

In a reprise of her journey aboard the *Ava*, Jane found the *Tonkin* stuffed with guns and ammunition bound for China. She was relieved when transshipped at Aden to the British *Huzara*. The slow passage to Karachi was only enlivened by the brilliant sunsets produced by the dust and ashes of the previous year's Krakatoa explosion still circulating in the earth's slipstream and bringing an exceptionally cold winter to Europe and Iran. At Karachi the *Assyria* was ready to depart, which deprived Jane of India. Hurrying aboard a ship crowded with pilgrims bound for the holy sites, she exclaimed as she saw the Arabs, Persians and Indians making their evening prayer, 'Allah keep me from doubting their fervent piety, but . . . can one attribute their ceaseless peregrinations to the pleasure of leaving their many wives, seeing new lands, and leaving behind their business worries under a true and laudable pretext?'[9] In the melee a crate containing hunting rifles and most of their dispensary was lost. Fortunately, the serious armaments supplied by the French ministry of war continued with them up the Persian Gulf.

The war ministry had appointed two Muslim soldiers from Algeria as servants and guards for the expedition, considering them less likely to offend the sensitivities of the fanatics patrolling Daniel's shrine in the shadow of the great mound. M. Babin, a young engineer, and M. Houssay, a science graduate of l'Ecole Normale, completed the party that disembarked in pouring rain at Bushire on the last day of January 1885.

The greedy governor who had pitilessly extorted taxes from the citizens while letting their city fall to pieces was gone, escaping dressed as a fisherman when the townspeople revolted, though his baggage was seized and pillaged. The new governor of Bushire, although awed by the royal firman awaiting the Dieulafoys, extended the Persian formalities for a week. Meanwhile, the British Resident conducted complex negotiations on their behalf, whereby the mission's funds would be accepted in Bushire by Zil-es-Sultan's representative and reimbursed in Dizful by the provincial governor. The Dieulafoys would carry no coin to attract attention, the precious receipt holding no interest for illiterate robbers.

The Europeans farewelling the Dieulafoys in Bushire on 7 February were hardly encouraging, reciting Loftus's difficulties during his explorations of Susa thirty years previously and recounting how the fanatics had chased him out. 'Loftus had diplomatic immunity, too, and he was driven out,' warned

Dr Ross as Jane brandished the royal firman, 'Be very careful,' but Jane was full of confidence. Rowed out to the *Arabia*, she was happy to be travelling among the Persians again. Forgetting illness and discomfort, she remembered the good things: the stoic endurance of the ordinary people, their charm and humour, the elegance of their language and the beauty of their country. With a light heart and a feeling of returning to old friends, she alighted at Fallahiyah and accepted Sheikh Mizal Khan's hospitality.

Going up the Karun in the sheikh's launch, its motor pushing through the deep water and riding over the shoals as it had refused to do when they were aboard three years earlier, Jane happily succumbed to the exoticism of the Orient. Snow-crested mountains rose like promises on the eastern horizon and gentle rain fell. At Mohammerah rustling date forests gave way to sprawling stretches of vivid-green young wheat. Beyond the crops, troops of camel, flocks of sheep and goats, and the sheikh's valuable horses grazed the pastures. The brown tents of nomads dotted the landscape. When the launch's wheelhouse rose above the river bank, women in long Indian-cotton chemises hoisted water jars onto their turbanned heads and drew their *abba*s around them, metal buttons and silver rings in their nostrils flashing with disdain.

By nightfall they had reached Ahwaz. Memories of their misery in that village of hovels refused to be banished. Ignoring the black-hearted mirza Akbar Ali, Jane rode away next day at the head of a caravan assembled from muleteers of the plain. Surrounded by ten of Sheikh Mizal's soldiers under the command of a black slave, the party could beat through the marshes and chase after wild boar during the day and did not need to seek out Arab tents at nightfall.

Holed up one night in a stable, Jane became aware of eyes gazing through the cracks. Opening the door she discovered the statuesque women of the Bend-Akhil tribe, red chemises and indigo veils clinging to their bodies, their brown wool *abba*s sodden, their amber and corral necklaces and the strings of silver money and coloured stones wound into their turbans shining in the rain. Curiosity outweighing their fear, they had brought yoghurt and goat's milk to sell to the foreigners.

At Shushtar the town governor's welcome was more civil now they rode with the authority of the shah and he lodged the Dieulafoys in his palace. Shushtar still groaned under extortion and crumbled in neglect, the streets appeared even filthier and the populace more oppressed. The women in the governor's *anderun*, whom Jane had treated for various maladies before her collapse in 1882, greeted her like a lost friend, stroking her strange hair and caressing her hands, approving her nails cut down to the quick by Golab *khanum* (the white of the nails is like animal claws! Let me cut it off, she had begged). They told her she would be perfect, if only she were a Muslim. Jane laughed, their warmth filling her with pleasure, yet she sensed their unhappiness. Of the twelve, four had never had a baby, six had lost their infants to smallpox, and the five surviving children were sickly and mal-formed. The same infertility affected all the Shushtari women and the town population was declining rapidly.

The Dieulafoys' concern was to arrange their financial affairs and physical safety. The governor of Khuzestan, who was to remit the funds entrusted to Zil-es-Sultan's representative in Bushire, was expected any day at his winter palace in Shushtar, they were told, a snowfall in his summer capital at Dizful reportedly hastening his departure.

While awaiting His Excellency, they called on Khuzestan's senior cleric, *hadji* sayyid Hussein, and were received in a vaulted *talar* by a man much younger than they had expected. Holding the staff of office and wearing the huge blue turban, he assured them they would have no cause to complain of the faithfuls' behaviour towards foreigners authorised by the shah to work at Susa. Satisfied by this and his promise that the senior cleric at Dizful, Sheikh Taher, would control the fanatics at Daniel's Tomb, the Dieulafoys were about to leave when the audience seated on their heels in a courtyard a little below the level of the *talar* pitched forward onto their faces. An aged man appeared, carried on the shoulders of two young clerics. The faithful snatched the hem of his robe as he passed and kissed it. This was the vener-ated *hadji* sayyid Hussein. Eighty years old and in poor health, he delegated the administration of the 'parish' to his eldest son, while he pleaded the cause of the poor and innocent before the powerful and cruel.

After Marcel had eased *hadji* Hussein's asthmatic breathing with medi-cation, the venerable one leant back on his cushions to listen to his son and Marcel discuss the relationship between God and Allah, the mute crowd, too, following the rational and amiable arguments. Marcel had been instructed in the niceties of Persian theological debate by Père Pascal in New Julfa, yet he was relieved when it ended.

It was already the middle of February and the Dieulafoys, recognising that the summer heat would force them out of Susa, were impatient to start. When told the governor's arrival would be delayed by eight days, Marcel became suspicious. 'We'll wait on him in Dizful,' he announced. Jane stirred the muleteers and the caravan set off across the winding Sasanid bridge on

Shustar wives

a three-day march into the ranges. The rain had left a green covering on the plains and wildflowers among the rocks. The beauty of Persia struck at Jane's heart and she travelled on elated.

The moment she saw mirza Abdoul-Rahim, Jane recognised a two-faced liar. He had all the handsomeness and quick intelligence of the men of Fars, his greeting was elegant, he presented the letter courteously, but his little button eyes were too alert to the effect it produced. Mozaffer el-Molk, governor of Khuzestan, instructed the Dieulafoys to wait for him in Shushtar. The letter was dispatched days ago, said mirza Abdoul-Rahim, we were delayed at the Konah River. One glance at their exhausted horses was enough to tell Jane they had spurred from Dizful in a single day. Why is he lying, she wondered. Abdoul-Rahim stroked his hennaed beard, straightened his high hat on his hennaed ringlets, and solemnly offered them tea.

He looks more youthful than is the case, Jane concluded as he declaimed his titles and explained his position in the governor's court. His duties included encouraging harmonious relations with the nomad chiefs by garnisheeing their income when they failed to pay their taxes. 'And now my heart dilates at the thought of living near you during your stay at Susa.'[10] Ah, sighed Jane, so this slippery customer is to be our gaoler, who will spy on us and report everything we do.

Suspecting the governor's motives, the Dieulafoys insisted that turning back the caravan was impossible, and continued on. Arriving at the Konah River when it was too dark to cross safely, they lodged at a deserted posthouse in the village. At midnight they woke to someone beating on its barred door. They heard it being cautiously opened and a whispered message – the posthouse must be cleared tomorrow to receive the governor's party. 'The mystery deepens,' said Jane to Marcel. 'We left Shushtar forty-eight hours ago, and a man who says he will not arrive for eight days is already leaving Dizful.'[11] Aware of the governor's greed, witnessed by every ruined village in Khuzestan, the Dieulafoys became even more suspicious.

Marcel left the posthouse on their best horse well before dawn to meet the advancing governor and insist on accessing their money, while Jane took the caravan on at its own sedate pace. As she emerged from the floodwaters swirling between sandbanks in the Konah River, Jane was surprised to see a red silk tent pitched in the shade of a stand of poplars. Servants were smoothing its creases, carrying in carpets and piling up cushions. Jane called to the tcharvadar bachy to move the caravan away and had barely cleared the track before an amazing sight appeared on the plain.

The first rank comprised a host of small donkeys over-burdened with rolled brown tents, sacks of grain, nets of dates, sheepskins, and small arms seized in the villages along the way. They were urged on by soldiers identified by metal plaques on their astrakhan hats and leather belts. Behind came dervishes, wild-haired and filthy, troops of horsemen, and officials holding their staffs of office. A bank of mounted men rolled by, followed by the poor half-naked wretches co-opted in the villages to porter the baggage of the governor's household, 'submitting, sad and resigned, to the hard laws of fate.'[12] After a short interval a large man dressed in scarlet appeared, waxed moustaches spreading almost to his ears – the executioner, a bundle of sharp-edged cutlasses bound to the pommel of his saddle ready for hand or head.

A troop of splendidly dressed horsemen followed, leading six horses. Two proud stallions and four superb Arab mares pranced along, gold-embroidered silks and velvets thrown over their backs, jewelled harness on their flanks, their bridles gleaming with gold plaques. Jane was jolted from a fantasy of riding such magnificent animals by a haughty soldier waving a lance at her and shouting at the caravan to move further off. Before she could speak, two grand personages on elaborately dressed horses came into view. Between them rode Marcel, his figure bearing all the dignity a French colonel could muster when wearing crumpled clothes and riding a hired hack in the company of the governor and his secretary. Ignoring the soldier, Jane gathered the reins, raised her whip and galloped towards her husband.

The governor graciously invited her to lunch in the silken tent, where he would attend to Marcel's concerns and direct his secretaries to draw up appropriate documents. A brief meeting of the eyes was enough for Jane and Marcel to agree it would be more politic for her to decline Mozaffer el-Molk's invitation and go straight to Dizful.

Lodged at the governor's palace, Jane waited for Marcel in a suite bare except for a mattress of palm fronds on the dirt floor. Carpets and furniture had followed the governor to Shushtar on the backs of the mules that had impeded her caravan as it made its way to Dizful. Only the fleas had been left behind. It was night before Marcel appeared, joyfully brandishing three letters authorising access to their money, the hiring of workers, and, most exceptional, use of the governor's hammam.

To bathe after weeks of rough travel was, said Jane, like a penitent removing the stones from his shoes. A dim light from windows high in the drum of a cupola lit up blue-and-white tiled rooms that provided steam, scalding hot water and a cold douse. Knowing it would be her last bath for

Young Dizfuli woman

many months, Jane's pleasure was profound. When the Dieulafoys returned glowing from the hammam, M. Houssay seized his chance. The governor's hospitality almost became Houssay's final tub – careless servants heating the water failed to open the flue and the young engineer almost succumbed to carbon monoxide poisoning.

Susa seemed very near, yet there were still affairs to attend to before they could take the path down the mountain and across the plain. A new cook had to be found, the terrible cuisine of Mçaoud, the Algerian soldier, having blistered their stomachs. Mirza Abdoul-Rahim had to be reimbursed for the comestibles he had supplied (at an extortionate price, but 'one must keep in good grace with one's spy,' said Jane). A vast painting on canvas had to be unrolled and placed on its stretchers and its gilded frame assembled before being entrusted to the deputy governor to present to the governor on his return to Dizful – the Wisdom of Solomon, a suitable subject for such a powerful man to contemplate – and lastly a call to be paid to Dizful's most senior cleric.

Sheikh Mohammad Taher wielded enormous influence over those who might oppose them at Susa. To appease him, Marcel presented a small wheeled cannon, an armament they had discussed during the Dieulafoys' 1882 visit. The sheikh was delighted and his followers thunderstruck by its wheels, items of wonder to people living in a province without roads. Sheikh Taher studied the instruction from his superior at Shushtar and nodded. Yes, he would calm the fanatics and do what he could to ensure the mission's safety in the vicinity of the tomb.

Cook, security, money, spy, all were in place. 'En avant,' Jane called to the tcharvadar bachy.

Chapter 16
First season: The Lion Frieze

With one knee on the ground Jane shouldered her rifle, sighted and fired. The shot rang out and a puff of white dust rose into the air. She fired again, and again, a fourth time, each time a loud crack and the little cloud spinning off the white rock. The Arab tribesmen shouted and raced towards her. 'Bismillah Ar-Rahman Ar-Rahim, may Allah preserve you forever,' they said, touching her rifle, kissing the hem of her jacket, hoping to receive some of her blessing. Sheikh Ali glowered and his eyes gleamed with malice. Swinging into the saddle, he galloped away, calling his men to heel with a furious fusillade of airshots.

'They won't be in a hurry to launch an attack after that,' said Marcel, which Jane recognised as enormous praise from that man of few words, though she regretted the sheikh's angry departure.

The wily sheikh had appeared out of the morning mist as it lifted from the mound, a figure of authority riding a grey mare, his beard henna-dyed, his head covering anchored by camelhair cords. The foreigners received him graciously, spreading a carpet in front of their tent, their Persian greeting, 'I live a thousand years in your visit,' wasted on a sheikh who claimed not to understand Farsi. Establishing a cordial relationship with the indigenes was of the greatest importance for the survival of the French mission. Four infidels with a guard of two Islamic soldiers in an antipathetic corner of Persia, their lives depended entirely on the local population.

In practical terms the shah who had authorised the mission and guaranteed their safety was as distant as the French government. Tehran was 550 kilometres away as the crow flies, crows not having to travel a twisting track over mountain ranges and along the edge of a great desert, while messengers took weeks to reach the capital. Telegraphy brought him no closer.

Unlike the well-maintained English telegraph line from Tehran to Bushire, the newly installed Persian line from Tehran to Shushtar functioned rarely, since camels used its cheap wooden poles as rubbing posts and brought them down, the Arabs stole the wire and repair was not a Persian habit. Between the shah and the local governor was Zil-es-Sultan, controller of all the southern provinces, equally distant and difficult to contact. Mozaffer el-Molk, governor of Khuzestan, was very powerful, very far from Qajar authority and, as long as he remitted the annual tax, able to do almost as he pleased. The mission's dealings with him had not made them confident of his support; in fact they suspected he opposed it, and they knew that his personal representative, mirza Abdoul-Kaïm, officially entrusted with the task of ensuring the foreigners' safety, was nothing more than a spy.

Besides security, the French mission needed a regular supply of food and labourers to excavate the huge site. Hoping the sheikh's tribe camped out on the plain might furnish both, the Dieulafoys had opened negotiations in Arabic, their failed Algerian cook interpreting. The tribeswomen would bring them butter, chickens and eggs, the sheikh agreed, and they could buy sheep, but as to workers: 'Arabs don't work, speak to the Persians at Dizful, a vile race only fit to be beaten.' Then, full of confidence in his English hunting rifle, the sheikh threw down his challenge. The French understood its significance and in the delicate moment weighed vulnerability against alienation. They dare not admit the former; they would have to risk the latter. In turn Marcel, Babin and Houssay addressed a white stone topping a pile of rocks 450 metres distant. Their shots blasted off the target, but the sheikh's fell far short. The faces of his armed troop lengthened. Those with rifles shrugged into the leather on their shoulders, men with lances stabbed at the ground. Then, thinking Jane the weak link, a malignant face spoke, 'Give the *khanum* a turn.'

Although in her usual dress of dark trouser suit, boots and white shirt she still looked a sweet boy, there was no longer any uncertainty about her gender. To live in safety on the mound Jane must be recognised as the *khanum*, the dear wife, but not discounted because of it. Her fair colouring and small size had already led to rumours she was a sorceress. In the Dizful bazaar they whispered that when she reached Susa three days ago she was seen diving head first into the river. She had not come up again, they said, she was still down there trying to get into Daniel's Tomb, drinking the water and living off crayfish. Realising it was imperative for their security that her four shots strike home, Jane faced down her challenger.

While it was vital that the Arabs and anyone else contemplating mischief should know she was a crack shot, Jane hoped her marksmanship had not destroyed the possibility of a respectful relationship with the sheikh. That too was important.

The two white tents appeared isolated among the spiny bushes on the most northerly of the three mounds that constitute the Susa site. Forty metres above the plain, ten kilometres in circumference, the uneven top of the tumulus was a vast, frightening place. Almost half of its 120 hectares (300 acres) were taken up by a buried city, asleep on the west beneath a great earth blanket. A deep ravine, where perhaps the river had once flowed, separated the city from a high rocky outcrop capped by a ruined citadel and the third mound, where Loftus had identified a palace. Shallower hazards hidden by a thick covering of prickly shrubs were perfect places for marauders to hide or wild animals to make their lairs.

The French set up their tents on a little hillock near the palace, from which they could observe the tomb and the winding path leading from it towards the tumulus. They could also see travellers on the road from Dizful, so the blue-turbanned sayyid and his twelve white-turbanned companions were not unnoticed when they hastened along in the afternoon. With them came their gaoler, mirza Abdoul-Rahim, disappointing their hope that he would linger in the town. The party rode through the gateway of the tomb and very soon afterwards were seen riding up the twisting pathway. A sour greeting and a brusque question: 'Why did you stay only one night at the Tomb?'

The Dieulafoys had been reluctant to stay at all, but when a thunderstorm broke over their heads on the ride from Dizful, even with the jagged flashes of lightning illuminating the darkness, they would not have been able to find a campsite and erect their tents. They were forced to take shelter under the only roof on the plain and to pass the night in a doorless space at the side of the courtyard, while rain and wind beat in upon them. Immediately yapping yellow dogs and ferocious mosquitoes announced the dawn, muleteers, servants and foreigners, all starving, began moving their baggage to the high ground. By three in the afternoon anything that must be protected from the rain was stacked inside the white tents, everything weatherproof made a wall alongside and the cook stood over a steaming pan of rice.

'The excavations demand my presence on the mound at all times, even though we will not be as warmly housed as at the Tomb,'[1] Marcel lied diplomatically and apparently effectively, for soon the blue and white turbans were bobbing away towards Dizful.

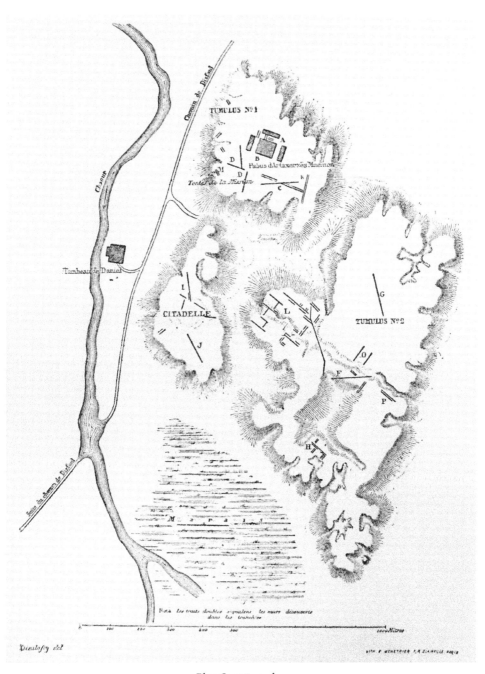

Plan Susa tumulus

The news that foreigners had come to look inside the mountain spread like gunshot, yet to the Dieulafoys' great disappointment no workers appeared. On 1 March 1885 nine people attacked a four metre by sixty metre oblong marked out by Marcel near the *apadana* where Loftus had dug thirty years before. An old Arab cast out of his tribe and who lived off thistles, two sons of a penniless widow, and a one-eyed ancient residing at the tomb while praying for his sight to be restored joined two soldiers of mirza Abdoul-Rahim's suite and the French contingent in taking up picks and buckets to dig a trench of undecided depth. Standing guard on the optimists were the two Algerians, one near the trench and one with the cook at the tents. Jane had the honour of turning the first sod.

The widow's boys had retired with blistered hands when three days later a party of Arabs carrying spades raised their hopes, only to hoist their lances and execute a noisy war dance around the dig before going off to turn an irrigation canal into their wheat field. With only two months before the summer heat would force them to abandon work, both Dieulafoys were close to despair when Ousta Hassan arrived, drawn by the myth of the sorceress living in the river. 'I have come to see the littlest foreigner emerge from the water.'

'I would like to meet her,' Jane laughed, and quickly suggested that the Dizfuli master mason might like some work since the good Dizfulis did not build during the winter. Jane summed him up as intelligent but reserved, 'his expression that mix of timidity and audacity known only to cowards,'[2] and didn't trust him. Jane's character judgements were not often wrong, but Ousta Hassan was to become one of their most loyal workers. If Marcel would pay him a head price, he would bring a band of men from Dizful, but first he would have to clear the matter with Sheikh Taher and the jume mullah, and with the deputy governor 'to whom I have access because my wife is the sister of the cousin of his favourite valet', and with the parents of his wives and with his own family. Also, he stipulated, his companion Dor Ali must be employed because he needed the money to buy a new wife, having lost one three years before.

Marcel would agree to anything that would progress the dig. 'I promise you,' he said to Dor Ali, 'that in six months you will be able to buy both a Persian and an Arab and compare their merits.'[3] With only limited hope for the outcome of Ousta Hassan's complex negotiations, he snapped up four passing soldiers. Amazed that the worker's wage equalled the pay of a colonel, they happily deserted the ranks. Marcel, accused Jane, was 'desperate enough to recruit Satan and his wife if they came looking for work.'

Ousta Hassan

When Ousta Hassan reappeared with forty builder's labourers, the usually solemn Marcel beamed, although a total of fifty men could only play at excavating such a vast area. Word of the generous pay brought a trickle of Bakhtiaris, then some Arabs, but not of Sheikh Ali's tribe. Soon there would be several hundred men working at the trenches, but only after the bluff of the devious mirza Abdoul-Rahim was called. Entrusted with the double-edged task of ensuring the safety of the foreigners while making their life sufficiently difficult to drive them out, that inventive man pursued his commission from several angles.

Abruptly Sheikh Ali cut off the meat supply. Chickens yes, eggs yes, butter yes, sheep no. The shepherds who herded their flocks into the courtyard of the Tomb each night also had no sheep for sale, not at any price. Speculating on why mutton had become unobtainable, the French were reduced to a diet of boiled chicken with rice in the morning and in the evening rice with fried chicken. If the following day the order was reversed it was still monotonous beyond bearing. Jane longed for green vegetables and fresh fruit. Golab *khanum* had advised her to eat field herbs, but on the mound there were only thistles. An occasional wild boar burst from the bushes and a cheetah's prints in the trenches once led them to a lair surrounded by bones. Panthers and lions roamed the banks of the Kerkhah. All were inedible, and without the hunting rifles lost in transit partridge and pigeon down on the plain and wild duck in the marshes were unattainable.

Their suspicions of mirza Abdoul-Rahim's machinations increased when a letter came from the governor still tucked up in his winter palace at Shushtar. 'Local Muslims are ignorant, uncivilised and out of control,' it began,

> and so they are a stumbling block to the advancement of your work. In my absence, I believe your mission will find them very difficult and I will be unable to restrain an increase in their Islamic fervour which may bring you great danger.
>
> It would be best for you to put your baggage in the care of mirza Abdoul-Rahim and come to stay near me in Shushtar.
>
> When I return to Dizful, you will be able to resume your work under the protection of an escort and with the power and counsel of the government.
>
> With best wishes, Mozaffer el-Molk[4]

Mirza Abdoul-Rahim, lurking in the background to see the effect of the epistle, was quick to dissociate himself, blaming the hundreds of impassioned faithful who had protested at the main mosque in Dizful the night after the Christians' departure for Susa. Incited by someone, no, certainly not himself, the mirza protested, and outraged that the infidels should be allowed near the Tomb of Daniel, they took to the road armed with lances and whips. Sheikh Taher sent his sons hurrying after them, to promise on behalf of their father that if the marchers would return peacefully emissaries would be sent to discover whether the foreigners had damaged the tomb. Suddenly Jane understood the cavalcade of blue and white turbans that came along the road from Dizful, and guessed that a messenger had been dispatched to Shushtar on their return. Now she knew why the unemployed Ousta Hassan had been so hesitant to accept their offer of well-paid work. Fear of the chain around the neck, the bastinado on the feet, of ears and noses tossed to the floor haunted every Persian.

With less than two months before the heat would became unbearable, the Dieulafoys refused even to think of packing up and deserting the workers who had put themselves on the line against such contrived opposition. Jane and Marcel would stay and the young Frenchmen Houssay and Babin, asked to decide for themselves, did not hesitate. They also would remain. Warmed by their confidence, Marcel replied to the governor:

> Excellency, I humbly thank you for the honour you have done in addressing a letter to me. Despite the pleasure it would be to spend time in your company, it is impossible to pack up here. My departure would seem like desertion.
>
> I promised you that no member of the French mission would interfere with Daniel's Tomb; but if I keep my promise I count on you to protect and ensure respect for representatives of a friendly government. Write in that sense to the senior cleric, who will then benefit from an opportunity to please his Imperial Majesty.

As soon as the letter was on its way, Marcel turned towards the fearful workers. 'Ousta Hassan, go to Dizful and engage as many men as you can: a hundred, five hundred, a thousand. Our work so far has been mere child's play.'[5]

Not wanting to show his hand, mirza Abdoul-Rahim held his fire when Ousta Hassan returned with a large troop of Dizfulis. Soon Bakhtiaris drifted onto the mound and, despite Sheikh Ali's words, many of his Arabs swelled the workforce. As the trenches opened, the mirza set his spies. He would know instantly if any treasure, silver, gold or precious stones, were found. The ban on supplying sheep to the foreigners remained in place, even the Bakhtiaris camped with their flocks on the banks of the Kerkhah refusing them. None of these actions generated income for the mirza, so he installed himself among the Dizfulis and imposed a daily levy. Though terrified of the threatened bastinado, the workers complained bitterly to Marcel, swearing they would rather leave the dig than cede him a single coin.

Furious, Marcel confronted the arrogant mirza, who blustered, 'Do you think me capable of taking bread out of the hands of those poor people? . . . The Dizfulis have offered me a little daily present, as is usual, but I have refused it . . . You humiliate me deeply in suspecting my best intentions.'[6]

The war was now out in the open.

The mirza looked for a new scheme. He would target the French directly; their hunger would fill his pockets. He bought up a flock of thirty sick old ewes and paraded them before the tents, offering them at five times their value. Disgusted by the ploy as much as by the rancid animals, the foreigners swore to starve rather than eat such meat.

Meanwhile the workers were excavating the mound with some success. Reporting each day at daybreak, they formed into gangs and were issued with a pick or bucket under the supervision of an overseer. Selected men acted as sentries, brought drinking water from the river or prepared the daily rice. The meal was the only official break during the day, but the men's efforts were lacklustre, their work ceasing as soon as the overseer turned his back. They lined up for their pay two hours before sunset, leaving them time to prepare for the evening prayer. The three ethnic groups neither worked together nor lived together. When the Arabs left their trench they drifted towards the tents on the plain, the Dizfulis climbed out of theirs and retired to Daniel's Tomb, while the Bakhtiaris handed their picks and buckets in at another site and returned to their twig-and-rush huts nearby on the tumulus.

For Jane the days were a tumult of emotions: anxiety about progress at the dig and excitement as finds were made, anger towards their gaoler and gratification at being involved in what she was confident would be a significant contribution to understanding the past. There were no comforts in life under the tent; even before the mirza's ban on their food supply the diet was spartan and the campbed unforgiving. The winter nights were extremely cold, but in the mornings when she ducked out of the tent's doorway and saw the snow gleaming on the crests of the Bakhtiaris she was filled with joy at her good fortune. On top of a tumulus in an exotic situation, when she saw the slanting light caressing the plain, saw how an overnight rainstorm had changed its sere yellow to softest green and tempted from the earth a carpet of scarlet anemones, she no longer felt the cutting wind and when she slipped in the mud near the trenches she was able to laugh with the workers.

As the weeks went by mutual respect grew between those who toiled in the trenches and those who decided where the pits should be dug. The Muslims saw their life as foreordained, so why should they struggle against its inevitability? They accepted with fortitude rain and cold, shrugged off ill treatment and endured whatever was the will of Allah – and it was obviously the will of Allah that the French colonel should not beat them on the soles of their feet, nor M. Babin cheat them of their money when they stood in line each evening. They were grateful, Inshallah, for the medicines dispensed so generously by the camp doctor, M. Houssay, and that the *khanum* would listen to their problems and acknowledge their human dignity.

It was Jane who was most responsible for the cordiality of the relationship. Marcel, an austere, introverted character, scrupulously fair in his dealings, was essentially wordless and remote. Jane had warmth and empathy. The maximum number of employees seems to have been 295 and only someone genuinely interested in people could have appreciated their individuality and come to know them all. They obeyed Marcel but returned Jane's consideration with small thoughtful acts. The servants planned and built a makeshift dining room and once, during exceptionally heavy rain, they stood out in the wet to light a fire in an excavation trench to prepare a hot evening meal. The foreigners had resigned themselves to dining off a cheese brought from the ship and Jane was very touched when the drenched cook arrived, smiling and carrying steaming rice and the inevitable chicken.

None of that constrained them from lying, cheating and robbing, nor from pitiless ferocity towards their enemies. Jane saw their defects clearly, but attributed them to the example set by those in authority. From the shah down to the town governor, the whole administration was corrupt and venal, its morality a model of wickedness. She believed that if the people were treated fairly and honestly, their considerable virtues would dominate.

The foreigners trod a careful path between the three distinct and mutually intolerant groups, above all trying not to become involved in their animosities. As far as the French were concerned, the Dizfulis were the least threatening. Dressed in rags and poorly nourished all their lives, they were thin and small and suffered from many sicknesses. They were poor workers, light-fingered and quick to profit from anyone else's misfortune. Never having had the benefit of education, their minds were fertile ground for the fanatic to sow hatred. Used to bending the high felt hat before arbitrary injustice, courage was not one of their qualities. At the sight of an authority figure, their bare legs trembled and their fingers pulled at the twisted shawl that held their two short sleeveless cotton coats together at the waist. On the mound they moved only in groups and in the evenings Ousta Hassan marshalled them down the twisting path to the security of Daniel's Tomb, since for them a night in the open was a fearful prospect.

Raiding and pillaging being their way of life, the nomads stole each other's camels and cows, stealing the same beasts back again, their tribal feuds manipulated by an administration addicted to the principle of 'divide and rule'. Guards were placed day and night to protect the white tents against the tribesmen. Not only was their thieving a direct threat, but during razzias between Bakhtiaris and Beni La'am the warpath sometimes ventured frighteningly close to the mission. To hear hooves in the night thundering across the mound or to wake to blood-curdling screams was a testing experience, but no concern of theirs, the French told each other, as they felt for the rifles that always shared their bed and the revolvers under the pillow. So when Jane's blood brother rode onto the mound and claimed her support, all her diplomatic skills were needed.

On the way into Susa in 1882 her party had been intercepted at the Kerkhah River by Bakhtiari horsemen, who took them to the tent of the tribal chief, Kerim Khan. There the khan's son, hooking his index fingers together, had promised, 'From now on we are brothers,' and Jane had responded, 'I am obliged to you, my dear Mohammad. In life as in death.'

What Mohammad thought when he discovered three years later that his 'brother' had reappeared at Susa as a *khanum* is interesting to speculate. However surprised he may have been, when Jane heard that Kerim Khan had pitched his tents some distance away, she knew the day would come when Mohammad would call in their pledged relationship. Several times the Khan visited the mound, the Dieulafoys receiving him formally, spreading the carpet and offering tea. His quick eyes darting about, he was never slow to ask for things: a rifle, a watch, a glass, unstated menace behind the unctuous request, but Mohammad did not appear until warfare between Bakhtiari and Beni La'am reached a bloody pitch.

In the fourth week of March, emboldened by the marriage of his daughter to the governor's son, the chief of the powerful Segvend[7] Arabs, Ali Khan, invaded the plain, pillaging caravans and killing travellers. When he raided the Bakhtiaris' tents and destroyed their barley fields, Kerim Khan gathered his warriors and sent them to do battle under Mohammad. Raiding and fighting was a formality, but if blood was spilled it became deadly. When Ali Khan's son was wounded the Bakhtiaris retreated in panic. Kerim Khan tore down his brown tents, rounded up his sheep, cattle and goats, loaded the chickens onto donkeys and hastened to pitch camp under the protection of the mound.

Mohammad climbed the steep flank of the tumulus and presented himself breathless at Jane's tent.

'They'll take all our wheat and cattle as the blood price. My brother, you must join our fight.'

'Sheikh Ali is your legitimate defender. He'll send you 300 mounted troops.'

'They're nothing compared to the terror that the sight of four white helmets will inspire. Foreigners with your courage will soon make those sons of dogs show the tails of their horses.'[8]

Since the mission depended on the goodwill of the tribes, the request challenged Jane's tact. The notion that foreigners must not interfere in the internal affairs of another country being beyond Mohammad, he departed angrily, throwing over his shoulder, 'What's the good of being your brother if you treat me like the lowest Dizfuli?'

With Mohammad's visit to his 'brother' unsuccessful, the tribe sent a woman to persuade 'Excellency *khanum*'. A head wrapped in a cashmere shawl rose above the bank, followed by a chemise patterned with red flowers and an emerald-green velvet vest decorated with chains of coins, then very full blue trousers appeared and at last the bare brown feet approaching the white tent. Jane invited Papi *khanum*, the second-ranking tribeswoman, inside. With much tinkling of glass beads, coral pieces and amber drops, she seated herself, gravely offering Jane all her mares, her camels, cows and sheep if the white helmets would ride with the tribe. Jane's diplomacy was severely tested, but her answer being essentially the same it was no coincidence that during the moonless night that followed the Mission's kitchen was raided.

Although Marcel's slippers had disappeared and in exchange Papi *khanum* had left some lively fleas, the visit had to be returned. At dawn, the hour for social calls among the tribes, Jane's white helmet disappeared down the slope and proceeded a short way onto the plain. The brown tents were planted in orderly rows around a central square where the animals were corralled at night. In the largest tent Kerim *khanum*, premier wife, surrounded by a crowd of women, received Jane most graciously. After tea was served Kerim *khanum* withdrew a jewel box from a hole in the earth beneath her carpet, an exceedingly secure place since Kerim *khanum* was extremely plump, and offered Jane the casket's contents, even her nose jewellery, as well as a packet of bright chemises. Jane softened her refusal with the gift of a mirror, something the tribeswomen had never seen. They thought the image was someone hiding behind the glass. Their shrieks of joy when they realised it was themselves brought Kerim Khan rushing in with his baton.

The following day the Bakhtiaris expelled the Dizfulis and Arabs, and took over the trenches. Marcel restrained himself until the evening. After the workers were paid, a soldier solemnly climbed onto a nearby hillock and in a loud voice proclaimed, 'Men of Dizful, of Shushtar and other places, Bakhtiaris of Kerim Khan . . . Arabs of Beni La'am and nomads of tribes whose name I do not know, listen well: there are guards here, the guards have rifles and the rifles are loaded,'[9] firing off a salvo as proof. In the moonless night prowlers again raided the fowlhouse, although unsuccessfully. Next morning when 600 Bakhtiaris appeared on the mound Marcel shut down the dig, which brought Kerim Khan rushing up the slope wielding his baton on his tribesmen's heads and shoulders. The expelled intruders, slipping sulkily away down the slope, vowed they would be revenged. Calm was restored by midday, only previously employed Bakhtiaris scowling at the Dizfulis and Arabs back in their separate trenches. The guard was doubled.

The new moon had risen and gone to bed again when shrieks and rifle fire filled the darkness. Bullets whistled around the white tents. Fully armed, the four foreigners emerged simultaneously from the canvas to see a whirlwind of Arabs galloping past, their arms filled with chickens, sheep hanging off their pommels. Behind them came the Bakhtiaris, screaming with rage, firing wildly. It was not their fight, the foreigners reiterated, and returned shaken to their beds. When a nervous guard raised the alarm again two hours later Jane and Marcel took up their rifles and patrolled the wild mound until dawn.

The rising sun lit up the rows of brown tents. In the large square at their heart, the brush barriers that had separated one flock from another, strings of camels from herds of cows, goats from sheep had been knocked down. Animals milled about, men and women screamed in despair as they counted their losses, roosters crowed for their hens and lambs bleated for their mothers. Only the yapping yellow bitches seemed as numerous as yesterday. 'Sons of dogs, sons of burnt fathers,' raged Kerim Khan, and then fell suddenly silent. At the foot of the mound lay a motionless brown *abba*; alongside was a blood-streaked cloth torn from its camel hair cords. Face down in the dirt was a Segvend Arab, half his head blown away.

Death demanded vengeance. A life for a life. Perhaps with interest. Collected quickly, the body was thrown across the back of a mule and dumped into a shallow grave near Daniel's Tomb. On the plain, wailing, serious discussion and random rifle fire filled the air; on the tumulus the dig proceeded. At night, fires burned among the brown tents and at the white tents the guards kept themselves awake by talking and reciting. When the workers entered the trenches at dawn the next day they found a bull-headed capital destroyed, its limestone shattered by pelted rocks. Nearby, carved inscriptions had been violated and spiteful vandalism perpetrated on many of the finds. Marcel was enraged. Marching down to the brown tents, he found the khan as white with apprehension as a man who never washed could be. Worse than his dread of inevitable Arab retaliation was trepidation that the Segvend daughter in the *anderun* of the governor's son might bring the governor's troops thundering towards him. His fear made him vulnerable to Marcel's anger; he threatened to cut off the head of

Shattered bullhead capital

anyone seen at night near the trenches. Jane spent the afternoon relocating the transportable finds to the tents.

Another night came when the mound seemed to roll away in sinister shadow, when every dog's bark jolted the foreigners awake and feeling for their rifles. In the morning the plain was alive – the tribe was on the move, its mules laden with folded tents and trussed chickens, its animals and children herded along. To the French the noise of their going was sweet music, the dust rising around them the most fragrant talcum. A group of horsemen broke away from the cavalcade, wheeled their horses in tight circles and fired off a volley of shots. 'My brother is wishing me adieu,' said Jane.

Forty kilometres distant from Susa the Kerkhah River looped towards the Turkish border. Encamped there, a wild ten-minute ride could take the Bakhtiaris safely across the frontier.

Despite the mirza and tribal warfare, the dig continued, methodically, systematically. Marcel conducted the investigation scientifically, laying out his trenches to seek the totality of the past, not its artistic and grandiose treasures alone and out of context. He first attacked the *apadana* to confirm Loftus's claims. The corner column bases were soon excavated, the trilingual inscriptions, whose cuneiform characters Loftus had copied and sent to Rawlinson for translation, revealed. They left no doubt that here lay an Achaemenid palace built by Darius, son of the great Cyrus, burned during the reign of his grandson Artaxerxes I, and repaired by his grandson Artaxerxes II. What was the appearance of the palace, how was it constructed, and how much remained were the primary questions the Dieulafoys sought to answer. They hoped to find evidence of how the kingdom was governed and relics explaining its relations with its ancient neighbours, so recently disinterred in Mesopotamia.

Clearing away the remains of a twelfth-century Arab town revealed evidence demonstrating that, like Persepolis later, Susa's *apadana* was built on a great elevated terrace, though they could find no trace of the staircase that must have led up from river level. After two weeks of digging Jane had written, 'Nothing worth mentioning discovered to date,' when suddenly the workers came upon a horde of elegant earthenware vases, sixty-five centimetres high, stoppered with black stone. Alerted by his spy and imagining treasure, the mirza was disappointed when the contents were sifted in his presence. Bones and skulls revealed they were Parthian funerary urns, their story only confirming that many dynasties had used the site after Alexander the Great defeated the Persians.

Dizfouli with funerary urns

Later that same day a single brick was unearthed, not a mud or clay brick, but a very distinguished brick, an intriguing brick. Its matrix was dense and white, and two sides were enamelled. On one, 'bands of yellow and blue, separated by black cloisons, framed white rosettes on a blue ground.'[10] The adjoining face carried a pattern of blue, white and green triangles. The colours were vibrant, the enamel lustrous but fragile, slipping off in little puffs of coloured dust. Jane recognised it immediately as a siliceous brick fired three times: once to meld its sand and limestone mix, again after the lines of the design had been drawn out in a black substance, and, finally, when it had cooled, and the cloisons – the outlined spaces – filled with coloured enamels, the brick had been returned to the kiln.[11] The sophistication of this cloisonné technique raised many questions. Though the workers searched the area diligently and Jane sifted the dirt where it was found, nothing more, not so much as a fragment, came to light and the brick remained a small lonely thing. She put it away packed in straw, her thoughts haunted by intriguing possibilities.

The next significant find represented the other end of the scale: broken pieces of a giant bull, its shank thicker than a Dizfuli waist, its hoof as high as an Arab knee, its neck encircled by central Asian rosettes; nearby lay its huge head. Carved from fine-grained grey limestone and 'evidence of a powerful decorative art and advanced technique', it confirmed that the Susa *apadana* had been a great open space punctuated by twenty-metre-high columns topped with bull-headed capitals to carry the roof beams, its design the prototype for Persepolis.

Marcel had brought a jack from France to manoeuvre heavy loads. When he set it up to raise the bull from the trench, the workers retreated in fear. Knowing nothing of mechanics and ignorant of the wheel, they were astounded by the jack. Their shocked faces became one of Jane's cherished memories. But the find posed a problem. Left at Susa, it would soon be vandalised, yet how to get it home to France? It was too big and too heavy for camel or mule. It seemed best to bury the bull for the present and delay its repatriation until the following season. Suspecting other bull heads lay beneath the debris still covering the marble-tiled floor, Marcel abandoned the *apadana* and set the workers to open trenches in the city and on the citadel.

While Jane photographed and measured the bull pieces prior to burial, the single enamelled brick teased her. None had been found at Persepolis. And why was it alone? Was it a solitary specimen brought as booty from another city? A few glazed sun-dried bricks had been found in Mesopotamian sites, but nothing comparable with this complex treatment. Were others hidden beneath the rubble? Within a week an excited shout brought her racing across the mound to be confronted by five baskets in which delicate enamelled bricks lay side by side. 'Where?' she screamed at the workmen, 'where?' and ran to the trench where what is known today as the *Frieze of the Lions* lay face down on the earth. Today, mounted on a wall at the Louvre Museum in Paris, the irascible lions once more march towards a doorway. Raised in relief against a delicate turquoise-blue background, their white bodies are lustrous, their muscles, highlighted by cloisons of blue and green, ripple as they stalk, their gold-tipped tails swish with rage, their jaws are wide and snarling. Exquisite bands of apple-green and turquoise triangles and tiny palm trees threaded on a yellow ribbon define the space above and below, creating a repetitive stillness, a calm counterpoint to the aggressive cats imperiously prowling the five-metre high wall. Topped by turquoise crenellations, the enamelled-brick wall carries the Achaemenid signature: a band of many-petalled rosettes set in yellow. Many laborious stages spanned the moment at Susa when Jane recognised an incomparable lost masterwork and the day the *Frieze of the Lions* was exhibited in Paris for all to enjoy – the delicate work of retrieving each individual brick or fragment without damaging its enamel; the charting of its position and its labelling; painstaking packing and transport; months of anxiety; chemical stabilisation of the fragile surface; and, finally, reassembly according to the record Jane made as she and her small group of specially selected workers disinterred it.

Jane was jubilant. If they found nothing more, the *Frieze of the Lions* justified the excavation. Greater than its intrinsic beauty was its revelation of the palace's appearance. She realised they had retrieved the beautiful façades of the palace. Susa's palace was exuberantly unlike anything they had imagined. Its walls and staircases were not faced with carved stone, as at Persepolis, but were built with colourful, shining enamelled bricks. The frieze told how impressive the palace must have appeared when it stood upright on the platform above the river. As the bricks yielded to her little trowel, Jane extracted the brilliance of the palace from the trench.

Jane had been obsessed by Persian enamel work since the day in 1881 when a peasant searching the rubble of Ghazan Khan's lost suburb near Tabriz brought her an enamelled eight-pointed tile, on its surface a golden dragon writhing in a net of stars and arabesques. She was fascinated by a medium which combined beauty and durability. She had followed the trail of enamelled tiles and bricks to Shiraz, lost it in the south and had never expected to find it again in an Achaemenid palace at Susa. But here they were, so old yet so skilfully crafted, enamelled bricks with designs in relief, enamelled bricks with flat surfaces, monochromatic bricks and polychrome bricks, each a tribute to the medium's durability, each an incredible surprise.

The frieze was not alone. A fantastic enamelled beast in relief was uncovered nearby and two yellow griffins, but before they could begin excavating in earnest a three-day deluge set in and the tribes remained tucked up under their tents, not venturing across the plain to bring the daily supplies to the mound. As lightning flashed and thunder rolled and the tent sagged under the weight of water, it was thrilling to think of the bricks, but their stomachs remained empty. With an advance on their wages, the Dizfulis bought dates from the Arabs, while the French sank to the humiliation of killing and eating one of mirza Abdoul-Rahim's mangy old ewes. It stuck in their throats, literally and metaphorically, but what was the alternative?

The mirza and the governor were tightening their embrace. When Marcel sent a messenger to the deputy governor at Dizful for an instalment of their funds he was beaten and returned empty-handed. Fearing financial strangulation, the French decided they must conserve what cash they had on site to pay expenses if they were forced to leave. While Houssay, escorted by the treacherous mirza Abdoul-Rahim, went off to confront the deputy governor, Babin closed the trenches, explaining to the workers why they were unable to continue. It testifies to the rapport the French had established that the men shrugged and said, 'You can pay us when you get your money,' and returned to the dig, confident that Marcel would overcome the Dizful tyrant.

The workers were not alone in believing the French would succeed. Sheikh Ali, who had stubbornly refused to understand Farsi during their encounters, rode onto the mound at the centre of a troop of his wild Arab tribesmen and said in excellent Persian, 'I hear the deputy governor refuses to advance the funds you left with Zil-es-Sultan. I have six million kran at your disposal.' Though Marcel politely declined his generosity, the sheikh sent a present of a fat lamb. With the mirza away, food was again abundant and the foreigners ate heartily. Before every meal, instead of saying Grace, they cursed mirza Abdoul-Rahim and Mozaffer el-Molk.

The next to offer his purse was Dizful's senior cleric, Sheikh Mohammad Taher. In that wet, wild winter of 1885, the earth's atmosphere still full of Krakatoa dust, the Dizfulis blamed the exceptionally heavy spring rains on the foreigners. When rivers rose above their banks and part of Shushtar's winding bridge was swept away, the Dizfulis knew it was the evil sorceress at Susa who had caused the disaster. Fearing trouble, Sheikh Taher had come to honour his pledge to protect the French mission. He visited Daniel's Tomb and then climbed the twisting pathway. The workers were delirious with pleasure that this much revered figure who spoke out for them against the oppression and venality of their rulers should visit them. They leapt from the trenches to kiss his hand, his robe, even, recorded Jane, 'the imprint of his foot.' He calmed their fears about excavating funerary urns, assuring them entombment in pots was not an Islamic practice. After matching Sheikh Ali's offer, Sheikh Taher revealed what was really distressing him: the deputy governor was beating the taxes out of the Dizfulis with such ferocity that they were begging him to intercede with the shah.

Sheikh Taher's visit was timely, because that night there was an eclipse of the moon. Superstition, fear and anger filled pilgrim and worker alike. They burst onto the mound, faces white, hands trembling. Even the most faithful supporters were shaken, crying to Marcel, 'Excellency! Excellency! What have you done? Allahu Akbar, why have you taken the moon?'[12] Jane and Marcel recognised a crisis and consulted a lunar calendar. Though the eclipse was nothing to do with them, they said, the moon would return at ten o'clock. When it reappeared on the hour many still saw the foreigners as sorcerers – otherwise how could they know when it would come back?

Twentieth-century excavators at Susa unearthed clay tablets inscribed with mathematical tables, geometrical calculators, and hundreds of years of astronomical data recorded in cuneiform characters. All that learning was lost, buried in the past, and in Jane's present no trace of it remained among the Persians. Only the spades could reveal it.

Monsieur Houssay returned in triumph across a carpet of flowers blooming on the plain following the rains. He had called the deputy governor's bluff by threatening to ride on to the English telegraph station. Recognising he was beaten, the miserable functionary had paid out, but mirza Abdoul-Rahim had taken his cut. For the present, the mirza remained in Dizful hoping Marcel's anger would recede. The mirza's influence with the governor had the foreigners in a stranglehold but, more dangerous to the mission, he was the official conduit between them and the world. Houssay also brought their first incoming post. Four months since they had left France, the letters precipitated an attack of acute homesickness, especially for Jane, who came from a very loving family. But the pages of the letters were out of order. Obviously, the governor's French-speaking doctor had read their mail for his master. The French realised that their outgoing mail, too, was being intercepted.

The blatant censorship immediately terminated the official channel for informing France of the *Frieze of the Lions*, so the Dieulafoys rode the forty kilometres to Kerim Khan's camp on the Kerkhah to ask him to send their letters across the Turkish border. The khan declined, saying he did not want to mix in affairs between them and the government, perhaps revenge for their not wanting to become involved in his fight with the Arabs, though it was more likely pressure from the mirza. With everyone playing two hands at once, either or both was possible. Foiled there, they recruited two Arabs from the trenches and sent them off across the marshes towards Amarah only hours before the mirza returned from Dizful. Hearing of it, he went red with rage and accosted Marcel, shouting at him, how dare he send mail other than through himself, the official channel.

Marcel, usually so cool, also became angry. 'Am I your prisoner?'

'Certainly not! But your letters will never reach their destination. The Arabs will throw them in the marsh and keep your silver.'

The mirza sent a party galloping after the messengers. One was beaten almost to death and the other chased into the desert, where the Beni La'am took care of him and tossed the letter to the wind. When Marcel learned their fate, 'I expected that from you,' he said, and went on the attack. 'Have you brought the money that you took [from our funds] at the deputy governor's residence?'

'By order of the governor, Mozaffer el-Molk, not a kran more will you receive until you give me Zil-es-Sultan's receipt.'[13]

And so the French learned that they were indeed prisoners. If they parted with the official receipt, they would never see the balance of their money and could never hope to escape. It became imperative that they communicate with France. The news of the Lions was nothing. Now their lives were at stake.

After much discussion it was decided to leave the two young Frenchmen in charge of the dig and the Dieulafoys would take the mail to Ahwaz. They called for their horses. Hired from Kerim Khan and cared for by a Bakhtiari groom, the mares had often taken the Dieulafoys out onto the plain for an evening gallop and had carried Houssay to Dizful. Now, suddenly, by order of Kerim Khan, the horses were not available.

It was time to show the iron fist. All the Bakhtiari workers were dismissed and their huts dismantled. With pity and regret, Jane watched them stream away across the plain towards the Kerkhah.

The next confrontation with the mirza was sweetened by the arrival of an Arab 'princess'. Daughter of M'sban, feared head of all the many Beni La'am tribes, she had come with an escort across the Turkish border, using a pilgrimage to the shrine as an excuse to meet Jane. While her curiosity attests to a greater than average intelligence and also speaks of Jane's reputation among the tribal women, whatever the reality, she could not have appeared at a better moment. The Dieulafoys would return with her into Ottoman Turkey, 'on foot if they must', Jane declared, and from there contact the French and Persian governments.

The mirza retired to his tent and sent a messenger galloping towards Dizful. The Dieulafoys got on with the dig and waited.

The excavations had been very rewarding. Among the tangible objects such as the bull-headed capitals, many single enamelled bricks and the entire Lion frieze, were broken glass vases iridescent with age, a green enamelled bracelet, inscriptions, elegant earthenware pieces, bronze lamps and carved ivory cones, which hinted at how the Susians had lived, their style and how they valued beauty. On the city mound, trenches cutting down beneath Shapur I's town, which had been destroyed by Shapur II's elephants sent in to trample its Christian residents, revealed the walls of a complex defensive structure and a suburb divided in two parts by a long alley. A potter's house, entombing the tools of his trade and domestic artifacts, bore witness to the life of a skilled Susian artisan. On the citadel, work had been less successful, uncovering few built structures, although many crafted objects such as seals.

The numbers in the trenches were declining, not only because the Bakhtiaris had been fired. The Arabs, too, were starting to slip away. Summer was beginning with rising temperatures and a sere-yellow plain, and the ripening winter wheat was calling the nomads back to the tribal lands to take up sickles for the harvest. Only the Dizfulis were constant, although soon they would be needed in the town for summer building projects. Jane and Marcel knew the dig must end and were making plans to repatriate, but everything was dependent on their gaining access to their funds. At this late stage three significant finds were made. Near the fortifications in the city a number of high-quality enamelled bricks were exposed, part of a frieze of splendidly dressed people. Jane was impressed by the bricks' fine, dense matrix, the precision with which their edges fitted together, the delicacy of the colours and the harmony of their design. While technically very advanced, Jane saw them as evidence of the Susians' high aesthetic sensibility.

Their recovery had barely begun when one evening Jane slipped on something hard near the white tents on the palace mound. The workers had already descended the twisting path but impatient Jane could not wait for morning. Her trowel quickly uncovered a parapet and then parts of a stairway lined with enamelled bricks. Between delimiting upper and lower rows of triangles and chains of rosettes were horizontal panels with a whirling, spinning circular motif in apple green, dark green and yellow. Subsequent excavation revealed it was Achaemenid material recycled by the Sasanids who later occupied the site.

Their next discovery, a bull in apparently very good condition, was quickly covered over and left for the next season's dig. Although the machinations of the bureaucrats made life hazardous and often miserable, the mission was determined to return with the winter.

Soon, the hundreds of men and women, students and mullahs, children and ancients streaming down the Dizful road on the annual pilgrimage to Daniel's Tomb ensured that their life became even more unpleasant. From before the morning prayer until nightfall, they arrived in waves on the tumulus, rolling the earth back into the trenches, breaching the barriers between them and, to the rage of the workers, shattering the fragments of a bull. Almost fifty funerary urns waiting to be photographed near the white tents were deliberately and irreparably smashed into small pieces. Musket balls raised a dust and catapults flung stones around the foreigners whenever they crossed the big ravine between city and palace sites. 'Kerim Khan's men were little saints compared with these devout worshippers,' Jane wrote angrily.

To save face the deputy governor used the excuse of paying his respects to Daniel to bring the balance of the mission's funds to Susa. In the ballet of intimidation danced by the two men, Marcel's threats had prevailed, but in the wings waiting for his entrance was Mozaffer el-Molk, the governor.

Why the governor was so ill disposed to the mission is hard to determine. His behaviour epitomised the 'mix of timidity and audacity known only to cowards' that Jane attributed to Ousta Hassan. Like all the functionaries he was terrified of the shah's arbitrary power, while never wasting an opportunity for his own financial gain. Had he hoped to expropriate the mission's funds? Were his agents stirring the fanatical pilgrims and Dizfulis whose opposition he used as an excuse to threaten the workforce? 'Scoundrels who continue to work for the foreigners will have their ears cut off,' he warned. When the Dizfulis, despite their fears, continued to labour he sent an order via the mirza for Marcel to shut down the dig. This rattled Ousta Hassan so much he let slip that when he had originally sought permission to work at Susa, the deputy governor, 'to whom I have access because my wife is the sister of the cousin of his favourite valet,' had told him to use the opportunity to earn as much silver as possible because nothing would ever leave the site.

Having excavated a tangible record of Susa's Achaemenid civilisation, the French would not consider leaving the material to be smashed, the fate of the urns, or broken like the bull, and as for the enamelled bricks, 'those useless old things,' sniffed the mirza, they would be powder before the next full moon if not expatriated. Marcel met the threat head on, sending Ousta Hassan to Dizful to hire a carpenter and make specific purchases, then joined the laughing French contingent in devising a way to overcome the censorship protocol. Their letter to de Ronchaud, director of the French national museums, 'announcing the ruin of the hopes raised by the early excavations, the only things of importance being the funerary urns, which could form the basis for a very interesting archaeological study of funerary practices,' ended with 'a eulogy to the Persian bureaucrats and a list of the presents, honours and decorations that should be awarded to each of them.'

'If M. de Ronchaud takes the epistle seriously,' wrote Jane in her diary, 'he will accuse Marcel of being sunstruck; but if the governor reads our correspondence!'[14]

When Ousta Hassan returned with a skilled carpenter and materials to construct stout wooden crates, he was escorted by a smiling mirza who brought permission for the Dieulafoys to expatriate all finds except the funerary urns.

As well as making crates, the carpenter erected a dig house, which would be a safer, warmer dwelling for the French when they returned the following winter. The greatest supporter of this plan was the tomb guardian, suddenly revealed as one of their truest friends, who 'every night climbed onto the roof of the Tomb to reassure myself that the foreigners' camp had not been pillaged.'[15]

As summer marched across the plain, it brought the temperature in the tent to unbearable levels, fiercely burning down on Jane as she supervised the packing of the enamelled treasures. One of Alexander's generals described Susa as 'scorchingly hot. At midday the snakes and lizards cannot cross the city streets for fear of being burnt alive; when the people want a bath they stand their water outdoors to heat it'[16] but for Jane a bath was only something she dreamed of. People walked in their own little cloud of dust and black swarms of mosquitoes penetrated even under the white helmets. Huge spiders and scorpions reared their pincers beneath every raised stone. Food turned rancid in an hour and dysentery struck Jane so badly she was too weak to walk to the trench to inspect a new lion.

A photograph from this time shows Jane seated in a makeshift shelter among the spiny bushes, leaning back against its one wall, sheltered from the sun by rush mats thrown over a short cantilevered roof. Instead of her white helmet she wears a black Persian felt hat, otherwise her dress is her usual uniform of boots and dark suit. Propped upright on their butts beside her are two rifles. Her eyes are closed. She looks drained and exhausted.

Seduced by what he had read in a letter he should not have opened, the mirza became as pliant as Torkhan *khanum*'s pet panther. For the moment his claws were sheathed and he purred when he was stroked. He watched serenely as the Dizfuli carpenter constructed crates for transporting their finds, approved the tcharvadar bachy, Attar, who had been contracted to take the Dieulafoys and their fifty-five cases to the Tigris and whose connections to the Beni La'am promised safe passage. The night before the mission's departure he attended a banquet given for the workers and the temple guardian, at which his scraggy old ewes were consumed as mutton pilau. What the duplicitous mirza made of a spontaneous speech by Ousta Hassan that praised the French excavators' integrity and begged them to return in the autumn is not recorded. Afterwards, the workmen lined up to salute Marcel in the Persian way by kissing his hand, while out on the plain red flames shot up into the darkness. The nomads were burning the vegetation before leaving for their summer pastures in the mountains.

Assembled on the banks of the Kerkhah, the caravan took two days to cross the river. Jane's heart was in her mouth as the heavy crates swung away from the bank on a raft made from lashed goatskin bladders. A lone Bakhtiari at the stern worked his paddle furiously, trying to edge the raft across the tumultuous waters, but the current seized it and he was hundreds of metres downstream before he could reach out and grab at the foliage on the far bank. Jane and Marcel swam their horses across and from the shelter of some trees watched the cases accumulate. Surrounded by shifting groups of fellow travellers, strings of camels still angry at being forced into the water, stinking dogs shaking themselves dry and flocks of drenched sheep, the couple were, for the first time in many months, pervaded by a feeling of freedom and safety. They were in Ottoman territory, away from the hatred of their gaoler, resting on soft green grass at the edge of a clean snow-fed river, the only shadow for Jane being her concern for Marcel. His appetite and his sleep had been destroyed by the strain of the last weeks. He looked old and gaunt.

As they prepared for the march at midnight on the second day, again red flames shot up into the darkness – Houssay and Babin signalling their departure from the tumulus. They were going into Fars for the summer to visit Persepolis and other ancient sites. In her diary Jane recorded how close they had become during the six testing months since leaving France: 'Never did any cloud come between us, each of them so intelligent and devoted'. She attempted to understand her very mixed feelings on leaving the tumulus, concluding, 'Some part of my spirit remains there caught on your spiny bushes.'[17]

It was now late May and the plain an inferno. Although they travelled at night, the stages were long and often the morning sun was high in the sky before they reached the next water. Chickens and lambs carried on mule-back died of dehydration and the travellers began to look like 'phantoms in the vestibule of Hell'. For two interminable stages the only water was salty and undrinkable and they relied on bladders filled at the previous camp. Marcel succumbed to malaria but clung grimly to the saddle.

When they reached the marsh where their caravan had lost its way in 1882, the Dieulafoys' caravan split from the larger party and travelled along slimy channels towards a Tigris tributary. Waiting on its bank to rendez-vous with native boats ordered up from Amarah, Jane counted off their fifty-five crates and ordered them stacked as shelter from the pitiless sun. She thought their precious contents had reached safety. In fact, there were to be two attacks against them and they would lose the second.

After fifteen hours on the water the contracted boatmen swinging into the backwater were desperate for rest. Marsh Arabs, slinking silently through the reeds, found the *belems* drawn up at the water's edge and saw the sleeping boatmen. Restless behind the makeshift shelter and taking her turn with malaria, Jane saw three dark shadows slipping away and knew they would return.

The attack was launched with a stampede of buffalo that split to left and right as they confronted the wall of crates. The Arabs rushing them from behind stalled when they saw the weaponry aimed at their heads. The siege lasted an hour, a long, long hour, and then gradually the rustle of reeds replaced low voices, as the Arabs melted into the darkness.

They had crossed the desert, negotiated the marsh, escaped the Arabs, but in Amarah the Turks defeated them. Customs agents seized the crates and impounded them, claiming the contents had come from digs in Ottoman territory. A sufficient bribe would have released them, but even if he had the money Marcel would never succumb to blackmail. All that could be salvaged from the imbroglio was to have the crates shipped down to Basra, where they were corded and sealed in the presence of the French Consul, and all that saved Jane from total despair was the foresight that had made her pack a selection of the Lion frieze bricks and all the small objects in her personal luggage.

Chapter 17
Second season: The Frieze of the Archers

'**Y**ou can no more depend upon the friendship of a king than you can upon the voice of a child; because the former changes on the slightest suspicion, the latter in the course of the night.'[1] Jane learnt the bitter truth of Sa'adi's proverb when she reached France on 1 July 1885 and was informed that Shah Nasr-al-Din had withdrawn permission for further excavation at Susa. The blow was unexpected. Instead of a joyous, careless summer with her family in the Languedoc, the months became a time of fretful uncertainty.

The shah's change of heart was prompted by a petition from Khuzestan's clergy claiming, 'the high cost of living at Dizful, the torrential rain, and the black storm clouds that gather every night on the horizon must be attributed to the coming of the French engineers ... who have extracted from the depths of the soil the talismans which our prophets had buried there to safeguard Susiane province ... the terrible floods are signs of divine rage.'[2] Conciliatory cables flew to Tehran asking Shah Nasr-al-Din to reconsider. After much nail-biting the shah yielded, reaffirming the firman of the previous year, changing only two clauses. Concerning the safety of the French mission: if any of them were killed, it was no business of his; and as to the dig's timing, they must be off the site before the annual pilgrimage began in early April.

Meanwhile, officials at quai d'Orsay fired off terse telegrams to Constantinople objecting to the seizure by Turkish customs of legally acquired French property. After several futile months the French government decided enough of diplomacy – they would send a gunboat. Consequently, in November 1885 Jane returned to Bushire in the ministry of war's *Scorpion*, a small warship with a high bridge and a low draught and so many guns there was no room for passengers. At night a tent was erected on the aft deck and at dawn it was thrown down. The Dieulafoys spent the daylight hours attempting to stay out of the way and out of the sun.

The ship's fire was aimed not only at the Turkish customs officers, but at the Persians, telling them plainly how the French government regarded its mission to Susa and the security of its agents. Nonetheless, when the *Scorpion* reached Bushire, the shah's promised document had not arrived, though Babin and Houssay had descended from Fars with several bales of newly acquired carpets. During twelve anxious days Marcel discreetly changed the mission's money into Persian kran, removing the mission's reliance on the honesty or otherwise of Khuzestan's governor and his minions, replacing it with the enormous risk of transporting a large sum through territory controlled by thieves. The Dieulafoys were still without an official document when, on 17 November, the *Scorpion*, already late for an assignment in Madagascar, weighed anchor and headed towards a show-down at the customs house at Basra. The Ottoman Turks, groaning in the death throes of empire, swallowed their medicine and coughed up all fifty-five crates with seals intact. Watching them being loaded for France, Jane farewelled them with the thought, 'If we die, at least the French nation will have a memento of us,'[3] and immediately trans-shipped to an English steamer ascending the Tigris.

In Amarah once more, the mission could only wait impatiently for the shah's dispatch to arrive and for an indigo caravan to come down from Dizful so they could hire its muleteers, the delay giving Jane time for reflection.

After her terrible experiences in Persia, what would prompt Jane's return? Was it only ambition, seeing the archaeological discoveries as her ticket to the Paris salons, or was the challenge of the search its own intellectual reward? Did the commanding beauty of the Bakhtiari ranges and the plain silvered by moonlight transcend the harsh reality of life on a mound exposed to winter storms and sullen heat? Did the humour and quick intelligence of the Persian workmen, even the oscillating friendship of the tribes, outweigh the antipathy of the governor and his bureaucrats and the fanaticism of the clerics? Perhaps her decision to return was influenced in some part by each of these.

Jane had a sensitive appreciation of the beautiful, a sensibility rewarded as much by the Persian landscape as by her enamelled finds at Susa. Her eye cherished the changes brought by the hours of the day and the seasons of the year. She noted:

From green the plain has become yellow, herbs replace their flowers with prickles, the chain of the Bakhtiaris show red crests where once glaciers lay,'[4] and advised, 'In the sparkling brilliance [of dawn] when the earth is lit by the rays of God himself . . . breathe in the gentle morning air, let your eyes roam that immense plain, bigger than an ocean, more iridescent than pearl shell, [and see] on the mountains the blue and purple ribbons, distant and final curtain of a sublime decor. Become one with the flocks going out into the desert, the bounding lambs and the kids butting each other, fighting for life. Watch the silhouettes of the camels and the buffalos . . . stomping along in the rising formless mists . . . and praise your supreme master, whatever name you care to call him . . . In the desert, while the mouth remains silent, the heart sings a spontaneous hymn of joy and recognition.

She suggests to those with troubled minds not to look for peace in the rationale of philosophers or the writings of theologians, but 'come to live in the solitude of the mountains, on the lonely plains. Their beauty and majestic eloquence will speak to your spirit more than the opinions of one or the contradictions of the other.'[5] Physical discomfort meant little to Jane compared with the exquisite pleasure, the sudden exhilarating surge when the strange and magnificent environment impinged upon her senses. It was like a drug without the dangerous consequences.

The cast of exotic characters who inhabited the mountains and deserts of Persia intrigued her. Men like Kerim Khan and Sheikh Mizal, Mozaffer el-Molk and even the devious mirza Abdoul-Rahim could hardly be said to walk through Jane's story, their egos too great and their power considerable. They marched. Yet it would seem that the people she had most rapport with moved more humbly: the workers, the tribespeople and, perhaps especially, the women. She understood their struggle and saw their faults as a consequence of the larger, darker picture which framed them. She admired the tribeswomen with their bright colours, she laughed at the hennaed palms in the *anderun*, and was charmed when a proud workman paraded his new clothes. While her experiences in that Muslim land reinforced her Christian faith, paradoxically they made her more tolerant. Aware of the hatred many directed towards her, the friendship of ordinary Persians affirmed her courage. Reviled by fanatical elements and tormented by corrupt officials, the qualities of the humble people endorsed her spirit with charity in the true sense of that word.

Enclosed by the walls of her Passy convent, the child Jane had quickly grasped the difference between bourgeois provincial and Paris intellectual. Belonging to one, she aspired to the second, despite having no idea of how she would attain it. She was confident that she had the intelligence required to make a mark there, but it needed more than brains to open the salon doors. She knew that to be admitted she must excel in some field, earn distinction in some way. In part, her love for Marcel sprang from a feeling that together they might find the key. When they married, she was unaware of its shape but she suspected the secret might be hidden in their mutual fascination with the East. After the powerful architect Viollet-le-Duc encouraged Marcel in 1879 to leave the security of his post in Toulouse for the possibility of finding official support in Paris for a journey to Persia, Jane felt she was getting closer to her desire. In Paris she sniffed the air of the salons and felt the excitement of the Third Republic's vibrant intellectual life, but she remained only an unknown provincial until presented to Louis de Ronchaud, then general secretary of the Ministry of Fine Arts. While de Ronchaud recognised Marcel's qualities and played a vital role in obtaining official support for his Persia project, it was the blue-eyed Jane who bewitched him. For decades de Ronchaud had quietly loved the comtesse Marie d'Agoult, whose writings under the name of Daniel Stern had put her at the intellectual heart of Paris. In Jane he found Marie's daughter. He was captivated by the same combination of physical beauty and ruthless intellect. De Ronchaud would give her the key, but first she had to prove herself in Persia.

On her return to France in 1882, her literary skills recognised by the publication of her diary in *le Tour du monde*, her courage and originality admired, de Ronchaud's endorsement made the doors swing wide. Then Jane learned how bitter it is to achieve one's goal, only to find it not enough. Having the entrée, she wanted more: her own salon where the distinguished would come to her. The distinction she needed to achieve that aim could be found only at Susa.

And there was a second disenchantment. The Parisienne intellectuals nourished a strong feminist movement. George Sand, Juliette Adam and de Ronchaud's beloved Marie d'Agoult were among those within the republican heart demanding equality for the sexes as well as equality among men. In Persia, as a sweet boy to Marcel's man, Jane was treated the same as he by the people they met (although often not very kind treatment, it was equal). When she returned to Paris and put on her frock she immediately became Marcel's dear wife, something altogether different in the public perception, a second-class person to be condescended to, while her achievements became curious rather than exceptional. She felt patronised by men whose minds were no better than hers, often much inferior, and who excluded her from an intellectual world in which she wished to participate. Their gallantry with its sexual edge offended her, and their presumption that her mind was occupied only with feminine trivialities incensed her.

Returned from the 1884–85 dig, she resented even more their dismissal of her as merely a woman. With her sparkling eyes and vivacious personality she could charm them if she chose, but that was not the relationship she wanted. She felt that to be physically desired but intellectually excluded was demeaning. On the Susa tumulus she had been one of four equals who had surmounted great emotional and physical difficulties to achieve laudable results; yet in Paris many saw her as nothing more than the mission's quaint mascot. That opinion was all the more unacceptable because to Marcel she was lover, companion, collaborator, forever his inspiration and always his equal.

Shortly before Jane left Paris for Persia in the autumn of 1885 a woman who had asked to be presented to the celebrated Mme Dieulafoy suggested that with a little more attention to her toilette she would make an admirable mannequin for French couture among the Persians. It seemed that even women belittled her achievement by not understanding the role she had played. Jane realised there were matters that needed deep consideration. There was a strategy to be determined. Some months on the mound at Susa might clarify her thoughts.

Impatient in Amarah, Marcel made a rash decision which placed them in tremendous danger. The season's budget was tucked away in the party's personal luggage. Recollecting from their previous crossings of the plain the thieving propensities of the Beni La'am, Marcel was concerned for the safety of the bulky Persian krans. If word leaked out that the mission was carrying its entire funds in tin chests crated up in four square wooden cubes the robbers would be tempted to more daring raids. Marcel's plan to avoid that possibility was based on the unfortunate presumption that M'sban, head of all the Beni La'am tribes, was as honourable as his friend Sheikh Mizal Khan, head of the Muhaisen tribes.

As soon as they stepped into the brown tent and saw M'sban they knew they were mistaken. Eighty years old, white-bearded, crooked-nosed, he sat among cushions on a threadbare carpet, not so much as a straw mattress under his old bones. His fierce black eyes burned with pride, though his robe was dirty and torn. When he blew his nose into his fingers he flung the result carelessly behind him. It was hard to believe that this was the king of the Beni La'am, a man greatly feared, with huge flocks and enormous wealth from the annual capitation fee demanded of his subjects, and who by trickery and cheating mostly managed to avoid Ottoman taxes. They had been warned against his avarice, but had not expected this picture of evil. He was a thief without honour, decidedly not a man to trust. To confide what they carried and expect his protection would be like dangling a lamb chop in front of a lion.

But they had to give some reason for riding five hours out from Amarah. 'The letters,' Jane whispered. Yes, the letters that the Beni La'am had stolen from the messenger dispatched last season from Susa! With grave courtesy Marcel asked him to guarantee their correspondence safe passage through his territories.

'Why concern yourself with bits of paper? The only letters I receive contain nothing but tax demands.'

'They bring us news of our families.'

Immediately M'sban called for his mirza and instructed, 'Write! "Take care! I tell you once, I tell you twice. No one bruise the bearers of this safe conduct nor stop the letters addressed to these Frenchmen."'[6]

Despite that firman and the sacred law of hospitality guaranteeing protection to anyone spending the night under the tent, their pockets were picked. When M'sban's seven-year old son was caught in the act of stealing Jane's handkerchief he proudly flourished all the things he had stolen before anyone had become aware. His unscrupulous parent lauded him. The child's father also felt deep in their pockets. At dawn, after a night spent on the cold winter earth, 'a foretaste of the tomb,' commented Jane, they called for their horses, only to have M'sban inform them their baggage mule had broken its leg. He had one they could hire. They paid out 10 kran, not realising this was only the first of M'sban's scams.

They had underrated the old nomad and aroused his interest. He was no fool. He knew they had entered his tent for a purpose, and not the one they gave. He did not know what it was, but he would find out and while he did so it was enough to collect his profit slowly and threaten their lives constantly. For the next thirteen days the French would wish Marcel had never assumed he could treat with a brigand.

M'sban's second scam concerned the hiring of horses, mules and camels in Amarah, in which both the French couple and Attar, the tcharvadar bachy who had brought them from Susa in May, were double-crossed. Attar's caravan was the first to come down since the route was released from the burning heat of summer. When rain filled the rivers, the route would close again. Travel was only possible in short intervals between the seasons and opportunities must be grasped.

Burning with fury at the cheating Beni La'am, the instant the shah's dispatch arrived, the Dieulafoys and Attar departed from Amarah. Their goods loaded on *belem*s, the first stage took the French deep into the marshes to a rendezvous with Attar's muleteers, who had travelled overland. Sneaking out of the darkness the Beni La'am discovered their camp in the reeds, cut the hobbles of the mules, leapt on their backs, and away at lightning speed went half the pack animals that had been hired at double price. Porterage of their goods after this third strike became slow misery. Though it was M'sban's last success, it was far from his last attempt.

As a twenty-four hour storm drenched the low-lying areas, the caravan struggled desperately to reach high ground along paths turned slippery as glass. When the overloaded mules fell, they had to be unloaded before being helped to their feet and reloaded, a time-consuming business. One of the camels broke its leg, another went lame and the travellers dripped with mud. Emerging onto the plain, they saw an Arab camp. 'Son of a dog, it's Menchet!' swore the tcharvadar, 'a brigand, a robber, an assassin who lets no one pass without stripping every fur and feather! Madness to make our own camp tonight. You must enter his tent resolutely and oblige him to receive you. He won't dare infringe the rules of hospitality. Pile your small luggage about you and we'll stack the bigger ones before the door where you can see them. You must keep your eye on them at all times.'

Looking like 'an evil bird of prey', Menchet welcomed them, called for mocha beans, roasted them and made coffee, but his piercing eyes missed nothing. 'What do you carry in those black chests in the crates? What makes them so heavy?' he asked.

'Bullets.'

Leaving Jean-Marie, the navy carpenter newly seconded to the mission, to guard their belongings, they paid a formal visit to the tribal tents. And returned to a shocked Jean-Marie. 'Madame, we have fallen into a nest of thieves. That child there, still at the breast, crawled underneath the saddles and tried to steal the girths. To be so wicked at that young age! Tonight they will cut our throats and steal everything we have.'

Dinner came. One pilau was placed before the unclean foreigners, another given to the Arab men seated by the fire. Bits of bone flung over the shoulder caused a frenzy among children crawling out from the shadows.

'Aren't you afraid under a nomad's tent?' Menchet asked.

'Why would we be afraid? Aren't we your guests?'

'You are braver than I. I fear a raid tonight, there are evil doers out there on the plain, but I will sleep soundly if you lend me your rifles.'

He had nothing to fear, they told him, they would watch all night. Menchet snorted. When the men retired to the women's tents, the French set up the four chests as a table and played dominoes, keeping their arms close. Towards one o'clock there was a rush of figures beyond the tent doorway and a volley of shots rang out in the darkness, yet the dogs had given no warning bark. Again the French refused Menchet's request for their arms, and neither would they go outside to chase off the robbers. Furious and sulky, Menchet retired knowing they understood his ploys.

Attar's animals, cruelly overloaded since M'sban's raid, were in a pitiful state. Menchet saw his chance. 'You can hire my mules and take my son as your guide.' Marcel accepted the mules and declined the son, impulsively boasting, 'I could show him the way to Susa.' But Menchet insisted and Marcel, resigned to the impost, offered the guide five kran.

'Have you lost your head?' Menchet shouted, demanding 150 kran, 'Tomorrow it will be double, after that three times. If you like you can spend the winter here or cede me your baggage. It's up to you,' he said, sweeping aside M'sban's letter of safe passage with a contemptuous hand.

Realising that Menchet was holding them to ransom the French arranged the baggage more defensively and positioned themselves to cover their backs. Soon their cook appeared: their sack of rice had been stolen and the tea caddy filled with cinders. No one would sell him sheep or chickens, all he had was stale bread and dates, he wailed.

At noon two strangers entered the tent, surveyed the embattled foreigners and quietly counselled Menchet, 'Fear of M'sban is the beginning of all wisdom,' but Menchet was not yet ready to be wise.

They were saved late in the afternoon when the huge commotion of a pilgrim caravan rolled in from the plain. To the French it was a joyful noise, the sound of freedom. A deal was done, the Dizfulis returning from Karbala only too happy to lease their mules and complete their pilgrimage on foot under the protection of French arms.

'Allah sees your wicked deeds,' was Jane's farewell to Menchet.

As the caravan struggled through the tamarisk trees on the far side of a swollen river, they found Menchet's son, Fellahyé, the guide they had declined, helping himself to the muleteers' breakfast. Dismissed and dismissed again, he clung on arrogantly. They knew he was not alone, that men from Menchet's tents were shadowing the caravan, only waiting for Fellahyé's signal to fall on them. When a posse of ten Arabs appeared in the distance late one day, the muleteers quickly formed a defensive square while the French loaded their weapons. To their surprise Fellahyé spurred his horse towards the troop, shouting at them to hold their fire. 'You won't intimidate these foreigners,' he warned, 'they're too well armed. They'll defend themselves and you'll get hurt.' They embraced Fellahyé and took his advice. Another band was seen in the evening, but galloped away after Marcel fired off a few airshots.

They slogged on towards Susa knowing the Arabs were always near – Menchet's men or M'sban's – awaiting their chance. The days seemed very long and the fashionable streets of Paris almost impossible to recall. At night the silence of the jackals betrayed the figures slipping through the darkness. The mission slept poorly, the watch, broken into three-hour turns, tense and anxious.

Late one afternoon when the sun broke through the storm clouds, there silhouetted against the sky was the mound of Susa, twelve kilometres away across the Kerkhah River in a direct line, days away by the caravan route. Jane knew a buried lion waited there; they had buried it themselves to keep it safe, but what, she wondered, was waiting for her to discover?

Shoals of gravel flung high up the bank warned them of the torrent before they saw the Kerkhah's swirling, treacherous waters. Recognising they would drown the mules if they tried to get the baggage across the swollen river on their backs, they resolved to send a man next day to find Kerim Khan's tents and buy dried animal bladders to make rafts, but tonight they would have to camp. Their tent sodden from nights of rain and days of cloud, the men went off along the bank to chop down bushes to make a shelter, leaving Jane to guard the piled baggage.

Now it was Jane's turn to make a wrong decision. Long days of travel and anxious nights ever-vigilant in defending the caravan, wearing the same damp clothes and being unable to undress or wash for ten days had exacted its toll. She was dirty and her skin itched. She was tired and on edge. When she heard shouts and wailing coming from a stand of trees, her response was instinctive. Bounding towards the noise she found the Dizfuli pilgrims wringing their hands and Fellahyé beating the old mullah, shouting, 'Give me your rice.' It is evidence of how overwrought she was that she abandoned all caution and seized the piece of wood from Fellahyé's hands. 'Shut your bags,' she screamed, 'and don't give anything to this brigand. As for you, son of a dog, how dare you beat these people.'

For anyone to come between an Arab and his prey was folly. For a tiny woman to do so was unimaginable idiocy. Fellahyé drew his pistol, Jane drew hers, and they stood there, for an eternity it seemed, separated by only a few paces, short white-helmeted figure and dark-robed nomad, furious eye staring into raging eye. Then gradually the barrel of the Arab pistol went down and the Arab eyes slid away. Fellahyé jumped on his mare and galloped off, throwing over his shoulder, 'I'll show you not to mix in my affairs! That pilgrim caravan belongs to me. I'll bring my friends and you can count on your fingers what will remain of it tomorrow.'

The pilgrims wailed more loudly, 'Allahu akbar, Allah is great, we will all be robbed and beaten. What will happen to our mules? Excellency *khanum*, let him take the rice.' Drawn by the noise, Marcel raced up out of breath and gasped, 'What's going on?' The Dizfulis turned to him and said, 'Excellency, it's all the *khanum*'s fault, she forbade Fellahyé to beat the mullah.'

When the cook regretfully informed her there would be no dinner that night, Jane began to understand. This was a double scam, directed as much by the cook for her benefit as by Fellahyé. Ever since their rice had been stolen while under Menchet's 'hospitable' tent, the cook had been buying where he could. Now only the mullah had any left – a whole sack, which he refused to sell to feed 'those Christian dogs'. In desperation the cook had turned to Fellahyé. 'Take the mullah's rice and I will buy it.'

As they feared, within the hour Fellahyé returned at the head of thirty tribesmen. In this country of mirages, where their best friend was the guardian of the fanatics' tomb and governors descended to petty theft and nothing was ever as it seemed, Fellahyé came to be paid off, claiming his five kran as 'guide'. Jane's bravery had brought about his downfall: having lost face he could no longer burden the pilgrims. Curiously, rather than reviling Jane for his humiliation, he praised her. 'Dizfulis have water in their veins and a lemon for a heart. Fifteen of them can't hold a candle to this brave woman,'[7] he said admiringly, presenting Jane with three ripe pomegranates and several sweet lemons obviously stolen from some other hapless traveller. Only Marcel remained agitated, angry with Jane for being so foolhardy. Since she had not reproached him for misjudging M'sban and leading them into the lion's den, it seemed a little unjust. Besides, news was swift on the plain and soon many people would hear this new evidence that they could not mess with Jane, something of vital importance should they need to recross that evil stretch of land.

Next day Jane's nerve was again challenged, this time in cold blood, in fear, without the bracing effect of an adrenalin rush. People who know only one thing about Jane Dieulafoy know this famous incident. Jane is dripping wet, alone on the far bank of a flooded Kerkhah confronting a band of eight armed nomads. Baggage is piled around her, two crates containing half the mission's funds stacked in front of her. On top of the crates are two loaded rifles. She aims her revolver and says, 'I have fourteen bullets at your disposal. Go and find yourselves six friends.'

Three hundred metres away across the flooded river, Babin and Houssay level their rifles at the troop. Marcel, who had thrown his rifle to Jane when the overladen raft threatened to sink and had swum back to the shore, peers through binoculars ready to give the Frenchmen the signal, but Jane is in their line of fire to the Arabs.

Understanding her threat, the nomads halt. They stand behind their leader and speak urgently to him. The breeze rustling in the trees further back lifts the corners of their head cloths. The river rushes wildly on. Pebbles grate as the man who ferried Jane across races upstream with the raft and launches it into the flood. Jane's eye does not falter, she gazes directly at the attackers, knowing the raft will be carried down and paddled to the other bank where Marcel will seize it and come to her support. It will take some time to make the two crossings of the tossing waters. She has never felt so alone. She has never been so afraid.

The Arabs are undecided. Should they rush her? She is only one, but they fear the deadly foreign weapons. Perhaps Fellahyé has told them of her courage. Yet a quick attack and they could be away with all the infidel goods. There is plenty of time to think how they would share them.

Jane's arm grows heavy but her aim is unflinching. She must not appear frightened, nothing must distract her. The minutes go by, the long, long minutes that will bring Marcel and Babin and Houssay. Though she reads uncertainty in the Arab eyes, she will not assume she is safe and lower her weapon. She must concentrate, it is a matter of wills as much as a matter of arms. Her will is fierce.

And then they are gone, slinking into the trees as the Frenchmen leap from the raft. Thirty minutes have gone by, perhaps thirty years.

Arab woman at Susa

Her heart warmed by the welcome of the workers and her head spinning with expectation of what the trenches would reveal, Jane knew in part why she had returned to Susa, why she had dared to cross the plain a third time, how she had found the courage to run the gauntlet of the Arabs. Led by Ousta Hassan, the workers kissed the hem of her mud-spattered jacket and offered presents: a first-born lamb, a brace of partridge, yoghurt. They erected the white tent on the mound and formed a guard around it while Jane fell into an exhausted sleep. They were elated to have the French back, perhaps for more reasons than simply money, as expressed by the chant of the night watchman, singing to keep himself awake,

> If the foreigners, who don't rob us and don't beat us, will come to Susa, the nomads will build their houses around their palace and the country will be prosperous.
>
> If a man has four kran, the governor says to him, give me five kran, and the unhappy one dies of hunger, without strength, without courage.
>
> If the foreigners, who don't rob us and don't beat us, will come to Susa, we will cultivate the soil, we will have a profusion of golden herbage, of calves, buffalo and sheep. No one will seize them and the people will live happy.[8]

Sheikh Ali, speaking perfect Farsi, paid a formal visit without challenging their marksmanship, but his eyes missed nothing. He guessed what was in the crates held under the fragile white tents and sent a detachment of mounted Bakhtiari to guard the mound against Segvend and Beni La'am. The tomb guardian, who had stored many of their goods during the summer, climbed the winding path and was overjoyed with a gift of a chandelier brought from across the world to light Daniel's Tomb. Kerim Khan appeared, more to beg, or steal if he could, than to welcome. Tribeswomen came to sell yoghurt and butter, chickens and eggs and to request healing powders and charms to make their husbands love them. Papi Khan brought his epileptic son in search of potassium bromide. 'Go to Hell,' he shouted angrily when Jane poured out an aliquot from the three bottles she had nursed across the plain, 'I want the lot. Now.' The Algerian soldier left under the protection of Sheikh Mohommed Taher in May returned from Dizful dressed as a Persian and accompanied by four wives, who retired to quarters under the arches of Daniel when Jane banned them from the mound. Within days the jume mullah himself, accompanied by many blue turbans, appeared on the road from Dizful, although not especially to visit the foreigners. In protest at Mozaffer el-Molk's newly imposed head tax on the clergy, the imam had resolved to reside with Daniel at the tomb until the tax was lifted. He too climbed the winding path to inspect the trenches and take tea at the white tent, spilling onto the carpet the misery and anger of the Dizfulis against their hated governor. And wonderfully absent from the ranks of the callers was mirza Abdoul-Rahim, redeployed to impoverish nomad lives far distant from Susa.

The 'house' built at the end of the previous season had been damaged by raiding Arabs searching for the gold they were sure the foreigners had sealed within the walls, but its roof was still sound. It was a basic structure, easily repaired by the marine carpenter and his team. By Christmas it had been completed: two bedrooms, a dining room, at whose table Jane wrote up her diary by the limpid light of a lamp, a fireplace, where flames leapt during the cold evenings, and a strongroom with a locked door. Lockable too were the stout outer doors also transported from France. The insecurity, temperature changes and stuffiness of the white tents were assigned to the French carpenter and the Algerian guard, happy to relinquish the draughts of the improvised twig and reed structure of the previous season.

Near the house Jane created a fenced vegetable garden to vary the monotony of a rice and meat diet, planting potatoes, radish, spinach and lettuce. The rich soil of the mound and abundant winter rain soon produced shoots to satisfy her craving for fresh greens. No longer prohibited by mirza Abdoul-Rahim, sheep and hens and eggs and milk flowed in from the plain. As insurance, the mission bought a small flock of sheep and employed a shepherd to graze them on the mound. By comparison with the past, they were safely housed and adequately fed.

The French reached Susa on 12 December 1885 and under the terms of the agreement they had to be gone by 1 April 1886. With a much restricted budget of 15 million francs, Marcel and Jane decided that the trenches on the citadel would remain closed and only exterior walls would be followed on the town tumulus. Their work must concentrate on the palace mound, proceeding systematically, seeking not random treasure, but Achaemenid art and architecture, from which they could deduce the lives and minds of the people who had dwelt there. On 13 December work began.

As was the way of the East, at Susa each new conqueror had levelled the remains of the immediately vanquished and built on top of the past, so the mound grew in height down the millennia. The mound was bare when Jane returned, herbs and bushes having succumbed to the winter cold. Dizfulis chopping away with curved knives soon removed their dead spiny framework. As the trenches opened, the picks and spades cut down through the debris – mostly clay from crumbled brick structures, the most recent being an Arab mosque collapsed in the thirteenth century – down through the remains of Shapur I's Sasanid palace, burnt by his son in revenge for Shapur's Christian faith and his Christian love, Shirin, down through what the Parthians had built and what the Seleucids had superimposed during their post-Alexander hegemony, and finally down to the Achaemenids. There was no timber to shore up the walls and, although Marcel used his engineering knowledge to calculate a safe slope, as the trenches deepened the threat of collapse increased. To the watchman on the crest the workers seemed like ants tunnelling to hell. From the bottom of the trench the view of a clear sky was reassuring, but the trenches cleared swiftly when black clouds appeared. After days of torrential winter rain the workers returned to a trench full of water and earth which had slipped down the sides, not to mention drowned spiders and snakes.

Towards the edge of the mound a gravel stratum was uncovered. Marcel's engineering experience recognised it as a drainage bed for roof water and he set a team to work inwards in search of the palace's outer walls. Jane returned to the court where the Lion frieze had been found and soon encountered a mass of similar enamelled bricks. Unlike that first wall, which had fallen in one piece so that its bricks remained in the original design, this wall had been torn down and used as fill for a new palace constructed above it. The pieces had been thrown in randomly, and were a devil's jigsaw. Made in the same moulds as those found last season, although enamelled in different colours, the bricks suggested a similar parade of proud lions. Their enamel was delicate and fragile and extracting the bricks with the point of a knife was tedious work entrusted only to Jane's best workers. Gradually hundreds were rescued and conserved.

With 250 workers on site, the palace structures were gradually revealed. Jane and her team found the remains of a monumental door, which closed the passageway between the *apadana* and the town. Although the wood had long rotted, its metal studs and fittings were still intact. Repeatedly, they came on Parthian burial urns concealed in the rubble of previous dynasties. The results were satisfying but not wildly exciting. On Christmas Day Jane had an uncharacteristic fit of despondency, which rapidly became an aching homesickness. Recalling the happy Christmas routine of her childhood at château de Terride in the Languedoc, she pined for the little niece she so dearly loved, having no children of her own to her bitter regret, and in Susa's savage loneliness she turned to her lover for comfort.

From the depths to the heights! Jane and Marcel were standing in a trench which Marcel planned to close that night, its rewards being so few and mostly irrelevant, when a worker shouted, 'I've found something beautiful. They think it's gold, but I know it's a gilded brick.' The brilliant *Frieze of the Archers*, buried 2400 years, was emerging from the earth.

It came at first as a mere glimmer: 'a block of faience white as snow; on one side a beautiful yellow enamel hemisphere sprinkled with circles inside which a white rose in high relief spreads its petals, the spaces between filled with alternating blue and green, each in its cloison . . . The piece is not complete, but, even so, it is a superb ceramic.'

'The lions are white. This must be part of a great panther,' speculated Marcel.

Jane was not convinced. She took it to the house and set it on a ledge in the bedroom, where it would be the first thing she saw in the morning, a technique she had used before when challenged by a difficult piece. The clarity of dawn released its essence. 'It's the shoulder of a man dressed in a splendid robe,'[9] she informed Marcel.

Over the next seven weeks, as their vivid colours were released from the clay, the bricks proved her right. Piece fitted to piece revealed figures in elaborate Persian dress, duckhead-tipped bow and leather quiver over the shoulder, a spear grasped in both hands, its ball resting on the forward foot. Some march to the left, others to the right, but all have their hair tied around with a thick golden filet and their feet wear leather shoes that fasten over the instep. Working at the puzzle Jane realised the archers matched Herodotus's description of the Ten Thousand, the elite Persian guard who became known as The Immortals: when one fell in battle another immediately replaced him. They marched with Darius across the Hellespont and into Macedonia and down to Marathon, where the Greeks defeated them in an heroic battle. They marched again under Xerxes and were revenged at the sack of Athens in 480 BC.

Today they march along the walls of a gallery at the Louvre, each almost two-metre-high archer gazing ahead, hair and beard neatly curled. The fabric of his long-sleeved garment is relief-patterned with a geometric design – central Asian rosettes or a tower motif; the tassel dangling from his quiver dances down the solid bricks. Above the archers horizontal bands of palmettes, triangles and many-petalled rosettes take the frieze to the top of the wall, just as they had done in Darius's east court. Jane's meticulous work reclaimed The Immortals for a world that knew them only as words.

The Archers brought with them from obscurity the oriental splendour of Darius I's palace. Exemplifying the originality and power of Achaemenid architecture, the palace stood on a great gravelled platform set eighteen metres above the plain. On its *apadana* and in its garden courts enamelled brick friezes soared to the tops of the high walls, enveloping the king and his subjects in brilliant colour. Through many reigns the palace was a centre of high culture and scholarship, a cosmopolis attracting people of many tongues and faiths, the setting for elaborate rituals. Until one night fire broke out. The loss of its wooden roof beams, lintels and doors destabilised the sun-dried brick walls, which collapsed inwards. Destroyed in the fire were its rich 'white, green, and blue hangings, fastened with cords of fine linen and purple to silver rings', and the carpets and cushions on the 'beds . . . of gold and silver.' The 'pavement of red, and blue, and white, and black, marble' cracked in the heat, the 'vessels of gold, (the vessels being diverse one from another)' were buried in ash and 'royal wine in abundance' fuelled the fire.[10]

Though Esther's embellishments vanished, the colourful bricks, already fired three times in the kiln, survived. For twenty-four years the palace was a haunted shell, until Artaxerxes II restored it, as inscriptions on the *apadana* record.[11]

Even before their return to the mound the Dieulafoys were haunted by the nightmare difficulties of getting the material safely to France. How were they to transport a weighty bull-headed capital out of Susa? How could they move a limestone column base? When Susa was the administrative and winter capital of the great Achaemenid Empire, it was the hub of roads and navigable rivers, a rich town where trade routes converged, bringing together people and goods from the Fars plateau, the mountains and the plains. Chariots rolled along the Royal Road sweeping out from Susa; royal messengers sped from staging post to staging post, carrying information as far as the Mediterranean and into Central Asia. Three rivers encircled the city, connecting it with the Persian Gulf and providing irrigation to the fertile cultivated plain that fed the permanent residents and the royal entourage when the king came to spend the winter in its relative coolness. But in January 1886 there were no roads and the plain was an uncultivated desert, the rivers had silted up and changed their course, and the seat of power was far away.

The obstacles seemed insuperable. More than an imaginative leap was required to move the great stones across desert and water, but Marcel was determined to meet the challenge. As for Jane, she was obsessed by fear of having to leave behind the beautiful *Frieze of the Archers*, becoming more complete each day as the bricks were gently freed from the debris. She knew that having recovered the masterwork there was only one way to conserve it. Left at Susa it would be lost within a month.

The nomads and the marshes made the route through Amarah impossible, and to run the gauntlet of hatred through Dizful and Shushtar would be madness.

'The river, the Ab-i-Diz, is the only way,' Sheikh Ali advised, 'It's navigable from the rocks at Kaleh-Bender right down to where it runs into the Karun. Of course,' he added, 'it's a violent stream, the jungle along the banks is full of lions and in many places overhanging bushes make it difficult to get through. You have to watch out for the whirlpools, and the sandbanks and gravel beds are flung about each winter so you never know where you're going to find them. You'd have to pole all the way, but it can be done.'

Not encouraged by this information, Jane and Marcel pondered alternatives, but without success. Forced back to the sheikh's river option, they confronted two problems. One was finding boats and boatmen willing to go down the Ab-i-Diz. Emissaries sent to the towns and villages returned with the news that no one would risk the Ab-i-Diz's 'pestilential air, the monsters that live in it or the wild beasts on its banks.' Shelving that problem for the moment, they addressed the second dilemma.

How would they get the loads to the river? Kaleh-Bender was eight farsakhs from Susa and several smaller rivers intervened. Marcel may have been a relative newcomer to archaeology, but he was grounded in engineering. Without his expertise, the treasures they had excavated would never have reached the European world, and without European appreciation of their cultural worth, they would almost certainly have been destroyed.

They had brought four large wheels from France in 1884 and, in 1885, pulleys and ropes to make a crane with which to raise large weights and load them onto transport. But what transport? In Persia, where all loads were transported on the backs and along the flanks of camels and mules, carts did not exist.

They would have to be constructed. Jean-Marie, the naval carpenter, who had proved himself a skilled and innovative craftsman while packing the previous season's finds, was now set to work building carts and wooden wheels. Next, the Dieulafoys turned to the question of motive power. The only horses trained to harness belonged to Sheikh Taher, who used them to draw the small wheeled cannon presented to him by the French mission, but the town governor forbade him to lend his team. It was out of the question, he said, the situation in the streets being so dangerous he might have to use the little toy. Blocked at every turn, it was difficult not to be discouraged.

Marcel took drawings and measurements to the Dizfuli leatherworkers, who were soon making pieces of harness, while the blacksmiths began hammering out rings and buckles and other metal pieces from Marcel's diagrams. The mission members became cheerful once again when saddliers, called to Susa to unite metal and leather, tailored and tested the new harness. But optimism vanished when Marcel tried to hire muleteers – they had all been warned off, in the towns, out on the plain, among the tribes. Attar, who had led them twice across the desert, hung his head in embarrassment. Papi Khan, who came to show off his young son, fully recovered under Jane's medication, even as he thanked her lied that his mules were not in good enough condition to draw the carts, and departed abruptly, looking ashamed.

Concerned at how little time was left to train harness teams, on 27 January Marcel sent Ousta Hassan to make approaches among his contacts in Dizful. 'What do you think you're doing? The foreigners are stupid to spend their money on crates and carts. The governor will wait till they've spent their last coin, then he'll stop them taking even one stone,'[12] they retorted. Returning dejected to Susa, the loyal worker ran across a bizarre character, Sayyid Ali, a rough muleteer who despised the governor and openly mocked the mullahs, confident his large blue turban bought him immunity from their heavy hands. Even a mad sayyid muleteer was better than none, thought Marcel, and sent a secret envoy.

Hope lumbered across the plain a week later with Sayyid Ali, three muleteers and eleven mules. In the house on top of the mound spirits lifted when the mad muleteer set to work to train the teams, dropping again when it was whispered through the Dizful bazaars that the shah wanted all the finds brought to Tehran so he could select his share. 'If the shah wants us to bring the bull-headed capitals across those mountains, he'll have to put his army and the revenues of a whole province at our disposal,' Jane said bitterly. Alarm and resilience fought for her mind as she watched the mules galloping away in terror of the cart careering behind them. Unless they could find boats, Sayyid Ali would have to take the loads all the way to Ahwaz, an impossibly demanding overland haul for such enormous weights.

Work continued in the trenches despite the uncertain future of the artifacts being uncovered. It was some comfort to think that no one could interdict the knowledge of the physical dimensions of the palace, its architectural disposition and its unique decoration. This at least they could give to the world, whatever the shah and his bureaucrats might do, but 'It would break my heart to have to leave the enamelled bricks,' agonised Jane. There was still no progress on the boat front, but a crane of sorts had been assembled from block and tackle, stays and sheerlegs. With its first load swinging in the air, the crane teetered and seemed about to fall on the workers manoeuvering a cart to receive the heavy crate. 'The foreigners have good machines for killing forty men at a time,'[13] one of them commented.

Another superb bull capital was uncovered on the *apadana*. Jane knew it was too heavy even for the crane. A perfect specimen of Achaemenid decorative art, muscles chiselled in high relief so that shadows gave life to the surface, ears and horns arranged to bracket a beam, legs folded to cap the scrolls of a column's capital, it weighed, at a guess, around 12 000 kilos. 'It will have to be reburied,' she said, angrily hitting the huge piece of white limestone with a small hammer. The tap echoed within the stone, and with a loud cracking noise the head split open. Jane's eyes widened as the two pieces rolled apart. She was speechless. That one blow from her small hand could break a twelve-tonne stone! A small Hercules, she thought, and was appalled at what she had done. Marcel was not. He understood at a glance that she had solved the cartage problem. A second glance explained her achievement. The broken surfaces were not white, they were stained. As the capital had languished beneath the ground, a plant root had penetrated what was originally only a fine flaw. By extraordinary chance Jane's hammer had struck exactly on the weak spot, but in the eyes of the workers Excellency *khanum* had added 'enormous strength' to her list of supernatural abilities.

A letter from Mozaffer el-Molk quickly followed the serendipitous event and as despair replaced elation the flux of emotions affected all the foreigners. Headaches were the least of it. Jane developed neuralgia and Marcel diarrhoea, Babin and Houssay equally unpleasant physical symptoms of the general distress. The governor's missive, stating that, having received orders from Tehran that the objects found at Susa must remain there, he had banned muleteers and nomads from leasing mules and horses to the Christians was a real blow. Marcel responded angrily:

The French government is the legitimate owner of half the objects extracted from the tumulus. I demand an immediate sharing and hold the governor personally responsible, if, by his acts, we are unable to leave before the pilgrimage begins.

The head of the mission advises his excellency that seven crates full of stones will shortly be leaving for Ahwaz.

Mozaffer el-Molk's reply came early one morning in the form of mirza Taguy's tent planted squarely in front of the house on the mound. Taguy, an offsider of the unsavoury mirza Abdoul-Rahim who had caused them so much misery in the previous season, asserted pompously, 'His Excellency has entrusted me with the care of His Majesty's interests.' It was now mid-February and this affront darkened their prospects even further. 'Unless we use him!' Jane suggested, 'He looks as hungry as Abdoul-Rahim.' Amenable to a percentage, Taguy accepted a commission to arrange all transport not already under the whip of the mad muleteer and sped off to Dizful on a horse confiscated from a furious Sheikh Ali.

Although Sayyid Ali could in theory now get started, the weather made it impossible. For four days it poured, saturating the plain. The cart wheels stood in muddy ruts, bogged to the axles. They had to wait until the ground dried out and it was 28 February before Houssay's white helmet led three carts out onto the track to Ahwaz. To the watchers on the mound their progress seemed snail-like.

Mozaffer el-Molk struck. Since their first meeting the governor had cast a malignant shadow. Early one morning a platoon of soldiers appeared on the Dizful road, followed by a string of laden mules, imparting substance to the shadow. As the troops began to erect the governor's tents, the workers rushed to Jane with their possessions, such as they were, cooking pots, clothes, begging her to hold them in the strongroom. 'The soldiers will seize everything,' they cried, 'They'll beat our women living at Daniel's Tomb, take them too.' Despite being banned from visiting the mound, the women with their quick, sticky little fingers had been a constant annoyance, slipping into the trenches and peering into the house. Jane accepted the parcels for safekeeping, but declined the women.

Jane's fears far outweighed the terror of the workers. For her, this visitation was about more than stones and bricks. Her Paris salon depended on it.

At sundown Marcel was received very coldly under the governor's tent. Beneath the roof of the house on the mound the evening passed in discussing strategy. It was time to be resolute. There was no point in explaining to Mozaffer el-Molk that what the French wanted to take from Susa would restore to the Persians and to the world some part of the lost Iranian heritage. To Mozaffer el-Molk it was pre-Islamic, it was nothing. Contemporary Persians took no pride in it. If the contents of the mound had any value to the superstitious population, it was only as a pile of talismans, more or less valuable than amulets. As witness to human achievement it was of no interest.

Their cards must be more material. Will the shah thank you if you send him half of these packing cases, they resolved to ask Mozaffer. You will gain no credit with the shah by confiscating what is rightfully ours. He will tip them out contemptuously and ask, why have you sent me chipped stones and broken bricks? And who will pay to cart them over the mountains? The shah won't and the cost will fall on you. Besides, you will have to reimburse us the cost of packing.

The sun had barely risen when they received the governor with formal dignity. The French opened with a short statement of the agreement between their government and the shah: the French nation was to bear the cost of the excavation and in return would receive half the finds, but all precious metal objects must remain with the shah. They had scrupulously observed that pact, they assured the governor. He inspected the house and accepted a gift of radish and lettuce from the garden, then toured the palace and *apadana*. 'As you see, your excellency, there are ten times as many stones lying here as we have in our crates.' The game was neither lost nor won when the governor invited them to lunch.

On the citadel a splendid carpet received the heavily armed guests. The view to the snow-crested Bakhtiaris was magnificent. The sun decorated the sky with winter splendour. The plain glittered with new-sprung flowers. The governor was frigid.

The French thought he had accepted their argument until, 'What of the cases?' he suddenly asked. 'The stones are one thing, what's in the cases another.'

'There are 250 cases. Take half,' Marcel replied grimly, 'but remember you must pay the costs of their packing.'

'They must be opened. We'll sort the bricks into piles. I'll take half the yellow, half the blue and half the green.' Jane felt sick in the pit of her stomach. Of what value would they be to anyone then? She heard Marcel responding, 'After lunch you and I will share them out. You don't trust my men, I don't trust yours.' Was it only bluff? Surely it could not happen.

In the cold silence that followed the governor considered the options and drew on his *kalian*. Was he thinking of what the shah would say when he looked at those broken pieces, the shah who glittered with jewels and lived in splendid palaces? Did it then occur to Mozaffer el-Molk that he could gain greater leverage by taking an approach that would advantage the shah's son? Or was it his intention all along to ask the French to honour Zil-es-Sultan with a decoration? It is impossible to know, but the question was put.

It had not been foreseen. Feeling ambushed, Marcel answered truthfully that he could only propose to the French government; he certainly could not guarantee they would award the shah's eldest son a glittering star to wear on his breast.

'You are a man of your word. Everyone acknowledges it. I will lift the embargo that is keeping you here.'

Jane looked down at the carpet so the governor would not see the joy leaping in her eyes.

In less than a month the pilgrims would come to Daniel's Tomb. There was much to do before 1 April, crates and cases still to be made and filled and everything to be dispatched. There were formalities too. When Jane and Marcel rode into Dizful to take leave of the town governor and say goodbye to their friend Sheikh Taher they found the streets in open revolt, Mozaffer el-Molk having thrown several local dignitaries into chains. Crossing the medan had become as dangerous for the town governor as for the foreigners. Stones singing about their heads did not encourage the Dieulafoys to linger.

Sayyid Ali returned halfway through the month. The punishing round trip to Ahwaz had taken sixteen days, yet despite raiding nomads, the difficulties of the river crossings and several mules having to be put down, he would accept another commission. But was there time? The carts had moved only three crates, and there were hundreds more too heavy to load on camel or mule. Even with the newly available muleteers the task seemed impossible. A letter forwarded through Tehran saying the *Sané* was being sent from France to collect the mission, decided them. They had to accept Sheikh Ali's advice and use the Ab-i-Diz River.

Houssay and Babin would direct the transport by cart of everything heavier than sixty-five kilos to the river bank eight farsakhs away, where, with Jean-Marie's help, the loads would be stacked and guarded. Taking the lighter cases loaded onto baggage mules, the Dieulafoys would face the desert and the Arabs a fourth time and travel to the Karun River. There they would arrange for boats to ascend the Ab-i-Diz River.

Farewelling Sheikh Ali was difficult. A bond of respect had grown between them, and a trust strong enough for Marcel to accept a loan from the sheikh after the cost of making harness and carts, hiring animals and buying mirza Taguy had exhausted the mission's meagre funds. The sheikh knew his French friends would not default. Saying goodbye to Babin, Houssay and Jean-Marie had to be done quickly, otherwise the lump in the throat might turn to tears: in the jungle on the banks of the Ab-i-Diz they faced as much danger as the Dieulafoys in the desert with the Arabs. The parting from most of the workers had occurred earlier when the dig was gradually shut down and only a few guards and carpenters remained to wave from the top of the mound as Jane looked back from the plain. She knew the guardian would be on the roof at Daniel's Tomb but she was unable to see him through her tears. All she could see was the great mound. Although they had cleared the years from the *apadana* and the palace and made deep cuts in the town and on the citadel, a vast mountain of hidden secrets remained. Others might reveal them; Jane knew she would never return.

The long caravan of mules and camels, muleteers and guards that left Susa on 29 March had only two white helmets to defend it. By heading to Ahwaz on the Karun the Dieulafoys hoped to avoid Menchet's robbers and M'sban's Beni La'am, who made travelling in Turkish territory a nightmare. Jane knew the Persian desert would not be empty, but she had not expected to be raided almost every night or stoned during the day by half-naked nomads armed with lances. Enraged when stones rebounding from Marcel's helmet blackened her shoulder, she turned her horse and fired over the heads of the tribesmen, routing them. Next day others were slinking forward, and the next. The map telling her there were no marshes to be crossed did not show the thistle forest, which took a whole day to beat through. The mosquitoes and humidity inside the forest were as unbearable as in the swamps, and like the swamps the thistles were hiding places for robbers, which became apparent when one of the muleteers who had left the group to attend to private business came bursting out of the thicket stark naked and bloodied.

'Why didn't he cry out?' she asked.

'When you fall into the hands of bandits, you let them steal your clothes

The departure, March 29, 1886

and you put up with it. Never call for help, that would endanger the whole caravan,'[14] cautioned Attar.

Nor did the map indicate that, when the spring floods arrived, the country north of the Karun became a lake that blocked access to Ahwaz. Forced to detour through Hawizeh, the caravan found lion tracks in the sand, and a feline odour in the air unnerved the camels. Jane was astonished to see a castle, backed by a dawn sky, poised on the crest of a mountain, a garden at its base full of grape vines and orange trees that promised shelter from the sun. 'Go towards it,' Attar warned, 'and you'll find nothing but desolate rock where a partridge won't discover so much as a sprig of herb to shade its head.' The mirage was cruel.

All day Jane and Marcel rode beside the caravan, ready to defend it should nomads appear. The heat, the flies and the mosquitoes were no less torturous than the Arabs. Each evening when they made camp the animals were unloaded, led to water, and then hobbled behind a barricade built from the cases, where people and animals passed the long night together. Since there were only two foreigners in the caravan, the Dieulafoys had to be on constant watch, always alert to seize the rifles lying beside them if the alarm were raised, always listening for a break in the guards' songs, which would indicate the guard had slipped into sleep. During one long night Jane heard a guard improvising to keep himself awake, 'If the shah were to sit at the muleteer's fire, I would tell him: Sultan, Allah will demand an account of all the crimes committed during your reign. Why then is your sleep so heavy that the weeping of your slaves does not wake you?'[15]

By the time they reached Djeria, a village on the Karun inside Sheikh Mizal's territory, Jane was exhausted. The physical demands and constant tension of the twelve-day journey were not the only cause. She was pregnant, nearly four months into term. In the hired boat that sped down the river towards Mohammerah she fell into a sleep as deep as the shah's.

The next four days became a nightmare of journeys up and down the rivers as Marcel tried to arrange the retrieval of the treasures accumulating on the bank of the Ab-i-Diz. Unsuccessful in an attempt to hire boatmen in Mohammerah, they went on to Basra. With no better luck there, the river men knowing too well the evil reputation of that violent stream and the wild, beast-infested jungle that overhung it, they returned to Fallahiyah where Marcel appealed to his friend, Sheikh Mizal. Immediately, the sheikh ordered the huge black slave who commanded his navy to find six large *belems* and twenty-four strong oarsmen and proceed at once to Kaleh-Bender. When the boats were underway, Marcel and Jane returned to Basra to access money wired from Paris, their own, not the French government's, so they could repay their banker, Sheikh Ali. Once again Sheikh Mizal proved his friendship, providing three trusted cavalry officers to take the bags of heavy krans to Susa.

There still remained the problem of the *Sané*, sent to return the mission and its treasures to France and presently stuck in the Persian Gulf, unable to cross the shallow bar at the entrance to the Shatt el-Arab. Afraid the *Sané* might depart, Marcel sent a cable begging the captain to wait another twenty days. To Jane, unwell and bitter, it seemed that 'when they counted on being succoured and supported, once again their country failed them and they were forced to rely only on themselves.'[16]

And for a third time Jane was in a vessel forcing its way along the Karun by day, lying by at night for fear of lions on the banks. As the mid-April temperature in the open boat rose into the high forties, the intrepid Jane was undermined by her condition and tortured by flies and mosquitoes. She found the journey unbearable.

Either side of their junction the waters of the Karun and Ab-i-Diz form three sides of a square. Leaving the oarsmen to take the boat through rapids and whirlpools, the Dieulafoys set off on hired horses to cross the theoretical fourth side, planning to rejoin the boat for its ascent into the upper reaches of the Ab-i-Diz, where Babin, Houssay and Jean-Marie waited with the collection. It was almost as hot on the treeless plain as on the jungle-overhung river, and as midday approached the sun burned down. Suddenly gripped by pain, Jane gave a deep groan, and said, 'I'm going to die,' and fell unconscious from her horse.

There was blood everywhere. Marcel was too shocked to understand immediately what had happened. He leapt to the ground and seized her hand, felt for her pulse, straightened her limbs, poured water over her forehead. The sun, he realised, would kill her, and he ordered the escort to unsaddle the horses and build a shelter from saddle cloths and saddles, and all the time blood was seeping into the sand and Jane was lying there white and still.

When Jane regained consciousness she and Marcel wept together, alone in the desert. The escort had drawn away, their pity invoking their courtesy, so no one heard their anguish. The child they had longed for had been given them at last in a country and under conditions where it would be most difficult to sustain the pregnancy. The child was lost. Jane was thirty-five and there was little chance she would conceive again. They were consumed by grief.

With the approach of nightfall Marcel gathered up his dear wife, laid her on the back of a horse and set off slowly towards Ahwaz. Jane lapsed in and out of consciousness, making no effort to hold onto awareness, even onto life itself.

In the pages of *le Tour du monde* Jane accounted for her bloody collapse by claiming a nose bleed. In a journal usually filled with the heroic paragraphs of male explorers, a bleeding nose read better than a miscarriage and a hemorrhage.

For more than a week Jane lay seriously ill at Ahwaz, Marcel afraid to leave her side. When the *belems* returned bringing the treasures from Susa safely down the river they were able to rejoice together that not everything was lost. Arriving with the stones, the three Frenchmen sensed the Dieulafoys' sorrow and understood their tragedy, but they had not lived at close quarters with Jane without recognising her dedication to living. They knew she would create a future from what was packaged in the crates and boxes and from her own talents. To lift her spirits they offered the news that the people of Khuzestan had risen and driven out their hated governor, Mozaffer el-Molk.

And once again, and finally, Jane left Persia too ill and fragile to mount a gangway. Carried aboard the warship *Sané* in the waters of the Persian Gulf, she was accompanied to France by 327 crates and forty-five tonnes of baggage.

Afterword

In the Louvre Museum in Paris today, Jane Dieulafoy's contribution to archaeology is still found in the Richelieu wing, although since Jane made her audacious appearance wearing a tailored trouser suit the displays have been rearranged. Among the friezes and bull-headed capitals in galleries number twelve to fifteen a laughing boyish figure receiving the cross of the Chevalier de la Légion d'honneur from the French President haunts the imagination.

Immediately she returned to Paris in 1886, Jane applied for a *permission de travestissement* and on receiving the licence she hastened to her tailor to have him build the first of the elegant suits she would wear for the rest of her life. Her decision to wear masculine clothes to the inauguration of the Dieulafoy Galleries at Musée du Louvre was not a rejection of her femininity, only of the perceived persona inherent in frocks. It was a demand that her achievements be recognised and judged on their literary and archaeological qualities alone, neither disparaged nor lauded because of her gender; an insistence that her intellect was her essence, not her body.

In Persia her strength of mind had triumphed over physical frailty, her intelligence had overcome the many obstacles to exploring Susa successfully. A frock, she felt, would obscure her mental qualities and encase her in conventionality.

She wanted to be a person, a whole, an entity respected for her mind and achievements.

Jane's unique quality was to ignore her physical beauty and to construct an allure that relied on personality and intellect. Her gaiety and love of life drew people to her, her charm was a mix of humour and astuteness, her eccentricity was magnetic. It attracted the progressive and liberal, those distinguished in the arts and literature, science and politics. Her rich intellectual life was envied and emulated and many aspired to enter her circle.

Yet much of her appeal was her ambiguity. Discarding women's dress, she espoused women's freedom to develop their abilities and live independent creative lives. Though rejecting divorce, she campaigned for the entry of women into the armed services. Eurocentric and with a Greek bias, she revealed the achievements of the East and spoke for their contribution to European civilisation.

If her Persian interlude brought recognition of her abilities and courage, her experiences in the splendour and squalor of Persia affected her profoundly. Physical suffering and ill health paradoxically toughened her psychologically; surviving aggression and rejection confirmed her self-respect, and witnessing the oppression and limitation of women in the *anderun* affirmed her feminism.

The eighteen-year-old Jane had hungered for the life she glimpsed across the wall of her convent school. That hint of something beyond social position, a world whose entrée was intelligence and wit, had determined her ambition to conquer the Paris salons. Her triumph in Persia bought acceptance: admiration from that elite world made her own salon possible. Her assemblies were much admired: in Jane's salon intellectual and social life was constructed on her terms. Never conventional, she challenged the ordinary and created her own style. She enjoyed the respect of people whose opinion she valued, the intelligentsia, the literati and the artistic elite. It was exactly the life Jane had dreamed of, made complete by sharing it with the companion she adored.

Jane did not ride into French intellectual life on Marcel's coat tails. Rather, it was she who brought him celebrity. Without her vivid account of their Persian travels and excavations, without the sensitive and restrained photographs that introduced Persia and her people to the French, Marcel and the mission would have remained in the academic twilight, celebrated by a small coterie of archaeologists and architects perhaps, but unknown in the wider world.

She used the respect earned by her Persian achievements to contribute more generally to society. Inspired by the early French feminist, Juliette Lamber, who argued that 'the degree of civilization of a nation is proportional to the role played by its women', Jane led an active public life, organising innumerable conferences and encouraging women to participate. She was also a prolific author. Honoured in 1890 by the Académie Française for her contribution to literature, she chaired a committee to establish La Vie Heureuse, which has evolved into today's Prix Femina.

Her diverse interests, her influence in French intellectual circles and her exceptional achievements 'caused her to be regarded as the most remarkable woman in France and perhaps in all Europe,' acknowledged *The New York Times* in its obituary.[1]

The core of Jane's life was her relationship with Marcel. Rejecting the role of 'wife' as defined by the bourgeoisie, Jane was always Marcel's companion and collaborator, always his equal. She lived with Marcel, not through him, her life never mediated through the mesh of another's decisions and preferences.

Because at eighteen Jane had been a passionate young woman too impetuous to consider the risks, her initial love for Marcel, predicated on the dangerous basis of admiration and expectation, could easily have foundered. If events had shown that what she admired in his character was only something imagined, her love would have shattered in a moment, as ice on a glass of water splinters at a note from a violin. Equally, her expectation of the life they would lead together made her attachment vulnerable. Either of these chances could have revealed that her love was imperfect.

During their long life together her romantic love was never challenged. Instead, not compressed into a mould, free to be herself, her passionate love for Marcel transformed into a more mature, deeper devotion. Their life together was always full of the unexpected, full of physical and intellectual demands, even to the very end. Their only regret, and it was bitter, was their childlessness.

Their last adventure was not one she would have chosen – in their sixties they went to war again, together, always together. When the First World War took Colonel Dieulafoy to North Africa, Jane was by his side, just as she had been as a bride of nineteen when he fought the Prussians. While the colonel attended to Moroccan military matters, Jane triumphed over heat, dust and hostility to excavate the ruins of Rabat's Hassan mosque in the mornings and in the afternoons worked as a volunteer in an unhygienic Rabat dispensary. When she became ill amoebic dysentery was diagnosed, but the long pain-filled course of her illness suggests cancer. Marcel took her home to France where she died in his arms on 25 May 1916.

Notes

Prologue

1 J. Dieulafoy, *La Perse La Chaldee et La Susiane*, Hachette, Paris, 1887, p. 133. (Author's translation, as will be all subsequent quotes; punctuation as in the original.)
2 ibid., p. 210.

Chapter 1: A daring destination

1 Often called Sasanians in the older literature.
2 J. Dieulafoy, 1887, p. 2.
3 A.U. Pope, *Persian Architecture: The Triumph of Form and Color*, George Braziller, New York, 1965, p. 76.
4 khanum: a suffix meaning Mme, Mrs.
5 J. Dieulafoy, 1887, p. 2.
6 ibid., p. 2.
7 ibid., p. 2.
8 ibid., p. 134.

Chapter 2: To a land without roads

1 J. Dieulafoy, 1887, p. 5.
2 ibid.
3 High official of the Ottoman (Turkish) Empire.
4 The excavation agreement between Persia and France stipulated the finds be shared equally, the Persians to retain all precious metals. Every item on the French invoice is extant today. The location of most of the items retained in Persia is unknown.
5 J. Dieulafoy, 1887, p. 6.
6 ibid., p. 9.

7 G.N. Curzon, *Persia and the Persian Question*, Longmans, Green, and Co., London, 1892, vol. 1, p. 63.
8 J. Dieulafoy, 1887, p. 10.
9 ibid., p. 11.
10 ibid., p. 21.
11 ibid., p. 22.
12 ibid., p. 24.
13 M.D. Dieulafoy, *L'acropole de Suse: d'apres les fouilles executes en 1884, 1885, 1886*, Paris, 1893, p. 277.
14 J. Dieulafoy, 1887, p. 30.
15 ibid., p. 31.
16 ibid., p. 38.

Chapter 3: A golden dragon caught in a net of stars
1 Curzon, vol. 1, p. 393.
2 Courtesy title similar to lord.
3 E.G. Browne, *A Year Amongst the Persians*, Adam and Charles Black, London, 1893, p. 84.
4 Religious schools.
5 J. Dieulafoy, 1887, p. 55.
6 Public baths.

Chapter 4: Saving Marcel
1 Browne, p. 75.
2 J. Dieulafoy, 1887, p. 68.
3 ibid., p. 95.
4 Browne, p. 72.
5 J. Dieulafoy, 1887, p. 72.
6 ibid., p. 76.
7 Forerunner of the Baha'i.
8 J. Dieulafoy, 1887, p. 106.
9 Pope, p. 129.

Chapter 5: The Golistan two hours before sunset
1 I. L. Bird, *Journeys in Persia and Kurdistan*, John Murray, London, 1891, vol. 1, p. 207.
2 Browne, p. 119.
3 Bird, vol. 1, p. 203.
4 ibid., vol. 2, p. 7.
5 ibid., vol. 1, p. 187.
6 Hasan-e Fasa'i', *Farsnama-ye Naseri History of Persia under Qajar rule*, translated by Heribert Busse, Columbia University Press, NY, 1972, p. 375.

7   Curzon, vol. 2, p. 15.
8   V. Sackville-West, *Passenger to Teheran*, Hogarth Press, 1926, p. 47.
9   J. Dieulafoy, 1887, p. 134.
10 Bird, vol. 1, p. 199.
11 When the author saw it in Tehran in 2001, though not in this audience
    hall, it was looking rather shabby after pillage at the palace during the1979
    revolution. The crown jewels, still on display, are mostly from the same
    looted treasure. (See M. Axworthy, *The Sword of Persia Nader Shah*, IB Taurus,
    London, 2006, p. 10.)
12 recess indicating the direction to Mecca.
13 J. Dieulafoy, 1887, p. 141.
14 mausoleum of a descendant of one of the twelve Imams venerated by the
    Shi'a.
15 J. Dieulafoy, 1887, p. 147.
18 ibid., p. 134.
17 ibid., p. 146.
18 Bird, vol. 1, p. 208.
19 J. Dieulafoy, 1887, p. 163.

Chapter 6: On business for the shah's son

1   Browne, p. 412.
2   J. Dieulafoy, 1887, p. 179.
3   ibid., p. 181.
4   Bird, vol. 1, p. 220.
5   Descendant of the Prophet through his grandson Husain.
6   Written with a capital, Imam refers to a descendant of the prophet recognised
    as caliph (successor) by the Shi'a. Lowercase imam refers to ordinary
    members of the clergy.
7   J. Dieulafoy, 1887, p. 193.
8   ibid., p. 287.
9   ibid., p. 209.
10 ibid., p. 210.
11 ibid., p. 194.

Chapter 7: Isfahan, rose flower of paradise

1   Browne, p. 199.
2   J. Dieulafoy, 1887, p. 216.
3   ibid., p. 239.
4   K. Casey, *The Middle Ages in Texts and Texture*, ed. Jason Glenn , University of
    Toronto Press, 2011, pp. 85–92.
5   J. Dieulafoy, 1887, p. 253.

6 J. Chardin, *Voyages de monsieur le chevalier Chardin en Perse et autres lieux de l'Orient* (ed. Langlès), vol. viii, p. 43.
7 J. Dieulafoy, 1887, p. 250.
8 Browne, p. 200.
9 Though Sar Puchideh has vanished the stone women now frame the corners of the Chihil Sutun pool.
10 J. Dieulafoy, 1887, p. 253.
11 Bird, vol. 1, p. 267.
12 In a curious quirk, during the Pahlavi era the caravanserai was saved by an inspired architect who reconciled it with the twentieth century. From the windows of the (misnamed) Abbasi Hotel's dining room the madrasa's dome seems to float into the sky.
13 Bird, vol. 2, p. 257.
14 J. Dieulafoy, 1887, p. 261.
15 ibid., p. 274.
16 M. Hattstein & P. Delius, *Islam Art and Architecture*, Könemann, Cologne, 2000, p. 511.
17 J. Dieulafoy, 1887, p. 296.
18 ibid., p. 302.
19 ibid., p. 309.
20 Hattstein & Delius, p. 369.
21 Pope, p. 107.
22 Bird, vol. 2, p. 370.
23 J. Dieulafoy, 1887, p. 319.

Chapter 8: Caravan to Pasargadae

1 J. Dieulafoy, 1887, p. 338.
2 Curzon, vol. 2, p. 61.
3 Sir R. Ker Porter, quoted by Curzon, vol. 2, p. 61.
4 J. Dieulafoy, 1887, p. 356.
5 Strictly defined, such seasonal movement between two permanent territories is transhumance, not nomadism
6 Curzon, vol. 2, p. 294.
7 J. Dieulafoy, 1887, p. 356.
8 J. Dieulafoy, 1887, p. 360.
9 ibid., p. 366.

Chapter 9: The Achaemenids

1 T. Talbot Rice, *Ancient Arts of Central Asia*, Thames and Hudson, London, 1965, p. 14.
2 Plutarch LXIX quoted in J.E. Curtis & N. Tallis, *Forgotten Empire: The World of Ancient Persia*, British Museum Press, 2005, p. 155.

3 J. Dieulafoy, 1887, p. 368.

4 D. Stronach, *Pasargadae*, Clarendon Press, Oxford, 1978, p. 36.

5 J. Dieulafoy, 1887, p. 387.

6 E. Gibbon, *The History of the Decline and Fall of the Roman Empire*, Folio Society, London, 1983, vol.1, p. 192.

7 Quoted in Curtis & Tallis, p. 153.

8 Browne, p. 251.

9 ibid., p. 219.

10 J. Dieulafoy, 1887, p. 393.

11 Medicine 1907.

12 A flame lit from that at Yazd burns in Bombay today to remind the many Zoroastrian Parsees living there to be diligent in the eternal fight of good against evil.

13 The last day of the old year is marked by bonfires, a relic of the even older sun god, Mithras. No Ruz begins with a family feast at which everyone wears new clothes. A bowl of water, candles and a mirror are set on a cloth on the floor and remain there for thirteen days while friends pay formal visits and exchange gifts. As at ancient Persepolis, the festivity ends on the fourteenth day.

14 E. Herzfeld, *Iran in the Ancient East*, London, 1941, p. 227.

15 J. Dieulafoy, 1887, p. 416.

Chapter 10: Shiraz, city of wine, of roses and of poets

1 J. Dieulafoy, 1887, p. 453.

2 ibid., p. 431.

3 ibid., p. 437.

4 ibid., p. 427.

5 This garden was restructured in 1935, and the headstones removed. Although still covered by the engraved Yazdi marble, his simple tomb has become the centrepiece of an octagonal columned temple.

6 Curzon, vol. 2, p. 105.

7 J. Dieulafoy, 1887, p. 435.

8 Pope, p. 231.

9 Browne, p. 285.

10 Hasan-e Fasa'i', p. 374.

11 J. Dieulafoy, 1887, p. 460.

Chapter 11: South to the Sasanids

1 Hasan-e Fasa'i', p. 412.

2 J. Dieulafoy, 1887, p. 469.

3 Sackville-West, p. 65.

4 E. Gibbon, *The history of the decline and fall of the Roman Empire*, Folio Society, London, 1983, vol. 1, p. 191.
5 Hasan-e Fasa'i', p. 413.
6 J. Dieulafoy, 1887, p. 475.
7 R. Byron, *The Road to Oxiana*, Penguin Books, London, 1992, p. 161.
8 D'Herbelot, *Bibliothèque orientale*, au mot *Ardshir*, Paris, 1697, quoted in Gibbon, vol. 1, p. 199.
9 J. Dieulafoy, 1887, p. 507.

Chapter 12: Smuggled into Babylonia, Iraq

1 Palm plantation.
2 Arabistan in the original. This province has since been amalgamated with the eastern half of Khuzestan.
3 J. Dieulafoy, 1887, p. 528.
4 Jane's Basra photographs were exhibited in the Louvre Museum, Paris, in 2005.
5 Patterned cotton square wrapped about the head.
6 Bird, vol. 1, p. 7.
7 J. Dieulafoy, 1887, p. 551.
8 ibid., p. 552.
9 ibid., p. 553.

Chapter 13: With the Shi'a to the Holy Places

1 J. Dieulafoy, 1887, p. 575.
2 Built 1221, now called Bab al-Wastani (Hattstein & Delius, p. 91).
3 J. Dieulafoy, 1887, p. 571.
4 Hattstein & Delius, p. 117.
5 It has since been incorporated into the twentieth-century Caliph's Mosque.
6 J. Dieulafoy, 1887, p. 585.
7 ibid., p. 588.
8 ibid., p. 611.
9 ibid., p. 613.
10 Babylon's Ishtar Gate, the Processional Way and its glazed-brick lion friezes were only revealed in the early twentieth century by German spades.
11 J. Dieulafoy, 1887, p. 624: The Holy Bible, Jeremiah 51, but note: the Bible which Jane carried is an independent French translation of original sources. It and the English Bible do not exactly match.
12 ibid., p. 632.
13 ibid., p. 583.

Chapter 14: The deadly price of Susa

1 Curzon, vol. 2, p. 277.
2 J. Dieulafoy, 1887, p. 635.
3 ibid., p. 639.
4 H. Rawlinson, 1839, p. 105, quoted in L. Adkins, *Empires of the plain*, HarperCollins, London, 2003, p. 71.
5 J. Dieulafoy, 1887, p. 646.
6 G. Rawlinson, *A Memoir of Major-General Sir Henry Creswicke Rawlinson*, Longmans, Green & Company, London, 1898, p. 63.
7 The 'beds' are the great cots on which the king and his retinue sat in state. The so-called Peacock Throne in Tehran, like the Marble throne, is a large high cot. In Central Asian teahouses men still sit cross-legged smoking the *kalian* on carpet-strewn cots beside tree-fringed pools.
8 J. Dieulafoy, 1887, p. 667.
9 The Holy Bible, Daniel 8:2.
10 Curzon, vol. 2, p. 317.
11 J. Dieulafoy, 1887, p. 694.
12 ibid., p. 697.

Chapter 15: Return to Susa: The cast assembles

1 J. Dieulafoy, *A Suse, journal des fouilles, 1884–1886*, Hachette, Paris, 1888, p. 55.
2 J. Dieulafoy, 1887, p. 708.
3 A.H. Layard, *Nineveh and its remains*, John Murray, London, 1849, vol. 1, p. 65.
4 H. Rawlinson, Letter to Layard 1846, British Library Add mss 38977, f 25–7.
5 A.H. Layard, *Nineveh and Its Remains: A Narrative of an Expedition to Assyria During the Years of 1845, 1846, and 1847*, John Murray, London, 1867, p. 316.
6 A.H. Sayce, A.H. *The Archaeology of the Cuneiform Inscriptions*, Brighton, New York, 1907, p. 448.
7 A.J. Booth, *The discovery and decipherment of the trilingual cuneiform inscriptions*, Longman, London, 1902, p. xvi.
8 J. Dieulafoy, 1888, p. 2.
9 ibid., p. 37.
10 ibid., p. 70.
11 ibid., p. 71.
12 ibid., p. 72.

Chapter 16: First season: The Lion Frieze

1 J. Dieulafoy, 1888, p. 92.
2 ibid., p. 95.
3 ibid., p. 96.

4 ibid., p. 101.
5 ibid., p. 104.
6 ibid., p. 112.
7 Transliterated as Sagwand in Bird, vol. 1, p. 19.
8 J. Dieulafoy, 1888, p. 136.
9 ibid., p. 143.
10 ibid., p. 107.
11 O. Harper, J. Aruz & F. Tallon (eds), *The Royal City of Susa*, Metropolitan Museum of Art, New York, 1993, Achaemenid brick decoration, p. 223.
12 J. Dieulafoy, 1888, p. 153.
13 ibid., p. 164.
14 ibid., p. 176.
15 ibid., p. 173.
16 Quoted in R.L. Fox, *Alexander the Great*, Folio Society, London, 1997, p. 243.
17 J. Dieulafoy, 1888, p. 182.

Chapter 17: Second season: The Frieze of the Archers

1 J.J. Morier, *The Adventures of Hajji Baba of Ispahan*, The Heritage Press, New York, 1947, p. 111.
2 J. Dieulafoy, 1888, p. 194.
3 ibid., p. 213.
4 ibid., p. 171.
5 ibid., p. 232.
6 ibid., p. 230.
7 ibid., p. 251.
8 ibid., p. 338.
9 ibid., p. 290.
10 The Holy Bible, Esther 1:1.
11 He also built a new palace across the river, which Jane and Marcel investigated but did not have the resources to excavate.
12 J. Dieulafoy, 1888, p. 316.
13 ibid., p. 319.
14 ibid., p. 341.
15 ibid., p. 338.
16 ibid., p. 344.

Afterword

1 *The New York Times*, 28 May 1916.

Selected bibliography

L. Adkins, *Empires of the Plain Henry Rawlinson and the Lost Languages of Babylon*, HarperCollins, London, 2003

Amis de la Bibliothèque Municipale du Blanc (ed.), *Eugène Flandin Voyage en Perse 1840–1841*, l'A.B.M.B., Le Blanc, 1995

M. Axworthy, *The Sword of Persia Nader Shah*, IB Taurus, London, 2006

P. Barr, *A Curious Life for a Lady The Story of Isabella Bird*, Secker & Warburg, London, 1970

I. L. Bird, *Journeys in Persia and Kurdistan*, John Murray, London, 1891

D. Blow, *Persia through writers' eyes*, Eland, London, 2007

A.J. Booth, *The discovery and decipherment of the trilingual cuneiform inscriptions*, Longman, London, 1902

B. Brend, *Islamic Art*, British Museum Press, London, 1991

E.G. Browne, *A Year Amongst the Persians*, Adam and Charles Black, London, 1893

R. Byron, *The Road to Oxiana*, Penguin Books, London, 1992

S.R. Canby, *Persian Painting*, British Museum Press, 1993

—— *The golden age of Persian art: 1501–1722*, Abrams, New York, 1999

S. Carboni (ed.), *Venice and the Islamic World*, Yale University Press, New Haven, 2007

K. Casey, *The Middle Ages in Texts and Texture* (ed. Jason Glenn), University of Toronto Press, 2011

J. Chardin, *Voyages de monsieur le chevalier Chardin en Perse et autres lieux de l'Orient* (ed. Langlès) Le Normant, Paris, 1811

N. Coldstream, *Medieval Architecture*, OUP, Oxford, 2002

J. Curtis, *Ancient Persia*, British Museum Press, London, 2000

J.E. Curtis & N. Tallis, *Forgotten Empire: The World of Ancient Persia*, British Museum Press, 2005

G.N. Curzon, *Persia and the Persian Question*, Longmans, Green, and Co., London, 1892

O.M. Dalton, *The Treasure of the Oxus with other examples of early Oriental metalwork*, British Museum Press, London, 1926

J. Dieulafoy, *La Perse La Chaldee et La Susiane*, Hachette, Paris, 1887

J. Dieulafoy, *A Suse, journal des fouilles 1884–1886*, Hachette, Paris, 1888

M.D. Dieulafoy, *L'acropole de Suse: d'après les fouilles exécutées en 1884, 1885, 1886 sous les auspices du Musée du Louvre*, [s.n.], Paris, 1893

M.D. Dieulafoy, *L'art antique de la Perse*, Librairie Centrale d'Architecture, Paris, 1890

Firdauzi *Shahname*, the Book of Kings, (trans. D. Davis) Viking Press, New York, 2006

A. Firouz, *In the Walled Gardens*, HarperCollins, Sydney, 2002

R.L. Fox, *Alexander the Great*, Folio Society, London, 1997

R. Ghirshman, *Iran: From the earliest times to the Islamic Conquest*, Harmondsworth, Middlesex, 1954

—— *Iran: Parthians and Sassanians*, Thames & Hudson, 1962

E. Gibbon, *The History of the Decline and Fall of the Roman Empire*, Folio Society, London, 1983

E. and J. Gran-Aymeric, *Jane Dieulafoy, une vie d'homme*, Perrin, Paris, 1991

Hafez, *Divan* (trans. S. Salehpour), Booteh Press, Tehran, 1998

O. Harper, J. Aruz & F. Tallon (eds.), *The Royal City of Susa*, Metropolitan Museum of Art, New York, 1993

Hasan-e Fasa'i', *Farsnama-ye Naseri History of Persia under Qajar rule*, (trans. Heribert Busse), Columbia University Press, NY, 1972

M. Hattstein & P Delius, *Islam Art and Architecture*, Könemann, Cologne, 2000

B. d'Herbelot, *au mot Ardshir*, Bibliothèque orientale, Paris, 1697

E. Herzfeld, *Iran in the Ancient East*, London, 1941

—— *Archaeological History of Iran*, OUP, Oxford, 1935

—— *The Magnificent Discovery at Persepolis*, Illustrated London News, March 1933

R. Hillenbrand, *Islamic architecture: Form, Function and Meaning*, Columbia University Press, New York, 1995

—— *Islamic Art and Architecture*, Thames and Hudson, London, 1999

P. Hobhouse, *Gardens of Persia*, Florilegium, Sydney, 2003

T. Holland, *Persian Fire*, Little, Brown, London, 2005

A. Hourani, *A History of the Arab Peoples*, Faber and Faber, London, 1991

L. Jebb, *By desert ways to Baghdad*, Thomas Nelson & Sons, London

D. Keys, *Catastrophe An investigation into the origins of the modern world*, Arrow Books, London, 1999

A.K.S. Lambton, *Qajar Persia*, I.B.Taurus, London, 1987

I.M. Lapidus, *A History of Islamic Societies*, Cambridge University Press, Cambridge, 2002

A.H. Layard, *Nineveh and its Remains*, John Murray, London, 1849

—— *Nineveh and Its Remains: A narrative of an expedition to Assyria during the years 1845, 1846, and 1847*, John Murray, London, 1867

—— *Nineveh and Babylon: a narrative of a second expedition to Assyria during the years 1849, 1850 & 1851*, John Murray, London, 1874

M.E.L. Mallowan, *Early Mesopotamia and Iran*, Thames & Hudson, London, 1965

S.A. Matheson, *Persia: An Archaeological Guide*, Noyes Press, Park Ridge, 1973

V.M. Manfredi, *Alexander The Ends of the Earth*, Macmillan, London, 2001

A. Molavi, *Persian Pilgrimages*, W W Norton, London, 2002

J.J. Morier, *The Adventures of Hajji Baba of Ispahan*, Heritage Press, New York, 1947

H. ST. L. B. Moss, *The Birth of the Middle Ages 395-814*, Folio Society, London, 1998

O. Pancaroğlu, *Perpetual Glory Medieval Islamic Ceramics from the Harvey B. Plotnick Collection*, The Art Institute of Chicago, Chicago, 2007

I. Plimer, *A Short History of Planet Earth*, ABC Books, Sydney, 2001

A.U. Pope, *Persian Architecture: The Triumph of Form and Color*, George Braziller, New York, 1965

G. Rawlinson, *A Memoir of Major-General Sir Henry Creswicke Rawlinson*, Longmans, Green & Company, London, 1898

D. Richards and J Videon, *Persia and Beyond Islam and Asia*, Art Gallery Board of South Australia, Adelaide, 1997

V. Sackville-West, *Passenger to Teheran*, Hogarth Press, 1926

Sadi, *Gulistan* (trans. E. Rehatsek), Mamod Hakimay, Shiraz, 1997

H. Sancisi-Weerdenburg (ed.), *Through Travellers' Eyes: European travellers on the Iranian monuments*, Nederlands Institut voor het Nabije Oosten, Leiden, 1991

A.H. Sayce, A.H. *The Archaeology of the Cuneiform Inscriptions*, Brighton, New York, 1907

D. Stronach, *Pasargadae*, Clarendon Press, Oxford, 1978

T. Talbot Rice, *Ancient Arts of Central Asia*, Thames and Hudson, London, 1965

D. Talbot Rice, *Islamic Painting A Survey*, EUP, Edinburgh, 1971

The Holy Bible

The Holy Koran

C. Waddy, *The Muslim Mind*, Longman, London, 1976

J.G. Westenholz (ed), *Royal Cities of the Biblical World*, Bible Lands Museum, Jerusalem, 1996

L. Woolley, *The Sumerians*, Clarendon Press, Oxford, 1928

Acknowledgements

During the long gestation of this work I have had the support and encouragement of my family and many friends and I thank them sincerely.

Of particular assistance has been Adelaide Titterton, who checked translations, formatted references, introduced French contacts, photographed images and much else besides. I am deeply indebted to her.

Margaret Frey and Leigh Finke read parts of an early draft, as did Ross Burn. Henrietta Clark commented on a later draft. Diana Hill's encouragement was vital. Chris Wood made many useful suggestions while making the impossible seem possible. Mary Hill searched Paris for out-of-print books; Effie of Mosman translated Iranian script; Sophie Morin, Senlis, France, facilitated access to Musée Fabre, Montpelier, France.

In Paris, Cultural Relations/ Australia France Foundation, Australian Embassy enabled my access to research facilities at Musée du Louvre, where Marie-France Lemoine, curator, l'Histoire du Louvre; Patricia Kalensky, chargée d'études documentaires, départment des Antiquités orientales; Nicole Chevalier, ingénieur d'études au départment des Antiquités orientales, Musée du Louvre, generously assisted with my research.

At the Victoria and Albert Museum, London, Barry Wood, then curator Islamic Gallery Project, allowed me to see the Natanz mihrab and other material despite it being in storage during the gallery renovation. Later, Olivia Stroud, also at the V and A, patiently assisted with image selection.

Librarians at Fisher Library, Sydney University, and, as always, my friends at the Mitchell Library, Sydney, were tireless in finding material.

My sincere thanks are owed to Justice Mary Finn for her meticulous reading and her generous assessment of the manuscript. My greatest debt is to Dr John Tidmarsh, whose knowledge was always available; his image files were generously put at my disposal and his belief in this work saved me many times from despair.

I am most grateful that he should write a scholarly Foreword while he was traversing the great spaces of Iran.

I thank the Iranians, met during several visits to their country, who offered Iranian history and achievements in accord with Persia's long tradition of hospitality.

Finally, I would like to acknowledge Clinton Ellicott, production manager, for his fastidious, insightful and sympathetic creation of these beautiful pages, and Michael Bollen, publisher, Wakefield Press, for realising the work.

List of illustrations

Black & white images

(Ex p. XX refers to *La Perse La Chaldee et La Susiane* page XX)

Page ii: Jane Dieulafoy. EX P. FRONTISPIECE
            Jane Dieulafoy signature
Page 1   and other chapter openers: Faience tile panel, Isfahan, Safavid dynasty.
            EX P. 239
Page 10:   Persian woman's street dress, 1880s. EX P. 119
Page 11:   Ziba Khanum. EX P. 271
Page 35:   Mujtahid, Tabriz. EX P. 57
Page 43:   Babi girl, Zendjan. EX P. 85
Page 56:   Shah Nasr-al-Din. EX P. 131
Page 78:   Governor's wife, Kashan. EX P. 214
Page 84:   Armenian woman, New Julfa. EX P. 235
Page 97:   Youssouf khanum, Isfahan. EX P. 269
Page 133:   Cyrus's tomb, Pasargadae. EX P. 365
Page 139:   Doorway, Persepolis. EX P. 400
Page 146:   Zoroastrian family from Yazd (Yazidis). EX P. 411
Page 150:   Wetnurse, Shiraz. EX P. 433
Page 153:   H.H.E. The Governor of Shiraz. EX P. 439
Page 186:   Sheik Mizal's coffeepot. EX P. 523
Page 189:   Torkhan khanum. EX P. 521
Page 201:   Left: Chaldean girl, Baghdad. EX P. 581
            Right: Jewish woman, Baghdad. EX P. 580
Page 211:   Beggarwoman, Amarah. *A SUSE, JOURNAL DES FOUILLES 1884–1886*
Page 216:   Beni La'am woman. EX P. 641
Page 222:   Bibi Dordoun, Dizful. EX P. 656
Page 245:   Shustar wives. *A SUSE, JOURNAL DES FOUILLES 1884–1886*
Page 248:   Young Dizfuli woman. *A SUSE, JOURNAL DES FOUILLES 1884–1886*

Page 253: Plan Susa tumulus. *A SUSE, JOURNAL DES FOUILLES 1884–1886*

Page 255: Ousta Hassan. *A SUSE, JOURNAL DES FOUILLES 1884–1886*

Page 263: Shattered bullhead capital. *A SUSE, JOURNAL DES FOUILLES 1884–1886*

Page 265: Dizfouli with funerary urns. *A SUSE, JOURNAL DES FOUILLES 1884–1886*

Page 288: Arab woman at Susa. *A SUSE, JOURNAL DES FOUILLES 1884–1886*

Page 301: The departure, March 29, 1886. *A SUSE, JOURNAL DES FOUILLES 1884–1886*

Colour images

Plate 1: Jane Dieulafoy aged 20, veteran of the Franco–Prussian War, wearing the grey blouse and trousers, uniform of a franc-tireur. Artist unknown. ROSSITER 2005

Plate 2: The enamelled-brick Frieze of the Archers excavated by Jane Dieulafoy in 1886. The Dieulafoy expedition retrieved the beautiful facades of Susa's palace, revealing that its walls and staircases were finished with colourful, shining enamelled bricks. PHOTO © RMN-GRAND PALAIS (MUSÉE DU LOUVRE) / HERVÉ LEWANDOWSKI

Plate 3: Top left: A visitor is diminished by the great Frieze of Lions, Musée du Louvre, Paris. Excavated 1885 by Jane Dieulafoy, it once decorated a wall of Darius I's 2500-year-old palace at Susa. ROSSITER 2005

Top right: Two details from Frieze of the Lions. ROSSITER 2005

Left: Detail, 2500 year-old enamelled bricks from Susa. ROSSITER 2005

Plate 4: Top: Detail of an Archer's tunic showing the cloisons that were filled with coloured enamel before the siliceous brick was refired. Excavated by Jane Dieulafoy 1886. ROSSITER 2005

Centre: A parapet built by the Sasanians from recycled Achaemenid enamelled bricks: 'panels with a whirling, spinning circular motif in apple green, dark green and yellow', wrote Jane in 1885. ROSSITER 2005

Bottom: Staircase adjacent to the parapet shown above, also made from recycled Achaemenid enamelled bricks, the spinning motif delimited by upper and lower rows of triangles and chains of rosettes. ROSSITER 2005

Plate 5: Top: A bullhead capital which capped one of the 36 huge columns on Susa's apadana. It held the wooden beams (shown in section) that supported the roof. Its huge size diminishes the door of the Dieulafoy gallery, musée du Louvre, Paris. PHOTO © RMN-GRAND PALAIS (MUSÉE DU LOUVRE) / HERVÉ LEWANDOWSKI / FRANCK RAUX

Bottom: Damaged bull-head capital at Susa 2004. Note the 'saddle' which carried the wooden roof beams, and the Achaemenid rosettes banding its neck. ROSSITER 2004

Plate 6: Top: Twelfth-century Seljuk tomb, its eight sides patterned with turquoise-blue enamelled bricks inserted into a background of soft-red unglazed bricks. 'The marriage of turquoise blue enamel and the rose tint of bricks is of exquisite delicacy', Marcel wrote. ROSSITER 2004

Bottom: Detail of Seljuk tomb. Unglazed bricks projecting from the plane form intricate laced designs, their shadows accentuating the textural effect. Beneath a muqarnas cornice is an inscription frieze: 'Everything passes. May this remain'. ROSSITER 2004

Plate 7:   Top: Oil painting of the Blue Mosque, Tabriz, by Frenchman Jules Laurens, 1872. In 1881 Jane was shocked by its derelict state. MUSÉE FABRE DE MONTPELLIER AGGLOMÉRATION - PHOTOGRAPH BY FRÉDÉRIC JAULMES
Bottom: The cable moulding spiralling around the portal arch of the Blue Mosque, Tabriz, had lost many more of its turquoise-blue tiles by 2001. Much of the mosaic tiling had also fallen. ROSSITER 2001

Plate 8:   Top: Moulded faience tile with dragon and cloud scroll enamelling, dated 1275 AD, Il Khanid era. A hexagonal tile of the same era with similar dragon-decoration inspired Jane's passion for enamelled tiles and bricks. © VICTORIA AND ALBERT MUSEUM, LONDON
Bottom left: Moulded enamelled cornice corner tile, Qazvin. Cobalt blue kufic lettering is raised on a lustre ground with white leaves and tendrils and Koran verses in nakshi script. Made in Kashan. ROSSITER 2013
Bottom right: Glazed ceramic tiles decorated with metallic lustre from the imamzadde Yaya, Varamin. Each design is surrounded by Koranic quotations. Made in Kashan 1262 AD. Much of the bright silver and copper lustre had lost its shine; Jane admired their subtle delicacy. © VICTORIA AND ALBERT MUSEUM, LONDON

Plate 9:   Top left: Portico, Shah Mosque, Isfahan, a riot of patterns and techniques. Turquoise cable moulding separates (left) mosaic-tiled muqarnas inside the half dome from (right) cuerda seca tiles on the flat facade. JOHN TIDMARSH
Top right: Tile mosaic with floral design, Iran (probably Isfahan), 1450–1500 AD. The stylised lotus flowers were made as composite tiles like that on the next page (bottom), then embedded in the plaster matrix alongside the simpler shapes. © VICTORIA AND ALBERT MUSEUM, LONDON
Bottom: Cuerda seca tiles, Shiraz, which Jane thought 'excessively pretty'. ROSSITER 2001

Plate 10:   Top: Craftsman at work in Isfahan 2004 repairing damaged mosaic tile panels. ROSSITER 2004
Centre: Damaged mosaic tile section to be repaired or replicated. ROSSITER 2004
Bottom: A composite tile made in Isfahan 2004. Various holes were cut out of a cobalt-blue tile, then the spaces filled with complementary shapes cut from other coloured tiles. Such a flower would then be included in a tile mosaic like that on the previous page (top right). ROSSITER 2004

Plate 11:   Top left: Wall painting, Ali Qapu, Isfahan. Painting and other arts flourished under the tolerant Shah Abbas 1642-1660. The opulent fabrics shown reflect the buoyant economy. ROSSITER 2001
Top right: Riding down the pass. ROSSITER 2001
Bottom: Wall painting in Chihil Sutun, Isfahan, built ca. 1644 during the reign of Safavid Shah Abbas. Shah Ismael is shown defeating the Uzbeks in 1511 AD. JOHN TIDMARSH

Plate 12:   North chamber, jume mosque, Isfahan, 'the masterpiece of medieval Persian architecture', Seljuk dynasty, 1088. Tri-lobed squinches support the dome, colonettes lead the eye upwards, the brickwork is exquisite. JOHN TIDMARSH

Plate 13:   Top: Persepolis at dusk, 2004. Few of the apadana's mighty columns remain. ROSSITER 2004
Bottom: Relief carving at Persepolis, a stone catalogue of Achaemenid footwear. ROSSITER 2004

Plate 14:   Top: Remains of a fifth century AD Sasanian palace at Sarvistan, which Marcel, ill and delirious, labelled Achaemenid. Rounded arches springing from short round columns were unknown to the earlier dynasty. JOHN TIDMARSH
Bottom: Sasanian palace, Sarvistan. Squinches, semicircular scallop-shell shapes, bridge the corners of a square room to support the circular base of the dome, an architectural legacy of the Sasanians. JOHN TIDMARSH

Plate 15:   Top: Darius I's palace, Susa, 2001. Excavated stubs of the apadana's huge columns diminish the figure on the far side. The modern brick wall is to stabilise the site. ROSSITER 2001
Bottom: Column base 'among the spiny bushes', Susa 2004. ROSSITER 2004

Plate 16:   Top: Stone billboard, Sakavand 500BC. A Zoroastrian priest prays at a fire altar above an empty tomb. The author accessed the carving, 350 m up a steep cliff, wearing full hijab. ANON 2001
Bottom: The landscape that captivated Jane, 'angular mountains rising abruptly from the plain, colours ranging from magenta through burnt umber to violet and even bright yellow'. ROSSITER 2004

Index

A

Abadeh 120
Abbas *see* Shah Abbas
Abdoul-Rahim *see* mirza
    Abdoul-Rahim
Achaemenid viii, xi, xiv–xv, 2,
    128–164, 171–172, 175, 217,
    224–225, 238, 264, 267, 272–
    273, 290, 293, 296
Afghani ix, 44, 79, 100, 113,
    119, 158
Aga Mohammad ix, 160
Ahura Mazda 55, 131, 144, 147, 177,
    197, 224
Ahwaz xi, 165, 227, 230, 232, 243,
    270, 295, 297, 299–300, 303
Akbar Ali *see* mirza Akbar Ali
Alburz Mountains 24, 41, 44, 50,
    59, 67
Alexander the Great viii, 15, 64, 122,
    129, 132, 135, 138, 140, 175,
    177, 224, 264
Ali 46–47, 53, 73, 163, 190
Ali Khan xi, 261
Amarah xi, 195, 204, 209, 210–212,
    219, 270, 275, 278, 281–283
Arabat x, 114, 167–168
Araxes River 22, 86, 196

Ardashir viii, 175–177, 196
Artaxerxes *see* Ardashir
Assassins ix, 41, 67
Assyria 242
Assyria viii, 129, 131, 194, 224,
    239–240
Athens 13–14, 225, 292
    Acropolis 13–14, 138, 144,
    224–226
Attar xi, 274, 283–284, 295, 301
Ava 13, 15
Avah x, 71
Azerbaijan ix–x, 17, 29, 32, 41, 85
Azerbaijan Mountains 24

B

Babi sect 42–43, 161
Babin, M. xi, 242, 251, 257, 259,
    268, 275, 278, 287, 296, 299,
    300, 303
Babylon viii, 129, 144, 175, 195,
    204–206, 224, 227, 238–240
Babylonia province 192, 195, 207
Baghdad viii, x–xi, xiv, 63–64, 165,
    192, 194, 199–205, 209, 214,
    235–236, 238–239
    al-Kadhimain shrine 204
Bagh-i-Sheykh 149, 167, 183

Bakhtiari Lurs x–xi, xv, 90, 95, 113, 120–123, 163, 165, 209, 212, 218–219, 223, 256–264, 270–271, 274, 289

Basra xi, 192–194, 233, 236, 240–241, 276, 302

Beni La'am xi, 196, 209–210, 212, 215–218, 260, 262, 270, 274, 281–283, 289, 300

Bibi Dordoun xi, 221–222

Bird, Isabella x, 50–52, 57, 68, 74, 109, 117

Bisitun 238

Botta, Paul 239

Browne, Edward G. x, 39, 51, 115

Bushire x–xi, 12, 95, 118, 124, 158, 166, 172, 182–185, 242, 251, 277

C

Caliph 209

Captain Dominici *see* Dominici

Caravanserais, construction and neglect ix, xv, 71, 76, 86, 93, 159

Carnot, President x

Caucasus 12, 17, 85, 172, 180

Chahar Bagh 82, 90–91, 93–94

château de Terride 4, 87, 200, 291

Chihil Sutun 90, 92

Constantinople 13–15, 17, 39, 104, 277

Crusaders ix, 7, 64–67, 107–108, 202

Ctesiphon viii, 192, 196, 199

Curzon, George N x, 23, 58, 79, 114, 230, 236

Cyrus viii, 129–131, 137, 195, 225, 264

Cyrus's tomb 129, 132–133

D

Daniel's Tomb 223, 226, 244, 251, 257–258, 263, 269, 272, 289, 297, 299–300

Darius I viii, xiv, 12, 122, 134, 137, 140, 144, 148, 225, 238, 264, 292

Darius III 135, 224

de Ronchaud, Louis x, 2, 12, 237, 241, 273, 280

Deh-i-No 130, 132, 134

Dieulafoy Galleries 3, 305

Dizful xi, 191, 195, 209–210, 214–215, 217, 219, 222, 226, 242, 244, 249, 251, 269, 277, 295, 299

Dizfuli 248, 254, 257–259, 262, 266, 268, 271–272, 274, 284–286, 290, 295

Dominici, Captain xi, 194–196

Dor Ali 254

Dr Olding *see* Olding

Dr Ross *see* Ross

Dr Tholozan *see* Tholozan

E

Elamites viii, 129, 137, 224–225

Elgin, Lord 14–15

Eqlid 120–123, 165, 218

Escombrera 209, 227, 229–230, 233, 235

Euphrates River 47, 176, 182, 191, 194, 196–197, 205–206, 235

F

Fallahiyah xi, 185, 191, 236, 243, 302

Fars x, 60, 89, 120, 125–126, 129, 141, 158, 163, 166, 175, 178, 184–185, 225, 237, 246, 275, 293

Farsi xv, 6–7, 21–22, 42, 45, 48, 55, 64, 76, 157, 250, 268, 289

Fath Ali Shah 29, 74, 160

Fatima 46–47, 53, 73

Fellahyé xi, 285–287

Ferhad Mirza x, 30, 140, 166, 167, 173

Fin 79

Firuzabad viii, xv, 7, 172, 176, 178, 196
Flandin and Coste 7, 223
Franco–Prussian War 1, 28, 57
Frieze of the Archers 2, 37, 292, 294
Frieze of the Lions 2, 267, 270

G

General Kouly Khan x, 69–70
General mirza Taqi Khan x, 82, 89–91, 99, 234
Georgia 17–19
Georgian (peoples) 17–19, 85, 89
Golag *khanum* xi, 236
Golistan palace 1, 54
Gothic architecture ix–x, xiv, 6–8, 107–108
Greco–Persian Wars 14, 138

H

hadji Houssein x, 96, 98
hadji Ibrahim Khan xi, 160
hadji Jabir Khan 185
hadji mirza Hosein Khan x, 53, 57, 70
hadji sayyid Hussein xi, 244
Hafiz 155–158
Hasan 47
Hasan-e Fasa'i' x, 53, 161
Hasht Bihist 91
Hillah 205, 206
Houssay, M xi, 242, 249, 251, 257, 259, 268, 275, 278, 287, 296, 297, 299–300, 303
Houssein *see hadji* Houssein
Hosein Khan *see hadji* mirza Hosein Khan
Houssein *khanum, see* Ziba *khanum*
Husain *see* Shah Husain
Husein Kuli Khan x, 122
Hussein 46, 163, 190, 205–207

I

hadji Ibrahim Khan *see hadji* Ibrahim Khan
Ilkhanids ix, 32, 39, 83, 102
Isfahan 61, 80–110
jume mosque 106–108
Ismael Safavi 85
Ispahanec 111

J

Jabir Khan *see hadji* Jabir Khan
Jean-Marie xi, 283, 294, 300, 303
Jesus xi, 210, 212
Jolfa 22, 86

K

Kaleh-Bender 294, 302
Kanat xv, 75, 81, 86, 93, 116, 142
Karbala 46, 116, 141, 161, 163, 192, 202, 204–207, 284
Karim Khan Zand 159
Karun River 51, 165, 185, 188, 191, 227–228, 230–235, 237, 243, 294, 300–303
Kashan 63, 75–80
Kashani scorpions 54, 70, 72
Kashquai xv, 178–179
Kerim Khan xi, 218, 260–263, 270, 272, 279, 285, 289
Kerkhah River 215, 217, 224, 256, 258, 260, 264, 270, 274, 285, 287
Khorsabad 204, 239
Khuzestan xiv, 74, 185, 190, 227–228, 234, 237, 241, 304
Kodja Youssouff x, 96, 98
Kouly Khan *see* General Kouly Khan
Kurds 12, 17, 24, 26, 38, 44, 55, 85

L

Layard, A. H. 223, 239–240
le Tour du monde 3, 8, 180, 237, 280, 303

Légion d'honneur 1, 3, 37, 305
Loftus, William Kennet xi, 165, 223,
    242, 252, 254, 264
Lord Elgin *see* Elgin
Louvre Museum xiv, 1–3, 15, 239–
    241, 267, 292, 305, 319

M

Magre family 4
Marv Dasht 134–135, 142–143, 148
Mashhad 38, 40, 58, 73, 119
Mausoleum of Uljaitu ix, xv, 38
Medes viii, 33, 41, 120, 129, 137
Menchet xi, 283–286, 300
Mesopotamia 32, 61, 74, 130, 137,
    193, 196–197, 203, 205–206,
    212, 223–224, 227
  archaeological exploration
    131, 238–240, 264, 266
mirza Abdoul-Rahim xi, 246,
    249, 252, 256, 268-269, 279,
    290, 297
mirza Akbar Ali xi, 232, 243
mirza Taguy xi, 297, 300
mirza Taqi Khan x, 79
Mizal Khan *see* Sheikh Mizal Khan
Mohammad, the prophet 8, 46, 141,
    190, 192, 198, 212
Mohammad, Kerim Khan's son
    xi, 219, 260, 264
Mohammad Taher *see* Sheikh
    Mohammad Taher
Mohammerah 185, 188, 191–192,
    227, 232–234, 243, 302
Mosul xi, 194–199
Mosul 239
Mount Ararat 12, 20, 21
Mount Damavand 48, 50, 59, 69,
    75, 80
Mozaffer el-Molk xi, 246–247, 251,
    256, 268, 270, 272, 279, 289,
    296–299, 304

M'sban xi, 271, 281–286, 300
Muhaisen Ka'b Arabs xi, 185
Muzaffar-al-Din Mirza x, 30, 89

N

Nadir Shah ix, 87, 158
Naib-es-Sultaneh ix–x, 68, 70–71, 83
Najaf 141, 163, 192
Naqsh-i Rustam viii, xv, 134, 143,
    145, 147, 171, 199, 238
Narchevan viii, 21, 37, 62
Nasr-al-Din ix–x, 29, 55–56, 59,
    77, 79, 89, 100, 108, 120, 131,
    162–163, 241, 277
New Julfa x, 82–113, 118, 124, 162,
    200, 244
Nineveh 204, 224, 239, 240
Nizam al-Mulk 64, 67, 107

O

Olding, Dr xi, 149, 152, 154
Omar 46–47
Ottoman Turks 17, 74, 85–86, 163,
    192, 203, 212, 278
Ousta Hassan xi, 254–255, 257, 260,
    273–274, 289, 295

P

Papi Khan (-*um*) xi, 289, 295, 261
Parthians viii, 175–176
Pasargadae viii, xv, 127–133, 225
Pendjab 182, 184–185
Père Pascal x, 83, 88, 92–96, 102–
    106, 108–110, 112–113, 115,
    200, 244
Péretié, M. xi, 200, 209
Persepolis viii, xv, 7, 115, 128,
    135–148, 171, 225, 238, 264,
    266–267, 275
Persian Gulf 12, 23–24, 74, 80, 85,
    95, 124, 158, 165–166, 172, 180,
    184, 192, 196, 242, 293, 302, 304

Polvar Gorges 129, 132–133, 143
Polvar Plain 128–130
Poti 15, 17
President Carnot *see* Carnot

Q

Qajar dynasty ix, xv, 29, 41, 50,
 53–54, 73, 76, 87, 89, 94, 108,
 117, 122, 141, 160, 184, 223, 241
 administration 38–39, 42, 45,
 47, 53, 67, 86, 159, 173, 178,
 221, 251
Qazvin viii, xv, 23, 38, 44–48, 59,
 61, 86
Qom 70–71, 73–74, 207

R

Rawlinson, Henry x, 143, 221–223,
 238–239, 264
Rayy viii, 59–62, 67, 104
Ross, Dr xi, 182, 243
Russo–Turkish War 12, 17, 19, 164

S

Sa'adi 155–158, 277
Safavid ix, xv, 76, 81, 85–87, 92–95,
 100–102, 119, 195, 203
Sahib Divan xi, 152, 160, 167, 169,
 173, 178, 184–185
Sané 299, 302, 304
Sar Pol-i-Zohab 174
Sarvistan 169–170, 173
Sasanid viii, 7–8, 44, 62, 64, 100,
 104, 134, 155, 165, 167, 171–
 172, 174–178, 192, 196, 206,
 217, 219, 228–230, 237, 272, 291
Saveh x, 68–71, 166
Sayyid Ali xi, 295, 297, 299
Scorpion 277
Segvend Arabs 261, 263, 289
Seleucia viii, 199
Seleucid viii, 175, 291

Seljuk viii, xiv, 8, 22, 44, 61, 63–65,
 67, 102, 107–108, 165, 203, 237
Seropa 232–235
Shah Abbas ix, 68, 81, 85–87, 90–93,
 100–103, 116, 160, 195, 203
Shah Husain 94, 100
Shahname 64, 123, 134, 157, 196,
 199, 228
Shapur 12, 134, 175, 196, 199,
 271, 291
Shatt al Arab 165, 182, 185, 194,
 227, 233–235
Shaur River 223, 227
Sheikh Ali xi, 250, 256, 261, 268,
 289, 294, 297, 300, 302
Sheikh Mizal Khan xi, 185–186,
 188, 231–232, 234, 236, 243,
 281, 302
Sheikh Mohammad Taher xi, 249,
 254, 257, 268–269, 294, 299
Shiraz ix, xv, 30, 111, 120, 122, 127,
 148–149, 151, 157–164, 185,
 237, 267
Shushan xi, 165, 225
Shushtar 185, 228–230, 243, 246,
 249, 251, 256, 262, 268, 294
Soltaniyeh ix, xv, 38, 41, 131
Sufi ix, 51, 64, 85, 93, 156
Sumer viii
Sumerian 131, 240–241
Surmaq xv, 121, 123
Susa viii–ix, xiv, 1–3, 14, 128, 165,
 182, 185, 193, 200, 204, 209,
 217, 223–227, 237, 241, 251–
 274, 278, 285, 289–300

T

Tabriz ix, xv, 29–37, 59, 64, 85,
 165–166, 267
Taguy *see* mirza Taguy
Taqi Khan, grand vizier *see* mirza
 Taqi Khan

Taqi Khan, Zil-es-Sultan's doctor *see* General mirza Taqi Khan
Tehran ix–x, 1, 8, 23, 29, 38, 42, 48–59, 66–68, 71, 74, 80, 82, 90, 99, 108, 160, 163, 178, 186, 237, 250, 277, 295, 299
Tholozan, Dr x, 50–52, 54–57, 82, 152, 241
Tiflis (Tbilisi) 15, 17–19, 165
Tigris viii, xi, 182, 191–199, 201, 205, 209, 212, 235, 239, 275, 278
Timur (Tamerlane) ix, 85, 158
Timurids ix, 17, 85, 102, 158
Tonkin 242
Torkhan *khanum* xi, 187–191, 236–237, 274
Toulouse 4–7, 38, 55, 200, 280
Trabzon 15
Troy 15

V
Valerian 134, 196–197, 228
Varamin ix, 59–66, 79, 87, 104, 232
Viollet-le-Duc x, 6, 209, 237, 280

X
Xerxes 14, 138, 144–145, 225, 264, 292

Y
Yazd-i Khvast 119
Yerevan, Armenia 20–22, 147
Youssouff *khanum* x, 96–98, 113

Z
Zagros Mountains ix, 24, 74, 158, 172, 193, 209, 212, 228, 229
Zand dynasty ix, 158–160
Zendjan 41–43, 162
Ziba *khanum*, aka Houssein *khanum* x, 9, 11, 96, 98–99, 163
Zil-es-Sultan ix–x, 89–94, 98–99, 101, 103, 112, 115, 118, 120, 122, 151, 166, 173, 178, 185, 210, 217, 229, 232, 234, 242, 251, 270, 299
Ziyanda River (Rud) 82, 87, 90, 99, 100
Zoroastrian 47, 59–60, 63, 93, 100, 145–148, 162, 173, 177, 312

Wakefield Press is an independent publishing and
distribution company based in Adelaide, South Australia.
We love good stories and publish beautiful books.
To see our full range of books, please visit our website at
www.wakefieldpress.com.au
where all titles are available for purchase.

Find us!

Twitter: www.twitter.com/wakefieldpress
Facebook: www.facebook.com/wakefield.press
Instagram: instagram.com/wakefieldpress

CPSIA information can be obtained
at www.ICGtesting.com
Printed in the USA
BVHW092330071121
621055BV00018B/527